SAP R/3 Plant Maintenance

SAP R/3
Plant Maintenance
Making it work for your business

Britta Stengl and Reinhard Ematinger

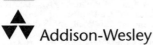
Addison-Wesley

an imprint of **Pearson Education**

Harlow, England • London • New York • Reading, Massachusetts • San Francisco • Toronto
Don Mills, Ontario • Sydney • Tokyo • Singapore • Hong Kong • Seoul • Taipei • Cape Town
Madrid • Mexico City • Amsterdam • Munich • Paris • Milan

PEARSON EDUCATION LIMITED

Head Office: London Office:
Edinburgh Gate   128 Long Acre
Harlow   London WC2E 9AN
Essex CM20 2JE   Tel: +44 (0)20 7447 2000
Tel: +44 (0)1279 623623   Fax: +44 (0)20 7240 5771
Fax: +44 (0)1279 431059

Website: www.informit.uk.com
www.aw.com/cseng/

First published in Great Britain in 2001

© Galileo Press GmbH 2000

The rights of Britta Stengl and Reinhard Ematinger to be identified as Authors of this Work have been asserted by them in accordance with the Copyright, Designs and Patents Act 1988.

ISBN 0-201-67532-3

British Library Cataloguing in Publication Data
A CIP catalogue record for this book can be obtained from the British Library

Library of Congress Cataloging in Publication Data
Stengl, Britta.
  [Instandhaltung mit SAP R/3. English]
  SAP R/3 plant maintenance: making it work for your business/Britta Stengl and Reinhard Ematinger.
    p. cm.
  Includes bibliographical references (p.).
  1. SAP R/3. 2. Marketing–Management–Computer programs. 3. Sales management–Computer programs.
  4. Plant maintenance–Computer programs. I. Ematinger, Reinhard. II. Title.

  HF5438.35.S7413 2001
  658.2'00285'53769–dc21   2001020277

10 9 8 7 6 5 4 3 2

Designed by Claire Brodmann Book Designs, Lichfield, Staffs.
Typeset by M Rules, London, UK.
Printed and bound in Great Britain by Biddles Ltd.

The Publishers' policy is to use paper manufactured from sustainable forests.

Contents

3   GETTING STARTED WITH RELEASE 4.6   29

4   OBJECTS IN R/3 PM   47

5   BUSINESS PROCESS: BREAKDOWN MAINTENANCE AND CORRECTIVE MAINTENANCE

9 INTERFACES TO NON-SAP SYSTEMS 317

Preface I

Given the current international discussion of changing markets, the accompanying trend towards globalization of business processes and the increasingly evident revolution in intercompany communication via the internet, it is all too easy to lose sight of the fact that optimized and harmonized production processes are the basic prerequisites for raising corporate IQ. It is precisely these aspects that form the starting point for the Plant Maintenance (PM) component in the SAP R/3 System.

This book has been written as a compendium for members of specialist teams. It provides interdisciplinary groups with a clear implementation guide, and aims at developing a new understanding of the software-assisted procedures in preventive and breakdown maintenance within a location. The book also presents a detailed discussion of technical implementation, thus enabling not only IT departments but also users to implement the process flows they actually require in the system. This knowledge will ultimately allow user departments to respond quickly and independently to changing demands, and adjust their workflows accordingly.

Using explanatory examples, the authors describe the practical day-to-day process flows clearly and unambiguously. The book is designed to cover all the topics relevant to maintenance planning and execution, as well as business processing of tasks, procurement, refurbishment of spare parts, and external services. Particular attention is given to integrating plant maintenance in the natural process flow of a company. To this end, integration of the PM component in the environment of Materials Management, Purchasing, Production, and Payroll is described in detail. Once the Plant Maintenance component has been successfully implemented, users can consider linking non-SAP systems at management level, as well as an Internet connection for quotation processing. When the internal process flows have been synchronized, companies have virtually unlimited options for optimizing their internal information flows.

Walldorf, January 2000
Ringo Kairies
Consulting Director
Process Industry
SAP AG

Preface II

The R/3 Plant Maintenance (PM) component from SAP is targeted at an area that may appear somewhat unspectacular when compared with business management in the areas of sales and production. As I will show, however, the PM component does more than merely add another cost planning area to those already covered by the R/3 System; it also provides specific new functionalities that enable SAP users to handle an area crucial for their strategic success.

In Western European economies, expenditure on maintaining production systems, public infrastructures and privately operated systems accounts for over 10 per cent of gross national product (Warnecke 1992). Although there are cases where it cannot be strictly delimited from investment costs (largely because there is a certain technical scope for substitution), plant maintenance planning accounts for an overwhelming volume of expenditure and must, therefore, be carried out efficiently. Economic planning of this type is of crucial importance, since the current trend is towards increased expenditure on plant maintenance. This is chiefly due to the growing complexity of production systems, which, in turn, is a result of progressive functional integration and automation. These production systems, which support the increasing productivity crucial for market competition, require ever more investible funds. While systems of this type continue to represent a structural increase in plant maintenance expenditure, this expenditure is, in some cases, being replaced by investment expenditure (partly as a result of the diminishing product and system life cycles as part of the optimization of life cycle/usage costs via asset management) (Biedermann 1990).

For these reasons, plant maintenance will remain an exceptionally important area for applying business methodology – above all, in the areas of process control and cost management. A significant number of companies are now able to leverage their specialized production know-how as a strategic competitive factor. In such companies, there is also the potentially profitable chance that plant maintenance will be innovatively extended, becoming a key factor for competitive expertise in managing production effectiveness.

Optimizing the overall effectiveness of systems and assets is a key goal for cost management in plant maintenance. One way of achieving this goal is to systematically deploy modern organizational methods and plant maintenance strategies – such as condition-based maintenance (CBM), continuous improvement programs (CIP), and specialist teams to ensure that plant maintenance is carried out as efficiently as possible. In addition to this, cross-sector benchmarking can be applied to provide further starting points for increasing plant maintenance efficiency in accordance with the principles of Business Process Reengineering (BPR) with innovative advances toward designing best practice processes. Given the advent of BPR and outsourcing, the pragmatic question that must be addressed is whether companies can ensure the diversity and depth of specialist knowledge required to continue autonomously developing practical expertise in production technology (to the extent that this represents a core competency). Finally, the increasing orientation of companies to monetary markets and customer demands has given rise to an area of business activity for plant maintenance specialists, the importance of which is not to be underestimated. Here, maintenance management plays an active part in the process of target costing, especially in the 'design to cost' development phase.

The predefined structures of the PM component provide comprehensive support for mapping the characteristic features of corporate plant maintenance in data processing systems. The component is also extensively integrated in a networked planning and financial environment, which covers all the activities of an enterprise. This ensures that all the information required for controlling plant maintenance is available holistically across all production activities involving systems. In addition to this, the powerful tried-and-tested tools for implementing targeted aggregation, as well as differentiated, comprehensible and assessable representations of company activities, help prevent those responsible for plant maintenance from being flooded with details, thereby enabling them to concentrate more on technical improvement considerations.

The comprehensive functionalities of SAP R/3 and the PM component will ensure targeted support for this welcome trend.

Leoben, January 2000
Jürgen Wolfbauer
Professor of Business Administration
and Industrial Management
Montanuniversität Leoben, Austria

Preface III

KEEPING THE ROLLING STOCK ROLLING

It is now a good few years since we at the transport companies of VOEST ALPINE Stahl Linz (Austria) realized that IT support was essential for repairing our own and external rolling stock efficiently. Back then, we tested the SAP RM-INST, which was still in its infancy, and came to the conclusion that it did not meet our specific requirements. The reason? Our plant maintenance processes (surprise, surprise) were totally different from those of other companies. Quick as a flash, we set two students to the task of developing a tailor-made system for making quotations and creating maintenance task lists. The years went by, technology rolled inexorably on, modern systems were installed throughout the company, and our process flows were optimized. Throughout the company, SAP applications were installed, and more and more interfaces had to be developed and maintained, until . . . well, until our system could no longer cope. By this time, the original developers had disappeared without trace, and our IT solution was creating more problems than it solved. Nothing matched up with anything else; we had reached the stage where we had to work in several systems to process business orders; and the problems were getting out of control.

EVERYBODY'S TALKING ABOUT SAP R/3. COULD THIS BE THE SOLUTION FOR US?

The answer is, of course, yes! It did not take long to convince our transport personnel of the benefits of the SAP R/3 Service Management and Plant Maintenance modules for their day-to-day work. Soon everyone was asking: if other people are satisfied with the system, why can't we use it too? After all, we already had the system in-house; we 'only' needed to implement it, didn't we?

We soon put together a team, which faced up to the challenge and got to work on putting ideas and potential improvements into practice. In addition to ensuring a friendly atmosphere, the project leader made sure that the team worked as a team. Not even a change in market requirements, which radically changed the direction of the project, could dampen the team's spirit. The plant maintenance personnel soon realized that the Plant Maintenance module contained everything they needed to carry out their work – and that our plant maintenance processes were not so different from those of other companies after all. With support from SAP, our highly motivated team achieved its goals and the users are more than satisfied with the result. They now work in one thoroughly stable, integrated system, and cannot imagine working any other way.

We can now honestly say that our decision was the right one. By opting for the PM component, we have invested in the future. Keeping up with the pace of development demands a constant supply of up-to-the-minute expertise. Our decision in favour of R/3 has not only provided us with a state-of-the-art system, it also ensures us further development by SAP.

Linz, January 2000
Peter Ustupsky
Information Systems (Production)
VOEST ALPINE Stahl Linz GmbH

CHAPTER 1

Introduction

This book is intended as an introduction to a small but sophisticated component of the R/3 System: R/3 PM (Plant Maintenance). Carrying out plant maintenance with SAP is not merely an option; it is a strategy with considerable practical benefits. This book aims, therefore, to provide more than a brief introduction to the functional scope of the component. Its main objective is, rather, to provide users with a practical guide to implementing PM.

In Release 4.6 (marketed under the banner 'Enjoy'), many functions in the R/3 System have been simplified. The entire user interface of the system has been redesigned, and now has a considerably more modern, lean and intuitive appearance. In the PM component, SAP began replacing long sequences of screens with tab pages as early as Release 4.0. With Release 4.6, this process of simplification has been consolidated. In terms of functionality as well as appearance, PM is now a mature logistics component, fully integrated in the R/3 System and equipped with useful interfaces.

1.1   BUSINESS PROCESSES AND ROLES

To enable the functions in PM to be presented as practically as possible, this book describes three main business processes:

1 Breakdown maintenance (repair)

2 Corrective maintenance (planning and control of maintenance tasks)

3 Planned maintenance (maintenance planning)

Other business processes are also considered as special cases:

■ Refurbishment of repairable spares

■ Processing of external services (outsourcing of maintenance tasks)

In companies, these business processes involve various people with different tasks. Irrespective of the job titles used in a particular company, three main tasks can be distinguished for each business process:

1 Planning

2 Execution

3 Verification for financial purposes

In small companies, these three tasks can be carried out by one person. In large companies, there may be a specific organizational form with numerous members of staff for each task, and it may be necessary to subdivide the tasks further as a result. All three tasks can also be carried out by one team. The business processes are subdivided into three roles corresponding to these three tasks:

1 Maintenance planner (PM planner)

2 Maintenance technician (PM technician)

3 Controller

Subdividing the PM functions according to business processes and roles simplifies the work carried out by project teams during PM implementation. The project team begins by selecting only the specific business processes actually required in the company. The subdivision into three roles enables the necessary Customizing settings to be carried out for each work centre in accordance with its particular role. Work centres for the individual roles can thus be set up step by step, and are available at a relatively early stage of the project. Role-based Customizing also makes it easier to train power users or end users. There is no need for a controller in a company to learn about functions that he or she will never use, such as creating a malfunction report or a time confirmation. By contrast, a technician in the company will be trained how to report malfunctions, request spare parts and carry out confirmations, but not how to call up planned/actual reports or carry out capacity requirements planning. Customizing should always be carried out taking the individual user into consideration, and never solely on the basis of certain abstract rules in the Implementation Guide. By the same token, user training courses are efficient only if they teach the individual user precisely what he or she requires in order to carry out his or her core tasks.

| 1.2 | **STRUCTURE OF THIS BOOK** |

The chapters in this book are divided into the following three areas:

1 Introduction to business administration and content of plant maintenance (Chapters 1–4)

2 Business processes (Chapters 5–7)

3 Integration and interfaces (Chapters 8 and 9)

Chapter 2 provides an introductory classification of plant maintenance from a business administration point of view. This chapter can be used by project teams during PM implementation to facilitate decisions concerning the best maintenance strategy. Students will find the chapter helpful for classifying maintenance tasks in terms of business administration models. The chapter provides a solid business foundation for the business processes described later in R/3 PM. In addition to an overview of the traditional organizational forms of maintenance departments, the chapter provides a synopsis of modern concepts of maintenance management and other related trends. Chapter 3 explains new features of Release 4.6, which affect not only R/3 PM, but can be used to help you work with R/3 PM – for example, defining your own menu, using a new interface to the SAPNet–R/3 Frontend (formerly the Online Support System OSS), or referring to the redesigned HTML documentation. Chapter 4 introduces and defines the master data and most important objects in R/3 PM. In Chapters 5 to 7, business processes and roles are used to describe the functions of R/3 PM. Chapter 8 discusses the integration of the PM component in the other components of the R/3 System. Chapter 9 presents the interfaces to non-SAP systems using the example of process/building control systems, CBR systems and CAD systems. The efficacy of each interface for plant maintenance is also considered from a business point of view. With regard to CBR and CAD systems, solutions available from two partner companies of SAP are presented.

| 1.3 | **TARGET GROUPS** |

The authors of this book are both certified consultants for PM and CS (Customer Service, formerly SM, Service Management), and work for SAP AG in Walldorf, Germany. As a result, this book is aimed primarily at project teams or consultants involved in implementing the PM component. This book, therefore, places particular emphasis on describing functions and the Customizing settings these require from a practical perspective. In practice, an extended knowledge of Customizing can often help avoid the need for modifications.

The book is also targeted at students who work with the Logistics component of the R/3 System and wish to gain an overview of the PM component. At colleges for higher professional training, where considerable attention is already given to the MM and PP components, knowledge of R/3 PM is still comparatively limited.

This book presupposes a basic knowledge of how to operate the R/3 System. It is aimed at readers who are not yet familiar with R/3 PM, as well as experienced consultants who have already worked with older releases of R/3 PM and want to find out about the new functions in Release 4.6.

Due to the practical nature of the descriptions given here, all the functions presented can be executed directly in an R/3 System. Almost all of the data used in the examples refer to an IDES system. The appendix contain a practical guide for a PM implementation workshop, as well as a case study based on IDES.

When you put the material in this book into practice, please note that the menu paths for the R/3 System and the Implementation Guideline (IMG) refer to Release 4.6B. The functions described in this book cover Releases 4.6A, 4.6B and 4.6C. However, since there are minor differences between the menu paths in 4.6B and 4.6C (for example, in the Customizing settings for notifications), transaction codes are generally used instead of menu paths.

CHAPTER 2

Classifying plant maintenance[1] from a business perspective

DEFINITIONS

In business administration, plant maintenance is traditionally classified as part of production (Nolden 1996; Hartmann 1995). The following definitions are intended to illustrate the many diverse ways of evaluating plant maintenance, as well as the different objectives these entail.

2.1.1 Plant maintenance to DIN 31051

According to the German standard DIN 31051, plant maintenance comprises 'all measures for maintaining and restoring the target condition as well as determining and assessing the actual condition of the technical equipment in a system'. These measures are subdivided into

- Preventive maintenance

---

1 We wish to express our thanks to Ms Renate Sommer (Business Administrations Department, University of Applied Sciences Coburg) for advice on the business administration aspects of this chapter. In numerous discussions, Ms Sommer established the links between traditional business administration and applied plant maintenance.

■ Inspection

■ Repairs

Preventive maintenance comprises all measures for maintaining the target condition of the technical equipment in a system. In addition to the maintenance task itself, this includes creating maintenance plans which are used to carry out the PM tasks at regular intervals.

Inspection comprises measures for assessing the actual condition of the technical equipment in a system. This also includes creating a plan for determining the actual condition, with information on the inspection date, method and tasks, as well as on the use of technical equipment. An inspection is carried out on the basis of the plan; in other words, specific characteristics are determined quantitatively. These results are then evaluated and any necessary PM tasks deduced.

Repairs comprise measures for restoring the target condition of the technical equipment in a system. This process includes the actual order, order documentation, and analysis of the order content. During order planning, alternative solutions should be isolated and evaluated to enable the best possible solution to be found. Preparing to execute tasks comprises costing, scheduling, provision of personnel, funds and material, as well as creating maintenance task lists. After the tasks have been completed, a functional test, acceptance inspection, notification of completion, and evaluation (including documentation, cost monitoring, and indication of suggested improvements or preventive measures) are carried out.

2.1.2 System-oriented plant maintenance

Whereas DIN 31051 applies to the individual parts of a system and associated measures, system-oriented plant maintenance focuses on safeguarding the functioning of a production system as a whole. Plant maintenance in this sense belongs to system logistics, the primary goals of which are planning, creating and maintaining system availability. System availability is planned taking the maximality and minimality principles into consideration.

The maximality principle aims at achieving the maximum possible yield from a given resource (yield maximization). For further information on this principle, see Schierenbeck (1995). The PM budget, for example, is a given quantity and is intended to ensure the highest possible level of system availability. By contrast, the minimality principle aims at keeping the resource required to achieve a particular result as low as possible (expenditure or cost minimization). For example, a particular system is to be maintained twice a year at as low a cost as possible. To ensure an optimum relationship between PM costs and system availability, the extremum principle is used. This aims at achieving the most favourable relationship possible between yield and expenditure. Yield and expenditure are optimized when the maintenance costs, as well as costs incurred through loss of output, are reduced to a minimum.

Costs related to system logistics include:

- Procurement costs of the system
- Preventive maintenance costs
- Stockholding costs for spare parts
- Procurement costs for replacement equipment
- Costs incurred through loss of output
- Costs incurred for shutting down and scrapping the system

The goals of plant maintenance here are subordinate to those of system logistics. As a result, the aim of plant maintenance is, by means of corrective maintenance, to prevent loss of output and maximize system lifetime. Other tasks include influencing the storage of spare parts so that, when required, spare parts are available at the right time and place. Ideally, plant maintenance should also ensure that maintenance tasks are scheduled to coincide with normal breaks in production or system downtimes. In production, this requires close coordination between maintenance planning and production planning. The basic dilemma in plant maintenance is that, while preventive maintenance initially increases plant maintenance costs, it can help to prevent even higher costs being incurred as a result of breakdowns in production. This means that every company has to determine a plant maintenance strategy located between the following positions:

- Risk-based plant maintenance with low maintenance costs, but with a high risk of system breakdown and high repair or replacement costs;
- Preventive maintenance with high regular plant maintenance costs, but with a low risk of system breakdown.

2.1.3 Extended plant maintenance

In recent years, plant maintenance has been freed from its original, purely production-based context. In addition to its traditional task of safeguarding system availability, plant maintenance has come to include disposal of basic materials in accordance with ecological considerations and environmental legislation. Another new aspect is facility management. In plant maintenance, this area encompasses preventive maintenance, inspection and repairs for utility installations (for example, power supply, water supply and air conditioning). Plant maintenance has now become an important issue not only in production environments, but also in building management. (Consider, for example, the costs that can be incurred due to a defective air-conditioning system in a computer centre.) The following definition takes these recent trends into account, without neglecting DIN 31051:

Plant maintenance comprises preventive maintenance, inspection, and repairs for operational facilities. In many cases, this also involves utility installations or disposal of materials. The purpose of plant maintenance is to ensure the availability of operational facilities at a minimal cost. (Index entry 'plant maintenance' in Sokianos (1998))

2.1.4 Malfunction and breakdown

Whereas inspection and preventive maintenance are carried out on a functioning system, repairs presuppose a malfunction or breakdown.

A malfunction (or defect) is an unwanted interruption to or impairment of the correct functioning of a unit; this definition does not take the cause of the malfunction into account. A malfunction can take the form of a brief interruption. The terms 'malfunction' and 'breakdown' are often defined in such a way that a breakdown is caused by factors in the actual unit in question. In the event of a malfunction, a unit can continue to carry out its required function (a ventilator filled with dust or leaves is an example of a malfunction, not a breakdown). A breakdown always implies a malfunction, not vice versa. (Hubert Becker: Grundbegriffe. http://home.t-online.de/home/becker2/log3_1_1.htm)

The criteria according to which breakdowns can be classified include

- The life cycle of the system
- The particular form breakdowns take
- The logical sequence of breakdowns

In the life cycle of a system, there are three breakdown phases:

1. Early breakdown phase; for example, due to incorrect operation or material weaknesses
2. Random breakdown phase during consolidation; for example, due to vibration or fluctuations in pressure, temperature, load, or voltage
3. Late breakdown phase; for example, due to aging, wear and tear, or fatigue

Depending on the particular form they take, breakdowns are classified either as total or partial. For example, if one motor breaks down in a system comprising a total of three motors, this is considered a partial breakdown.

The logical sequence of breakdowns can be used to distinguish primary and secondary breakdowns, as well as breakdowns with a common cause. A primary breakdown is the breakdown of a unit due to a failure in the unit itself. In the case of a secondary breakdown, the unit either breaks down due to the failure of an upstream unit or has to be deactivated for safety reasons. A breakdown with a common cause involves several units breaking down simultaneously.

Documenting and analysing breakdowns is one important task of plant maintenance. In this context, the technical breakdown (failure) rate in VDI (Association of German Engineers) Guideline 2893 is particularly significant.

The technical downtime comprises all the downtimes attributable to technical malfunctions. According to VDI Guideline 3423, the target running time is the running time of a machine (according to capital investment planning, for example). The aging of a unit can be deduced from the characteristic of the technical breakdown rate; in other words, if the technical breakdown rate increases, scrapping a unit could, in certain circumstances, entail lower costs than maintaining it.

2.2   TRADITIONAL FORMS OF ORGANIZATION IN PLANT MAINTENANCE

2.2.1 Plant maintenance in line organization

Line organization is the oldest and most basic form of organization (Steinbuch 1997: 172ff). The characteristic features of line organization are:

- Centralization of tasks
- Simple subordination
- Full authority only

In line organization, each job is allocated only one manager, and each manager has several subordinate members of staff. This is a form of organization in which the manager plays an authoritarian role and each member of staff is answerable to only one level of authority. In other words, every PM technician is answerable to the PM manager. Line organization is the most common organizational form in small and medium-sized companies, in which all decisions are made by one person.

The advantages of this form of organization include unambiguous relationships between superiors and subordinates, uniform channels for communication and reporting, as well as clear demarcation of tasks, authority and responsibility. The responsibility of the manager for the decision process ensures that all process steps can be interpreted easily, and facilitates control and supervision of members of staff.

One of the disadvantages of line organization is the excessive load it puts on management. The emphasis on hierarchical thinking hinders cooperation between members of staff and also runs the risk of increasing bureaucracy. With line organization, a limited number of intermediate authorities results in a broad organizational plan and, therefore, large spans of control. A large number of intermediate authorities in line organization, however, results in long communication and reporting paths.

Figure 2.1 illustrates plant maintenance in line organization as a subarea of production. The PM manager is subordinate to the production manager here. Figure 2.2

illustrates plant maintenance as a separate area on a par with production. The PM manager here shares the same hierarchical level as the production manager, and both are subordinate to the corporate management.

2.2.2 Plant maintenance in the line-staff organization structure

To relieve the excessive load on management staff, which is a disadvantage of line organization, this organization structure assigns authority to staff units (Steinbuch 1997: 173ff). These staff units do not usually have competence to issue instructions; their tasks are, rather, in the areas of decision preparation, planning and support, as well as monitoring. A characteristic feature of the line-staff organizational structure is its separation of decision-making powers (for example, of the production manager) and the expert knowledge of the staff (for example, of the PM manager and his staff). Further characteristic features of this organizational form are:

- Centralization of tasks
- Simple subordination
- Full and partial authority

In addition to relieving management staff, the advantages of the line-staff organization structure include improved decision quality by incorporating specialists, the uniform

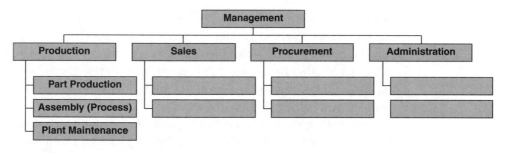

FIGURE 2.1 Plant maintenance in line organization as a subarea of production
(© SAP AG)

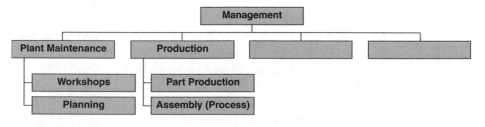

FIGURE 2.2 Plant maintenance in line organization as a separate area (© SAP AG)

line of command and communication channel, as well as the clear demarcation of responsibility.

The disadvantages of this organizational form include the potential for conflict between the line position and the staff unit assigned to it (for example, between the production manager and the PM manager), the danger of staff units becoming too large for the line position, as well as the possibility of the staff unit using its specialist knowledge manipulatively.

> As a rule, the staff units in plant maintenance are entrusted with long-term planning tasks, such as drawing up maintenance strategies for individual production plants, creating budgets, determining personnel capacity, elaborating maintenance task lists, and administering and maintaining the plant maintenance data. (Grobholz 1988: 84ff)

The planned PM tasks can actually be carried out either by the specialists of the PM staff unit, or by production staff. External processing (outsourcing) managed by the staff unit is also conceivable. Figure 2.3 represents plant maintenance as a staff unit assigned to the line position 'Production'.

2.2.3 Plant maintenance in matrix organization

With matrix organization, specific functions are not assigned to the business areas but are carried out centrally for the entire company (Steinbuch 1997: 185ff). Central departments are set up for this purpose and carry out their tasks for all business areas. At a second level, a horizontal functional organization is combined with this vertical organization of business areas, thereby creating a matrix. The characteristic features of matrix organization are:

- Centralization of objects
- Multiple subordination
- Full authority, or partial and full authority

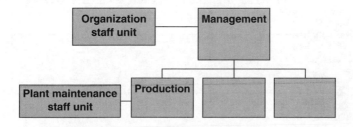

FIGURE 2.3   Plant maintenance in the line-staff organization structure (© SAP AG)

This organizational form is primarily used by large companies which have diverse product groups, a marketing orientation and high management potential.

Some of the advantages of matrix organization are that it safeguards corporate unity, generally confers the advantages of specialization, relieves the strain on management, and provides a large variety of response options.

The disadvantages of matrix organization, however, include the risk of conflict due to multiple subordination, the danger of entering into unsatisfactory compromises, the tendency towards greater bureaucracy, as well as high costs due to the large number of managers required.

Within matrix organization 'the PM unit that carries out the maintenance tasks is assigned to the (horizontal) central Maintenance division, as well as to the vertical division of the relevant product group' (Grobholz 1988: 35ff). In general, strategic PM planning is located in the central division, while the vertical divisions carry out PM planning for their product division and also perform the PM tasks. Figure 2.4 shows an example of the central Production and Plant Maintenance divisions for three product divisions.

2.2.4 Classification of external plant maintenance

Generally speaking, internal plant maintenance can be combined with external plant maintenance (outsourcing) in all of the three traditional forms of organization. In this case, the maintenance department is responsible for planning and monitoring the PM measures but not for carrying them out. Of course, it is also possible to transfer planning, control and execution of maintenance tasks entirely to the external provider.

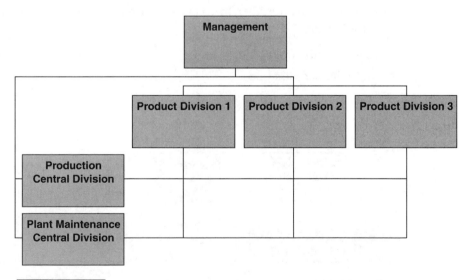

FIGURE 2.4   Plant maintenance in matrix organization (© SAP AG)

In all three organizational forms, external plant maintenance can result in leaner structures. Figure 2.5 illustrates the structure of integrated fixed-asset management and the inclusion of internal and external plant maintenance.

If maintenance is placed at the core of this type of fixed-asset management, it is clear that choosing between internal and external maintenance has consequences not only for the area of maintenance, but for all of the remaining activities in fixed-asset management. Depending on the particular tasks carried out by fixed-asset management, these consequences can affect the planning, execution, and control of the various activities in fixed-asset management. (Grobholz 1988: 54)

The evaluation technique used in decision making can be applied as a basis for deciding for or against external plant maintenance. This technique centres on creating a value profile which comprises the variables criterion, weighting, degree of fulfilment, and evaluation. Specific criteria are assigned a weighting from 1–10, for example. In addition to this, the degree of fulfilment is specified; in other words, which maintenance provider fulfils which criterion, and to what extent. The external maintenance provider is then evaluated on the basis of the criteria, weighting, and degree of fulfilment. Multiplying the values in the 'Weighting' and 'Degree of fulfilment' columns yields values per line, the sum of which constitutes the final value. Comparing the final values for the various external maintenance providers with the final value for internal plant maintenance provides a basis for deciding whether external plant maintenance is a viable option and, if so, which external provider should be commissioned.

The following criteria can be used for decision making (Grobholz 1988: 66ff):

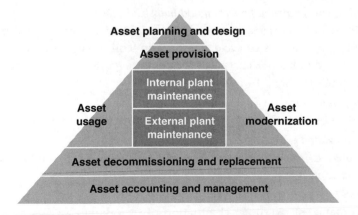

FIGURE 2.5   Integrated fixed-asset management (from Grobholz 1988: 55) (© SAP AG)

1 *Quality*
Deployment of well-trained specialists; use of precision tools; experience with similar cases; selection of repairs, spare parts, repairable spares and operating supplies appropriate to the specific demands involved; procedure in accordance with state-of-the-art technology.

2 *Time*
Time savings during execution of measures by means of deploying specialists in parallel; use of planned downtimes in production.

3 *Capacity*
Improved utilization of internal plant maintenance capacities; internal PM capacities relieved of routine tasks; short-term and cost-saving satisfaction of peak demand for PM activities.

4 *Elasticity*
External PM provider adapts to meet fluctuations in demand and changes in type of PM requirement.

5 *Planning*
Planning on the basis of data provided by system user (wear-and-tear profiles, lifetime statistics and operating efficiency analyses); determination of optimum PM strategy for the system user.

6 *Information processing*
Development and/or maintenance of specific software for IT-assisted plant maintenance; entry of existing PM data.

7 *Provision and storage*
Provision of spare parts, repair materials, repairable spares and repair operating supplies; knowledge of input/procurement market for spare parts, and so on.

8 *Finance*
Funds required remain constant due to long-term service contracts.

9 *Safety, environmental protection and industrial safety*
Elimination of risks to personnel, such as risk of internal specialists being unavailable due to illness or accident; warranty confirmations and good-will services; improved industrial safety and accident prevention by adopting tried-and-tested concepts; transfer of waste disposal issues.

10 *Human resources*
Reduction in staffing requirements; reduction in internal training measures.

11 *Organization*
Improved process structure in plant maintenance; centralization of decision-making authority.

12 *Costs*
Avoidance of overtime; elimination of reworking costs by means of warranty claims; falling fixed costs; cost-saving execution via plant-scale/quantity reductions.

EXAMPLE Your company operates an ice-cream production plant. You are planning external maintenance for the cooling systems in this plant, since these require highly specialized
maintenance and sophisticated precision tools. You now have the task of creating a value
profile for selecting the most suitable external maintenance provider.

You choose quality, time, elasticity, planning, corporate finance, safety/environmental pro-
tection/industrial safety, human resources, and costs as criteria with a high weighting. Since
you consider support during PM planning and saving training costs to be less important, you
assign these criteria a weighting of 5 on a scale of 1–10. You consider environmental protection to be very important for the cooling system, since you also intend to transfer disposal
of the coolant to the external maintenance provider. You consider it equally important to
conclude a long-term service contract with favourable conditions, and therefore assign
these criteria a weighting of 10. You assign all the remaining criteria a weighting of 8. Table
2.1 illustrates the resulting value profile with entries for an external maintenance company
X. In this way, you can evaluate the potential external maintenance providers, and decide on
the company with the highest final value.

TABLE 2.1   Value profile for an external maintenance provider

Criterion	Weighting	Degree of fulfilment (from –2 to +2)	Evaluation of company X
Quality	8	+1	+8
Time	8	–1	–8
Elasticity	8	–1	–8
Planning	5	+1	+5
Finance	10	+2	+20
Environmental protection	10	+1	+10
Human resources	5	–1	–5
Costs	8	+1	+8
			Final val.: +30

2.3   PLANNING IN PLANT MAINTENANCE

2.3.1 Planning and control

Planning in plant maintenance comprises 'all activities, tasks and actions, process
flows, technical data, economic criteria and costs, which affect the labour productivity
of the plant maintenance department and the adjoining enterprise areas or the enterprise as a whole' (Grobholz 1988: 38).

Control in plant maintenance comprises order-related scheduling and capacity determination, as well as monitoring the execution of PM tasks. Whereas planning is intended for the medium or long term, control is always short-term in nature. Figure 2.6 shows how planning and control interact in the order processing cycle.

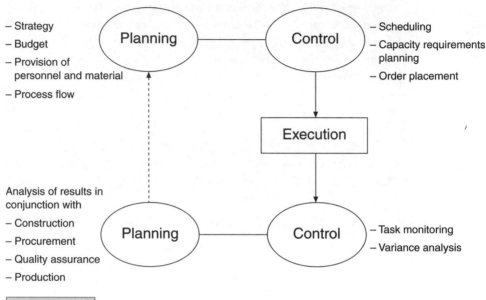

FIGURE 2.6   Planning and control (© SAP AG)

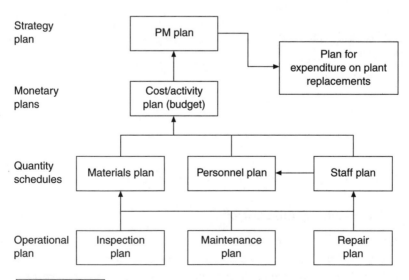

FIGURE 2.7   Strategy plans (from Grobholz 1988: 40) (© SAP AG)

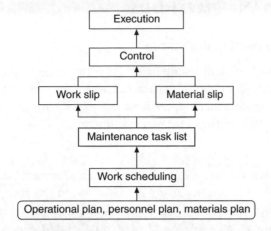

FIGURE 2.8   Work scheduling (from Grobholz 1988: 41) (© SAP AG)

2.3.2 Strategy plans and maintenance task lists

On the basis of Recommendation No. 10 of the Deutscher Komitee für Instandhaltung (DKIN: German Committee for Maintenance), a distinction is drawn in plant maintenance between strategic planning and work scheduling using maintenance task lists. Strategy plans are always created for the medium term or long term, and apply to a cycle or a period of time. By contrast, maintenance task lists are short-term in nature, and apply to a specific date.

> Strategic planning includes creating the operational plans (activities: preventive maintenance, inspection, repair), the quantity schedules (the personnel plan as well as the materials plan including the machine and equipment plan), the cost/performance plans, and the strategic overall plan. (Grobholz 1988: 40)

Figure 2.7 shows the strategy plans in context.

The maintenance task list is the instrument for controlling the PM tasks and is based on the operational plans. For example, a maintenance task list based on a repair plan contains detailed instructions on repair tasks as well as information concerning the execution date. After the repair tasks have been executed, the maintenance task list is returned to the preparation stage to allow an analysis to be carried out during planning. Figure 2.8 shows the work scheduling cycle in plant maintenance.

2.4.1 Damage-based plant maintenance

The damage-based method of plant maintenance (in extreme cases, also known as the breakdown or 'run-to-failure' method) is characterized by the fact that no preventive maintenance is carried out. System components are installed with no PM outlay, worn out, and replaced completely in the event of a malfunction.

EXAMPLE The service life of a seal is used up completely until a malfunction occurs. A damage-based plant maintenance task is then carried out to install a new seal. In this case, the damage-based plant maintenance method is worthwhile, since regularly inspecting and maintaining a seal would cost more than the seal itself. The situation is rather different, however, if the seal is classified as a system component presenting a danger to production or safety. In this case, the method would not only be foolish, but would also give rise to high downtime and follow-up costs.

The damage-based plant maintenance method is financially viable, therefore, only under the following conditions:

- If the system components involved cost considerably less to acquire than to maintain.
- If system components involved present no danger to either production or safety in the event of a breakdown, and can be repaired without significant outlay (for example, without shutting down the system).
- If the system components involved have a limited service life that it is neither feasible nor desirable to extend (no refurbishment).

The business process for this method begins with the notification that a malfunction has occurred. The second step involves specifying the nature of the malfunction. The PM planner responsible can either ask the notification creator for more details or investigate the malfunction himself. If the notification creator is a PM technician, he can also specify the nature of the malfunction himself in the second step. As soon as the details have been established, planning and control of the repair task can be carried out. The amount of time available for planning and control varies depending on the severity of the malfunction and its effects on production. If sufficient time is available, the PM planner can specify repairable spares, workflows, or the tools to be used. If little time is available, the PM planner provides a PM technician with a roughly specified work order.

In the event of serious malfunctions, this sequence can also be reversed. In this case, the repair is performed first, and official notification and specification of the malfunction are carried out only afterwards.

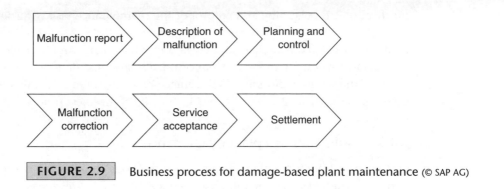

FIGURE 2.9   Business process for damage-based plant maintenance (© SAP AG)

After the malfunction has been corrected (repaired) by an internal or external PM technician, the PM planner (as the ordering party) signs off the service performed. In the concluding step, the order is settled by accounting. Figure 2.9 presents an overview of this business process.

2.4.2 Time-based plant maintenance

With time-based (or periodic) plant maintenance, preventive maintenance of a system component is carried out regularly after a specific period of use. One advantage of this method is that regular preventive maintenance increases the service life of a system component. In some cases, statutory or safety regulations require proof of regular preventive maintenance (for example, fire extinguishers and automobiles are subject to inspection at regular intervals). One disadvantage of time-based maintenance is that the service life of a system component always depends on its level of usage.

EXAMPLE A pump in an ice-cream production plant has to be replaced after every 10,000 litres at the latest. From a statistical point of view, this limit is reached every two months. As a result, a maintenance cycle of two months is specified by time-based plant maintenance. In March, this pump is replaced after 9000 litres; in May, after 4000 litres; and in July, after 9200 litres. In May, the utilization level was considerably lower than in the other months, which means that the pump only really needed to be replaced in June. However, time-based plant maintenance takes only the maintenance cycle of two months into account, and not the actual wear and tear. As a result of replacing a pump that was still functioning in May, the company incurred additional costs.

The business process for time-based plant maintenance begins with notification (generally output by a computer system) that the specified date has been reached. The specified date is the finish date of a particular maintenance cycle. Following notification, the planning and control of the maintenance task is carried out on the basis of a maintenance plan. Since the maintenance tasks are known in advance, this maintenance plan can also be output by a computer system. An internal or external PM technician carries out the maintenance on the specified date, and the PM planner signs off the service performed. As in damage-based maintenance, this step is followed by settlement. Figure 2.10 shows an overview of this business process.

2.4.3 Condition-based plant maintenance

Of the three traditional plant maintenance methods, condition-based plant mainte-nance is the one that enables the service life to be leveraged optimally and economically. In condition-based maintenance, a maintenance task is required only if a specific level of wear and tear has been reached (for example, if and only if the value for the pump has actually reached 9900 litres).

To enable condition-based plant maintenance to be carried out, the actual condition of the system component must be measured precisely by means of regular inspections. For example, the pump can be fitted with a meter that measures the flow in litres and is read regularly.

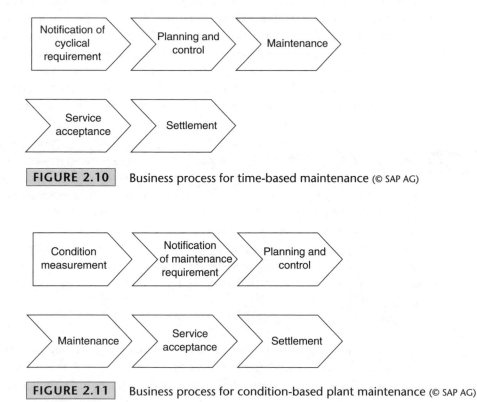

FIGURE 2.10   Business process for time-based maintenance (© SAP AG)

FIGURE 2.11   Business process for condition-based plant maintenance (© SAP AG)

The business process for this method begins with regular measurements of the condition. When this measurement determines that a specific value has been reached, notification of the maintenance requirement is issued. The PM planner plans and controls the maintenance tasks on the basis of a maintenance plan. As in the other business processes, maintenance is then carried out, signed off and settled. Figure 2.11 shows an overview of this business process.

A company can use all three of the above methods in parallel, or combine them as required. The particular method used often depends on the type and value of the material in question. Damage-based plant maintenance can be used as a method for parts subject to wear and tear, whereas time-based or condition-based plant maintenance can be used for system components with a long service life. It can also be expedient to combine time-based and condition-based plant maintenance.

EXAMPLE The pump should always be replaced after 10,000 litres, but only after a minimum usage time of two months. Or the pump should be replaced by an external company every two months; if the value of 9900 litres is reached, however, the pump can also be replaced within the two-month cycle.

2.5   BENCHMARKING IN PLANT MAINTENANCE BASED ON KEY PERFORMANCE INDICATORS

Benchmarking involves using specific criteria to define various subareas of plant maintenance, and then comparing these within one's own company or with other companies. To enable plant maintenance management to be improved, the particular demands that have to be satisfied are specified for the criteria. Two of these subareas are, for example, corporate management and asset management.

In the corporate management subarea, the following criteria must be evaluated as regards their level of maturity and the results achieved in comparison with the benchmarking partner (Biedermann 1998: 34):

1   Written version of the plant maintenance philosophy

2   Target-based formulation of continuous improvement

3   Cross-departmental teams with target achievement monitoring

4   Cross-departmental controlling with PM contribution as regards
    - Quality (key performance indicators)
    - Productivity (key performance indicators)
    - Utilization of system capacity (key performance indicators)
    - Safety (internal area) and environment (external area)

5 Standardization (standards, guidelines, instructions)

6 Staff commitment and delegation

7 Risk profile for organization (division) of work between system operator and maintenance provider

8 Catalogue of criteria for transferring tasks to production

9 Analytical evaluation of the optimum level of decentralization

10 Strategic orientation in assigning external services

11 Controlling functions

In the asset management subarea, the following criteria must be evaluated as regards their level of maturity and the results achieved in comparison with the benchmarking partner (Biedermann 1998: 35):

1 Documentation of critical systems/assemblies and description of relevant maintenance strategy

2 Systematic process of weak-point elimination
  – Technical assessments
  – Business assessments

3 Assessments with regard to occupational and operational safety, as well as environmental protection, with associated documentation

4 Classification of systems with regard to their significance and place in the production process, with associated documentation (key performance indicators)

5 Definition of targets in the areas of reliability and availability

6 Use of methods and tools or techniques to increase actual production time

7 Routine evaluation for reliability engineering

8 Use of information technologies for supporting reliability management

9 Visualization by means of reports, graphics and diagrams as means of organizing information in accordance with demands

10 Inclusion of plant maintenance concepts in the drafting and construction of new systems

11 Use of methods to compare the economic efficiency of asset investment as regards plant maintenance or replacement

In this context, some of the PM key performance indicators in VDI Guideline 2893 are significant. You can use key performance indicators 1–4, for example, to analyse PM costs. Key performance indicator 1 is the PM cost rate; in other words, the total costs (costs for personnel, labour, materials and external services) for PM tasks to DIN 31051 divided by the indexed acquisition value, the asset value in the year of procurement multiplied by the price index (index figures of the Federal Statistical Office Germany) for the year in question.

Key performance indicators 2–4 provide a further breakdown of the total cost. Key performance indicator 2 is the PM cost portion for personnel; in other words, the labour and salary costs for PM personnel, including the total cost divided by the total PM costs in accordance with key performance indicator 1.

Key performance indicator 3 is the PM cost portion for materials; in other words, the costs for material used for plant maintenance (spare parts, operating supplies and consumables) divided by the total PM costs in accordance with key performance indicator 1.

Key performance indicator 4 is the PM portion for external services; in other words, the costs for PM tasks carried out by external companies divided by the total PM costs in accordance with key performance indicator 1. It is advisable here to list separately the labour and material costs for the external service in accordance with key performance indicators 2 and 3.

The PM personnel cost rate (key performance indicator 17) and PM material cost rate (key performance indicator 18) can also be calculated in accordance with key performance indicator 1. With the PM personnel cost rate, the personnel costs in accordance with key performance indicator 2 are divided by the indexed acquisition value in accordance with key performance indicator 1. With the plant maintenance material cost rate, the material costs in accordance with key performance indicator 3 are divided by the acquisition value in accordance with key performance indicator 1. (For further PM key performance indicators, refer to VDI Guideline 2893. On PM key performance indicators, see Gamweger 1998: 101–112.)

2.6   MODERN PLANT MAINTENANCE MANAGEMENT

2.6.1 Total Productive Maintenance (TPM)

The TPM concept was developed in Japan in the 1970s, but only became more widespread during the 1990s. The main characteristic of TPM is that the tasks formerly planned and carried out by central PM departments are transferred gradually to the machinist.

> In contrast to traditional plant maintenance, which is regarded as an auxiliary plant or service function of production, TPM pursues considerably more extensive objectives, since all members of staff are included in the improvement process. (Matyas 1999: 31)

Training the operating personnel is an important prerequisite here for overcoming the traditional organizational separation of machine operation and machine maintenance. According to Matyas, the objective of TPM is 'autonomous operator maintenance'.

This is evident, for example, in the Japan Technology Group's mission statement for TPM:

> Total Productive Maintenance means that operators are empowered to maintain continuous production on totally efficient lines. (Japan Technology Group, Nippon Lever BV, Japan. http://www.bekkoame.or.jp/~axeichi/n_lever)

Within the scope of TPM, the actual PM department analyses the PM tasks carried out by the operating personnel. The PM department also carries out strategic planning, administration of maintenance task lists and maintenance plans, as well as cost control.

2.6.2 Reliability Centred Maintenance (RCM)

RCM, also known as Reliability Based Maintenance (RBM), is concerned specifically with system breakdowns, the associated follow-up costs, and how to avoid them. The aim of this method is to use a risk analysis and risk evaluation (as a separate method, Risk Based Maintenance) to decide whether preventive PM tasks could incur higher costs than a system breakdown and its consequences.

> The question of whether preventive measures are expedient arises especially where redundant (bypass) or multiply redundant systems are used. This is because the bypass is intended to take effect if the component breaks down. What is the use of prevention where a safeguard is already installed? This should be taken into consideration particularly in the case of systems with a high level of redundancy determined by technology or legal stipulations (for example, in systems involving nuclear technology). (Stender 1999: 43)

The most important prerequisites for RCM are calculation and evaluation of a system breakdown.

2.6.3 Life Cycle Costing

Life Cycle Costing is a tool used in cost management for a product or a system.

> Life Cycle Costing is not a separate method; it is based on a number of well-known methods from capital budgeting (for example, system evaluation methods, cost forecasting procedures, and methods for taking risk and inflation into account). (Günther 1997: 900)

When a system is procured, for example, Life Cycle Costing facilitates the decision between alternative products offered by rival providers. This method is used to compare not only the procurement and initial costs, but also (and more importantly) the operating and follow-up costs in the life cycle of a system. The operating and follow-up costs essentially contain the costs for preventive maintenance and plant maintenance, as well as the operating and disposal costs. Even after a system has been procured, Life Cycle Costing contributes to optimizing costs and performance throughout the life cycle of the system:

> In contrast to capital budgeting, Life Cycle Costing does not end when the analysis of life cycle revenues and costs is complete. To achieve its goal as regards design, Life Cycle Costing employs a continuous process for optimizing the design of the particular product or system throughout its entire life cycle (. . .). (Günther 1997: 912)

Life Cycle Costing is particularly worthwhile for systems involving high capital investment and with a long service life, as well as where the follow-up costs accrued by the system are high in comparison to the initial costs. Life Cycle Costing is, therefore, an important method for classifying and planning the scope of plant maintenance strategically.

2.6.4 Decentralized Equipment and Process Responsibility (DAPV)

DAPV was developed by the Fraunhofer Institute for Production Engineering and Automation (Germany). The method focuses primarily on the organizational structure of the PM department; in other words, on creating decentralized structures and transferring responsibility to work groups and teams.

> With a centralized form of organization, personnel and organization in the four elements of planning, control, execution, and monitoring are separate. In fact, it can even be said that the greater the separation of these elements with regard to persons and departments, the higher the level of centralization. By contrast, the characteristic feature of a decentralized organization is that these four elements or tasks are performed by a group or team (and possibly even by only one person). (Stender 1999: 51)

Former members of the PM department can be integrated in the production team that performs plant maintenance tasks. The team calls in external maintenance providers only in the event of more extensive and complex plant maintenance tasks. These providers come either from an internal 'plant maintenance service centre' or from an external company.

> The obvious thing to do, then, is to eliminate function-oriented departments, such as production (quantity), plant maintenance (system), logistics (time), and quality, in order to establish process-oriented departments (fractals), in which part

tasks of the original logistics, plant, maintenance and quality functions are carried out, as well as production. The former logistics, plant maintenance, and quality departments are retained in cases where specific tasks requiring a high level of function-specific know-how have to be carried out. If they are retained, however, these departments give up personnel, since the overall scope of their tasks is reduced. In addition to this, the role of persons responsible changes, since they are now only engaged by the production fractals as service providers within a clearly defined customer/vendor relationship. (Stender 1999: 56)

As with TPM, the organizational role of the PM department within the company is changed, while the actual PM tasks are now carried out as a role in a production team.

2.6.5 Other trends

System engineers as service providers

In addition to the PM management concepts outlined above, a number of other trends for modernizing traditional plant maintenance are currently developing. Some manufacturing companies are now carrying out not only traditional system engineering, but also production optimization and system maintenance.

This means that erstwhile producers are increasingly becoming providers of holistic product solutions extending from system planning and construction through to system support during operation. This establishes a control loop that also sets important new trends for maintenance. The total asset history costs of a machine or system from construction through to system operation are now relevant for system engineers. This means that they not only have to take the costs of the first phase of the product life cycle into consideration, but also have to allow for the subsequent costs of ensuring the availability of their system. This involves giving particular consideration to influences on system behaviour arising from the construction of assemblies and operational methods, the use of basic materials, and the quality of internally produced as well as externally purchased parts. (Proksch 1999: 14)

Remote diagnosis and virtual service groups

Virtual service groups are specialist teams for High Intelligence Maintenance (HIM), which work together on projects and are organized via virtual markets.

Virtual service groups will be created, in which companies (particularly PM service providers and component suppliers, but also system manufacturers) cooperate to provide services. The global options for accessing system data enable highly qualified specialist plant maintenance teams to be assembled internationally as and when required. This is especially useful in the case of more complex malfunctions, system optimizations, modifications, or other large-scale measures. (Slender and Proksch 1999: 14)

This scenario offers following remote diagnosis options:

- Process supervision and weak-point analysis
- Process management and control
- Business reengineering, process optimization
- Remote programming and control of machines
- Remote control and fault correction for control software
- Teleservice with sensors, video/audio monitoring (on teleservice, see Stoll 1999))

Internet technologies can be used to create a virtual marketplace (or portal) operated by providers of software for PM planning and control systems, for example. In this portal, providers of PM services, suppliers of spare parts, and systems engineers can advertise their products and services under the heading 'Sell'; companies seeking to purchase plant maintenance services in the short-term or mid-term can advertise under 'Buy'. This marketplace can be used not only to level out supply and demand, however, but also to exchange information (for example, on benchmarking results, key performance indicators, and PM strategies, as well as experience with modern PM management concepts or technical innovations). Some of the above options for remote diagnosis could also be implemented directly via a marketplace of this type.

Facility management

Building maintenance is a subarea of facility or building management. The greater the level of automation via building control systems, the more important it is to integrate the PM processes smoothly. If computers are used to support plant maintenance operations, an interface must exist between the maintenance planning and control system (MPC) and the building control system so that a malfunction report is generated automatically in the MPC as soon as the building control system detects a malfunction.

Graphical user interfaces for MPC

Traditional MPC systems can be made easier for PM planners or technicians to operate by means of intuitive user interfaces. Malfunctions in a system can be localized more easily if the MPC system is equipped with a user interface supporting CAD drawings, three-dimensional images, construction plans, or process and instrumentation diagrams. Drawings or images of this kind can be made available throughout the company on the internet/intranet and accessed via a browser. This means that users do not require a technical key for the system component affected in order to enter data and trigger events in an MPC system (for example, to initiate a malfunction report).

Solution databases

Analysis procedures, such as 'Safety through organizational learning' (SOL), are centered on the concept of learning from experience. (On SOL, see Geipel-Kern (1999).) Breakdowns, malfunctions, accidents and near-accidents are evaluated systematically to enable processes to be improved and similar malfunctions to be corrected more quickly. Tried-and-tested solutions can be stored in solution/task databases. By means of Case-Based Reasoning systems (CBR), the system can link the description of a particular problem to descriptions of similar problems. These descriptions are connected, in turn, to a tried-and-tested solution that has already been used successfully and linked to the descriptions of problems via SOL, for example. This enables company-internal knowledge relating to plant maintenance processes to be stored in a knowledge base. Some system engineers or manufacturers of spare parts supply product-specific knowledge bases with their products. The PM technician (as customer) can then call up the manufacturer's knowledge base directly or via the internet should problems arise.

Simulation programs

Simulation programs can be used, for example, to show how the breakdown of a subsystem will affect the system as a whole.

> In the simulation system itself, the behaviour of the system is mapped via events, which are triggered at the appropriate times by means of the determined characteristics. These cause changes in the system condition, which trigger further events (discrete event simulation). This not only enables the behaviour of real systems/system components to be described, but also allows supplementary levels of analysis to be integrated in the simulation model in parallel with the actual process flows. (Feldmann 1999: 54)

When used as part of a preliminary economic evaluation of the simulated malfunction, this procedure enables the costs for PM personnel to be calculated directly according to the duration of the malfunction and the hourly rate, for example.

CHAPTER 3

Getting started with Release 4.6

Even if you have already worked with earlier releases, you will find some of the new R/3 functions unfamiliar. This chapter introduces you to useful new features in the areas of navigation, communication, error handling and documentation, which support your day-to-day work in plant maintenance.

3.1 THE PM MENU WITH EASY ACCESS

3.1.1 How to display the Maintenance Processing menu after logging on to R/3

If your work mainly involves maintenance processing, you may find it useful to hide the other menus in the R/3 System so that you can work in the processing menu as soon as you log on. This one-off setting is carried out via the user profile (Fig. 3.1).

1   After logging on, choose SYSTEM | USER PROFILE | OWN DATA.

2   In the DEFAULTS tab page, enter IW00 as the start menu and save your data.

The next time you log on, the R/3 System displays the new Easy Access navigation menu for maintenance processing that you have chosen. None of the other R/3 components are displayed in this menu (Fig. 3.2).

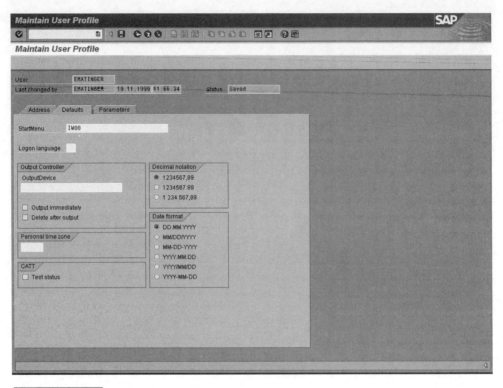

FIGURE 3.1 Start menu as a user profile (© SAP AG)

You open the individual folders by double-clicking them. Double-clicking one of the cube-shaped transaction icons starts the corresponding transaction.

3.1.2 How to display a role-specific PM menu after logging on

As you will see in the subsequent chapters, we recommend that you use three roles in maintenance processing:

- Plant maintenance technician (PM technician)
- Plant maintenance planner (PM planner)
- Controller

You can group together the transactions used frequently for each role as 'Favorites' in a separate folder. For example, after the PM technician has logged on to the R/3 System, he or she can store the frequently used transaction CREATE MALFUNCTION REPORT, together with any number of other transactions, as favorites in a 'Technician' folder. To do so, you proceed as follows:

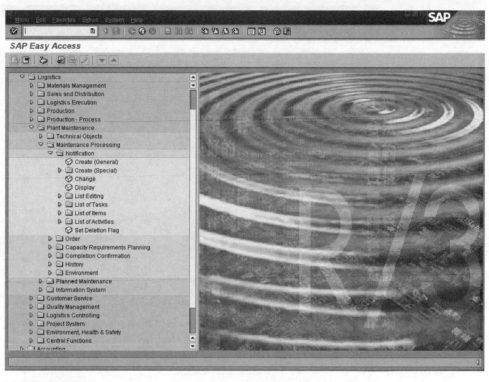

FIGURE 3.2   Maintenance Processing menu (© SAP AG)

1 After logging on to the R/3 System, you will see the general navigation menu (Fig. 3.3). CHOOSE FAVORITES | INSERT FOLDER.

2 Enter 'PM Technician' as the name of the folder and confirm your entry.

3 Open the Logistics menus by double-clicking the folders until the notification transactions are displayed.

Now place the cursor on the transaction NOTIFICATION | CREATE (SPECIAL) | MALFUNCTION REPORT. While holding down the left mouse button, drag the transaction to the 'Technician' folder.

Using this method, you can create any number of folders and fill them with transactions. To start a particular transaction, simply double-click it.

3.1.3 How to add internet pages and files to your menu

In addition to transactions, you can include links to frequently used internet pages or files in your folders. Choose FAVORITES | ADD WEB ADDRESS OR FILE. In the text field, enter a text of your choice for the link. In the second field, you can specify either the

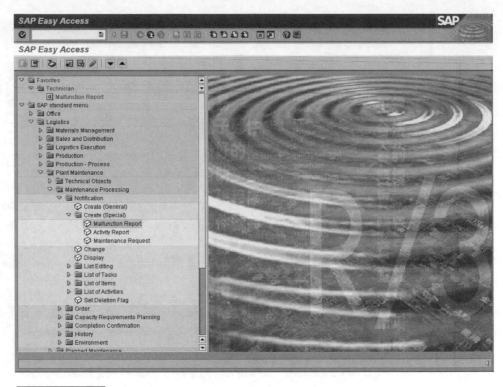

FIGURE 3.3 Choosing transactions as favorites (© SAP AG)

WWW address or the file storage path. Alternatively, you can press F4 and search for the desired document on your hard disk (Figs 3.4 and 3.5).

3.2 THE BUSINESS WORKPLACE

The Business Workplace provides a standard working environment in which you can carry out your share of the tasks in the business and communication processes of your company. For example, the PM technician's Inbox shows him the orders for execution that the PM planner has sent him. Other scenarios could involve several PM planners from different departments working together via Business Workflow and sending each other orders for planning; or the controller could use the Business Workplace to inform the PM planner if the planned costs for an order are too high.

In the Workplace, you receive all the work items assigned to you in a workflow. The Business Workplace is required by every user who participates in the SAP Business Workflow in your company. Data sent to and from the R/3 applications is also handled via the Business Workplace. For this reason, many applications include a direct link to the Business Workplace.

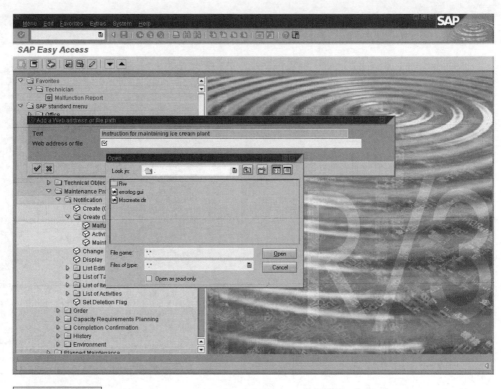

This component can also be used to process all the internal and external mail of a company. In the Business Workplace, you can process all the mail documents sent to you by people or by R/3 applications. You can organize the folders in which you manage documents and tasks. You can read information published within a work group or throughout the company, or make it available to others. You can also use the Business Workplace via the interface of MAPI-capable clients (such as Microsoft Outlook). In addition to this, the Business Workplace is available as an Internet Application Component.

3.2.1 Working with the Business Workplace

To start the Business Workplace, choose OFFICE | WORKPLACE. The Business Workplace screen comprises the following three elements (Fig. 3.6):

■ *Structure*

The folders in your Business Workplace are displayed here in a tree structure. Clicking a folder calls up its contents.

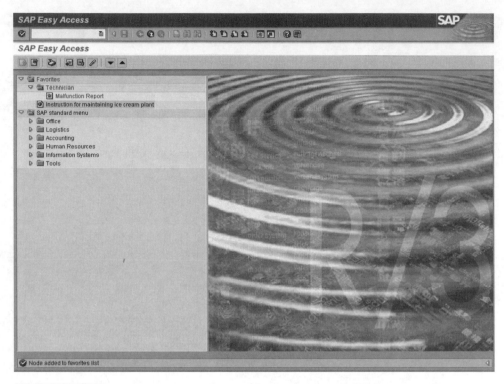

FIGURE 3.5   Transaction, WWW address, and document as favorites (© SAP AG)

■ *Folder contents list*

This displays a list of the work items, documents, distribution lists, folders, and objects in the folder you have selected in the folder tree. Clicking an entry in the list calls up a preview. Double-clicking an entry calls up its screen.

■ *Preview*

The list entry selected in the folder contents list is displayed here – if the entry supports the preview function. The work item preview provides you with further functions. You can hide the preview, if necessary.

The default settings are such that the workplace is always displayed as it was when you last exited it. This does not apply to the sort sequence of the folder contents list. If you change the settings so that the Workplace display is not saved, every time you access the Workplace it will be displayed the way it was the first time you called it up.

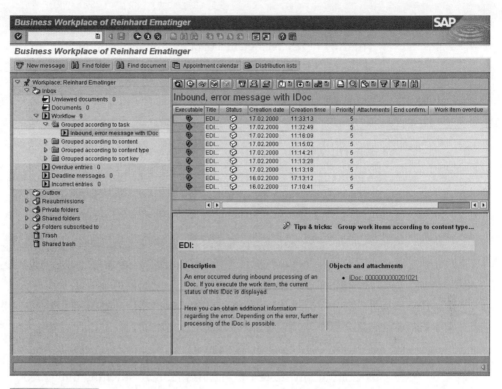

FIGURE 3.6   Incoming mails and work items in the Business Workplace (© SAP AG)

3.3   SUPPORT LINE FEEDBACK AS AN INTERFACE TO SAP

In the past, if you encountered a program error while working with the R/3 System, you had to call up the OSS system (new name: SAPNet–R/3 Frontend) and enter a notification for SAP. Release 4.6 of the standard system gives you the option of sending a notification directly to SAP from the current R/3 application (Support Line Feedback). A new notification type has been created for this purpose, the 'R/3 notification'. R/3 notifications automatically include your most important system and user data, which means that you only have to enter the problem and assign it to a component. SAP treats R/3 notifications in exactly the same way as OSS notifications.

The aim of this new interface to SAP is to support R/3 users with enquiries and problems by enabling them to:

- Create notifications in the local R/3 customer system

- Supplement their notification with R/3 system data automatically

- Integrate in-house support (Customer Competence Centre, CCC) in the notification flow

Other advantages of this interface to SAP include:

▨ Transfer of reliable detailed data to in-house support/CCC or to SAP

▨ Direct, tool-based link to in-house support/CCC via 'Link to CCC', or to SAP via 'Link to SAP'

3.3.1 How to create an R/3 notification

The feedback functionality of the SAP Support Line enables you, as a normal R/3 user, to contact your support unit directly from the R/3 System (in-house support/CCC or SAP). The Support Line has advantages for all user groups:

1 R/3 users can enter their notification via a simple notification screen and send it to their support unit. This means that users do not have to enter notifications in a different system.

2 While the R/3 user is entering the notification, the system automatically adds important data to the notification, thereby providing the basis for effective processing.

3 The R/3 user can enter a notification containing his or her comments or questions at any time. This means that users are fully integrated in the R/3 feedback process.

4 Members of the in-house support/CCC staff can forward notifications directly to SAP from their R/3 system. It is not necessary for them to log on to the OSS System (SAPNet–R/3 Frontend) to enter and forward notifications.

FIGURE 3.7   SAP logo for calling up an R/3 notification (© SAP AG)

The feedback notifications can be used either as 'Link to CCC' or directly as 'Link to SAP', depending on whether individual R/3 users in your company are authorized to send notifications directly to SAP. The 'Link to CCC' is intended specifically to aid in-house support when a support structure is being created.

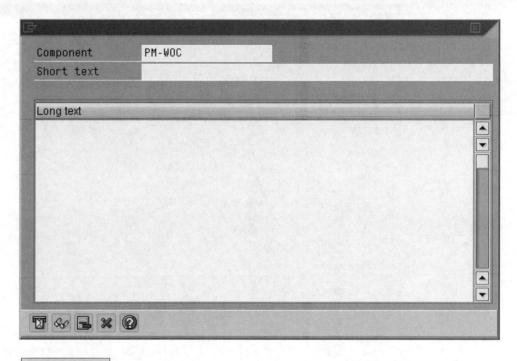

Component   PM-WOC

Short text

Long text

FIGURE 3.8   R/3 notification with sections for short text and long text (© SAP AG)

To create an R/3 notification from any transaction, choose HELP | FEEDBACK. Alternatively, you can double-click the SAP logo at the top right of the screen (Fig. 3.7). This calls up the entry screen for your R/3 notification, in which you can enter a short text and a long text. The system determines the component automatically from the transaction that you are currently working with. In Figure 3.8, the PM planner has called up the R/3 notification from order processing, so the PM-WOC component appears automatically.

All the other important data for processing the notification is provided by the R/3 System itself and added to the notification; for example, the R/3 installation number, R/3 Release, current transaction, and support package (Fig. 3.9). This data enables SAP to respond quickly and effectively to your notification. The data involved here is user-independent data, which you can call up at any time when entering the notification. To do so, choose the DISPLAY icon in the R/3 notification.

When you have entered the short text and the long text, you can send the R/3 notification. To do so, choose the SEND icon. In Figure 3.10, the PM planner has sent the notification to in-house support first, and not directly to SAP.

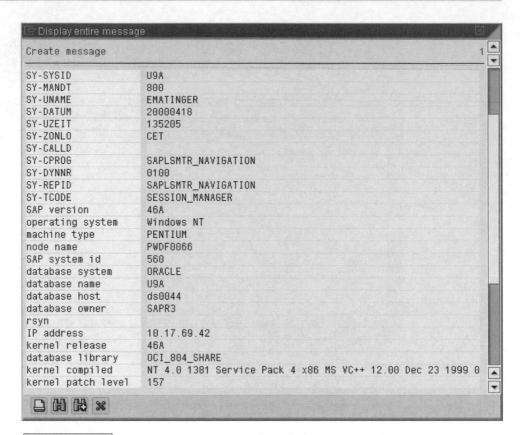

```
Display entire message                                                          ☒

Create message                                                            1

SY-SYSID          U9A
SY-MANDT          800
SY-UNAME          EMATINGER
SY-DATUM          20000418
SY-UZEIT          135205
SY-ZONLO          CET
SY-CALLD
SY-CPROG          SAPLSMTR_NAVIGATION
SY-DYNNR          0100
SY-REPID          SAPLSMTR_NAVIGATION
SY-TCODE          SESSION_MANAGER
SAP version       46A
operating system  Windows NT
machine type      PENTIUM
node name         PWDF0066
SAP system id     560
database system   ORACLE
database name     U9A
database host     ds0044
database owner    SAPR3
rsyn
IP address        10.17.69.42
kernel release    46A
database library  OCI_804_SHARE
kernel compiled   NT 4.0 1381 Service Pack 4 x86 MS VC++ 12.00 Dec 23 1999 0
kernel patch level 157
```

FIGURE 3.9   Some of the system data for an R/3 notification (© SAP AG)

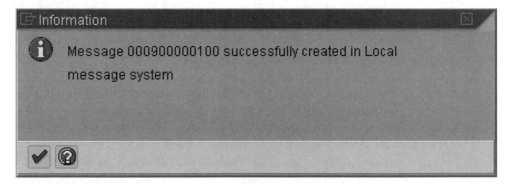

Information   ☒

Message 000900000100 successfully created in Local
message system

FIGURE 3.10   Creating an R/3 notification in the local support system (© SAP AG)

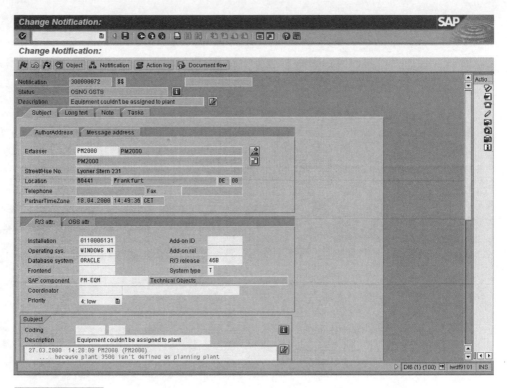

FIGURE 3.11   R/3 notification received by the support team (© SAP AG)

3.3.2 How your support team processes the R/3 notification

To send the notification, you have to enter your user ID and password. When you have done so, a complete R/3 notification is created automatically in the support team's R/3 System (Fig. 3.11). In addition to the short text and long text you have entered, this R/3 notification contains your address data and all the system data you have transferred. The members of the support team can then process the notification in their R/3 System and inform you of the solution.

The functions for notification processing are the same as those for a PM notification, since the R/3 notification is, in a sense, simply another notification type in PM. What is new in the R/3 notification is the option of searching for related notes in SAPNet directly from the notification. To do so, the members of the support team choose the NOTE tab page and then the NOTE pushbutton. The selection criteria are entered on the left of the search screen, where the hit list is also subsequently displayed. The appropriate note is displayed on the right of the screen (Fig. 3.12).

If the member of the support staff is unable to solve the problem, he or she forwards it directly to SAP via a bi-directional interface. To do so, he or she chooses SEND TO SAP in the action box of the R/3 notification (Fig. 3.13). The member of the support staff

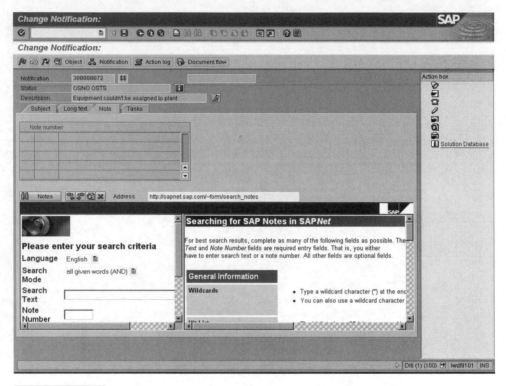

FIGURE 3.12   Notes search in SAPNet (© SAP AG)

does not have to log on to the OSS System (SAPNet–R/3 Frontend) to create notifications, track statuses and search for R/3 notes. These actions can be executed directly in his or her R/3 System. From a technical point of view, several R/3 Systems can send notifications to a central R/3 System of the in-house support/CCC (via a Remote Function Call). The member of the support team can process or forward the R/3 notification in the same way as any other PM notification.

3.3.3 How to activate support line feedback

As of Release 4.6A, Support Line Feedback is a standard feature of the R/3 System. This release includes the technical interfaces, as well as all the required Customizing settings, enabling the Feedback functionality to be activated very quickly.

For further tips on installing the Feedback functionality, refer to SAPNet: http://sapnet.sap.com/support_line. Then choose 'Feedback Messages'. In SAPNet, you will find complete documentation for the functionality, as well as SAP Note number 153743 on immediate installation.

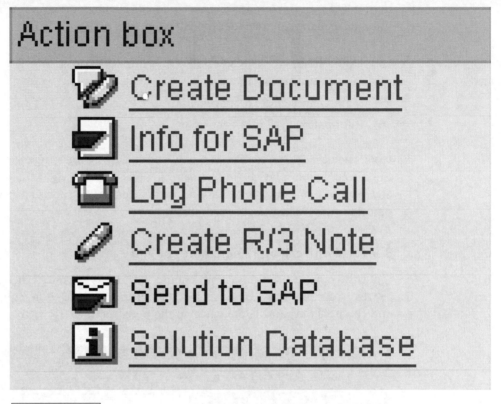

Action box

- Create Document
- Info for SAP
- Log Phone Call
- Create R/3 Note
- Send to SAP
- Solution Database

FIGURE 3.13   Sending an R/3 notification from the support team to SAP (© SAP AG)

3.4   PM DOCUMENTATION IN THE SAP LIBRARY

For every release, SAP provides a CD-ROM containing the current documentation in English and German. Your system administrator should install the documentation on a server in the desired help display format. In the examples given here, the documentation is displayed as plain HTML in an internet browser and is taken from the SAP Knowledge Warehouse database.

3.5   HOW TO CALL UP PM DOCUMENTATION IN THE SAP LIBRARY

From the current PM transaction, choose HELP | APPLICATION HELP. This immediately calls up the section of the PM documentation on the appropriate transaction. Via HELP | SAP LIBRARY, you can call up the documentation on the entire R/3 System from any transaction (Fig. 3.14). From there, choose the 'Logistics' area (Fig. 3.15). Then call up the 'PM Plant Maintenance' area by double-clicking it (Fig. 3.16). You will find the individual chapters here under the following four nodes:

1 Equipment and Technical Objects

2 Preventive Maintenance

3 Maintenance Order Management

4 Information System

Open the desired chapter. You can now navigate using the structure tree on the left of the screen, and display the individual info objects on the right. Each info object here always corresponds to a link in the structure. Figure 3.17 shows an example of an info object for the PM notifications.

3.5.1 How to call up release notes on PM

From the current PM transaction, choose HELP | SAP LIBRARY. Then choose RELEASE NOTES in the blue navigation bar. Find the release for which you require release notes, and choose 'PM Plant Maintenance' in the tree structure (Fig. 3.18).

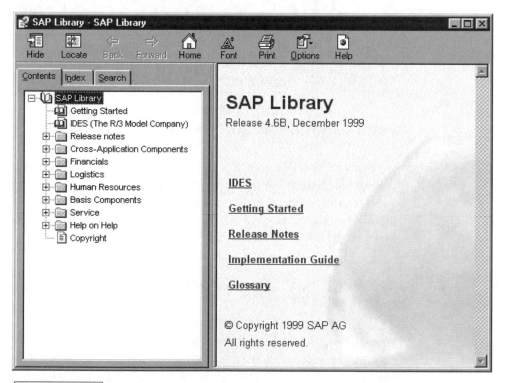

FIGURE 3.14 SAP Library initial screen as plain HTML in browser (© SAP AG)

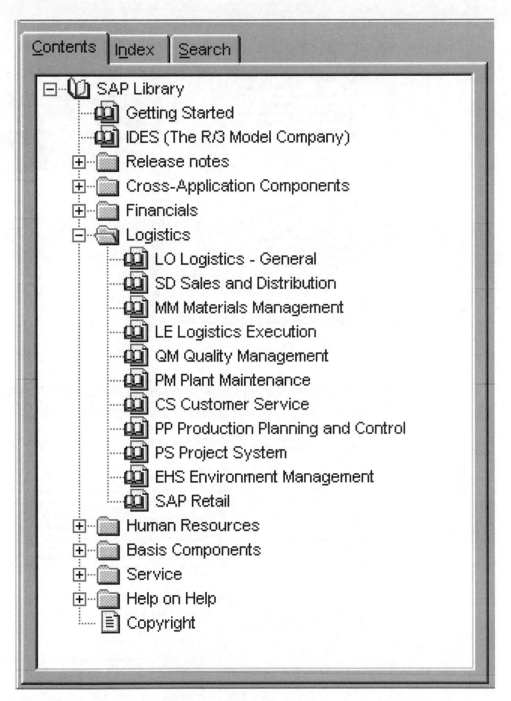

FIGURE 3.15   Logistics components (© SAP AG)

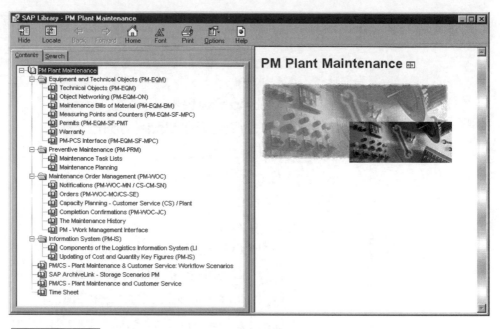

FIGURE 3.16 PM documentation in the SAP Library (© SAP AG)

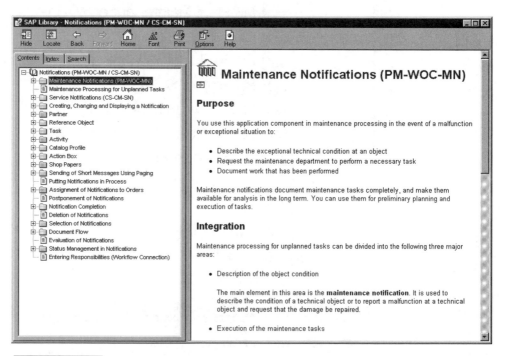

FIGURE 3.17 Info object for the PM notifications (© SAP AG)

3.5.2 How to call up PM documentation in the implementation guide (IMG)

From the current PM transaction, choose HELP | SAP LIBRARY. Then choose IMG in the blue navigation bar. Next choose 'Plant Maintenance and Customer Service' in the tree structure (Fig. 3.19).

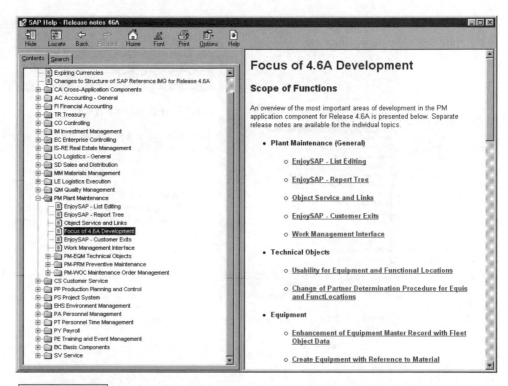

FIGURE 3.18   PM release notes (© SAP AG)

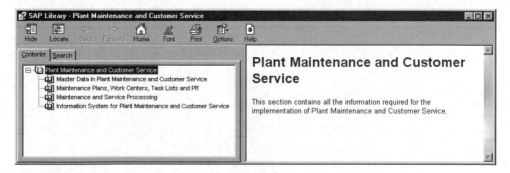

FIGURE 3.19   PM documentation in the IMG (© SAP AG)

3.5.3 How to call up PM terms in the glossary

From the current PM transaction, choose HELP | SAP LIBRARY. Then choose GLOSSARY in the blue navigation bar. Next, click the initial letter of the term you want to find (Fig. 3.20).

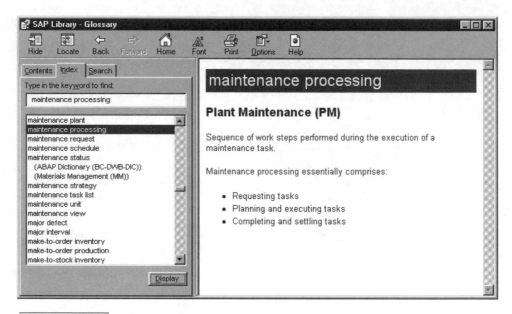

FIGURE 3.20   PM terms in the glossary (© SAP AG)

CHAPTER 4

Objects in R/3 PM

4.1 MANAGING TECHNICAL OBJECTS

If companies wish to use IT-assisted plant maintenance efficiently, they must structure their existing technical assets; in other words, these assets must be divided into technical objects (PM master data) and organized hierarchically. In order to use R/3 PM effectively, you first have to map the objects for maintenance as master data in the R/3 System. For PM processing proper, the object for maintenance is used as a reference object. Various data from the reference object can be transferred to the maintenance order.

Advantages of structuring are that it:

■ Reduces the outlay for managing technical objects

■ Simplifies maintenance processing

■ Considerably reduces the outlay involved in entering data during maintenance processing

■ Improves targeting, comprehensiveness and the speed with which plant maintenance data is analysed

Before starting to map technical objects in the system, you should form a clear picture of how maintenance planning is organized in your site. To achieve this, you must focus primarily on the structure of the company as a whole. This involves defining the maintenance plants and maintenance planning plants (PM planning plants) correctly in your system.

Do not underestimate the length of the planning phase required for structuring. Consider very carefully the comparative advantages and disadvantages of every structuring approach for your site. Remember that it will take you longer to restructure objects than to create a new structure. If entered incorrectly, technical objects cannot simply be deleted from the R/3 System; rather they have to be reorganized via the archiving program.

4.1.1 The concept of plants in the R/3 system

In the R/3 System, the plant is a place of work or a branch within a company. The plant is integrated in the organizational structure as follows (Fig. 4.1):

- The plant is assigned to exactly one company code. One company code can have several plants.
- One plant can have several storage locations at which material stocks are stored.
- Exactly one business area is assigned to a plant and a division.
- A plant can be assigned to several sales organizations/distribution channel combinations.
- A plant can have several shipping points. A shipping point can be assigned to several plants.
- A plant can be defined as a PM planning plant.

A plant has the following attributes:

- It has an address.
- It has a language.
- It belongs to a particular country.
- It has its own material master data. Data can be maintained at plant level specifically for the following views of the material master record: materials planning, purchasing, storage, work scheduling, production resources/tools, forecast, quality management, sales and distribution, and costing.

The plant plays an important role in the following areas:

- *Material valuation*

  If the valuation level is the plant, the material stocks are valuated at plant level. If the valuation level is the plant, the material prices can be defined per plant. Each plant can have its own account determination.

■ *Inventory management*

The material stocks are managed in a plant.

■ *Material requirements planning*

Material requirements planning is carried out for each plant. Each plant has its own material requirements planning data. Cross-plant reports can be carried out for material requirements planning.

■ *Production*

■ *Costing*

With costing, the valuation prices are always defined within a plant.

4.1.2 Maintenance plants and maintenance planning plants

The maintenance plant of a technical object is the plant in which that object is installed. The maintenance planning plant of a technical object is the plant in which the maintenance tasks for that object are planned and prepared. PM planner groups work in the maintenance planning plant. These groups plan and prepare the maintenance tasks for the plants assigned to the maintenance planning plant. Maintenance planning plants are standard plants, which have been identified as maintenance planning plants in Customizing.

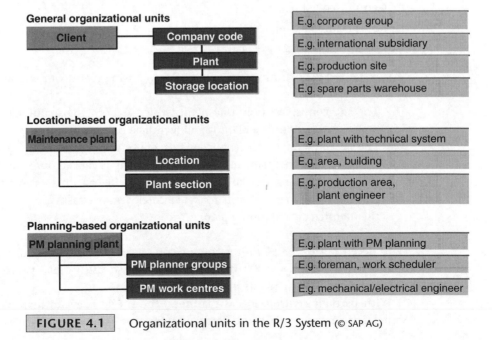

FIGURE 4.1   Organizational units in the R/3 System (© SAP AG)

The following activities are carried out in the maintenance planning plant:

- Definition of maintenance task lists
- Material planning on the basis of bills of material in maintenance task lists and orders
- Administration and scheduling of maintenance plans
- Entry of PM notifications
- Execution of PM orders
- Maintenance of master data (administration of technical objects)

In the majority of cases, PM planning is carried out in the plant in which the object is located. There are, however, scenarios in which cross-plant PM planning is carried out for various locations. In other scenarios, a location is divided logically into several plants, but PM planning is carried out centrally for the location. The main work centre, which performs or, at least, coordinates the PM activities for the object, is usually located in the maintenance planning plant. It is also possible, however, for this work centre to be located in the maintenance plant or in a third plant. The important point here is that the plant of the PM work centre is located in the same controlling area as the maintenance plant of the object, otherwise internal activity allocation cannot be carried out.

How you map the organization of PM planning in your site depends on the structure of the company as a whole. You have three options:

- Centralized PM planning
- Decentralized PM planning
- Partially centralized PM planning

Centralized PM planning can involve the following plant combinations:

1. The site consists of only one plant, which is both the maintenance plant and maintenance planning plant for all technical objects.
2. The site has several maintenance plants, but only one plant in which PM planning is carried out. The plant in which PM planning is carried out is identified as the maintenance planning plant in the system. All the other plants are assigned to this plant as maintenance plants for which maintenance tasks have to be planned in the maintenance planning plant.

With decentralized PM planning, the site consists of several maintenance plants. Each plant carries out its own PM planning. In this case, all the plants are identified as maintenance planning plants in the system.

With partially centralized PM planning, the site has several maintenance plants. Some of the maintenance plants carry out their own PM planning, while others do not.

The plants that do not carry out their own PM planning are assigned to maintenance planning plants, in which planning is carried out for them; the plants in which PM planning is carried out are identified as maintenance planning plants in the system.

EXAMPLE Maintenance planning plant 1000 is responsible for maintenance plant 1200 or, if necessary, for other maintenance plants. In this scenario, plant 1000 and plant 1200 can also belong to two different company codes in one controlling area. The work centres (in other words, the PM technicians) are administered in plant 1000. The spare parts warehouse is located in plant 1000 (Fig. 4.2).

EXAMPLE Maintenance planning plant 1000 is responsible for one maintenance plant (1300) or, if necessary, for several other maintenance plants. In this scenario, plant 1000 and plant 1300 can also belong to two different company codes in one controlling area. The work centres (in other words, the PM technicians) are administered in plant 1000 and in plant 1300. Plant 1300 tries to use its own technicians wherever specialists from plant 1000 are not required. The spare parts warehouse is located in plant 1000 (Fig. 4.3).

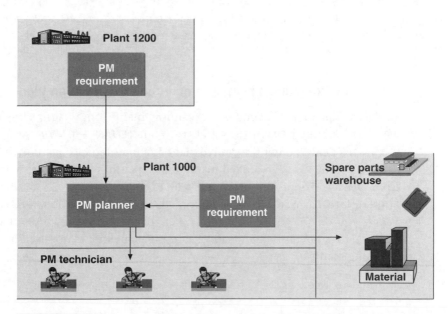

FIGURE 4.2   Plant 1000 plans and carries out maintenance (© SAP AG)

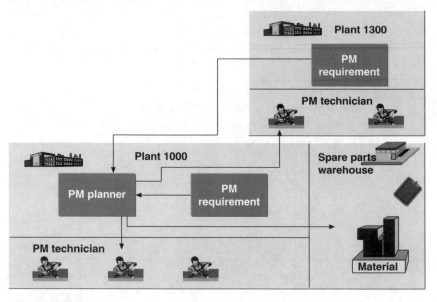

TIP   The R/3 System assumes that the spare parts warehouse is located in the maintenance planning
plant. Whenever you carry out material planning in the PM order, the system proposes that
material be withdrawn in the maintenance planning plant. You can, however, overwrite this
default setting with another plant from the same controlling area, if necessary.

4.1.3 How to define a plant as a maintenance planning plant

To define a plant as a maintenance planning plant from Customizing, choose ENTER-
PRISE STRUCTURE | DEFINITION | PLANT MAINTENANCE | MAINTAIN MAINTENANCE
PLANNING PLANT. Enter the desired plant as a maintenance planning plant.

 If you want to assign a fixed maintenance planning plant to a maintenance plant
from Customizing, choose ENTERPRISE STRUCTURE | ASSIGNMENT | PLANT
MAINTENANCE | ASSIGN MAINTENANCE PLANNING PLANT TO MAINTENANCE PLANT.
When you do so, you should remember that a maintenance plant that is already
assigned to a different maintenance planning plant should not itself be a maintenance
planning plant.

Two items of PM master data are designated technical objects in the R/3 System – the functional location and equipment. When you have mapped the organizational structure of your company, you can choose between three options for mapping technical objects:

1 Functional structure (functional locations only)

2 Object-based structure (equipment only)

3 Combination (equipment at functional locations)

In addition to this, you can structure technical objects according to technical or accounting criteria.

With structuring according to technical criteria, you assign the technical objects of the system to specific object classes (classes of equipment, functional location, and assembly). You can use this type of structuring to supplement functional and/or object-based structuring.

With structuring according to accounting criteria, you assign the system and its technical objects to specific cost centres or tangible assets. In this way, equipment for maintenance in a technical system can be grouped together according to accounting criteria to form system units. In this case, the higher-level technical system is understood as a tangible asset in the business sense of the term. Grouping together equipment to form tangible assets enables you to carry out comprehensive evaluations at a level higher than that of the individual item of equipment. You can also use this type of structuring to supplement functional and/or object-based structuring. To do so, you must use the R/3 component FI-AA (Asset Accounting).

4.2.1 Functional locations

Functional locations are elements of a technical structure (for example, components in a system as a whole). You create functional locations hierarchically and can structure them according to the following criteria:

- Functional (for example, pumping station, drive unit)
- Process-based (for example, polymerization, condensation, and so on)
- Spatial (for example, bay, location)

Functional locations have a structure indicator (in other words, a key for an edit screen). You can use the structure indicator to specify the generic structure of the location number and to make the hierarchy levels within the location structure visible in the location number. Figure 4.4 shows the structure indicator for functional locations in an ice-cream factory. The structure indicator AAA-AX-XX-XX specifies that a location

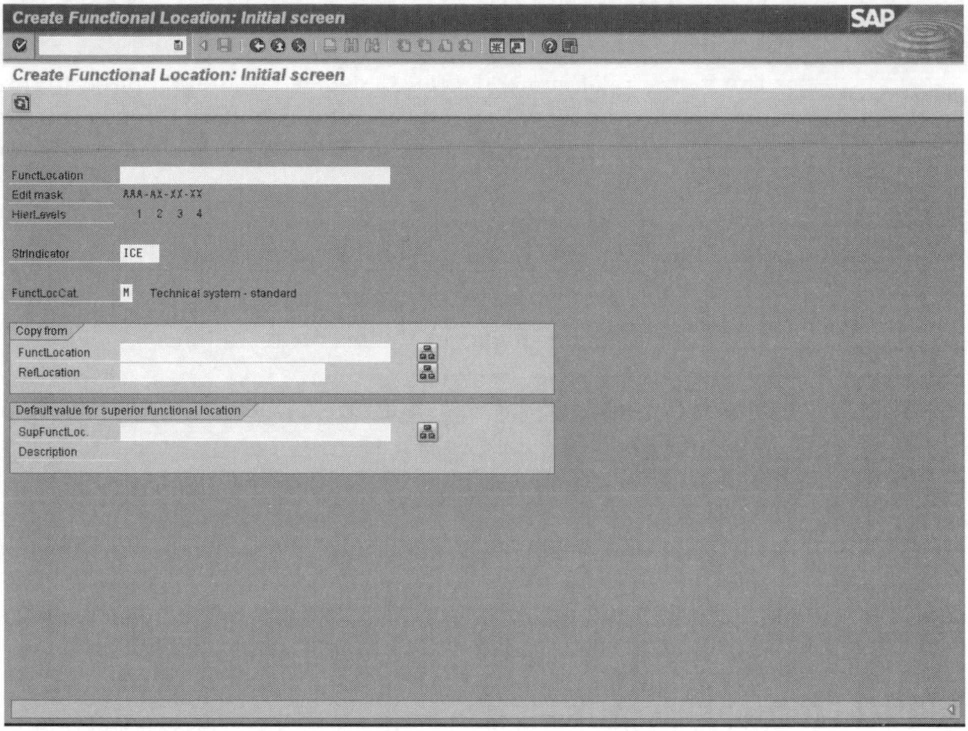

FIGURE 4.4   Functional location initial screen with structure indicator (© SAP AG)

at the first hierarchy level has three alphanumeric characters (for example, ICE). A location at the second hierarchy level has another two characters (for example, ICE-M1); and a location at the third hierarchy level has a further two characters (for example, ICE-M1-01). The indicator of a location, therefore, automatically shows the names of the locations above it in the hierarchy (for example, ICE-M1-01 is located directly under ICE-M1 in the hierarchy). The master record of a functional location comprises the following data groups (Fig. 4.5):

▨ General data

   – Technical data
   – Acquisition value
   – Manufacturer data

▨ Location data

   – Maintenance plant
   – Details of location and room
   – Address

- Organization data
  - Account assignment data
  - Maintenance planning plant
  - Planner group
- Structure data
  - Superior functional location
  - Equipment installed

In Customizing, you can display or hide other tab pages (for example, Sales and Distribution data). Additional functions can be called up via pushbuttons or menus (for example, classification, document management, permits, measuring points).

You use functional locations if

- you want to map system/site structures according to functional criteria
- maintenance tasks (in the broadest sense) have to be carried out for the individual areas of your site/system structure
- verifications should/must be stored for future reference for the maintenance tasks executed in the individual areas of your site/system structure

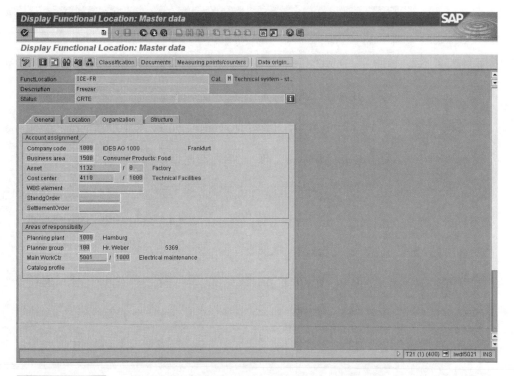

FIGURE 4.5   Organization data in the master record of a functional location (© SAP AG)

- technical data has to be collected and evaluated over a long period of time for the individual areas of your site/system structure

- the costs of maintenance tasks have to be tracked for the individual areas of your site/system structure

- you want to analyse the influence the usage conditions have on the susceptibility to damage of the installed equipment

- you require various views of the location structure (for example, process engineering view and measurement/control engineering view)

EXAMPLE You use functional locations to map your ice-cream factory on a process basis (Fig. 4.6). The functional location at the top of the hierarchy is the plant itself (ICE). At the second hierarchy level, you map the stages of the production process one after the other. First comes the mixer (ICE-M1), then the tanks for the semi-finished material (ICE-TA), then the second mixer (ICE-M2), the freezer (ICE-FR), the packager (ICE-PK), and finally the blast freezer (ICE-BF). At the third hierarchy level, you map the inflows and outflows of the plant, as well as the actual tanks, mixers and functional units. Figure 4.7 shows an overview of the structure of the plant.

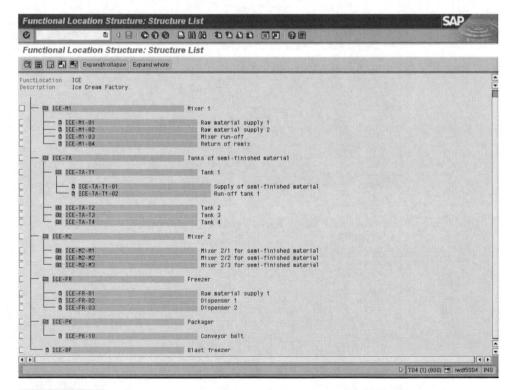

FIGURE 4.6 Structure of the functional locations in an ice-cream factory (© SAP AG)

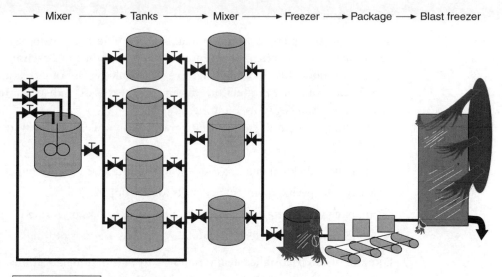

Mixer ⟶ Tanks ⟶ Mixer ⟶ Freezer ⟶ Package ⟶ Blast freezer

FIGURE 4.7   Structure of the ice-cream factory

What are the effective differences between functional locations and equipment?

▪ After you create a functional location, you can change its indicator; if you have made a typing error, you can change the indicator whenever you wish.

▪ When you create functional locations, the structure indicator assigns them automatically to their position in the structure (in accordance with the top-down principle, from top to bottom). This reduces the time and effort required to enter data when you are setting up a structure for functional locations.

▪ The strictly hierarchical structure of functional locations allows data (for example, costs) to be summarized at every hierarchy level.

▪ A functional location can be an item of real estate within the Real Estate management industry solution IS-RE.

What do you have to remember when working with functional locations?

▪ In Customizing, you must create a structure indicator for each structure.

▪ Functional locations can only be installed at functional location positions, or exist as individual objects.

▪ A functional location installed at another functional location cannot store the history of its installation locations; it only displays the current installations.

▪ If you modify the structures of functional locations to have different structure indicators, automatic assignment will no longer function. As with equipment, you then have to assign the superseding functional location manually.

4.2.2 Equipment

An item of equipment is an individual, physical object that is to be maintained as an autonomous unit. An item of equipment can be installed in a technical system or in a system component. You can manage every possible type of object as an item of equipment: for example, production resources, means of transport, test equipment, production resources/tools, buildings and PCs.

Each item of equipment is administrated individually in the system. This enables you to

- manage individual data for the object from the plant maintenance view
- carry out specific maintenance tasks for the object
- manage verifications of the plant maintenance tasks performed
- collect and evaluate technical data over longer periods of time

Equipment can be installed at and removed from functional locations. The usage times of an item of equipment at a functional location are documented on a time line. The master record of the item of equipment contains the same data groups as the master record of the functional location (Fig. 4.8). Via menus or in Customizing, you can

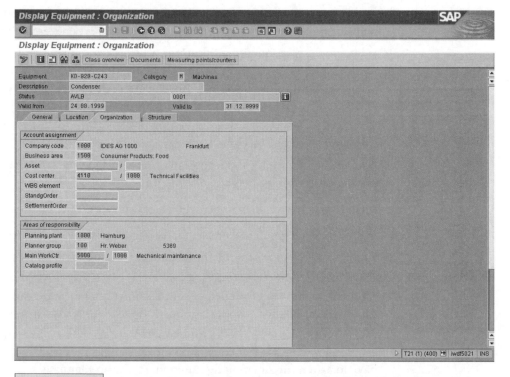

FIGURE 4.8   Organization data in the master record of an item of equipment (© SAP AG)

display or hide other tab pages, such as data on production resources/tools, serialization data, configuration data, and Sales and Distribution data. You can call up additional functions via pushbuttons or menus.

You use equipment if

- individual data has to be managed for the object (for example, year of construction, warranty deadlines, installation locations)
- breakdown, prepared or preventive maintenance tasks have to be carried out on an object
- verification of the maintenance tasks carried out has to be managed for this object (for example, for official inspections or insurance purposes)
- you want to collect and evaluate technical data for this object over a longer period of time
- you want to track the costs of maintenance tasks for this object
- verifications of usage times at functional locations are required for this object

EXAMPLE You install equipment at the existing functional locations of your ice-cream factory. You map the motor of the freezer as an item of equipment and not as a functional location, since you may also want to install the motor in the blast freezer and require an installation history. You map the compressor of the freezer as an item of equipment, since the material master record involved is serialized. You map the container for the semi-finished material in the freezer as an item of equipment, since you want to manage the year of construction and warranty deadlines for this system component. Figure 4.9 shows an overview of the installed equipment.

What are the differences between equipment and functional locations?

- You can serialize an item of equipment by assigning a material and a serial number to it. This enables you to carry out inventory management for the item of equipment.
- You can create an item of equipment with a material as a template, and copy material data to it. As of Release 4.6, you can also classify the material.
- An item of equipment can be configured (via super BOM/variant configuration).
- Equipment can be installed at functional locations or in other items of equipment, or can exist as individual objects.
- An item of equipment can be a vehicle within Fleet Management.
- An item of equipment can be a device within the Utilities industry solution (IS-U).
- An item of equipment that is installed in a technical object can store the history of its installation locations. The system writes a time segment for each installation location, thereby enabling you to track the installation history as a whole.

■ Via menus, you can call up other tab pages (Sales and Distribution data, data on production resources/tools, and configuration data) in addition to the standard tab pages in the equipment master record. No additional Customizing settings have to be made for this purpose.

■ You can map warranties in the system by means of the Customer Service (CS) component.

Examples of other areas in which you can use equipment include:

■ Production Planning and Control (PP): production resource/tool

■ Quality Management (QM): test equipment

■ Materials Management (MM): serialized material

■ Sales and Distribution (SD): customer equipment

What do you have to remember when working with equipment?

■ When you create structures, equipment is not assigned a position automatically. As a result, you have to assign the equipment manually for each master record.

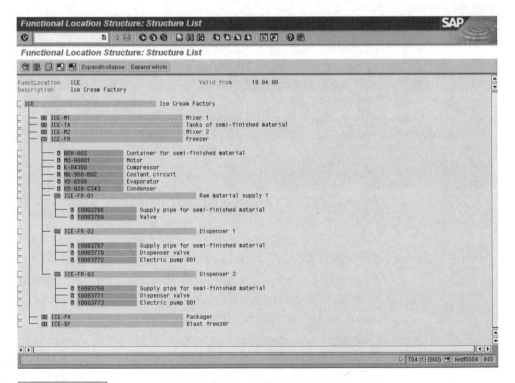

FIGURE 4.9 Structure of equipment at functional locations (© SAP AG)

■ Once you have created an item of equipment, you cannot change the equipment number. If you have made a typing error when entering the external number, you have to archive the item of equipment.

■ If you use many items of equipment as individual objects or as an equipment hierarchy, without using functional locations, you should classify the items of equipment. You will find this helps you find equipment more easily.

4.3   THE MOST IMPORTANT TRANSACTIONS FOR FUNCTIONAL LOCATIONS AND EQUIPMENT

Table 4.1 provides an overview of the most important master data transactions.

TABLE 4.1	**Transactions for functional locations and equipment**	
Transaction	**Technical name**	**Comments**
Create Functional Location	IL01	Individual entry
Change Functional Location	IL02	Individual processing
Functional Location Structure	IH01	Display location hierarchy with installed equipment
Create Functional Location: List Entry	IL04	List entry
Change Functional Location	IL05	Change from list
Functional Location List (Multi-Level)	IL07	Multi-level list with transaction data for master record
Create Reference Location	IL11	Functional locations referenced to reference location for data transfer
Change Reference Location	IL12	Changes transferred to referenced functional location
Create Equipment	IE01	Individual entry
Change Equipment	IE02	Individual processing
Equipment Structure	IH03	Display equipment hierarchy
Collective Equipment Entry	IE10	List entry
Change Equipment	IE05	Change from list
Equipment List (multi-level)	IE07	Multi-level list with transaction data for master record
Create Production Resource/Tool	IE25	Master record for production resources/tools
Create Vehicle	IE31	Master record for vehicles, ships, containers, and so on

In addition to the PM-specific master data (the technical objects), master data from other R/3 components is used in PM. This master data is managed mainly in the R/3 Materials Management (MM) component.

4.4.1 Material

If, in the event of damage, an object is not replaced but repaired, you should map it as a technical object. In this case, you map the object as an individual object (functional location, item of equipment) with a clearly defined maintenance history.

You should not map an object as a technical object if it is replaced in the event of damage, since the low value of the object means that repairs are not worthwhile. In this case, you map the object as a material or an assembly.

The material master contains descriptions of all the articles and parts that a company procures, manufactures and stores. The material master is the central source for calling up material-specific information within the company (for example, material stocks). Since all the material data is integrated in one master record, the problem of data redundancy does not arise. This integration also enables the stored data to be used jointly by purchasing and other areas (for example, inventory management, material requirements planning and invoice verification). Descriptions of the individual materials used in a company are stored in the material master records. The complete set of material master records constitutes the material master.

In the following, the various types of information in a material master record will be listed and illustrated by means of examples:

▪ *Accounting*

  Information specific to accounting and costing (for example, standard price, former and future price, as well as current valuation)

▪ *Material requirements planning*

  Information on material requirements planning (for example, safety stock, planned delivery time, and reorder point for a material)

▪ *Purchasing*

  Data provided by purchasing for a material (for example, the purchasing group responsible, permissible overdeliveries and underdeliveries, as well as the order unit for a material)

▪ *Engineering/design*

  Technical information on the engineering/design of a material (for example, CAD drawings, basic dimensions and design data)

■ *Storage*

Information on warehouse processing and storage of the material (for example, unit of issue, storage conditions and packaging sizes)

■ *Forecast*

Information for forecasting the material requirement (for example, type and method of material procurement, forecast period and previous usage)

■ *Sales*

Information on sales orders and pricing (for example, sales price, minimum purchase order quantity, and name of the sales department responsible for a particular material)

From the point of view of plant maintenance, all technical objects are primarily materials that have to be purchased, stored and installed in technical systems; in other words, each functional location and item of equipment is based on a material master record. You do not, however, have to turn all material master records into technical objects from the point of view of plant maintenance. This is only necessary for those objects with a maintenance history that you are interested in. A combination of

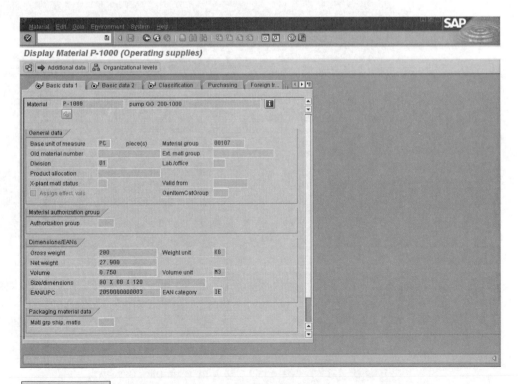

FIGURE 4.10   Material master – basic data (© SAP AG)

material master record and a serial number or an assembly can also be a reference object for maintenance tasks.

In maintenance processing, you use materials when you order spare parts or reserve them in the warehouse. Via the master record of the materials kept in stock, you can (with appropriate authorization) call up all of the above views of the material in question. You should ideally have created bills of material (BOMs) for the location, equipment or material of your technical objects, in which the spare parts for the technical object are mapped as materials or assemblies.

Figure 4.10 shows the example of the basic data for material P-1000, a pump installed in the ice-cream factory.

4.4.2 Assembly

For production, an assembly of a BOM denotes a group of semi-finished products or parts, which together form a component of a finished product or the finished product itself. An assembly is identified by a material number. As a rule, an assembly is a group of components with a shared function.

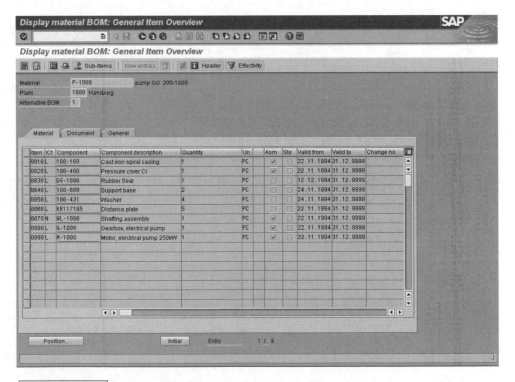

FIGURE 4.11 Material BOM with assemblies (© SAP AG)

For plant maintenance, there are also PM assemblies, which are materials of the material type IBAU. The material master record of PM assemblies contains only basic and classification data; in other words, you cannot carry out inventory management for PM assemblies.

You use PM assemblies as structure items in a BOM

- if you want to group together materials of the same type under one node

- if you do not require inventory management, but intend to track the costs, for example, in the PM Information System.

The PM assembly indicator can only be maintained for items relevant to plant maintenance. When maintenance tasks are processed, items identified as PM assemblies are displayed as structure items of a technical system. They can be used to provide a detailed description of an item in a technical system (for example, potential damage location).

Figure 4.11 shows the material BOM for material P-1000. All the materials with a tick in the Asm box in the BOM are assemblies. Figure 4.12 shows the structure list for the same material BOM.

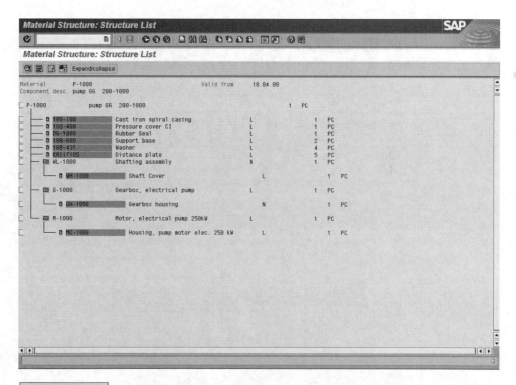

FIGURE 4.12   Structure list for material BOM (© SAP AG)

4.4.3 Serial numbers

Serialized materials are assigned a serial number in addition to their material number. This enables a single item to be differentiated from all the other items of the material. The combination of material number and serial number is unique. From a plant maintenance point of view, this combination can correspond to an item of equipment. This does not mean that you have to create a separate equipment master record. Instead, you can assign an equipment number to the material and serial number (serialized equipment).

Figure 4.13 shows how to create a serial number for material P-2002. The assignment of material P-2002 and serial number 307 is unique and enables the item of material to be identified. Figure 4.14 shows the combination of material P-2002 and serial number 11. From the plant maintenance point of view, this combination is equipment 10003429.

The serial number profile is combined data, grouped under a four-figure abbreviation that determines the conditions and business transactions for issuing serial numbers to serialized materials. Examples of this type of business transaction include assigning serial numbers with goods receipts, goods issues, stock transfers, stock transport orders or physical inventory.

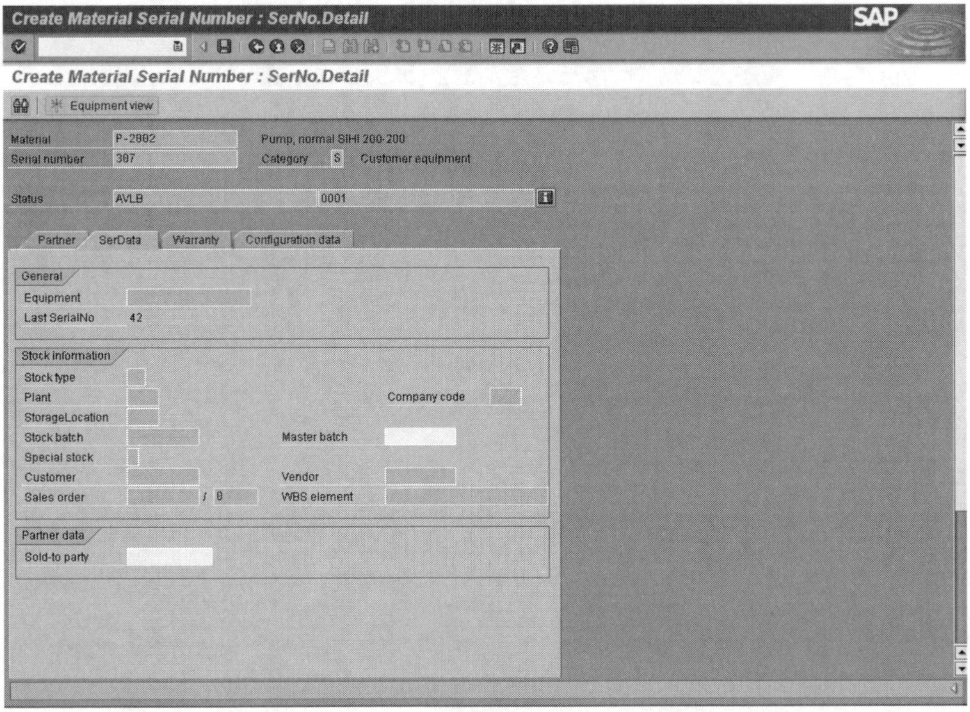

FIGURE 4.13   Material and serial number (© SAP AG)

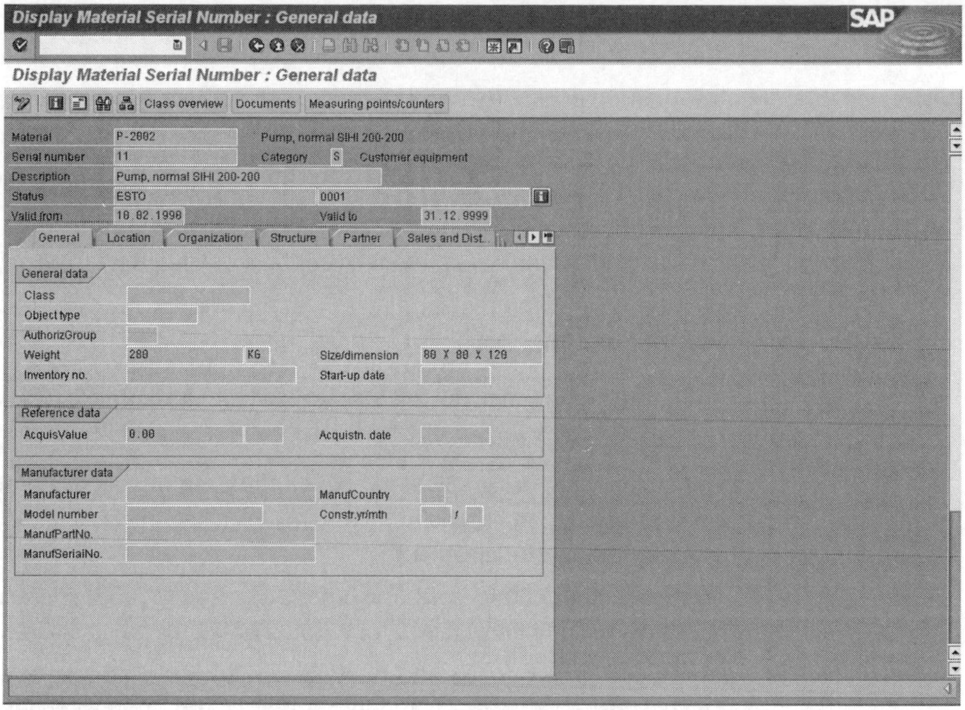

FIGURE 4.14 Material and serial number with equipment (© SAP AG)

You enter the serial number profile at plant level in the master record for materials you want to manage using serial numbers. This means that a separate serial number profile can be assigned to one material per plant. As a result, a material can require a serial number in one plant, but not in others. If you use different profiles for one material, the plants must be logistically independent of each other; this is because a stock transfer can only be carried out if the profiles are the same in both plants. Serial number profiles are defined in Customizing for Plant Maintenance.

The serial number profile contains the following information:

- The business transactions in which serialization
  - can be carried out
  - must be carried out
  - is carried out automatically
  - is not carried out

- Information on whether, in a business transaction,
  - serial numbers can be assigned for which the system does not yet contain a master record

– serial numbers that already exist as a master record in the system have to be specified

■ Information on whether a stock check is carried out in transactions affecting stocks, and how the system should respond in the event of inconsistencies

■ The business transactions in which an equipment master record has or has not to be created for each serial number

You will find out more about serial numbers in Chapter 7, 'Special cases'.

4.4.4 PM bill of material

In companies, bills of material (BOMs) are used for various purposes. Various usages are distinguished, depending on the particular enterprise area involved:

■ The engineering/design BOM records all the components of a product according to engineering/design criteria and contains their technical data. As a rule, this BOM category is order independent.

■ The production BOM records the items according to production criteria and assembly statuses. Only items relevant to production with process-based data are required for the assembly process, for example.

■ The costing BOM maps the product structure and provides the basis for automatic determination of the direct material costs for a product. Items that are not relevant for costing are not recorded in this BOM.

■ The plant maintenance BOM (PM BOM) differs from the other categories in that it contains only items relevant to maintenance.

The PM BOM has two main functions:

1 *Structuring objects*
The structure of an object should be represented as clearly as possible from the PM point of view.

2 *Spare parts planning in orders*
If a PM object has a BOM, this can easily be used for planning spare parts in a PM order.

To enable PM structure items or items relevant to maintenance to be maintained for a functional location BOM and an equipment BOM, you must select a BOM usage that provides items relevant to maintenance. BOM maintenance is carried out separately for the different areas (for example, engineering/design, production). If you create several BOMs for different usages of the same material, the system stores the BOMs under a separate internal number for each usage.

In general, a distinction is drawn between two types of PM BOMs:

1 *BOMs for technical objects (functional location BOMs, equipment BOMs)*
BOMs for items of equipment or functional locations are used to describe the structure of a particular item of equipment or functional location and assign spare parts to it for plant maintenance. This is carried out by means of direct assignment. With direct assignment, a BOM is created directly for the object (functional location or equipment). A material master is not used here.

2 *Material BOMs*
Material BOMs are created with a link to a material master record. The material master record contains descriptive data (for example, dimensions and weight) and control data (for example, material category and industry sector). The material BOM contains the single parts of the object (materials or assemblies). Technical objects are assigned indirectly to a material BOM. With indirect assignment, you can assign a BOM to master records of technical objects via a material master record. You carry out the assignment by entering the material number in the CONSTRUCTION TYPE field of the master record of the technical object (Fig. 4.15).

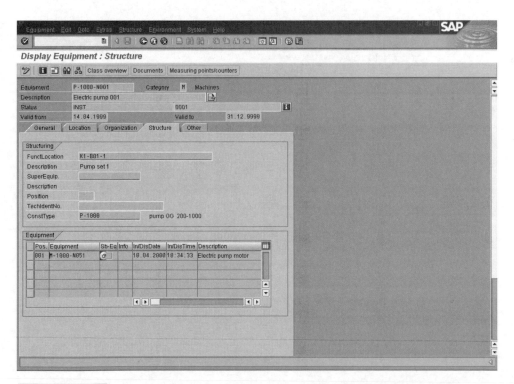

FIGURE 4.15   Linking a material BOM via the 'Construction type' field (© SAP AG)

The BOM is then linked to the material, and not directly to the technical object. This is expedient if a company has grouped together several identical technical objects under one material number. You can call up the material BOM directly from the master record of the technical object by choosing STRUCTURE | STRUCTURE LIST (Fig. 4.16).

A BOM can manage data that is binding for production. The plant, as the area of validity, is derived from this data. In this case, you create a plant-specific BOM. Diverse checks are then carried out at plant level; for example, with a material in the material BOM header, a material master record with plant data on the chosen plant has to exist. When items are entered, the system checks whether plant data also exist for the material components. If the checks are successful, the system transfers the material to the material BOM.

You can also create BOMs without reference to a plant. These are known as group BOMs. For example, this is expedient if, during the design phase, the design engineer maintains a BOM that is subsequently assigned to one or more plants for production. In this case, the system only checks whether material master records exist. Plant-specific material checks are not carried out.

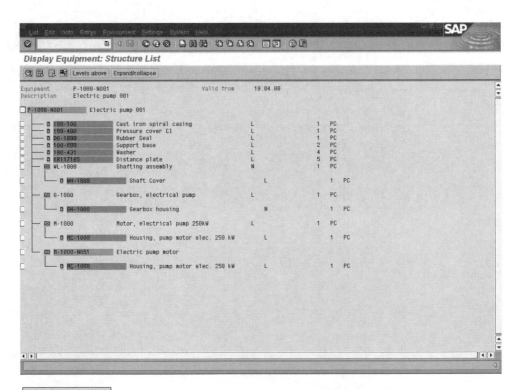

FIGURE 4.16 Structure list of material BOM for equipment (© SAP AG)

4.4.5　The most important transactions for other Logistics master data

Table 4.2 provides an overview of the most important transactions for using materials, assemblies, serial numbers and BOMs.

TABLE 4.2	Transactions for other Logistics master data

Transaction	Technical name	Comments
Create Material	MM01	Individual entry
Change Material	MM02	Individual processing
Create Maintenance assembly	MMP1	PM assembly with material type IBAU as structure item
Create Material Serial Number	IQ01	Individual entry
Change Material Serial Number	IQ02	Individual processing
Create Functional Location BOM	IB11	Direct assignment to functional location
Change Functional Location BOM	IB12	Individual processing
Create Equipment BOM	IB01	Direct assignment to equipment
Change Equipment BOM	IB02	Individual processing
Create Material BOM	CS01	Indirect assignment to technical object
Change Material BOM	CS02	Individual processing

4.5　MEASURING POINTS AND COUNTERS

In the R/3 System, measuring points are the physical and/or logical places at which a condition is described (for example, the temperature of the coolant in the freezer of the ice-cream factory, or the pressure in the pressure tank). In plant maintenance, measuring points are located on equipment or at functional locations.

At measuring points, measurements are read at regular intervals in specific measurement units (for example, the temperature of the coolant pipe is measured in degrees centigrade). Measured readings describe a condition at a measuring point at a particular time, and constitute the transaction data for the measuring points in the R/3 System. Measured readings are recorded as measurement documents.

In the R/3 System, counters are means that enable you to map object wear, consumption, or reduction of a working supply (for example, a counter for measuring operating hours in a pump, or a counter for measuring electricity consumption for an electrically powered system). In plant maintenance, counters are located on equipment or at functional locations. Figure 4.17 shows the master record of a counter for operating hours. Figure 4.18 shows the link between a counter and an item of equipment, where the counter measures the operating hours of the pump.

Counter readings are also taken at regular intervals in specific measurement units (for example, in operating hours). Counter readings describe a condition at a counter at a particular point in time, and constitute the transaction data for counters in the R/3 System. Counter readings are also recorded in the form of measurement documents (Fig. 4.19).

A counter is a special form of measuring point, since counter readings either rise or fall continuously over time. In addition to this, counter overflow can occur in most counters. For example, the highest value that a kilometre counter can display is 99,999. If this value is exceeded, a counter overflow occurs, and the counter starts counting from 00,000 again. Counter readings can be entered in the system in two forms. The valuation involved in both forms is quantitative:

1 The absolute counter reading is entered in the system; in other words, the counter reading displayed by the counter at a particular moment (02/01/2000, 2 p.m., 42 operating hours).

2 The difference between the last and the current counter reading is entered in the system (for example, 02/01/2000, 2 p.m., 2 more operating hours).

You use measuring points and counters for the following reasons:

- You want to document the condition of a technical object at a particular point in time.

  Documenting the condition of a particular object is always important where the law requires companies to keep detailed verifications of the correct condition. This can apply to critical values in environmental protection, hazardous work areas in industrial safety, devices in hospitals (in intensive care), as well as to the monitoring of emissions and ambient air quality in objects of every type.

- You want to carry out counter-based maintenance.

  Condition-based and counter-based maintenance are tasks of preventive maintenance. These tasks are essentially intended to reduce breakdowns in the objects to which they apply. With counter-based maintenance, maintenance activities are always carried out when the counter on a technical object reaches a certain value (for example, every 100 operating hours).

- You want to carry out condition-based maintenance.

  With condition-based maintenance, maintenance activities are always carried out when the measuring point at a technical object reaches a specific condition (for example, every time a brake lining is worn down to the minimum reserve).

You will find out more about measuring points and counters in Chapter 6, 'Business process: planned maintenance', and Chapter 9, 'Interfaces to non-SAP systems'.

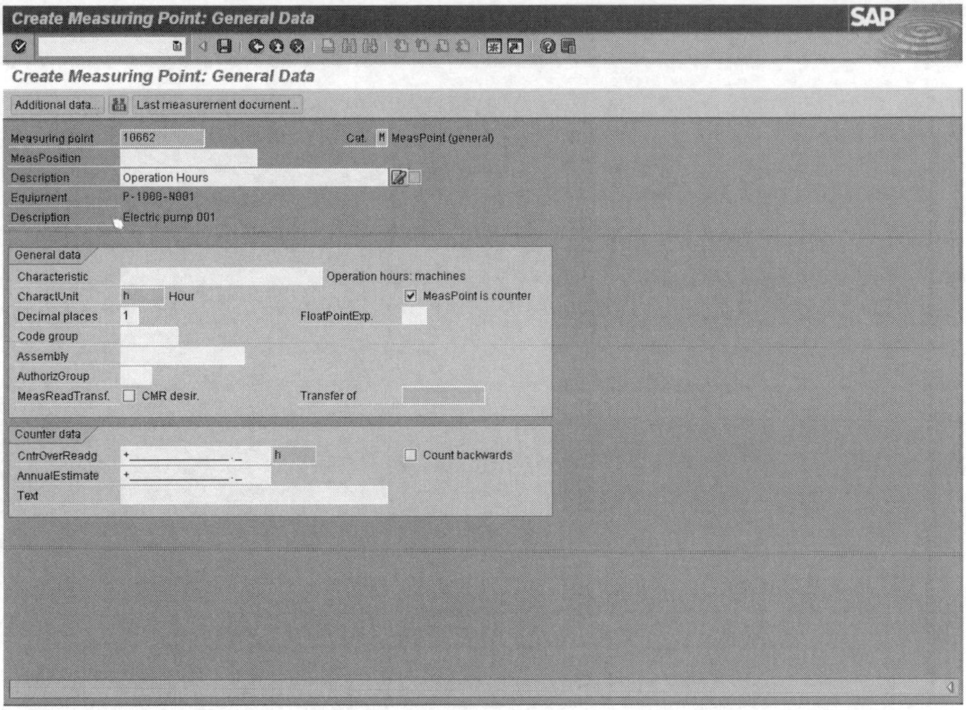

FIGURE 4.17   Master record of a counter (© SAP AG)

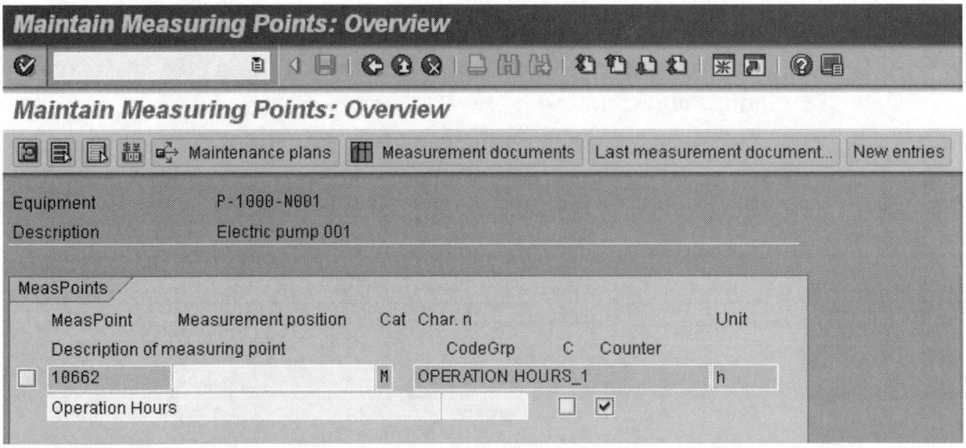

FIGURE 4.18   Link between counter and an item of equipment (© SAP AG)

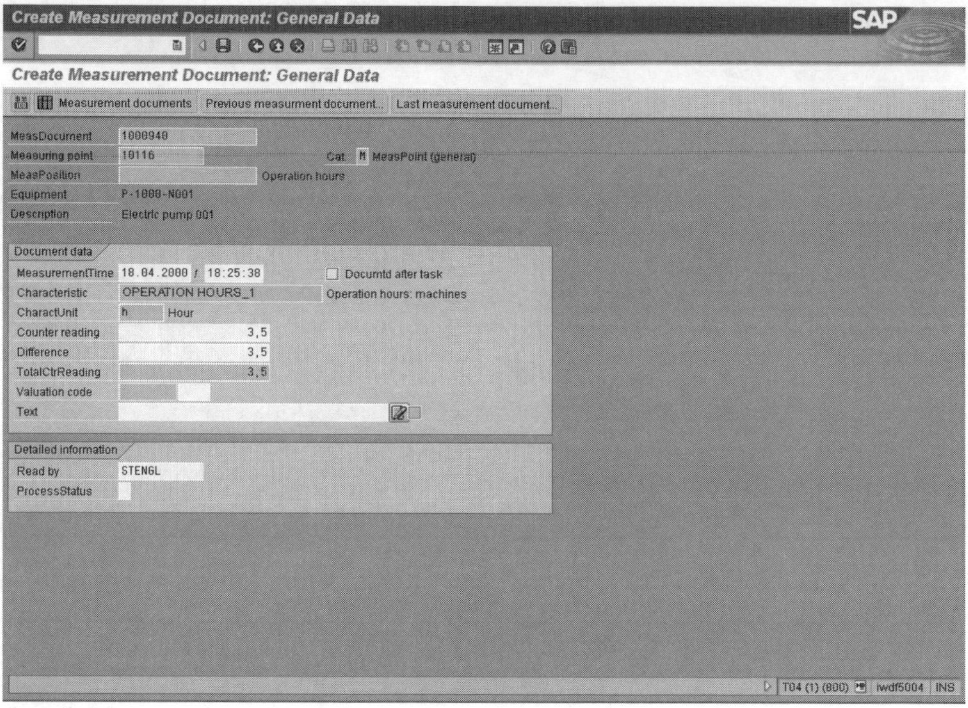

FIGURE 4.19   Measurement document (© SAP AG)

4.5.1 The most important transactions for measuring points and counters

Table 4.3 provides an overview of the most important transactions for using measuring points and counters.

TABLE 4.3   Transactions for measuring points and counters

Transaction	Technical name	Comments
Create Measurement Document	IK11	Enter measurement document for a measuring point/counter at functional location
Change Measurement Document	IK12	Individual processing
Create Measurement Document	IK11	Enter measurement document for a measuring point/counter on equipment
Change Measurement Document	IK12	Individual processing
Create Measuring Point	IK01	Individual entry
Change Measuring Point	IK02	Individual processing

PM WORK CENTRES

In Logistics, work centres are organizational units that specify where an operation should be carried out and by whom. Every work centre has a particular available capacity. The activities performed at or by the work centre are valuated by charge rates, which are determined by the cost centres and activity types. The following units can be defined as work centres:

■ Machines
■ People
■ Production lines
■ Maintenance groups

Work centre categories are used to distinguish work centres in the R/3 System (for example, production work centre, PM production centre). The data that can be maintained in the master record of a work centre depends on its work centre category. Figure 4.20 shows the basic data of a work centre master record in Plant Maintenance. Figure 4.21 shows the people linked to this work centre.

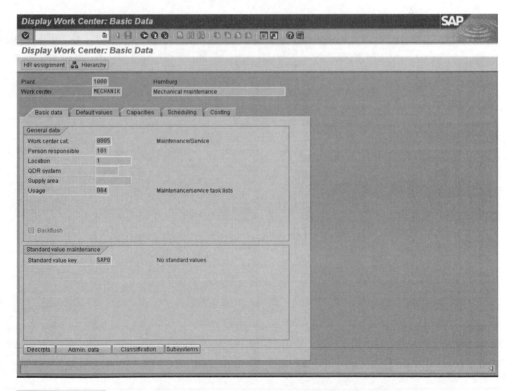

FIGURE 4.20   Basic data – work centre master record (© SAP AG)

Two different work centres are used in plant maintenance:

- the main work centre
- the performing work centre

The main work centre is generally used to map a person or a department who/which is responsible for ensuring that the maintenance tasks of an order are carried out by the work centres planned in the individual operations. The main work centre must be specified in the order header to enable the master record data to be copied to the order by default. In internal processing, the main work centre is also used by default for the performing work centre. In addition to the main work centre, you can appoint a specific member of staff as the person responsible. This member of staff is mapped with his or her own master record in the Human Resources (HR) component.

The performing work centre is generally used to map a person or a group of people that performs the maintenance tasks planned in the operations of an order. A specific member of staff, created in the Human Resources (HR) component with his/her own master record, can be assigned to the performing work centre via his/her personnel number. In addition to this, you can also use the requirements assignment function to assign other members of staff to an operation. The performing work centre is

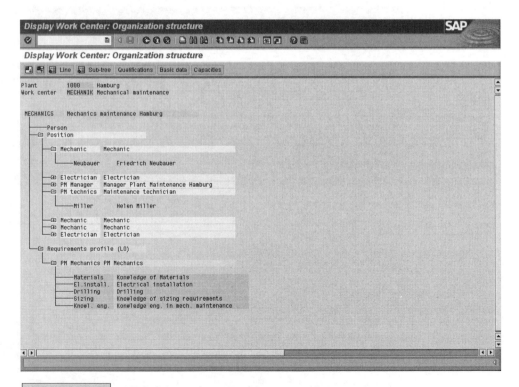

FIGURE 4.21　　HR link in work centre master record (© SAP AG)

maintained in the operation data of an order and is defaulted as the performing work centre for the operations in the order. Since capacities and (via the activity type) costs are assigned to the performing work centre, it is required primarily for capacity requirements planning, scheduling, and cost determination.

You can also create operations without specifying the performing work centre. A control key, which is linked neither to a cost centre nor to an activity type, then has to be assigned to these operations. The operations involved may be used solely for documentation purposes (for example, operations containing only safety instructions or information on the production tools/resources that have to be used). Operations in which a performing work centre is not specified are also used in external processing.

4.7   MAINTENANCE TASK LISTS AND MAINTENANCE PLANS

Maintenance task lists describe a series of individual maintenance activities that have to be performed repeatedly at a site. Maintenance task lists are used to standardize these repetitive procedures and plan them more effectively. Although many manufacturers include maintenance task lists with their technical objects, maintenance task lists are often created within the company itself. If standardized procedures are changed (for example, due to new legal regulations), maintenance task lists can considerably reduce the time and effort required to maintain data. In cases of this type, you only have to make changes to one specific place in the appropriate maintenance task list. All PM orders and maintenance items that refer to the maintenance task list then receive the updated version of the procedures automatically.

There are three types of maintenance task list. These are distinguished from each other by an indicator:

1 Equipment task list
2 Task list for functional location
3 General maintenance task list (without reference to an object)

All three types of task list can be used for continuous and preventive maintenance. If you want to use maintenance task lists for preventive maintenance, you assign the maintenance task list to a maintenance plan or to one or more maintenance items. The operations described in the maintenance task list are carried out on all the technical objects you have assigned to the maintenance item. The operations are due at the points in time calculated by the system during scheduling of the maintenance plan.

A maintenance plan describes maintenance and inspection tasks to be performed on maintenance objects. Using the maintenance plan, you can describe the dates and the scope of preventive maintenance and inspection activities for technical objects. You can ensure that your technical objects are always maintained on time and thus function

optimally. In maintenance planning, a distinction is drawn between different maintenance plan types. You can create a maintenance plan – as well as the associated
maintenance call objects – at the following levels, for example:

■ at the equipment level

■ at the level of the functional locations

■ at the material level

■ at the level of material number and serial number

■ at the assembly level

To map simple maintenance cycles, you use a single cycle plan. Single cycle plans are
the simplest form of maintenance plan. You create a single cycle plan and define
exactly one time-based or activity-based maintenance cycle, in which you specify the
interval after which the maintenance plan should be executed (for example, annual
maintenance of a system component or repair of a motor every 100 operating hours).

Should you require more than one cycle (for example, maintenance every 100 operating hours and/or every two months), you can no longer use a single cycle plan. In this
case, you require a strategy plan. Strategy plans with maintenance strategies are used to
map more complex maintenance cycles. You create a strategy plan and assign it a
maintenance strategy in which the maintenance cycles (called maintenance packages
in the strategy) are specified. A maintenance strategy contains general information on
scheduling and can be assigned to as many maintenance plans and maintenance task
lists as necessary. It would be expedient to use a strategy plan if, for example, various
maintenance tasks for a car arise in different cycles (oil check every 2000 km, oil change
every 10,000 km).

You will find out more about maintenance task lists and maintenance plans in
Chapter 6, 'Business process: planned maintenance'.

4.8 MAINTENANCE NOTIFICATIONS

In maintenance processing, maintenance notifications are the means you use in the
event of malfunctions or exceptional operational situations

■ to describe the exceptional technical situation of an object

■ to request a required task in the maintenance department

■ to document tasks that have been performed

Maintenance notifications provide comprehensive documentation of maintenance tasks,
thereby making them available for evaluations in the long term. You can use them to
carry out rough-cut planning and perform tasks. In the R/3 System, maintenance notifications, service notifications and quality notifications are distinguished by means of
notification categories. Within maintenance notifications, a similar function is performed

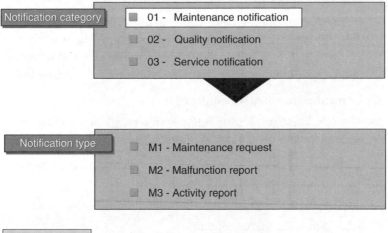

FIGURE 4.22   Notification category and notification type (© SAP AG)

by notification types. The notification type is a key that determines the origin, content and other features of maintenance, service or quality notifications. The following three types of maintenance notification are available in the standard system (Fig. 4.22):

- Malfunction report
- Activity report
- Maintenance request

You will find out more about maintenance notifications in Chapter 5, 'Business process: breakdown maintenance and corrective maintenance'.

4.9   MAINTENANCE ORDERS

Maintenance orders are used to carry out maintenance tasks. They contain the following information:

- Dates
- Resources (material, working hours for the tasks to be performed, data on operations performed by external companies)
- Settlement rules for the costs arising as a result of the order

Maintenance orders can be distinguished according to their plannability.

- Preventive maintenance orders

    Orders are created for specific dates via the maintenance plans and their scheduling functions. The tasks to be performed are derived from the maintenance plans.

■ Planned maintenance orders

In addition to maintenance plans, planned maintenance orders can be generated from maintenance notifications (for example, as the result of inspections, the findings of which flow into maintenance notifications and which, in turn, are used by the PM planning group responsible as a worklist for future tasks).

■ Unplanned maintenance orders

As a rule, these result from unforeseen damage or accidents, which require a maintenance task to be performed immediately.

The maintenance order is the data object in PM with the largest number of interfaces to other components of the R/3 System.

Integrative aspects of maintenance orders:

■ MM – Materials Management

Mapping of the processes required for managing materials; administration of the repairable spares to be refurbished; external procurement of materials and services; inventory management.

■ PP – Production Planning and Control

Provision of data on (preventive) maintenance activities at PP work centres via the graphical planning board.

■ QM – Quality Management

Automatic inspection lot creation during calibration inspection; documentation of results of inspections with subsequent usage decision; administration of the test equipment.

■ PS – Project System

Mapping of complex tasks comprising several orders and with specific dependencies between the orders.

■ FI – Financial Accounting

Administration of customer and vendor data; creation and verification of invoices.

■ FI-AA – Asset Accounting

Maintenance activities that must be capitalized are settled directly to the asset affected; representation of the link between maintenance-specific and business view of assets.

■ IM – Investment Management

Detailed account-based monitoring of complex PM tasks; cross-task administration of budgets; use of investment orders.

- CO – Controlling

  Monitoring, distribution and evaluation of internal costs incurred as a result of maintenance activities.

- PA – Personnel Management

  Provision of data on qualification of plant maintenance employees.

- WFM – Workflow Management

  Control and processing of cross-job process flows during planning and performance of maintenance tasks.

You will find out more about maintenance orders in Chapter 5, 'Business process: breakdown maintenance and corrective maintenance'.

Business process: breakdown maintenance and corrective maintenance

The main task of PM technicians is to implement the maintenance orders received from PM planning and confirm their activities as well as the quantity of spare parts, repairable spares and operating supplies required. Their tasks also include writing malfunction and activity reports, as well as documenting measurement/counter readings.

5.1.1 Basics of maintenance notifications

In the event of malfunctions or exceptional operating conditions, PM notifications enable employees in plant maintenance to describe the condition of an object, request required tasks, and document the work carried out.

The following notification types are preconfigured in the standard R/3 System:

- Activity report – documentation of activities already carried out
- Malfunction report – notification of malfunctions and problems that have occurred
- Maintenance request – request to perform specific tasks

Notifications can be created for PM objects such as functional locations, equipment and maintenance assemblies. For example, if a maintenance notification is created for an assembly of an item of equipment and this item of equipment is assigned to a functional location, the system copies all the relevant data from the higher-level item of equipment and functional location.

You can also create maintenance notifications without specifying the technical object. You would do so, for example:

- if a malfunction report refers to an object not stored under a number in the system
- if the damaged object cannot yet be localized precisely
- if a PM request refers to an object that is to be provided as part of an investment measure

The data in the maintenance notification is transferred to the maintenance history, where it remains available for evaluations as well as planning future PM tasks.

TIP   **INTEGRATIVE ASPECTS OF MAINTENANCE NOTIFICATIONS**

Maintenance processing for unplanned tasks is subdivided into the following areas:

- *Description of the object condition*

  This is the most important element of the maintenance notification. Its purpose is to describe the condition of the technical object, or to report a malfunction in a technical object, and request that the damage be corrected.

- *Performance of the maintenance tasks*

  The most important component in this context is the maintenance order. This is used to plan the performance of maintenance tasks, track the progress of the work, and (once the maintenance activities have been completed) to apportion the costs – for example, to the cost centres that gave rise to them.

- *Completion of the maintenance tasks*

  Via the maintenance history, important maintenance data is stored long term and kept available for evaluations.

These instruments enable you to process all the tasks that have to be performed in plant maintenance, as well as operations that do not belong directly to plant maintenance (such as investments or modifications).

All maintenance notifications comprise the following areas (see Fig. 5.1):

- *Header data*

  Every maintenance notification has a notification header, which contains the header data (information used to identify and administrate the maintenance notification) (Fig. 5.2). The header data is valid for the entire notification.

| Notification | System availability | Location data | Items | Tasks | Activities |

FIGURE 5.1   Tab pages in a notification (© SAP AG)

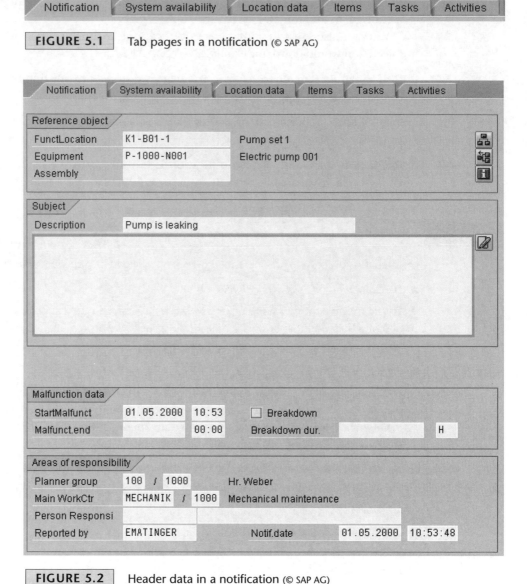

FIGURE 5.2   Header data in a notification (© SAP AG)

■ *Location and account assignment*

This data (Fig. 5.3) is copied by the system from the master record of the reference object and applies to the entire notification. The location data provides information on the actual physical location of the functional location or equipment in the company. The account assignment data specifies from whom the maintenance costs should usually be debited.

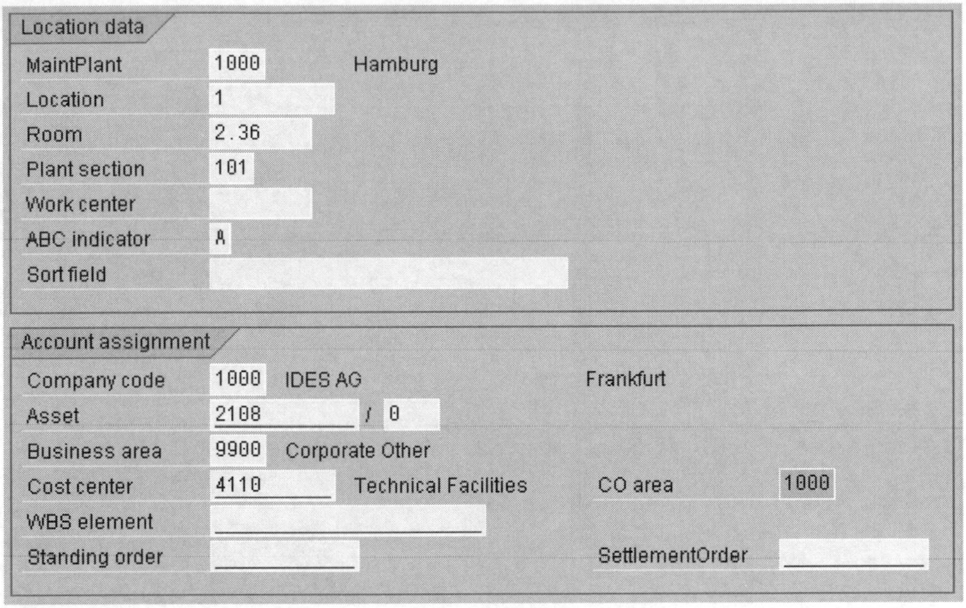

Location data

MaintPlant	1000	Hamburg
Location	1	
Room	2.36	
Plant section	101	
Work center		
ABC indicator	A	
Sort field		

Account assignment

Company code	1000	IDES AG	Frankfurt
Asset	2108	/ 0	
Business area	9900	Corporate Other	
Cost center	4110	Technical Facilities	CO area 1000
WBS element			
Standing order			SettlementOrder

FIGURE 5.3   Location and account assignment data in a notification (© SAP AG)

Reported by

Reported by	EMATINGER	Notif.date	01.05.2000 23:15:29

Start/end dates

Malfunct.start	01.05.2000 20:00:00	Req.start	01.05.2000 23:15:29
Malfunction end	00:00:00	Required end	00:00:00

Completion dates

Completn date	00:00:00	TechInspectn by	
Reference date	00:00:00	TechInspec on	

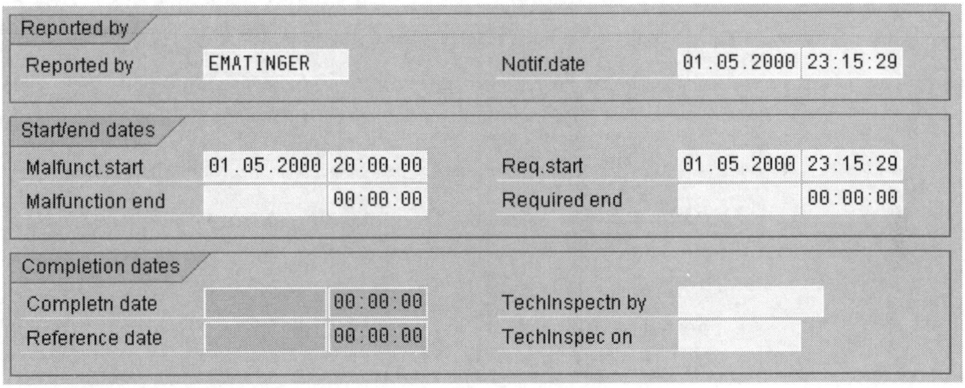

FIGURE 5.4   Scheduling overview in a notification (© SAP AG)

▪ *Scheduling overview*

All the dates stored previously for the maintenance notification are listed here (Fig. 5.4).

▪ *Items*

A notification contains one or more items (Fig. 5.5). These items describe the symptoms that have occurred, the cause of the problem, the object part affected, as well as the tasks decided on and actions performed.

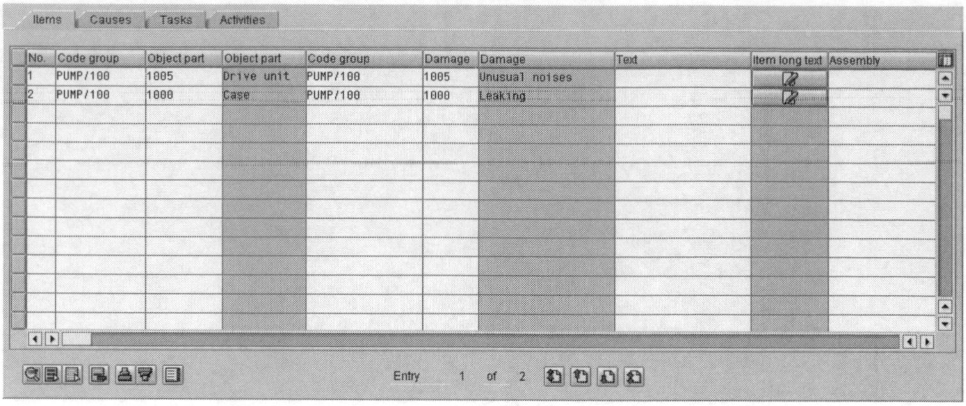

No.	Code group	Object part	Object part	Code group	Damage	Damage	Text	Item long text	Assembly
1	PUMP/100	1005	Drive unit	PUMP/100	1005	Unusual noises		✎	
2	PUMP/100	1000	Case	PUMP/100	1000	Leaking		✎	

Entry   1   of   2

FIGURE 5.5   Item data in a notification (© SAP AG)

No.	Code group	Task code	Task code text	Task text	Task long text	Status	User status	Func. of per. resp.	Responsible	List name
1	PM01	1001		Take a picture of damage	✎	TSOS		ER		
2	PM01	2000		Process warranty	✎	TSOS		ER		
								ER		
								ER		
								ER		
								ER		
								ER		
								ER		
								ER		
								ER		
								ER		
								ER		
								ER		
								ER		
								ER		

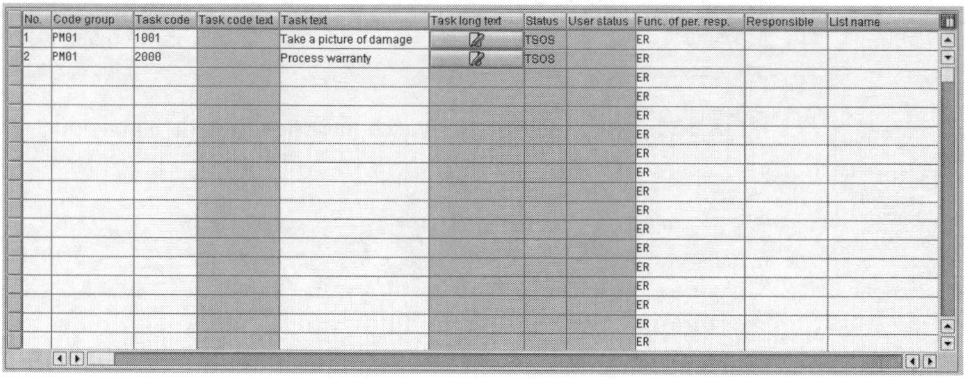

FIGURE 5.6   Task data in a notification (© SAP AG)

■ *Tasks*

These describe tasks to be performed (Fig. 5.6). The most important aspects here are planning and organization.

■ *Activities*

The work carried out for a notification is documented here (Fig. 5.7). Activity data is particularly important when inspections are performed, since it provides verification that specific tasks have been carried out.

■ *Catalog profile*

This profile comprises a combination of code groups, which specifies (according to functional criteria) the code groups that can be used for a technical object (Fig. 5.8). The catalog profile thus ensures that only suitable and useful codes can be used for any particular object.

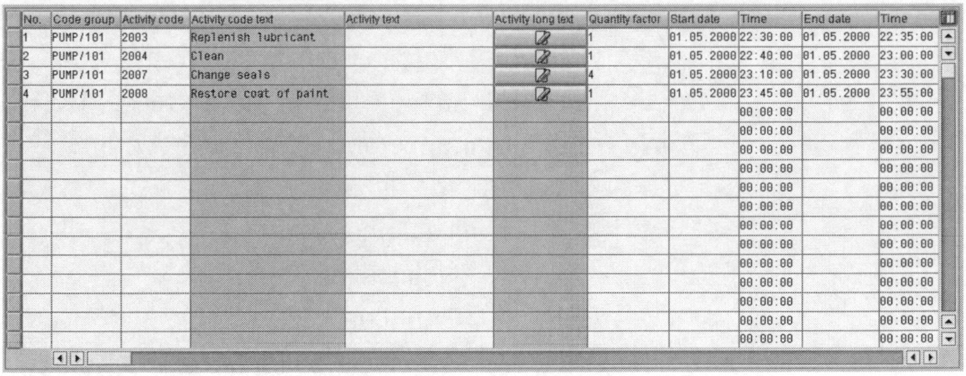

No.	Code group	Activity code	Activity code text	Activity text	Activity long text	Quantity factor	Start date	Time	End date	Time	
1	PUMP/101	2003	Replenish lubricant		✎	1	01.05.2000	22:30:00	01.05.2000	22:35:00	
2	PUMP/101	2004	Clean		✎	1	01.05.2000	22:40:00	01.05.2000	23:00:00	
3	PUMP/101	2007	Change seals		✎	4	01.05.2000	23:10:00	01.05.2000	23:30:00	
4	PUMP/101	2008	Restore coat of paint		✎	1	01.05.2000	23:45:00	01.05.2000	23:55:00	
								00:00:00		00:00:00	
								00:00:00		00:00:00	
								00:00:00		00:00:00	
								00:00:00		00:00:00	
								00:00:00		00:00:00	
								00:00:00		00:00:00	
								00:00:00		00:00:00	
								00:00:00		00:00:00	
								00:00:00		00:00:00	
								00:00:00		00:00:00	
								00:00:00		00:00:00	
								00:00:00		00:00:00	

FIGURE 5.7   Activity data in a notification (© SAP AG)

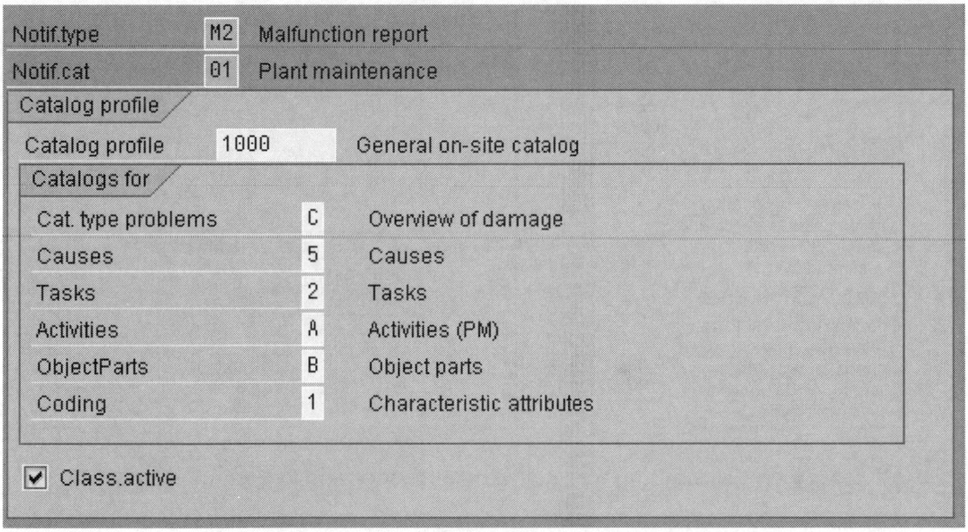

Notif.type	M2	Malfunction report
Notif.cat	01	Plant maintenance

Catalog profile

Catalog profile	1000	General on-site catalog

Catalogs for

Cat. type problems	C	Overview of damage
Causes	5	Causes
Tasks	2	Tasks
Activities	A	Activities (PM)
ObjectParts	B	Object parts
Coding	1	Characteristic attributes

☑ Class.active

FIGURE 5.8   Settings for catalog profile and catalogs (example: malfunction reports) (© SAP AG)

The Customizing path shown in Figure 5.9, PLANT MAINTENANCE AND CUSTOMER SERVICE | MAINTENANCE AND SERVICE PROCESSING | NOTIFICATIONS | CATALOG MAINTENANCE AND SETTINGS FOR REPORTING, calls up the settings of the maintenance notification that are relevant for Reporting. A hierarchically structured cross-application catalog system is used for this purpose, which permits structuring according to functional criteria.

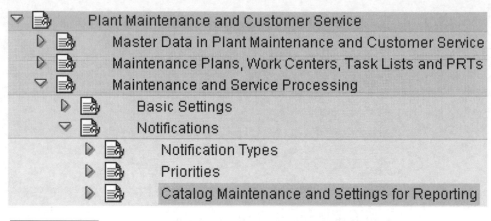

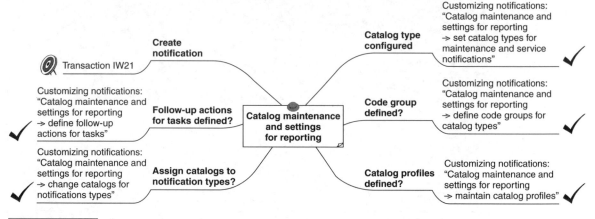

FIGURE 5.10 Customizing for catalog maintenance and Reporting settings

- Catalog types are the first level in this catalog system. Each of these plant mainte-nance catalog types represents a specific directory (for example, directories of possible activities, possible forms of damage, or object parts affected). Each catalog type can be broken down further via code groups, in which individual codes can be defined.

- *System availability*

  This data describes the system breakdown, as well as the system availability before, during, and after detection of the malfunction.

5.1.2 Activity reports

An activity report describes a maintenance activity that has already been carried out and

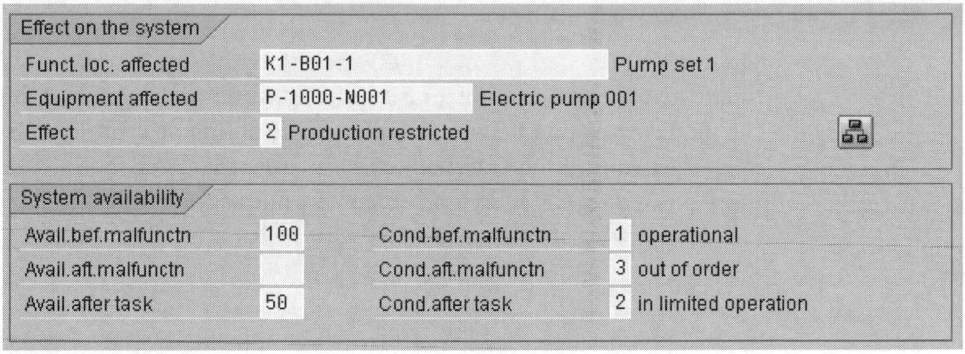

FIGURE 5.11   Display of system availability in a notification (© SAP AG)

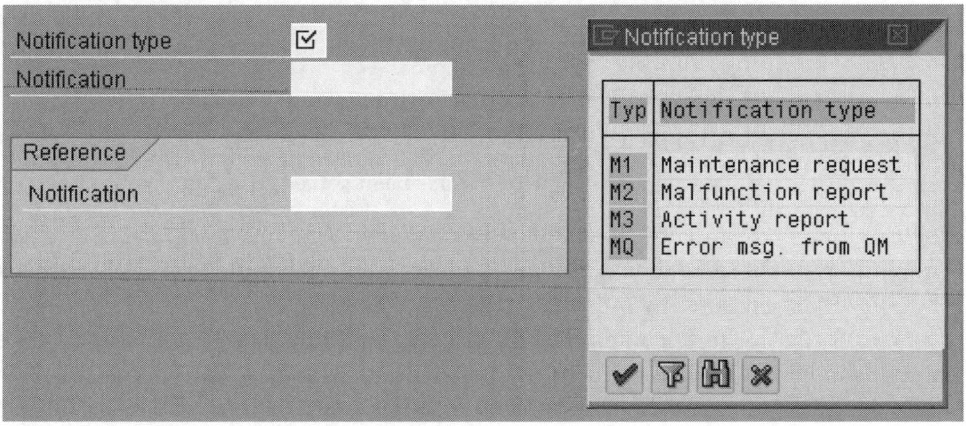

FIGURE 5.12   Choosing the notification type during creation of a maintenance notification (© SAP AG)

was not necessitated by a malfunction, problem or damage. An activity report is a technical document and is used to verify which activities were carried out when, and for what reason, as well as the result of these activities. Typical examples of activity reports include inspection or maintenance findings. These document all the results of an inspection, or the technical values of an object determined during or after regular preventive maintenance work. Inspection tasks are not requested explicitly via a malfunction report and are usually based on inspection orders. Preventive maintenance work is carried out to preserve the target condition of the object, and is based on preventive maintenance plans.

To enter activity reports in the system, you first choose LOGISTICS | PLANT MAINTENANCE | MAINTENANCE PROCESSING, followed by NOTIFICATION | CREATE (SPECIAL) | ACTIVITY REPORT. Alternatively, you can choose CREATE (GENERAL), followed by notification type M3 (Activity report) in the Notification type field.

How to document tasks

The term 'tasks' denotes activities planned within the scope of a notification. With tasks, the focus is on the planning and organizational aspects of the notification. You can plan cooperation between various people during processing of the notification, and track the completion of the activities in a particular time frame. A task can refer to the header as well as the individual items of a notification, and can have various statuses.

The following specifications can be made for all individual notifications:

- Planned start and end times
- Key of the task to be performed
- Operational method sheet
- Status of the task

The individual processing phases that a task passes through can be recorded by means of three different statuses:

- Released: the task can be performed
- Completed: the task has been carried out
- Successful: the problem has been solved; the damage has been corrected

To enter the individual tasks in the system, you call up the maintenance notification in create or change mode. If you want to create tasks that apply to the entire notification, choose the TASKS tab page.

To document tasks that apply to a single notification item, choose the ITEMS tab page. This contains the TASKS group, where you can specify the planned start and end times of the task. To call up the task detail screen, choose DETAILS. Figure 5.14 shows this detail screen with the TASK and TASK PLANNING groups.

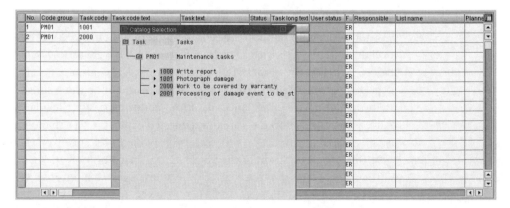

FIGURE 5.13 Choosing tasks: the example shows the 'Maintenance tasks' code group (© SAP AG)

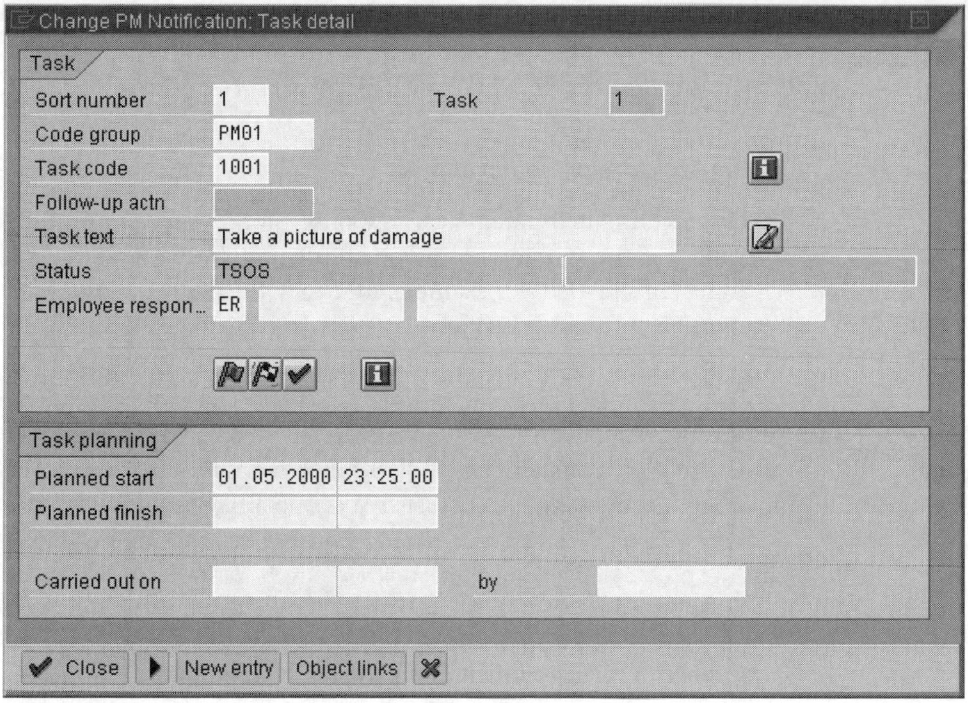

FIGURE 5.14   Detail screen of a task for a maintenance notification (© SAP AG)

If you want to create a new task from the detail screen, choose NEW ENTRY.

Possible tasks in a malfunction report can often involve forwarding information to the company department, central purchasing or engineering/design, for example. Tasks such as 'Contact customer as soon as possible' are often found in service notifications.

Provided that the appropriate data is maintained in Customizing, the system can trigger follow-up actions defined via the task code, such as printing specific papers or calling up SAP functions. These follow-up actions are defined by the customer to meet his or her specific requirements. The status of a task is only used to inform the members of staff involved in maintenance planning. In programming terms, the individual statuses are as independent of each other as possible.

A notification can, for example, be put in process even if it contains tasks that have not yet been released. A notification cannot be completed, however, if it still contains outstanding tasks. The system does not distinguish here between tasks entered in the header of a notification, and tasks in the notification items. If the status of a notification indicates that tasks are outstanding, the tasks involved may be in the notification header and the individual items.

A notification has the status 'outstanding tasks' as long as one or more tasks have not been completed – even if these tasks have already been released.

Automatic determination of tasks

The preconfigured parameters 'response profile', 'service profile' and 'priority' are required if the system is to automatically determine tasks for a notification. These parameters are used, for example, to specify the period of time within which a notification must be responded to.

You create a notification in the system in the afternoon. In the response profile, a time interval of one hour for the task code 'Call back customer' and a time interval of five hours for the task code 'Check whether technician is at customer site' are defaulted. The service window is from 6.00 a.m. till 9.00 p.m. You must, therefore, call back the partner by 1.00 p.m. to discuss the problem. If required, a technician must be at the partner's site by 5.00 p.m.

Automatic task determination is particularly important in connection with service and maintenance contracts, in which defined responses at specific time intervals have been agreed on.

In order to carry out automatic task determination, you must maintain the following settings in Customizing:

- Define response and service profiles
- Assign response and service profiles to notification types
- Define priority types
- Define priorities for each priority type
- Assign priority types to notification types

You maintain the priorities in Customizing under PLANT MAINTENANCE AND CUSTOMER SERVICE | MAINTENANCE AND SERVICE PROCESSING | GENERAL DATA | DEFINE PRIORITIES. You can here define priority types and priorities for each priority type, and also assign priority types to notification types. Figure 5.15 shows the Customizing activity DEFINE PRIORITIES FOR EACH PRIORITY TYPE. In this activity, you specify, among other things, the relative start and end times of tasks and the texts for priorities.

Response and service profiles can be set under the Customizing menu path PLANT MAINTENANCE AND CUSTOMER SERVICE | MAINTENANCE AND SERVICE PROCESSING | NOTIFICATIONS | RESPONSE TIME MONITORING. Here you can define response and service profiles, and also assign notification types to the response and service profiles you have generated.

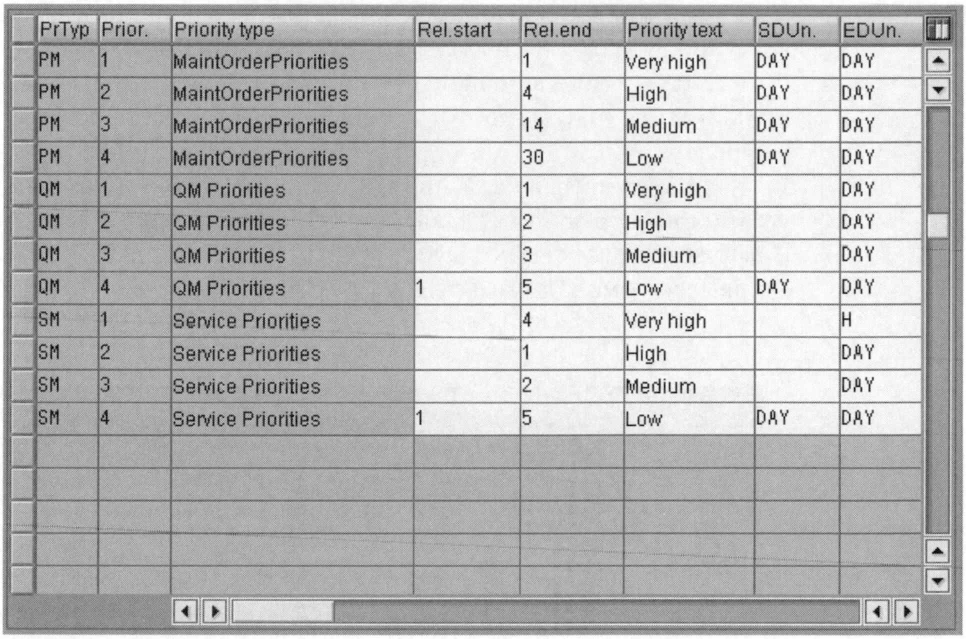

	PrTyp	Prior.	Priority type	Rel.start	Rel.end	Priority text	SDUn.	EDUn.
	PM	1	MaintOrderPriorities		1	Very high	DAY	DAY
	PM	2	MaintOrderPriorities		4	High	DAY	DAY
	PM	3	MaintOrderPriorities		14	Medium	DAY	DAY
	PM	4	MaintOrderPriorities		30	Low	DAY	DAY
	QM	1	QM Priorities		1	Very high		DAY
	QM	2	QM Priorities		2	High		DAY
	QM	3	QM Priorities		3	Medium		DAY
	QM	4	QM Priorities	1	5	Low	DAY	DAY
	SM	1	Service Priorities		4	Very high		H
	SM	2	Service Priorities		1	High		DAY
	SM	3	Service Priorities		2	Medium		DAY
	SM	4	Service Priorities	1	5	Low	DAY	DAY

FIGURE 5.15   Customizing activity 'Define Priorities for Each Priority Type' (© SAP AG)

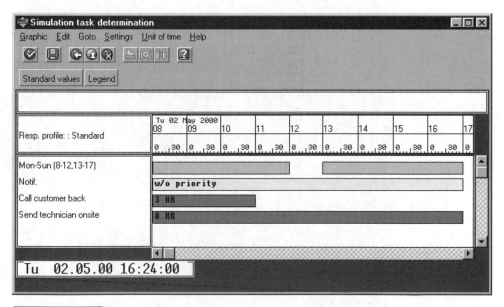

FIGURE 5.16   The result of simulating task determination (© SAP AG)

If you want the system to determine a task for a notification (starting from the notification), you have to choose EDIT | TASKS | DETERMINE. If you want to simulate one or more tasks before automatic determination is carried out, choose EDIT | TASKS | SIMULATION (DETERMINATION). Figure 5.16 shows the result of a simulation of this type.

As shown in Figure 5.17, the settings for the follow-up tasks are called up via the Customizing path PLANT MAINTENANCE AND CUSTOMER SERVICE | MAINTENANCE AND SERVICE PROCESSING | NOTIFICATIONS | CATALOG MAINTENANCE AND SETTINGS FOR REPORTING | DEFINE FOLLOW-UP ACTIONS FOR TASKS.

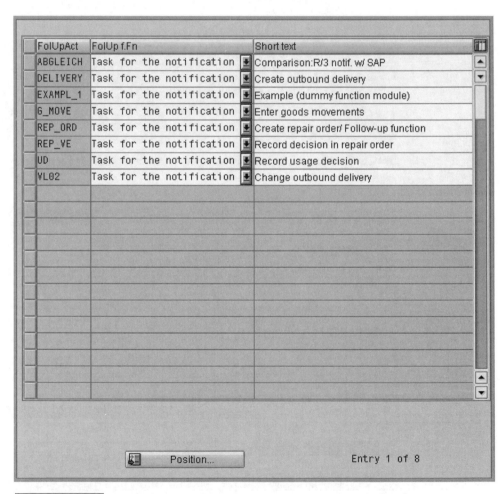

	FolUpAct	FolUp f.Fn		Short text	
	ABGLEICH	Task for the notification	⬇	Comparison:R/3 notif. w/ SAP	
	DELIVERY	Task for the notification	⬇	Create outbound delivery	
	EXAMPL_1	Task for the notification	⬇	Example (dummy function module)	
	G_MOVE	Task for the notification	⬇	Enter goods movements	
	REP_ORD	Task for the notification	⬇	Create repair order/ Follow-up function	
	REP_VE	Task for the notification	⬇	Record decision in repair order	
	UD	Task for the notification	⬇	Record usage decision	
	VL02	Task for the notification	⬇	Change outbound delivery	

Position...   Entry 1 of 8

FIGURE 5.17   Settings for the follow-up actions for tasks (© SAP AG)

How to document actions

Actions are activities that have been carried out in the context of a maintenance notification. Actions are distinct from tasks, in that the former denote the steps already taken towards solving a particular problem.

The following information can be included in individual actions:

- Key for the action carried out
- Short description
- Start and end time of the action
- Quantity factor for the action

An action can refer to the header of a notification as well as to the individual notification items.

When you create an activity report, your aim is to document an action you have already carried out. The activity report should contain information on the action that was carried out, as well as its scope and effects. In contrast to a malfunction report, an activity report describes the actions carried out, but not malfunctions or problems.

The action data is displayed in various levels of detail at two points in the notification, in the action overview and in the action detail screen. The action overview and the action detail screen are the same for all notification types. Figure 5.7 shows the action overview in a maintenance notification.

5.1.3 Malfunction reports

A malfunction report describes a malfunction on an object, which restricts the performance of that object in some way. An employee (for example, from production) can use a malfunction report to inform the maintenance department that a system is not functioning correctly, is not working at all, or is producing poor results. Malfunction reports are intended to prompt the maintenance department to carry out a maintenance task to restore the target condition of the object (to DIN 31051).

How to create malfunction reports

In most companies, the first step in creating a malfunction report only involves reporting a problem, a malfunction, or damage – and the report merely provides data on the malfunction. Data referring to technical findings or correction of the malfunction is not recorded until the second step. This is entered as changes in the report.

The malfunction report constitutes a special case if an employee detects a malfunction, corrects it immediately, and then writes a malfunction report documenting the nature and cause of the malfunction, as well as the action taken to correct it. In this case, the maintenance notification is entered as a completion confirmation after the maintenance task has been completed.

To create a malfunction report, choose LOGISTICS | PLANT MAINTENANCE | MAINTENANCE PROCESSING, followed by NOTIFICATION | CREATE (SPECIAL) | MALFUNCTION REPORT.

TIP When you create a malfunction report, it should provide the maintenance department with as much information as possible.

You can ensure that the report is processed quickly and smoothly by specifying the following:

- The malfunction/problem that has occurred
- The technical object affected
- The effects of the malfunction
- The person reporting the malfunction/problem
- Any other damage and problems

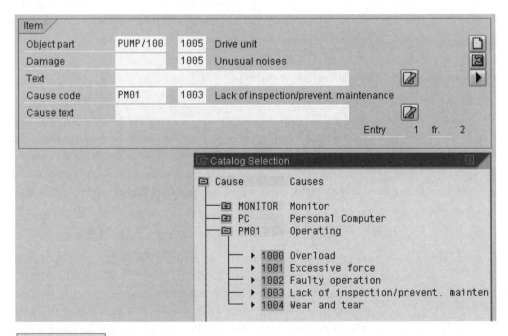

FIGURE 5.18 Selecting the code group (example: cause code PM01 Operating)
(© SAP AG)

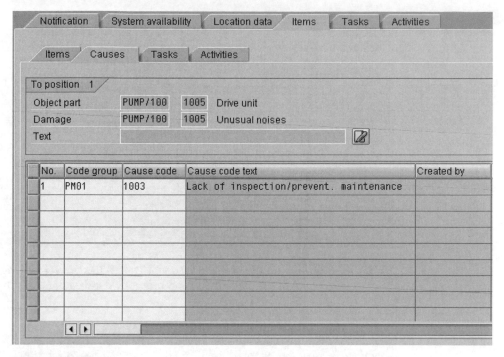

FIGURE 5.19   CAUSES tab page in the notification items (© SAP AG)

How to enter causes

If you want to enter a cause in a notification, choose the NOTIFICATION tab page and the ITEM group. Figure 5.18 shows the catalog selection for the cause code.

If you want to enter a cause for a notification item, first choose the ITEMS tab page followed by the CAUSES tab page, as shown in Figure 5.19.

How to specify breakdowns and breakdown durations

If a problem or the performance of an activity causes the assembly in question to break down, you can document the breakdown at two points in the system: in the notification header or in the breakdown data screen.

If you are in the create or change mode for the notification, choose the MALFUNCTION, BREAKDOWN tab page (Fig. 5.20). You can enter the start and end of the malfunction here. If you want to indicate that the malfunction resulted in a functional breakdown, select the BREAKDOWN checkbox. The system calculates the breakdown duration automatically and displays it in hours.

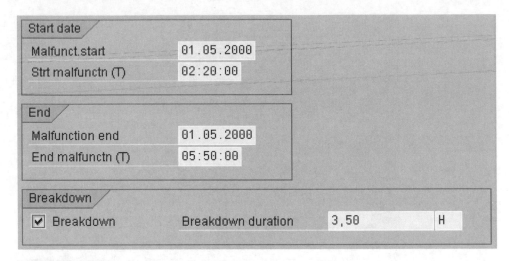

FIGURE 5.20   Content of the MALFUNCTION, BREAKDOWN tab page: start and end of the malfunction and breakdown indicator (© SAP AG)

	Funct	Name	Partner	Name	AddInd
	PR	Position Responsible	50011826	Work preparation	☐
	SH	Ship-to party	1000000019	Oliver Lipp	☐
					☐

FIGURE 5.21   Partner data in a maintenance notification (© SAP AG)

How to display partner information

A partner is a person within or outside your company, whom you can or must contact in the course of a business transaction. Details on partners are located in a separate screen of the notification. If you are in create or change mode for the notification, choose GOTO | PARTNERS or the PARTNERS icon. If partner data has already been entered for this notification, the system then displays the partner function, number, and name (as shown in Figure 5.21).

5.1.4 Maintenance requests

Maintenance requests are notifications used to request the maintenance department to perform an activity. Unlike malfunction reports, maintenance requests are not used in the event of malfunctions. They are typically used in conjunction with investments, reconstruction or replacement (involving systems or buildings, for example). During the first step of generating a maintenance request, it is important that you list the maintenance activities you require. The data referring to the performance of the request (for example, date and time) is not entered until the second step, and is included as changes in the maintenance request.

TIP

When you create a maintenance request, you should provide maintenance planning with as much information as possible on the type of activities you require from the maintenance department. If possible, you should, therefore, specify the following:

- The activity requested
- The object that the request applies to
- The person requesting the activity

To create a maintenance request, choose LOGISTICS | PLANT MAINTENANCE | MAINTENANCE PROCESSING, followed by NOTIFICATION | CREATE (SPECIAL) | MAINTENANCE NOTIFICATION.

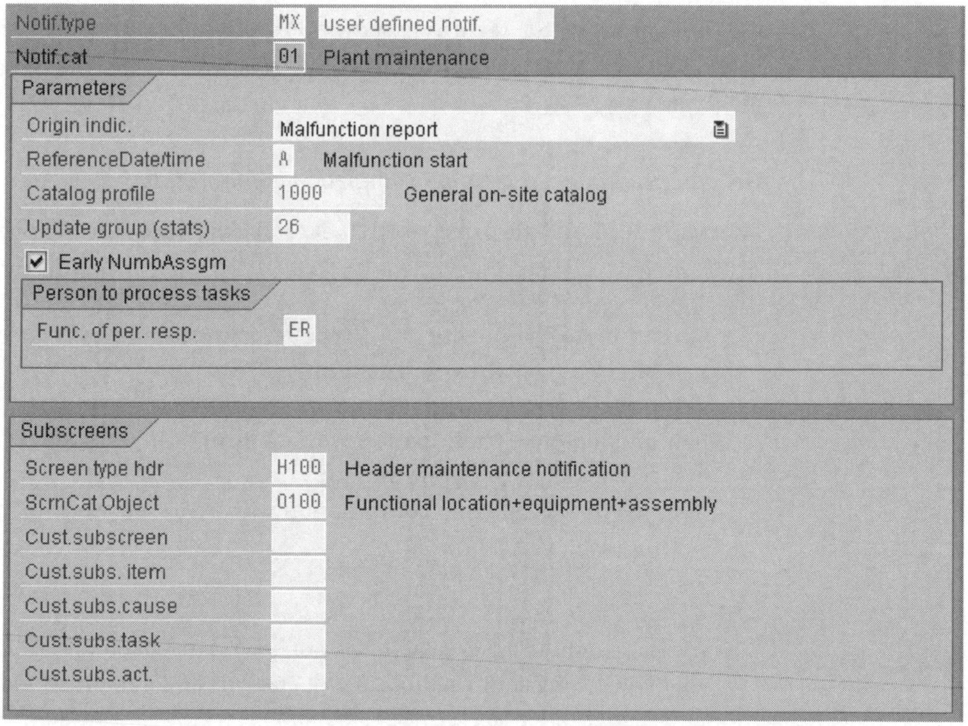

FIGURE 5.22 Customizing activity: Change View 'Notification Types' (© SAP AG)

5.1.5 User-specific notifications

A user-specific notification is a notification of a type not included in the standard notification types. User-specific notifications are based on standard notification types. As shown in Figure 5.22, the screens for notifications of this type can be configured in Customizing via PLANT MAINTENANCE AND CUSTOMER SERVICE | MAINTENANCE AND SERVICE PROCESSING | NOTIFICATIONS | NOTIFICATION TYPES | DEFINE NOTIFICATION TYPES.

To create user-specific maintenance notifications, choose LOGISTICS | PLANT MAINTENANCE | MAINTENANCE PROCESSING, followed by NOTIFICATION | CREATE (GENERAL).

5.1.6 Completion confirmations

Completion confirmations document the processing status of operations or sub-operations of maintenance or service orders. They are, therefore, part of order monitoring in the system.

The uses of completion confirmations include documenting and updating the following information in the system: the work centre that carried out one or more operations in an order; whether operations have been started or performed completely; the times at which the tasks were started and when they were completed; whether and where equipment has been dismantled or installed at functional locations, and which materials were used.

General procedure for creating completion confirmations

The following are all the process steps that can be included in a completion confirmation:

1 *Choose desired entry transaction*
   According to the quantity and type of confirmation, various entry transactions can be chosen for the confirmation:
   – Individual time confirmation with order/operation number
   – Individual time confirmation with confirmation number
   – Overall completion confirmation
   – Collective completion confirmation with/without selection
   – Time sheet (CATS)

2 *Confirm time data*
   Various options are available for entering data, depending on the type of data involved. Time confirmations for operations and sub-operations in maintenance and service orders are created to document the processing status for the operations in these orders.
   The following time data can be confirmed:

- Person or work centre who/that processed the operation/sub-operation
- Duration of processing and the period during which the activity was performed
- Duration of further work required
- Time required for the operation
- When operation is expected to be finished
- Whether work for this operation/sub-operation is finished, and whether the open reservations for the operation/sub-operation should be cleared.

3 *Confirm material used*

Various types of entry are also available for confirming material. The system allows you to confirm which materials were used to carry out an operation and in which quantities, and to document returns of unused material to the warehouse.

The following materials are taken into consideration:

- Unplanned materials; these are materials not taken into consideration when the order for this operation was planned, but which were used to execute the order.
- Planned materials: these are materials scheduled in the order for this operation, and used to execute the order.
- Backflushed materials: these are low-value small parts but are nevertheless subject to inventory management in the system. In the order, the maintenance planner has the option of flagging materials of this type as backflushed. This avoids having to post each of the materials separately when they are released.

4 *Confirm measurement/counter readings*

In the completion confirmation, you can also enter measurement/counter readings for specific order operations. These are entered in the form of measurement documents with data on the measuring point and measuring result, and additional information in short/long texts.

5 *Confirm installation/dismantling information*

You can also enter information on the installation or dismantling of technical objects in the completion confirmation, provided that the related order has been released for execution.

6 *Confirm goods receipts for refurbished material*

In the R/3 System, you can also post the goods receipt for materials that have been refurbished. In accordance with planning in the order, the goods receipt returns repaired/refurbished repairable spares to the warehouse, where they are posted and, if necessary, valuated. At this point in time, they are functional again and can be planned and used.

The value yielded by the quantity delivered and the current price is credited to the maintenance order.

7 *Technical completion confirmation*
In the completion confirmation, you can also enter technical data and findings, such as cause of damage, location of the damage on the object, work and activities performed, findings, as well as system availability during and after the task.

8 *Completion confirmations for services*
You can also confirm services performed internally, provided that the default values of the plant maintenance and customer service user have been assigned a confirmation profile that enables the service table to be displayed. In addition to this, the order operations for which services are confirmed must be assigned a control key that permits this confirmation to be carried out.

9 *Confirmation of external services or external material*
Services and materials purchased from external companies can also be confirmed for a maintenance order. The procedure for confirming external materials or external services is as follows:
On the basis of the purchase requisition generated in the order, the vendor is sent a purchase order for a material or external service. The delivery or service is treated as a goods receipt and posted directly to the order for which the material or external service was requested. When the goods receipt is carried out, the order is debited with the corresponding costs. Any changes in costs are updated in the order during invoice receipt.

10 *Display completion confirmations*
Various options are available for displaying confirmations. You can either display all the completion confirmations for an order, or display a confirmation list according to defined selection criteria. These options will be discussed in greater detail in section 5.1.7, 'Displaying completion confirmations'.

11 *Cancel completion confirmation*
Because completion confirmations are sometimes accidentally entered for the wrong operations or sub-operations, or contain incorrect data, the system provides you with the option of cancelling confirmations. The section 'How to cancel completion confirmations' discusses these operations in greater detail.

12 *Display costs*
Actual costs are accrued for the order as soon as maintenance or service activities begin to be performed, and completion confirmations (either time confirmations or material withdrawals) are entered for the order. Various options are available for displaying these costs: they can be displayed according to cost elements, or according to value categories.

TIP
When materials are withdrawn, the system generates a goods issue document automatically. If you want to enter completion confirmations in the system, you must use the MAINTENANCE ORDERS component. Technical confirmations can only be entered if the MAINTENANCE NOTIFICATIONS component is used.

If you have entered completion confirmations for operations or sub-operations of an order, and processing has not yet been completed, the system automatically assigns the operations/sub-operations 'partially confirmed' status. As soon as all the operations and sub-operations of an order that are intended for a completion confirmation are finally confirmed, the order is assigned the status 'finally confirmed'.

How to use individual time confirmations to confirm activities

Individual time confirmations are used to enter detailed time confirmations for individual operations, and splits. This is particularly useful if other data (such as material used or damage information) is only occasionally entered. The confirmation can only be carried out if the order to be confirmed has been released.

To enter an individual time confirmation with the order or operation number, choose LOGISTICS | PLANT MAINTENANCE | MAINTENANCE PROCESSING | COMPLETION CONFIRMATION | ENTRY | INDIVIDUAL TIME CONFIRMATION. Figure 5.23 shows the initial screen for individual time confirmations. In the ORDER group, you can enter the order number and/or operation and sub-operation numbers.

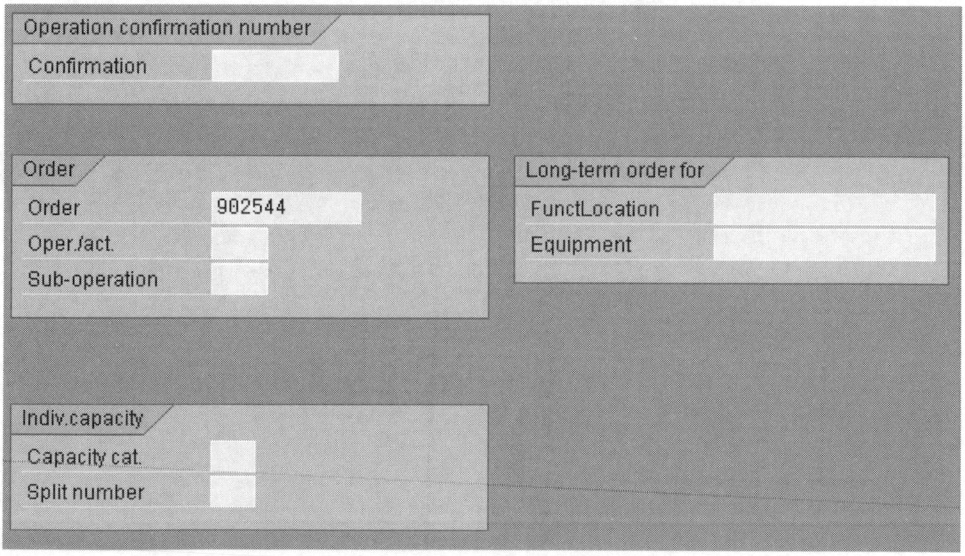

FIGURE 5.23   Initial screen for individual time confirmations (© SAP AG)

As shown in Figure 5.24, choosing ENTER calls up an overview of all the operations and sub-operations in the order that correspond to the parameter settings.

Select the operations/sub-operations for which you want to enter the completion confirmation, and choose GOTO | ACTUAL DATA. This calls up the screen containing details of the completion confirmation for the first operation/sub-operation you have selected. Enter the desired confirmation data here, as shown in Figure 5.25.

To enter an individual time confirmation with confirmation number, choose LOGISTICS | PLANT MAINTENANCE | MAINTENANCE PROCESSING | COMPLETION CONFIRMATION | ENTRY | INDIVIDUAL TIME CONFIRMATION. Figure 5.23 shows the initial screen for individual time confirmations described above ('Individual time confirmations with order or operation number'). In this screen, you enter the

Order	810740	Routine Check Pump									

Operations and sub-operations

Co	OpAc	SOp	Sp	Work ctr	Plnt	Work	Un.	Short text	Actual start	Act.finish date	Forecast work	Actual work
	0010			MECHANIK	1000	0,5	HR	Check Engine			0,0	0,0
	0020			MECHANIK	1000	1,0	HR	Change Sealings			0,0	0,0
	0030			MECHANIK	1000	0,3	HR	QA			0,0	0,0

FIGURE 5.24   Operation overview for completion confirmation of order (© SAP AG)

Order	810740	Routine Check Pump
Oper./act.	0010	Check Engine
System status	REL	

Confirmation data

Confirmation	50692				
Work center	MECHANIK	1000	Mechanical maintenance		
Personnel no.				Wage type	
Actual work	0,5	HR	Activity type	1410	Posting date	01.05.2000
Final confirmat	☐		No rem.work	☑	AcctIndicator	
Clear open res.	☐			Remaining work		HR
Work start	01.05.2000	23:13:58		Actual duration		HR
Work end	01.05.2000	23:30:00		Forecast end		24:00:00
Reason					
Confirm. text					

Total confirmation data

Cum.actual work		0,0	HR	ActualDuration	0,0	HR
Forecast work	0,5	HR		PlannedDuration	0,5	HR
Actual start		00:00:00		Actual finish	00:00:00

FIGURE 5.25   Confirmation detail screen (© SAP AG)

confirmation number in the CONFIRMATION field, choose ENTER, and enter the data for the completion confirmation.

TIP Choosing the SAVE function when processing a completion confirmation will always save all the data previously entered for the operations you have processed, and will take you back to the initial screen for the completion confirmation.

How to use individual time confirmations to confirm material used

In the confirmation detail screen, call up the material list by choosing ENVIRONMENT | GOODS MOVEMENTS. The system displays these goods movements as shown in Figure 5.26.

Make all the entries you require in this list. If the quantities of material required were smaller than planned, correct the quantity specified for the material in the list. Save the completion confirmation, or return to the confirmation detail screen for the operation to enter other data.

How to use overall completion confirmations to confirm activities and materials

In the R/3 System, overall completion confirmations provide useful support if you confirm data in addition to the working time (for example, materials used, damage information, work/tasks and actions performed, as well as measurement/counter readings).

TIP In the standard R/3 System, a default profile is set for overall completion confirmation. You can modify this profile to match your individual requirements by choosing LOGISTICS | PLANT MAINTENANCE | MAINTENANCE PROCESSING | COMPLETION CONFIRMATION | ENTRY | OVERALL COMPLETION CONFIRMATION, followed by EXTRAS | SETTINGS. This enables you to display fields for frequently used functions in the top area of the screen and locate less frequently used functions further down or on pushbuttons.

Order	810740	Routine Check Pump
Oper./act.	0010	Check Engine

Material	Description	Quantity	Entry unit	Plant	Stor. loc.	Batch	Valuation type	Item	Movmt type	Vendor	Compltd	AInd	Order	
AM2-311	basic motor 112 KW	1,000	PC	1000	0001				261		☐		810740	▲
400-431	Washer	3,000	PC	1000	0001				261		☐		810740	▼
400-200	Fly wheel CI	1,000	PC	1000	0001				261		☐		810740	
											☐			

FIGURE 5.26 Material list in a completion confirmation (© SAP AG)

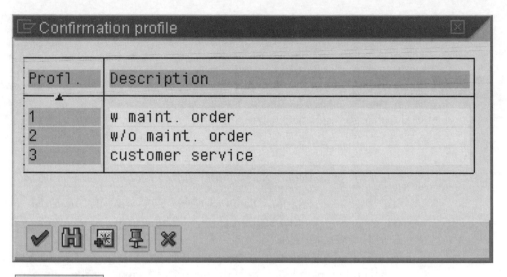

FIGURE 5.27   Dialog box for choosing the confirmation profile (© SAP AG)

In the dialog box displayed, specify the desired profile (as shown in Figure 5.27) and save your data. The next time you call up the overall completion confirmation, the user interface will be displayed in the form specified for the profile you entered.

With overall completion confirmations, the time confirmation, confirmation of goods movements and services, and technical confirmations are combined. Overall completion confirmations enable you to enter time data, causes, actions, tasks, goods movements and measurement/counter readings for the operations of an order without having to call up other screens.

To enter an overall completion confirmation with confirmation number, choose LOGISTICS | PLANT MAINTENANCE | MAINTENANCE PLANNING | COMPLETION CONFIRMATION | ENTRY | OVERALL COMPLETION CONFIRMATION. Figures 5.28a and b show the various areas of the initial screen for overall completion confirmations.

When you enter the ORDER NUMBER, you can see:

- All the operations to be confirmed for the order in the time confirmations table
- All the measurement/counter readings already entered for the order
- All the tasks, causes, and actions already entered in the notification for the order header

When you enter the order number and the desired operation number, or the confirmation number, you can see:

- The operation in the time confirmation table
- The planned materials for the operation
- All the measurement/counter readings already entered for the operation

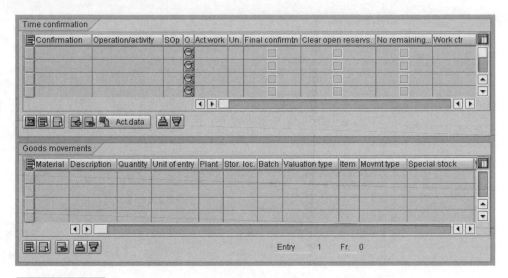

FIGURE 5.28a Initial screen for overall completion confirmations (Part 1: Time confirmation and goods movements) (© SAP AG)

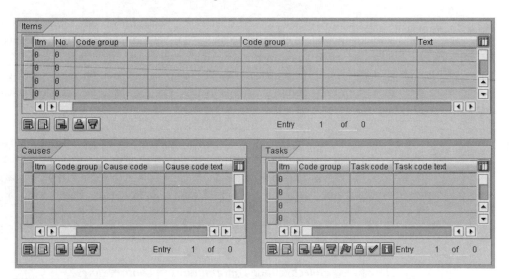

FIGURE 5.28b Initial screen for overall completion confirmations (Part 2: Items, causes and tasks) (© SAP AG)

▪ All the tasks, causes and actions already entered in the notification for the order header

By choosing ENVIRONMENT | CHANGE FUNCTION LOCATION, or ENVIRONMENT | CHANGE EQUIPMENT, you can call up master data to document the installation/dismantling of technical objects. You can process the notification for the order header by choosing the NOTIFICATION pushbutton.

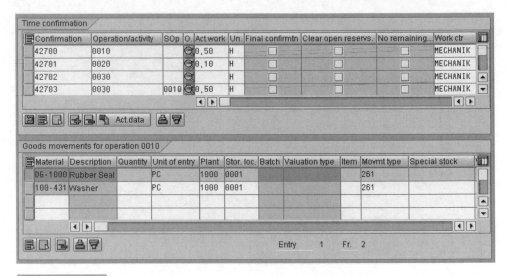

FIGURE 5.29 Data for the operation (example: goods movements) (© SAP AG)

To display the data of the operation in the appropriate tables of the overall completion confirmation, choose the DATA FOR OPERATION icon for the desired operation (Fig. 5.29), in the time confirmation table.

This function enables you to display planned materials, planned services, as well as measurement/counter readings in the appropriate tables, and enter the confirmation data required.

TIP The overall completion confirmation saves all the data entered via the entry screen or associated dialog boxes in one process step, including default data. If you do not wish to save specific confirmation or default data, you must delete these rows from the tables before saving your data.

How to use collective time confirmations to confirm times

Collective time confirmations are useful if you enter large quantities of time confirmations in the system and rarely make entries in the confirmation detail screen, or rarely enter data such as material used or damage information.

You call up the entry screen for collective time confirmations by choosing LOGISTICS | PLANT MAINTENANCE | MAINTENANCE PROCESSING | COMPLETION CONFIRMATION | ENTRY | COLLECTIVE TIME CONFIRMATION | WITHOUT SELECTION or WITH SELECTION.

As Figure 5.30 shows, the screen for entering collective time confirmations comprises two tables. In the upper table, you enter the data that you want to apply to all the operations in the list. This data can be stored on a user-specific basis so that it is automatically proposed by the system the next time you call up the collective entry screen. In the lower table, you can enter the data for the individual operations in the system. When you choose ENTER, the default data from the upper block is copied to the entry fields in the lower block.

Collective time confirmation without selection

You call up collective confirmation without selection (for example, for orders or operations) by choosing LOGISTICS | PLANT MAINTENANCE | MAINTENANCE PROCESSING | COMPLETION CONFIRMATION | ENTRY | COLLECTIVE TIME CONFIRMATION | WITHOUT SELECTION.

You can have the system propose all the actual data for the selected operations by choosing EDIT | PROPOSE ALL ACTUAL DATA or the ALL ACTUAL DATA pushbutton. If

-->	Confirmation	Order	Oper./act.	SOp	Capacity cat.	Split	Act.work	Un.	F.	C.	N.	Work ctr	Pint	ActTyp	A.	Postg date	Pers. no.	WageTy	R
		902544																	

C.	Confirmation	Order	Oper./act.	SOp	Capacity cat.	Split	Act.work	Un.	F.	C.	N.	Work ctr	Pint	ActTyp	A.	Postg date	Pers. no.	WageTy	F
	42780	902544	0010				0,5		✓	☐	☐	MECHANIK	1000						
	42781	902544	0020				0,1		☐	☐	✓	MECHANIK	1000						
	42782	902544	0030				0,40		✓	☐	☐	MECHANIK	1000						

FIGURE 5.30　Collective confirmation for a maintenance order (© SAP AG)

Pers.no	1045		Name	Karl-Heinz Schibulski	
Pers.area	1300 Frankfurt		Cost ctr	1230	Power
EE subgrp	DN	Monthly wage earner	WS rule	NORM	

Week	2 Tuesd...	3 Wedn...	4 Thurs...	5 Friday	6 Saturd...	7 Sunday	1 Mond...	
17 / 18	25.04.00	26.04.00	27.04.00	28.04.00	29.04.00	30.04.00	01.05.00	
	NORM	NORM	NORM	NORM	OFF	OFF	NORM	
Standard	7,50	7,50	7,50	7,50	0,00	0,00	0,00	30,00
Abs. hrs	0,00	1,67	0,00	0,00	0,00	0,00	0,00	1,67
Atl.hrs	0,00	0,00	0,00	0,00	0,00	0,00	0,00	0,00
Rec.hours	0,00	1,67	0,00	0,00	0,00	0,00	0,00	1,67
Rest	7,50	5,83	7,50	7,50	0,00	0,00	0,00	28,33

D	Start date	End date	Hrs	From	To	P	Type	Att./absence type	OC	Cost ctr	Order	WBS element	Cost
3	26.04.2000	26.04.2000	1,67	10:20	12:00	☐	0230	Doctor's appointment					
						☐							
						☐							
						☐							
						☐							
						☐							
						☐							
						☐							
						☐							

FIGURE 5.31　Maintaining attendances and absences (© SAP AG)

you want to enter more data for specific operations in the detail screen, select the operations you require and choose GOTO | ACTUAL DATA.

Functions for attendances/absences and time levelling are available in the ENVIRONMENT menu, as well as via the appropriate pushbuttons. These functions allow you to enter basic time information for evaluating working absence times of employees. You can use ATTENDANCES to document actual times, deviations from the work schedule, and deviations from an employee's usual activity. ABSENCES are used, for example, to enter periods of leave, doctor's appointments, or illness. Figure 5.31 shows the screen for entering this data.

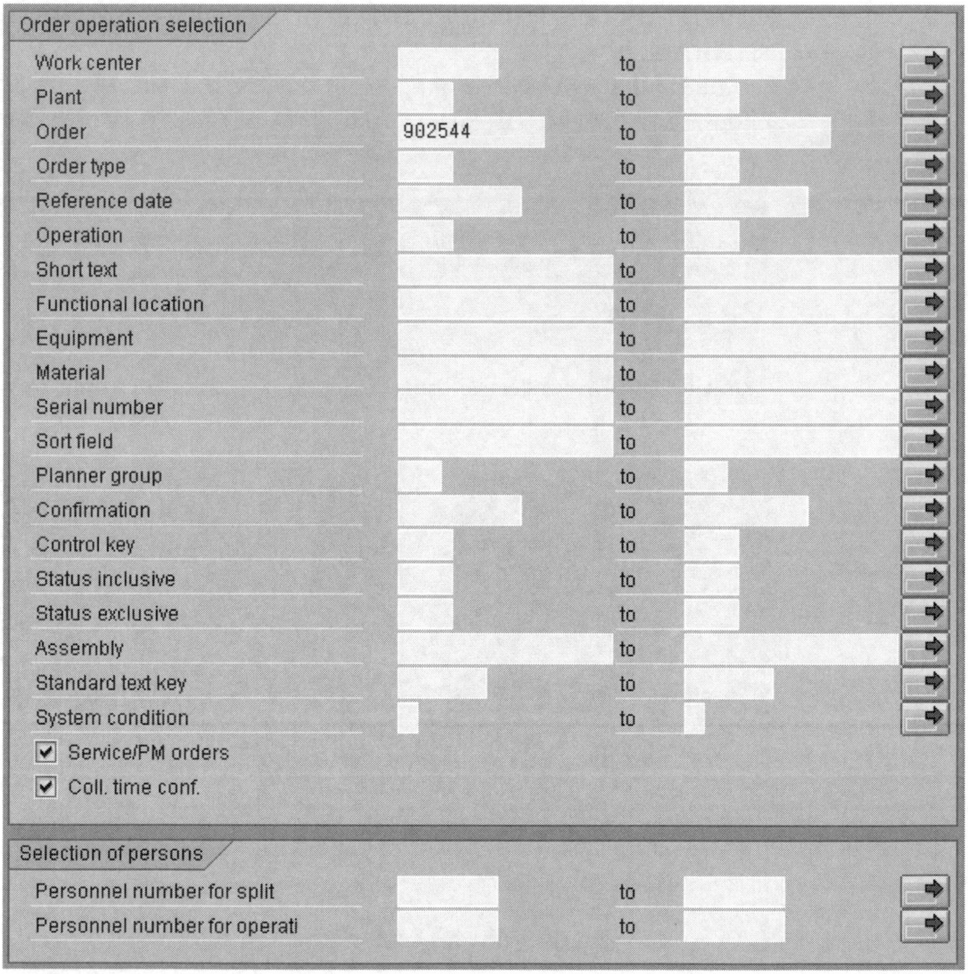

Order operation selection		
Work center		to
Plant		to
Order	902544	to
Order type		to
Reference date		to
Operation		to
Short text		to
Functional location		to
Equipment		to
Material		to
Serial number		to
Sort field		to
Planner group		to
Confirmation		to
Control key		to
Status inclusive		to
Status exclusive		to
Assembly		to
Standard text key		to
System condition		to
✔ Service/PM orders		
✔ Coll. time conf.		
Selection of persons		
Personnel number for split		to
Personnel number for operati		to

FIGURE 5.32 Selection screen for collective time confirmations (© SAP AG)

Collective time confirmations with selection

You call up the selection screen for order operations by choosing LOGISTICS | PLANT MAINTENANCE | MAINTENANCE PROCESSING | COMPLETION CONFIRMATION | ENTRY | COLLECTIVE TIME CONFIRMATION | WITH SELECTION.

If you flag the COLL. TIME CONF. checkbox as shown in Figure 5.32, the system copies the result of the operation selection directly to the entry screen for collective time confirmations, without proposing an additional selection list. If the SERVICE/PM ORDERS checkbox is flagged, only service and maintenance orders are selected. Choosing PROGRAM | EXECUTE calls up the screen shown in Figure 5.30.

TIP The pool function is useful for entering data when specific orders or operations have to be processed several times. The pool enables you to call up these operations again for processing. To save a pool, first select the operations you want to assign to it, and then choose CONFIRMATION | CREATE POOL. To call up this pool again for processing, choose CONFIRMATION | GET POOL. The data of the pool you require is displayed in the list screen for entering collective confirmations and is available for further processing.

How to use time sheets to carry out confirmations

The Time Sheet (Cross Application Time Sheet, CATS) is a cross-application component, which enables you to carry out standardized, application-independent personal time recording for internal and external employees.

The purpose of the Time Sheet is to record employee work times for various applications in one standardized transaction. The transaction enables internal employees and service providers to personally maintain their attendance times as well as specific periods of absence and working times together with information (for example, for an order or a purchase order). The data is then transferred to the appropriate applications in Logistics, Accounting and Human Resources, where it is processed.

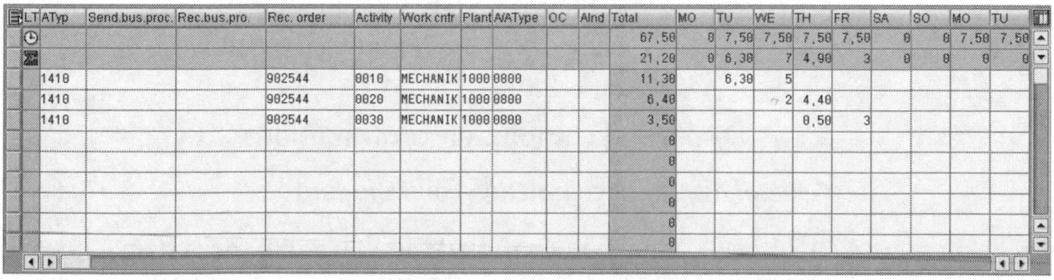

LT	ATyp	Send.bus.proc.	Rec.bus.pro.	Rec. order	Activity	Work cntr	Plant	A/AType	OC	AInd	Total	MO	TU	WE	TH	FR	SA	SO	MO	TU
											67,50	0	7,50	7,50	7,50	7,50	0	0	7,50	7,50
											21,20	0	6,30	7	4,90	3	0	0	0	0
	1410			902544	0010	MECHANIK	1000	0800			11,30		6,30	5						
	1410			902544	0020	MECHANIK	1000	0800			6,40			2	4,40					
	1410			902544	0030	MECHANIK	1000	0800			3,50				0,50	3				
											0									
											0									
											0									
											0									
											0									
											0									

FIGURE 5.33 Entering working times in the Time Sheet (© SAP AG)

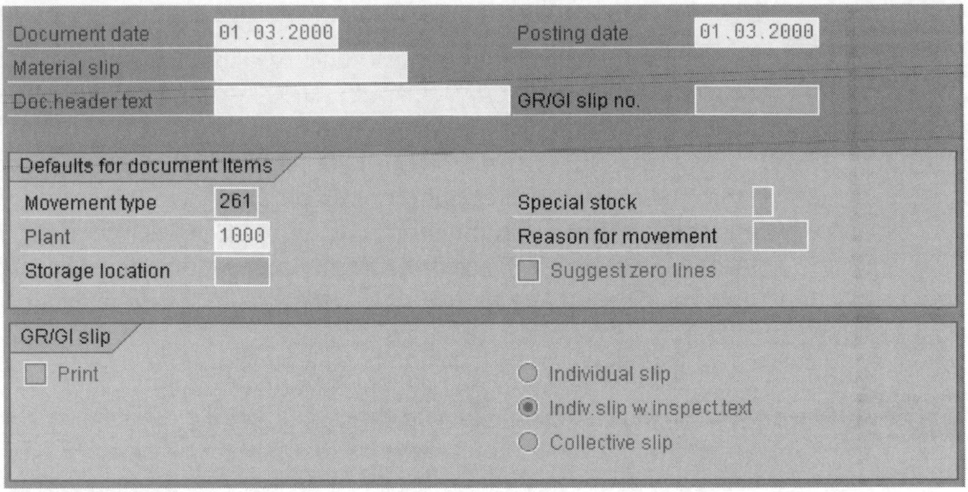

Document date	01.03.2000		Posting date	01.03.2000
Material slip				
Doc.header text			GR/GI slip no.	

Defaults for document items

Movement type	261	Special stock	
Plant	1000	Reason for movement	
Storage location		☐ Suggest zero lines	

GR/GI slip

☐ Print

    ○ Individual slip
    ◉ Indiv.slip w.inspect.text
    ○ Collective slip

FIGURE 5.34 Initial screen for entering goods movements (© SAP AG)

You call up the entry screen for the Time Sheet by choosing TIME SHEET | TIME DATA | ENTRY. This displays the data entry view, in which you enter your personnel number as well as a data entry profile, and then choose ENTER. When you first call up the Time Sheet after logging on to the system, the KEY DATE field is displayed. This is used to specify the period for which you call up the Time Sheet. Choose EDIT | ENTER TIMES. You can now enter the working times spent on an order (as shown in Figure 5.33) and save your data.

If you choose ENVIRONMENT | MATERIAL WITHDRAWAL in the Time Sheet data entry view, you can document goods movements in the system. This calls up the initial screen shown in Figure 5.34, where you can enter data for the movement type, plant and storage location of the material movement.

The system also allows you to select components generated with the maintenance order and copy or change the default quantity. These options are called up by choosing the menu path GOODS ISSUE | CREATE WITH REFERENCE | TO ORDER, or by clicking the TO ORDER . . . pushbutton, and then entering the order number in the appropriate field. Figure 5.35 shows the corresponding selection screen.

5.1.7 Displaying completion confirmations

General display of completion confirmations

To display completion confirmations entered in the system, choose LOGISTICS | PLANT MAINTENANCE | MAINTENANCE PROCESSING | COMPLETION CONFIRMATION | DISPLAY | CONFIRMATION LIST. After you choose PROGRAM | EXECUTE, the system displays a list of completion confirmations corresponding to your selection criteria.

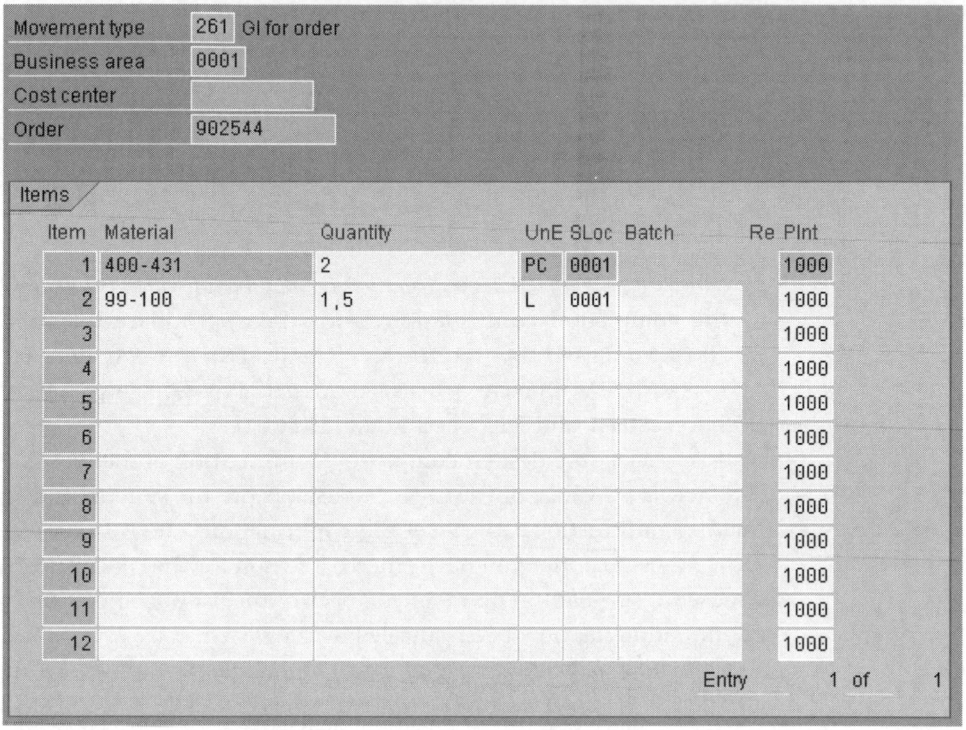

Movement type	261	GI for order
Business area	0001	
Cost center		
Order	902544	

Items

Item	Material	Quantity	UnE	SLoc	Batch	Re Plnt
1	400-431	2	PC	0001		1000
2	99-100	1,5	L	0001		1000
3						1000
4						1000
5						1000
6						1000
7						1000
8						1000
9						1000
10						1000
11						1000
12						1000

Entry   1 of   1

FIGURE 5.35   Selection screen for entering goods movements for an order (© SAP AG)

Displaying completion confirmations for an order: To call up the initial screen for displaying completion confirmations, choose LOGISTICS | PLANT MAINTENANCE | MAINTENANCE PROCESSING | COMPLETION CONFIRMATION | DISPLAY | COMPLETION CONFIRMATION. Depending on your entries, after you choose ENTER, one of the following screens will be displayed containing the completion confirmations already entered:

■ The confirmation detail screen

■ A list of the operations and sub-operations for the order

■ The selected operation with its sub-operations

■ The selected sub-operation

You can display the detail screen for the individual completion confirmations by positioning the cursor on the desired completion confirmation and choosing EDIT | CHOOSE.

How to cancel completion confirmations

If completion confirmations have been accidentally entered for the wrong operations or sub-operations, or if they contain incorrect data, the system allows you to cancel these confirmations.

Cancelling a completion confirmation the number of which is unknown: To display a list of the completion confirmations with the appropriate selection criteria, choose LOGISTICS | PLANT MAINTENANCE | MAINTENANCE PROCESSING | COMPLETION CONFIRMATION | DISPLAY | CONFIRMATION LIST. Enter the selection criteria in the selection screen, and select PROGRAM | EXECUTE.

If you select the desired completion confirmation and choose COMPLETION CONFIRMATION | CANCEL or the CANCEL pushbutton, the system displays the detail screen for the confirmation. To cancel the confirmation, choose COMPLETION CONFIRMATION | CANCEL. After you have entered a reason for the cancellation in the text editor, choose GOTO | BACK. This takes you back to the list of completion confirmations. The confirmation has now been canceled by the system.

Cancelling a completion confirmation the number of which is known: Choose LOGISTICS | PLANT MAINTENANCE | MAINTENANCE PROCESSING | COMPLETION CONFIRMATION | CANCEL. This calls up the initial screen for canceling order confirmations. After you choose ENTER, the system displays one of the following screens:

- The detail screen of the confirmation
- The selected operation with its sub-operations
- A list of the operations and sub-operations for the maintenance order
- The selected sub-operation

To call up the detail screen for the confirmation you want to cancel, select the confirmation and choose GOTO | ACTUAL DATA. The remaining steps for cancelling the confirmation are the same as for cancelling confirmations that have unknown numbers.

How to specify the control parameters for completion confirmations

In CUSTOMIZING, choose PLANT MAINTENANCE AND CUSTOMER SERVICE | MAINTENANCE AND SERVICE PROCESSING | COMPLETION CONFIRMATIONS | DEFINE CONTROL PARAMETERS FOR COMPLETION CONFIRMATIONS. This calls up a table with an overview of plants and maintenance order types that are assigned to an order type. Selecting an entry and choosing DETAILS calls up the detail view shown in Figure 5.36, where you can maintain the control parameters for completion confirmations for maintenance orders.

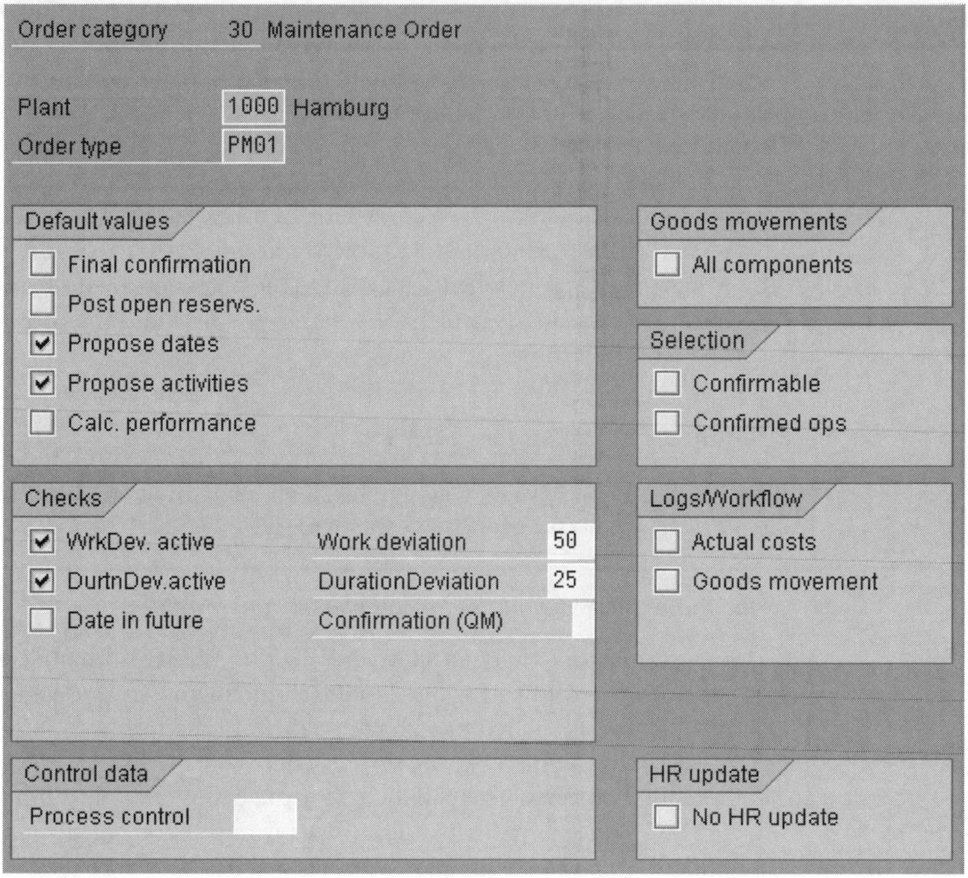

Order category	30 Maintenance Order		

Plant   `1000` Hamburg
Order type   `PM01`

Default values
- ☐ Final confirmation
- ☐ Post open reservs.
- ☑ Propose dates
- ☑ Propose activities
- ☐ Calc. performance

Goods movements
- ☐ All components

Selection
- ☐ Confirmable
- ☐ Confirmed ops

Checks
- ☑ WrkDev. active   Work deviation   `50`
- ☑ DurtnDev.active   DurationDeviation   `25`
- ☐ Date in future   Confirmation (QM)

Logs/Workflow
- ☐ Actual costs
- ☐ Goods movement

Control data
Process control

HR update
- ☐ No HR update

FIGURE 5.36   Detail screen for confirmation parameters (© SAP AG)

You use these control parameters to specify:

■ Which values are defaulted when completion confirmations are entered

■ The extent of the checks carried out

■ How the processes of the completion confirmation are controlled

The settings in the DEFAULT VALUES group are used to specify the outstanding confirmation data that you want the system to propose automatically as default values. In the case of activities, the system proposes the difference between the default values and the values already confirmed. By setting the FINAL CONFIRMATION indicator, you can specify whether the system should default a partial confirmation, a final confirmation, or a final confirmation with clearing of open reservations for the confirmation. The CALCULATE PERFORMANCE entry is used to specify whether the actual work should be calculated automatically, taking the remaining work and the final confirmation indicator into account.

You can use the CHECKS group to specify that values for deviations in work and duration are taken into account in the completion confirmation. In addition to this, the group enables you to control whether future dates can be used in a confirmation (such as posting date or end of execution time). The CONFIRMATION (QM) indicator specifies the system message that appears when you confirm a maintenance order (no message, information message, or error message). Messages of this type are displayed if QM inspection results have to be recorded for an order, but no results are available yet.

You use the ALL COMPONENTS indicator in the GOODS MOVEMENTS group to specify whether all the components assigned to the operation are displayed in the overview of goods movements, regardless of whether the backflushing indicator is set for the component in the order.

How to define reasons for variance

This Customizing activity enables you to define reasons or causes for variance at the plant level. Figure 5.37 illustrates this activity.

How to set screen templates for completion confirmations

This Customizing activity enables you to set up the screen templates for completion confirmations according to your specific requirements. Individual user profiles can be defined here and assigned to each user via the user settings.

As shown in Figure 5.38, the system offers you a choice of five screen areas, each comprising two parts. The data fields for the completion confirmation are grouped according to contents. The individual groups here are also displayed on the templates.

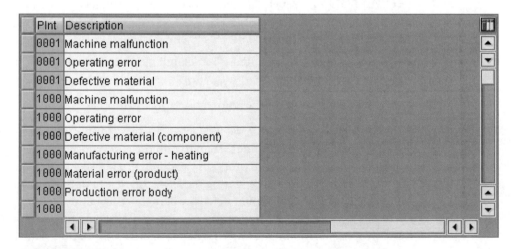

Plnt	Description
0001	Machine malfunction
0001	Operating error
0001	Defective material
1000	Machine malfunction
1000	Operating error
1000	Defective material (component)
1000	Manufacturing error - heating
1000	Material error (product)
1000	Production error body
1000	

FIGURE 5.37 Defining reasons for variance (© SAP AG) (© SAP AG)

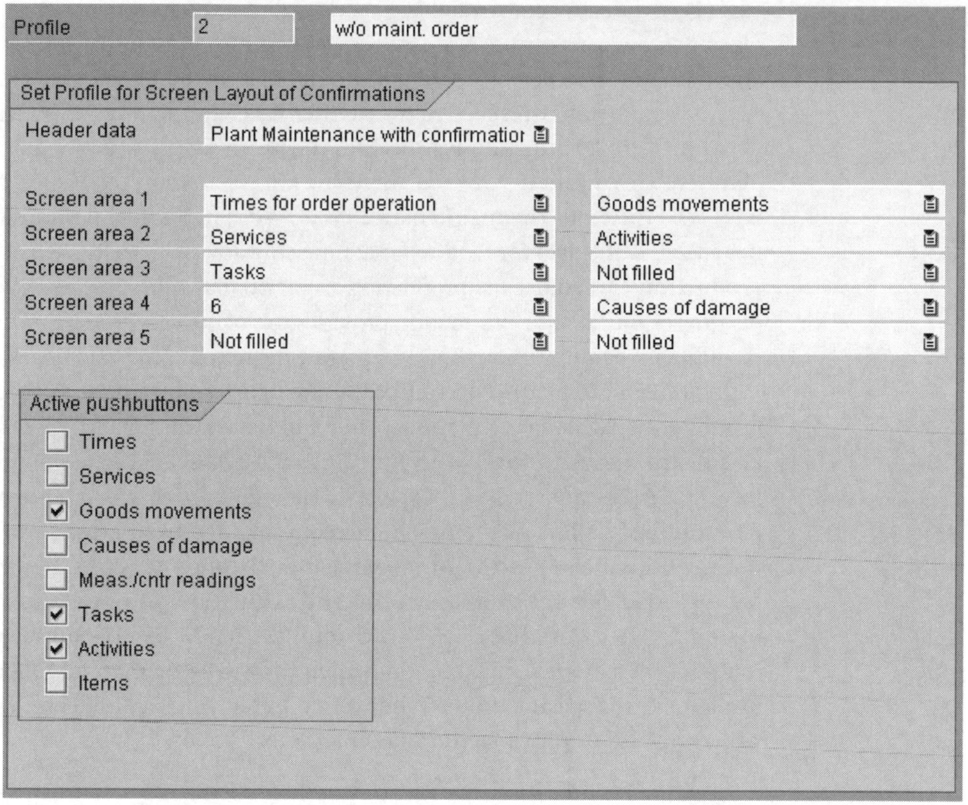

Profile	2	w/o maint. order

Set Profile for Screen Layout of Confirmations

Header data	Plant Maintenance with confirmatior 🗎		
Screen area 1	Times for order operation 🗎	Goods movements	🗎
Screen area 2	Services 🗎	Activities	🗎
Screen area 3	Tasks 🗎	Not filled	🗎
Screen area 4	6 🗎	Causes of damage	🗎
Screen area 5	Not filled 🗎	Not filled	🗎

Active pushbuttons

- ☐ Times
- ☐ Services
- ☑ Goods movements
- ☐ Causes of damage
- ☐ Meas./cntr readings
- ☑ Tasks
- ☑ Activities
- ☐ Items

FIGURE 5.38 Defining the screen layout for completion confirmations (© SAP AG)

When you carry out these settings, you can also activate pushbuttons to access frequently used confirmation functions.

5.2   TASKS OF THE PM PLANNER

The role of PM planner can be taken by the plant engineer, production engineer, work scheduler or shop foreman. The planner is primarily responsible for strategic maintenance planning, which includes material planning and resource planning, as well as planning the workflows. To avoid bottlenecks in material procurement, the planner should recognize in good time if replacement parts or utilities and process materials have to be reserved or reordered for larger maintenance tasks. As a rule, the planner is also the person responsible for the personnel of the maintenance workshop. This function involves coordinating personnel availability with the maintenance tasks that have to be performed. If lack of specialist knowledge or availability (for example, because of capacity overload, deployment abroad, leave, or illness among his own staff) prevent the planner's own personnel from performing the maintenance tasks, the planner must apply for external personnel in good time, or transfer all the maintenance tasks to an external company. Irrespective of whether tasks are performed by internal or external personnel, the planner always specifies the precise workflows for the maintenance task planned. He can then print out these workflows as shop papers for the PM technician who is to carry out the maintenance tasks. Working closely with production, the planner specifies the data for required machine shutdowns so that the person responsible for production can adjust his production capacity planning accordingly. For his part, the person responsible for production provides the planner with dates when the production machines are in low enough use to permit normal maintenance tasks to be performed.

In addition to planning, controlling the maintenance work is the second important task of the maintenance planner. The planner coordinates the work to be performed and distributes it to the PM technicians who are available at the required times and have the necessary technical expertise. He regularly checks whether new outstanding malfunction reports or maintenance requests have been created, or whether existing notifications are in process. At the same time, he monitors whether the PM technicians have carried out the work correctly and with the appropriate amount of time and material. After work has been carried out, every PM technician creates a time confirmation and material confirmation, which shows the planner whether it was possible to implement his specifications. When a maintenance task has been performed, the planner completes it from a technical point of view. Following this, the data is forwarded to accounting or to the controller.

The planner's tasks can also include maintaining the master data (in this case, maintaining the system structure). Some companies employ administrators specifically for this purpose.

5.2.1 Structure of the order

In the standard R/3 System, the screen for maintenance orders contains ten tab pages (Fig. 5.39).

Header data (Fig. 5.40)

This data includes details of the PM planner or planner group responsible, the PM technician who normally performs work on this object (also known as the main work centre), the date and priority of the work to be performed, as well as the object on which the work is to be carried out (reference object).

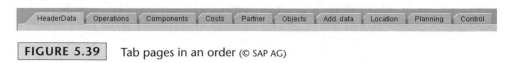

FIGURE 5.39   Tab pages in an order (© SAP AG)

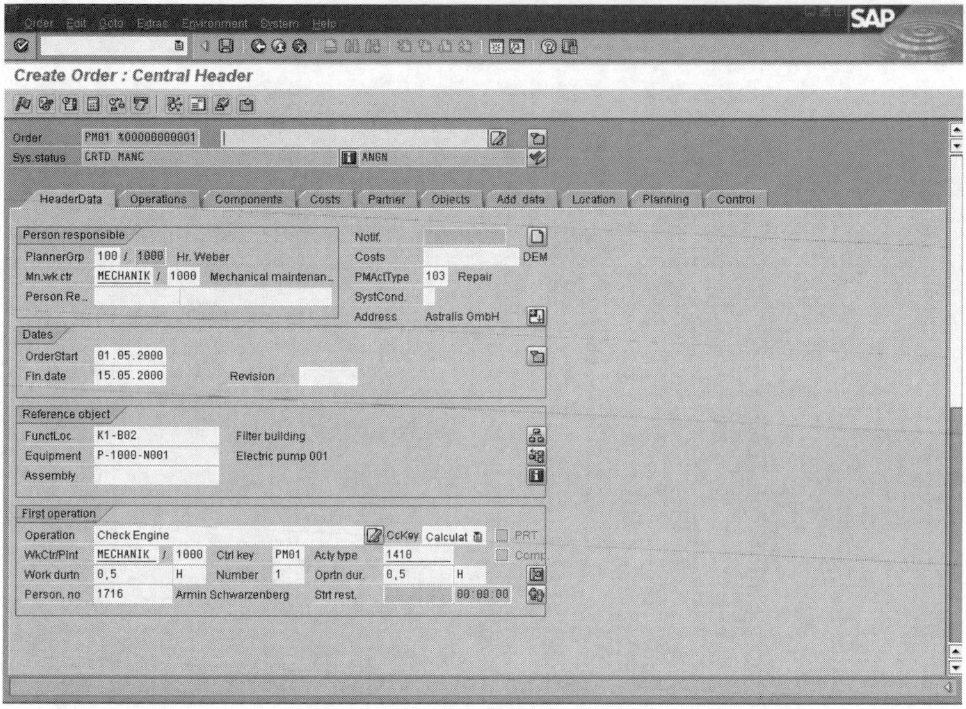

FIGURE 5.40   Header data in an order (© SAP AG)

In addition to this, the header data also contains the data of the first operation. You can use various operations to structure an order, just as you can use various items to structure a notification. If you use only one operation, enter the data in the header data screen. In this case, you only use the OPERATIONS tab page from the second operation onwards.

Operations (Fig. 5.41)

If you use more than one operation, you enter the operation data in this tab page. The most important data includes the operation number, the work centre that carries out the work (this can be the same as the main work centre, but does not have to be), the short text for the operation, the total amount of work (WORK), and the actual duration of the activity (DURATION). The total amount of work can differ from the activity duration. For example, the operation 'painting' is completed after an hour, but the overall amount of work is two hours (including the time required for the paint to dry).

You can further subdivide operations by means of sub-operations. In Figure 5.41, for example, operation 30 comprises two sub-operations. If you want to use sub-operations, you always have to create an operation for this purpose first. You can either enter the amount of work and activity duration at the level of the operation for all sub-operations, or for each sub-operation individually.

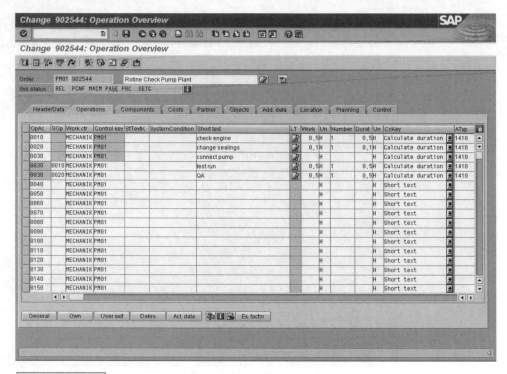

Components (Fig. 5.42)

This is the tab page where you enter the components; in other words, the material numbers for the materials required by the PM technician. Each material is assigned to an operation from the operation list. For each material, you enter the quantity you require, and indicate whether the material in question is a stock material or a non-stock material. A material reservation is generated for stock materials, and a purchase requisition is generated for non-stock materials. This ensures that the spare parts are available when the PM technician actually takes the material withdrawal slip to the material warehouse.

You can either take the material numbers from the BOM of the reference object or enter a number of your choice. Non-stock materials generally do not have a material number; for materials of this type, the short text is sufficient.

Costs

Maintaining the cost data is one of the tasks carried out by the controller, and will be discussed in section 5.3, 'Tasks of the controller'.

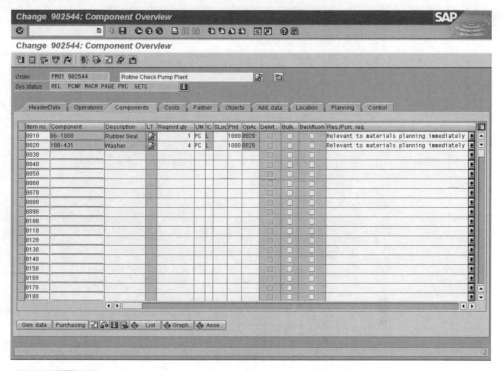

FIGURE 5.42   Component data in an order (© SAP AG)

Partner (Fig. 5.43)

The partner data enables you to store the addresses and communication data of various locations or individuals relevant to the order. In the FUNCTION field, you enter the type of link to the order; in the PARTNER field, you enter the number of the address master record that you want to link to the partner function. In Figure 5.43, you can see the function 'AB' for the address of the department responsible for the pump plant. The contact person is Mr Mayer, whose communication data is displayed. If partner data is maintained in the master record of the reference object, it is copied to the order automatically.

Objects (Fig. 5.44)

In this tab page, you can assign other technical objects to the order, for which you want the operations in the order to be performed. These can be other items of equipment, other functional locations, other assemblies, or other combinations of materials and serial numbers. In the object list, you can also assign other notifications to the order. Figure 5.44 shows that two objects have been assigned:

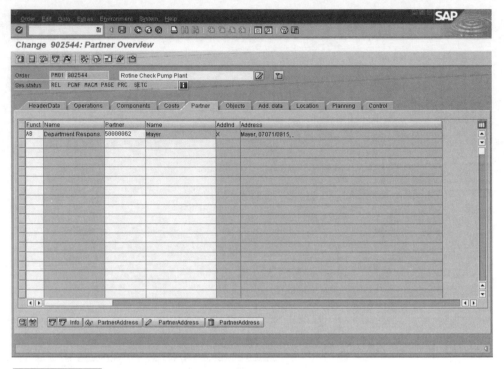

FIGURE 5.43   Partner data in an order (© SAP AG)

- An item of equipment, for which a check should also be carried out
- An activity report which precisely describes and later technically confirms the tasks to be performed

Additional data (Fig. 5.45)

In this tab page, the organizational data from the work centre master record and the plant data is defaulted. This organizational data includes the company code and controlling area, as well as the cost centre of the PM technician (performing cost centre).

Location (Fig. 5.46)

The data of the reference object is displayed in this tab page. The location data provides you with more detailed information on the physical location of the reference object. The account assignment data of the reference object is also displayed with the location data, and includes the cost centre to which the maintenance tasks are finally settled (receiving cost centre).

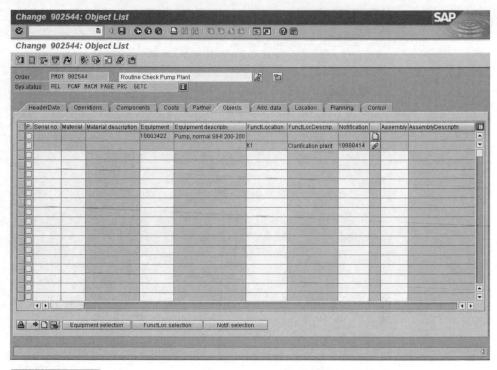

FIGURE 5.44 Object list in an order (© SAP AG)

Planning

In an order, the planning data refers to orders generated automatically during maintenance planning. Maintenance planning will be discussed in greater detail in Chapter 6, 'Business process: planned maintenance'.

Control (Fig. 5.47)

The control data includes details of the person who created the order, the parameters set in Customizing, and the order type (planned, unplanned or immediate order).

5.2.2 Notifications and orders

The R/3 System provides planners with two data objects: notifications and orders. The system allows you to work with notifications and orders separately, or with both together. You also have the option of specifying one of these procedures throughout your company, or deciding on a case-to-case basis.

You use the notification introduced in the preceding section if you merely want to document technical information. In the notification, you can record the start and end

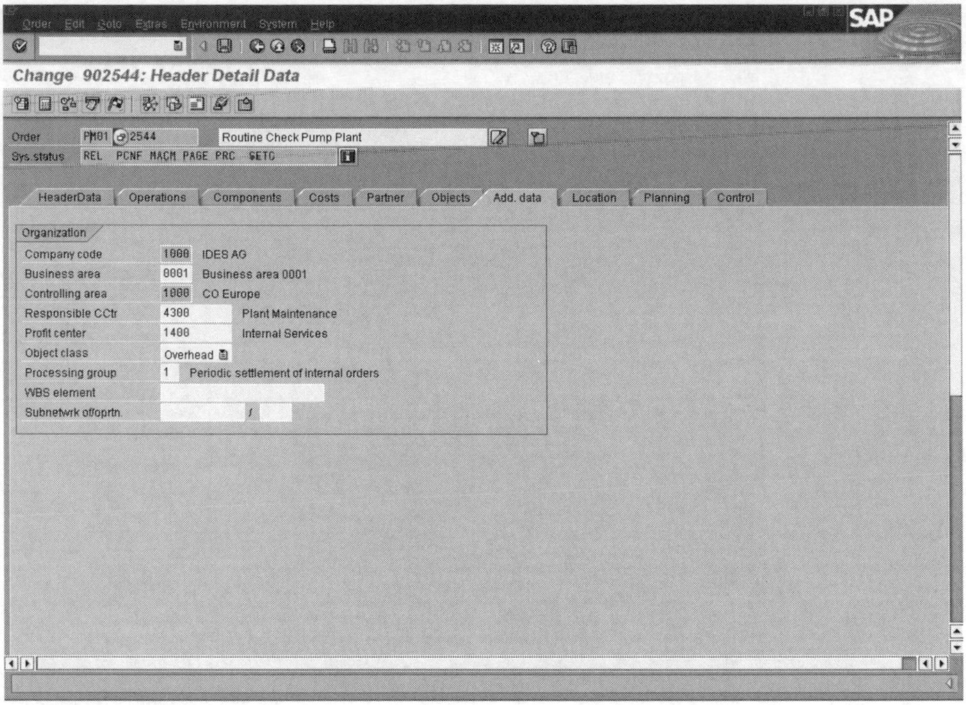

FIGURE 5.45 Additional data in an order (© SAP AG)

of a malfunction, breakdown duration, damage, cause of damage, planned tasks, and actions performed. This information is usually adequate if you want to document and track maintenance tasks, but is not sufficient for settling them. Small-scale repairs are more easily mapped with a notification than with the more extensive functional scope of an order.

If you want to track the costs of a maintenance order, you must use an order. Planned, actual, and estimated costs can only be mapped in orders, and not in notifications. In addition to this, Materials Management can only be integrated by means of an order. While a notification does allow you to record the materials you want to be used in performing repairs, this information has no effect whatsoever on material planning. Only orders allow you to reserve stock material and create a purchase requisition for non-stock material; and only orders enable you to schedule external work centres, or assign orders completely to external companies. Planning standard times for workflows, and scheduling production resource/tools are other useful functions provided by orders, but not by notifications.

In the business process illustrated here, a notification is used in conjunction with an order. The PM technician uses a notification to report and describe the malfunction that has occurred. The planner uses this notification to create an order, which is used

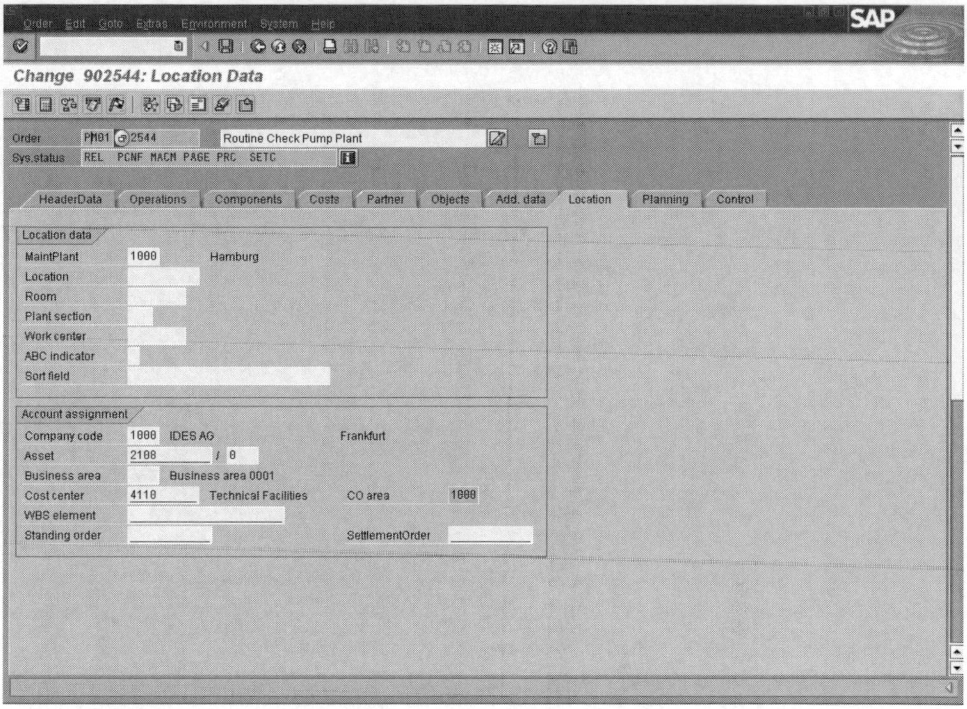

FIGURE 5.46   Location data in an order (© SAP AG)

as a planning basis by the planner, and as an operational method sheet by the PM technician. As soon as the maintenance tasks have been completed, the planner completes the order and the notification jointly.

You have the following options for combining a notification and an order:

1   You can create an order from a notification.

2   You can create an order by grouping together several existing notifications.

3   You can create an order directly without a notification.

4   You can create the notification and the order at the same time.

5   You can create an order and then create an activity report for it.

6   The order is created automatically without a notification as part of planned maintenance.

The first five of these six options are briefly outlined below. Figure 5.48 provides a graphical overview of all the options; the sixth option will be described in the next chapter as part of planned maintenance.

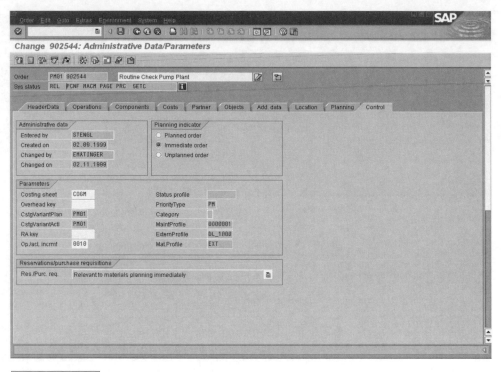

FIGURE 5.47 Control data in an order (© SAP AG)

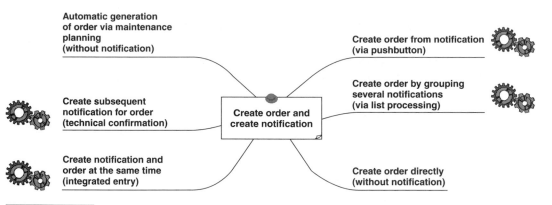

FIGURE 5.48 Order creation and notification creation

How to create orders from notifications

The most common situation in which you need to create an order from a notification is if you discover a new outstanding malfunction report, process it, and create an order directly from the message processing screen. To do this, choose the CREATE icon in the ORDER field (Fig. 5.49).

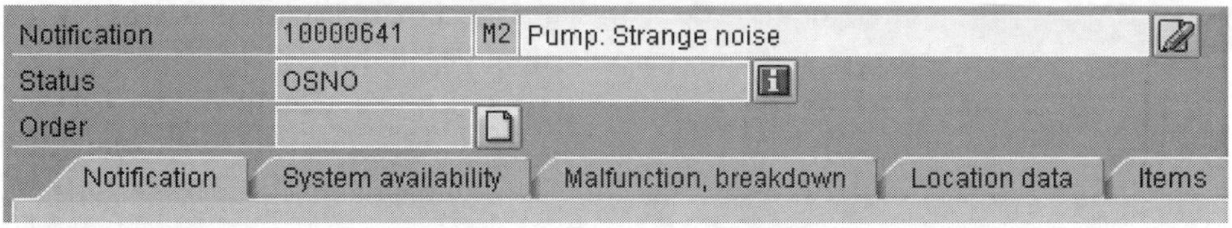

Notification	10000641	M2	Pump: Strange noise	
Status	OSNO			
Order				

| Notification | System availability | Malfunction, breakdown | Location data | Items |

FIGURE 5.49 Order field in the notification header (© SAP AG)

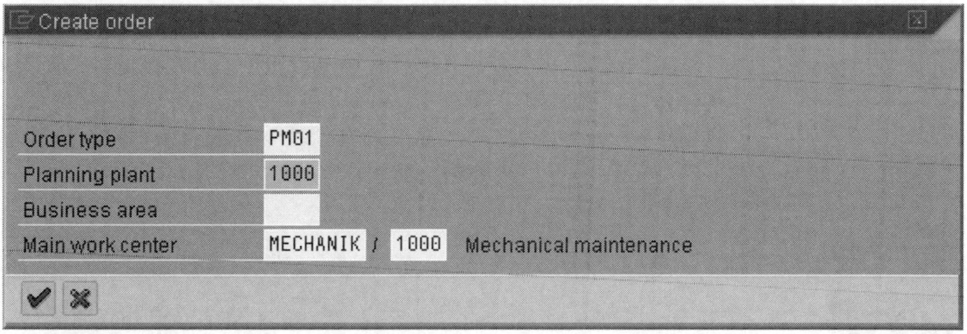

Create order

Order type	PM01
Planning plant	1000
Business area	
Main work center	MECHANIK / 1000 Mechanical maintenance

FIGURE 5.50 Creating an order from a notification (© SAP AG)

Create Order : Central Header   SAP

Create Order : Central Header

Order	PM01 %00000000001	Pump: Strange noise		
Sys.status	CRTD MANC NTUP		ANGN	

| HeaderData | Operations | Components | Costs | Partner | Objects | Add. data | Location | Planning | Control |

Person responsible
PlannerGrp	100 / 1000	Hr. Weber
Mn.wk.ctr	MECHANIK / 1000	Mechanical maintenan_
Person Re...		

Notif.	10000641	
Costs		DEM
PMActType	103 Repair
SystCond.	
Address	Astralis GmbH

Dates
| OrderStart | 01.05.2000 | |
| Fin.date | 01.05.2000 | Revision |

Reference object
FunctLoc.	K1-B02	Filter building
Equipment	P-1000-N001	Electric pump 001
Assembly	M-1000	Motor, electrical pump 250kW

First operation
Operation	Pump: Strange noise			CcKey Calculat	PRT
WkCtr/Plnt	MECHANIK / 1000	Ctrl key	PM01	Acty type	1410	Comp
Work durtn		H	Number		Oprtn dur.	H
Person. no				Strt rest.	00:00:00

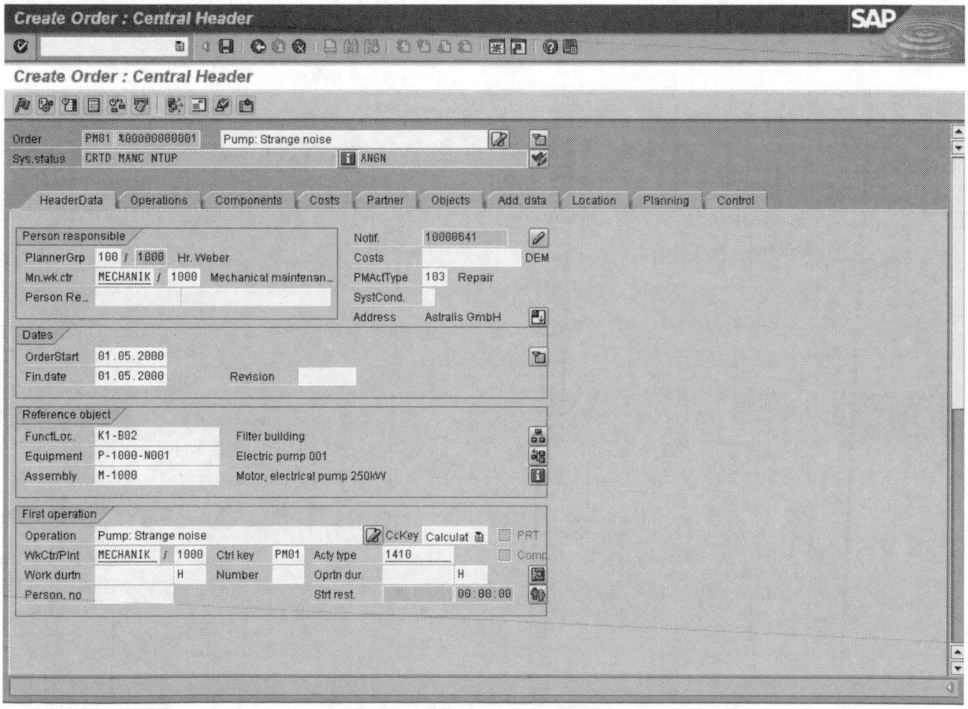

FIGURE 5.51 Creating an order with defaults from a notification (© SAP AG)

After you have done this, a dialog box is displayed, in which the field contents have been copied from the notification (Fig. 5.50).

You can change the field contents, supplement them, or leave them as they are. Choose ENTER. A new order is now displayed, to which some data has already been copied. This data comes from the following objects:

■ The notification

■ The reference object (for example, functional location, equipment, or assembly)

■ The main work centre (maintenance work centre)

The order does not yet have a number. This will only be assigned when you save your data (Fig. 5.51).

When you save the order, the system returns to the message processing screen and displays an information message (for example, ORDER 902539 SAVED WITH NOTIFICA-TION 10000411).

TIP In the order, the number of the notification from which the order was created is displayed in the NOTIFICATION field (Fig. 5.52). By double-clicking this notification number, you can call up the notification again whenever you wish. Similarly, you can call up the order again from the notification by double-clicking the notification number in the ORDER field.

TIP The system copies the short text of the notification to the order automatically. This is not always expedient, since the notification short text formulates a problem, and the order short text is an operational methods sheet. If necessary, change the order short text and the text for the order operation.

TIP The long text from the notification, which may contain a more detailed description of the malfunction, is not usually copied to the order. Since the planner and technician have different views of the problem, the long text field in the order should be available to the planner without default entries. The long text of the notification can be called up from the order via the notification if necessary. In response to numerous customer requests, it is planned to enable the long text from the notification to be copied to the order. This functionality may be available for 4.6C, but not for Releases 4.6A and 4.6B.

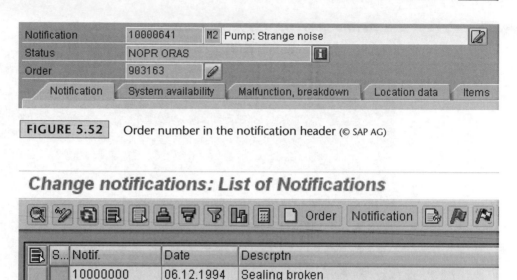

FIGURE 5.52 Order number in the notification header (© SAP AG)

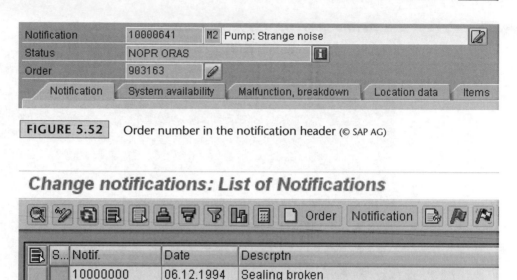

FIGURE 5.53 List of outstanding notifications (© SAP AG)

How to group together several notifications to form one order

It can sometimes happen that different people create different malfunction reports for the same malfunction. Another scenario that can arise is that different notifications result in small-scale repairs, which can be performed by one person in one operation. In both cases, you (as planner) process outstanding notifications and group them together in work scheduling to form one order.

Starting from transaction IW28 (CHANGE NOTIFICATIONS), you edit a list of all outstanding notifications (Fig. 5.53). While doing so, you discover, for example, that four different malfunction reports all refer to the same pump (P-1000-n001). You decide to group these four notifications together in one order 'Pump: Strange noise'. To do so, select the three notifications.

Next, choose the CREATE ORDER pushbutton. This calls up a screen in which the data of the first notification in the list (notification 10000408) has been entered in the fields. You can also change, supplement, or copy the data here. After you choose ENTER, a new order is displayed. Only the first notification in the list (notification 10000641), however, has been entered in the NOTIFICATION field in the header data (Fig. 5.54).

Since notifications and orders are always assigned on a one-to-one basis, only one notification is entered in the order header. The data of the two remaining notifications can be found in the object list of the order (Fig. 5.55). To call up the object list, choose the OBJECTS tab page.

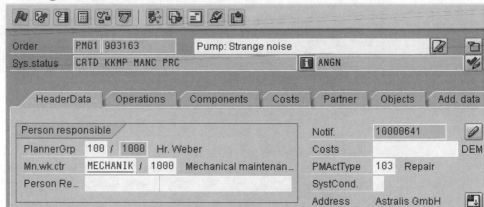

FIGURE 5.54   Notification field in the order header (© SAP AG)

When you save your data, the system returns to the list editing screen and displays a message (which, however, refers only to the first notification in the list).

How to create orders directly

If you work without notifications, you can create orders directly (for example, on the basis of a malfunction report made via telephone). You also create orders directly if you plan maintenance tasks that are not based on a malfunction report or maintenance request. To do so, you use transaction IW31 (CREATE PM ORDER). In the initial screen, you specify the reference object of the order. This can be a functional location, an item of equipment, or an assembly. When you choose ENTER, the order is created.

How to create notifications and orders at the same time

In urgent cases, malfunctions have to be corrected as quickly as possible. If the person who reported the notification does not have time to create a malfunction report, or if the malfunction is reported via telephone, this does not mean that you (as the planner) have to do without a notification. The solution here is known as 'integrative notification entry'. This involves creating an order with integrated notification data so that you can put the order in process as quickly as possible. The system also creates a malfunction report in the background, which you can edit when you have the opportunity to do so.

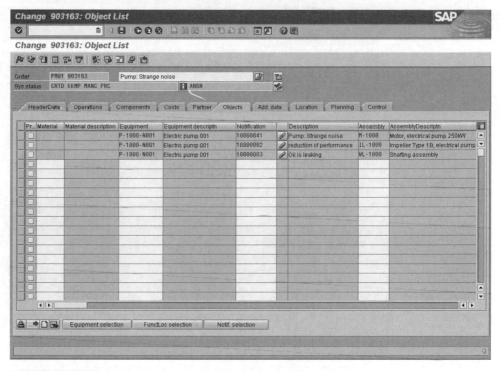

FIGURE 5.55 Object list with notifications (© SAP AG)

To create a notification and an order at the same time, you use transaction IW31 (CREATE PM ORDER). In the initial screen, enter 'PM05' in the Order type field (Fig. 5.56). More information on order types will be provided in the next chapter. Enter the reference object of the order and choose ENTER.

A new order is displayed, which contains a separate screen area for the notification data. This area is located at the bottom of the screen shown in Figure 5.57. The system has created malfunction report 10000642, which is displayed in the NOTIFICATION field.

All the data you enter in this screen area are copied to the notification automatically. You can, therefore, enter the most important data here and put the order in process. This allows you to take time to enter all the other notification data after the malfunction has been corrected.

The screen area in the order comprises the following tab pages:

▓ *Malfunction data*

You can display the breakdown data from here. The system automatically enters the creation date of the order in the START OF MALFUNCTION field. In most cases, the malfunction occurs before the order is created. If this is the case, change the date for the start of the malfunction manually.

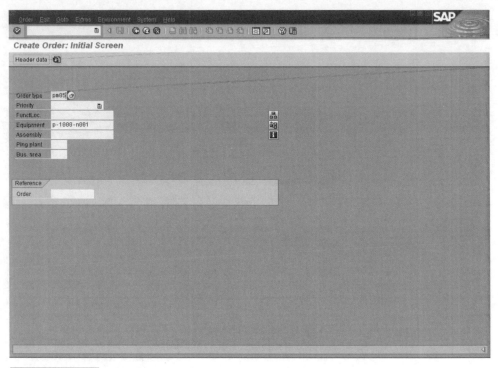

FIGURE 5.56   Initial screen for integrative notification entry (© SAP AG)

◼ *Damage*

As shown in Figure 5.58, you can call up the damage and cause catalogs from here.

◼ *Notification dates*

Here you can call up the basic dates for the notification, as well as the person who reported the notification.

When you have the opportunity, you can call up and edit the malfunction report created in the background. The examples of damage codes and reason codes in Figure 5.59 show that all the notification-relevant data you entered in the order has been copied to the malfunction report.

How to create an activity report for an existing order

In addition to confirmations of working time and material, there are also technical completion confirmations. These involve creating an activity report for an existing order. This is useful if you require technical documentation of the maintenance task, if you want to map the cause of damage via damage codes, or if you have to document the start and end of the malfunction as well as breakdown data.

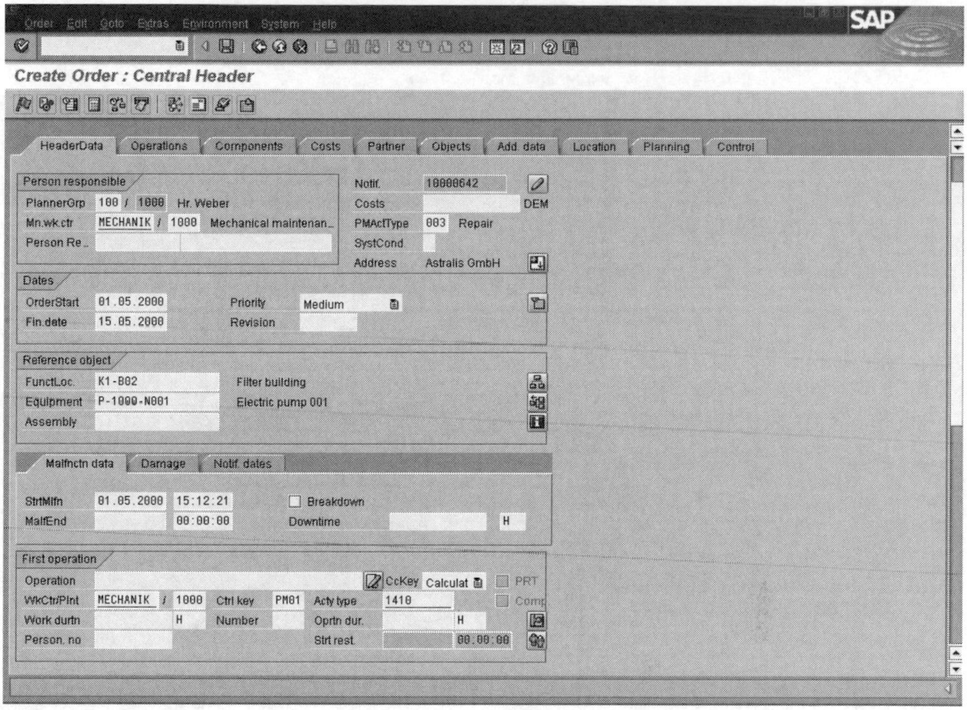

FIGURE 5.57   Order with notification data (© SAP AG)

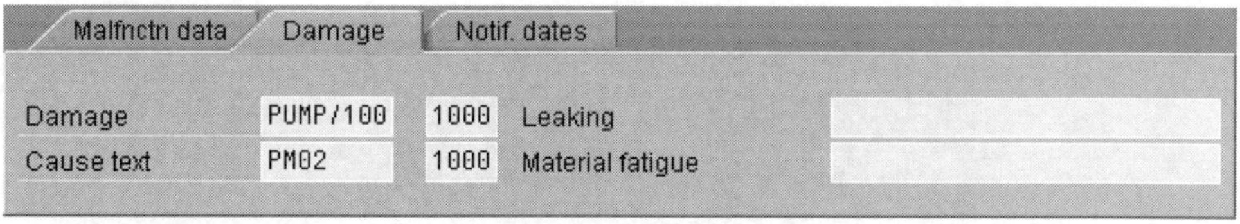

FIGURE 5.58   Damage data in the order with integrative notification entry (© SAP AG)

If a notification has not yet been assigned to the order for which you want to create an activity report, simply chose the CREATE icon beside the NOTIFICATION field in the header data. A dialog box is then displayed, in which you enter notification type 'M3' for activity report (Fig. 5.60). Choose CONTINUE, and the activity report is created.

If a notification is already assigned to the order for which you want to create an activity report, you have to first create an activity report and then assign it to the order. You use transaction IW25 to create activity reports. After you have created the activity report, call up the order in change mode and choose the OBJECTS tab page. In the NOTIFICATION field, enter the number of the activity report you created, and choose CONTINUE. The activity report is now linked to the order.

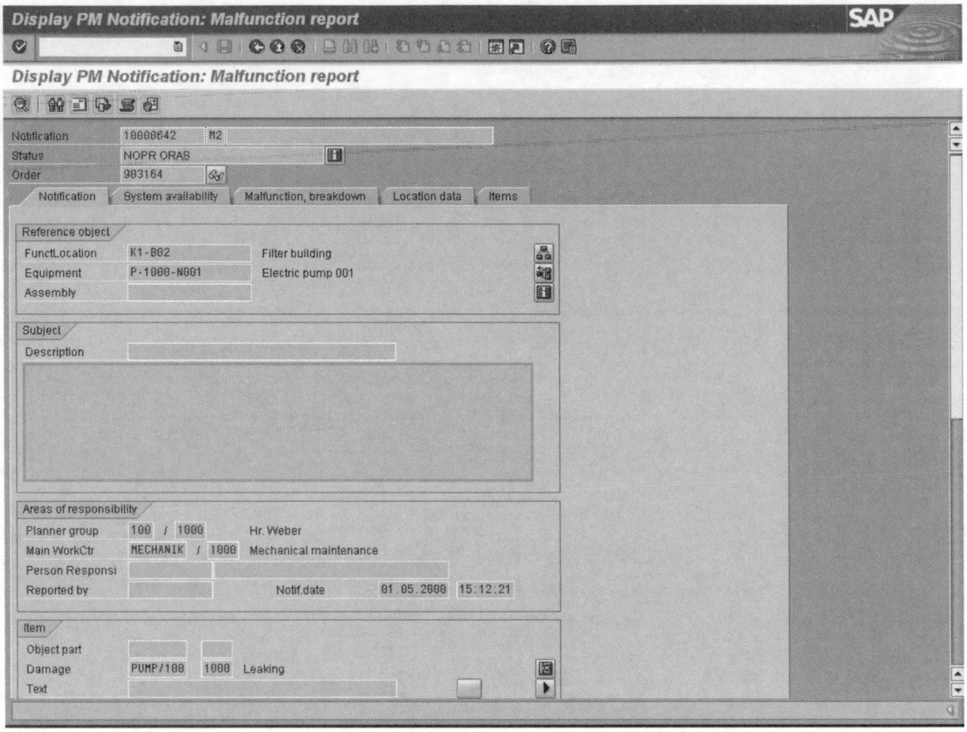

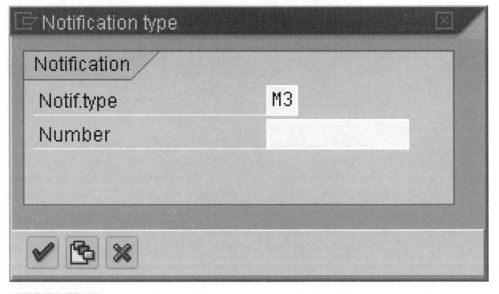

FIGURE 5.59   Notification in the background (© SAP AG)

FIGURE 5.60   Creating an activity report for an order (© SAP AG)

TIP
You can only undo the link between a notification and an order if the order and notification were created independently and assigned to one another subsequently, as was the case with the activity report just described. To undo the link, select the line with the notification you want to delete in the object list and choose the DELETE LINE icon. The link is then deleted. The link generally CANNOT be deleted in the following cases:

■ If the order was created directly from the notification
■ If the order has been completed

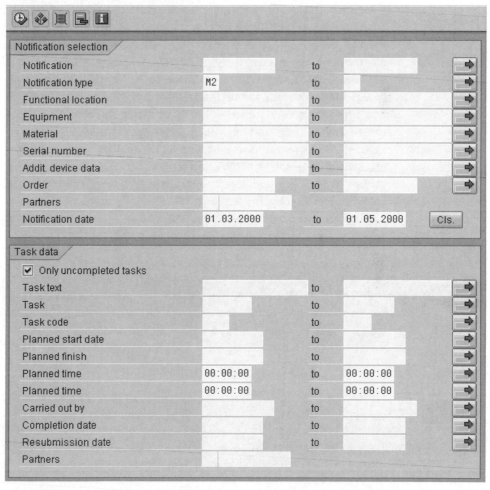

List of Notification Tasks

Notification selection

Notification		to
Notification type	M2	to
Functional location		to
Equipment		to
Material		to
Serial number		to
Addit. device data		to
Order		to
Partners		
Notification date	01.03.2000	to 01.05.2000

Cls.

Task data

☑ Only uncompleted tasks

Task text		to
Task		to
Task code		to
Planned start date		to
Planned finish		to
Planned time	00:00:00	to 00:00:00
Planned time	00:00:00	to 00:00:00
Carried out by		to
Completion date		to
Resubmission date		to
Partners		

FIGURE 5.61 Selection screen for the report for displaying tasks (© SAP AG)

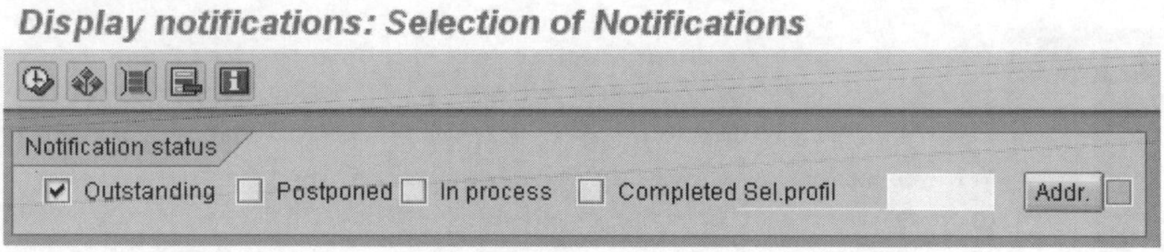

Display notifications: Selection of Notifications

FIGURE 5.62 Selection flags for the report for displaying notifications (© SAP AG)

5.2.3 Monitoring outstanding notifications

As a planner, you have to be constantly informed of outstanding notifications, for which you may want to create orders. To carry out monitoring, you can use either the single-level and multi-level lists for the notifications (described in section 6.1 'Tasks of the PM technician') or standard reports. The general report selection functionality for all standard reports in the R/3 System is called up by choosing INFORMATION SYSTEMS | GENERAL REPORT SELECTION. To display the reports for notifications, choose PLANT MAINTENANCE | MAINTENANCE PROCESSING.

To find out which new notifications have been created, or which tasks in a notification are still outstanding, you can call up the DISPLAY TASKS report, for example. Figure 5.61 shows you how to call up all the malfunction reports (report type M2) created within a specified period, and which still contain outstanding tasks. The system groups the notifications together in a standard notification list, from which you can create orders directly, if necessary.

You can also use the DISPLAY NOTIFICATIONS report for monitoring purposes. In the selection screen, select the status OUTSTANDING (Fig. 5.62).

TIP By choosing the SETTINGS | MONITOR ON/OFF function, you can display the priority of notifications in a notification list (or data in any other list) by means of traffic lights. This enables you to see at a glance which notifications should be processed first.

TIP It is often more convenient to control the monitoring of outstanding notifications via a workflow. In accordance with the priority or damage code, for example, the new notifications that fulfil certain criteria can be 'collected' by a workflow every morning. The results are then sent directly to the planner's inbox via SAP Office Mail or an external mail system.

5.2.4 Order types in PM

You can use order types to distinguish orders, just as you can use different notification types to distinguish notifications. You define various settings for each order type in Customizing under FUNCTIONS AND SETTINGS FOR ORDER TYPES.

Figure 5.63 shows the order types available in the standard R/3 System, which you can expand as required. Using order types PM02 and PM03 in maintenance planning is described in Chapter 6 'Business process: planned maintenance'. Order type PM04 (refurbishment order) will be discussed in Chapter 7 'Special Cases'. Order type PM06, which is used to link the Plant Maintenance and Quality Management components of the R/3 System, is not considered in this book.

The following general system settings depend on the order type.

- Number ranges
- Settlement rule or account assignment rule
- Default values for control keys
- Permissible maintenance activity types and default value of a maintenance activity type
- Permissible order types per maintenance planning plant
- Increment in assignment of operation numbers
- Costing parameters
- Retention period of orders following completion (residence time)
- Default values for completion confirmation procedure
- Default settings for the reference object screen
- Budget profile
- Immediate order release

Order type	Text
PM01	Maintenance Order
PM02	Planned Maintenance
PM03	Preventive Maintenance
PM04	Refurbishment Order
PM05	Order + Notification
PM06	PM/QM

FIGURE 5.63   Standard order types in Customizing (© SAP AG)

In this chapter, order type PM01 will be used to illustrate the most important Customizing settings for you (as a planner). You begin by defining the order types you require. To do so, you choose FUNCTIONS AND SETTINGS FOR ORDER TYPES | CONFIGURE ORDER TYPES. You then link the defined order types with appropriate settings.

TIP With regard to program control, it is not necessary to define different number ranges for the individual order types under FUNCTIONS AND SETTINGS FOR ORDER TYPES | CONFIGURE NUMBER RANGES. If your business does not require several number ranges to be defined, you can use the same number range for all order types.

By choosing FUNCTIONS AND SETTINGS FOR ORDER TYPES | ASSIGN ORDER TYPES TO MAINTENANCE PLANTS, you can specify which maintenance plant can use which order types. For example, it may be the case that you use maintenance orders or refurbishment orders in only one maintenance plant. If you want to allow all maintenance plants to use all order types, you must enter all the order types for each plant. Figure 5.64 shows an example of settings for five plants.

By choosing FUNCTIONS AND SETTINGS FOR ORDER TYPES | DEFINE DEFAULT VALUE FOR PLANNING INDICATOR FOR EACH ORDER TYPE, you can assign a planning indicator to each order type. The planning indicator is used for selection and statistical evaluations in the PM Information System. There are three standard planning indicators (Fig. 5.65):

▓ *Planned order*

You should use this indicator for order types with planned tasks.

▓ *Unplanned order*

You should use this indicator for order types that do not contain planned tasks or contain tasks that do not have to be performed immediately.

▓ *Immediate order*

You should use this indicator if you want the system proposal for the planning indicator in the maintenance order of this type to be a rush order.

By choosing FUNCTIONS AND SETTINGS FOR ORDER TYPES | MAINTAIN INDICATOR FOR NOTIFICATION AND ORDER DATA ON ONE SCREEN, you can define the order type with which an order and a notification are created at the same time. Figure 5.66 shows that, when an order is created with order type PM05, for example, a malfunction report is generated with notification type M2.

Change View "Valid Order Types by Planning Plant": Overview

New entries

PlPl	Name 1	Type	Order type text
3000	New York	PM01	Maintenance Order
3000	New York	PM02	Planned Maintenance
3000	New York	PM03	Preventive Maintenance
3200	Atlanta	SM01	
3200	Atlanta	SM02	
3700	Plant Orlando	PM01	Maintenance Order
5000	Tokyo	PM01	Maintenance Order
5000	Tokyo	PM02	Planned Maintenance
5000	Tokyo	PM03	Preventive Maintenance
5000	Tokyo	SM01	
5000	Tokyo	SM02	
5100	Kobe	PM01	Maintenance Order
5100	Kobe	PM02	Planned Maintenance
5100	Kobe	PM03	Preventive Maintenance
5100	Kobe	SM01	
5100	Kobe	SM02	

FIGURE 5.64   Linking order types and maintenance plants (© SAP AG)

Change View "Default Planning Indicator for Order Types": Overview

New entries

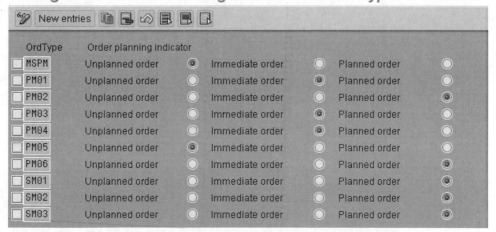

OrdType	Order planning indicator		
MSPM	Unplanned order	Immediate order ●	Planned order
PM01	Unplanned order	Immediate order ●	Planned order
PM02	Unplanned order	Immediate order	Planned order ●
PM03	Unplanned order	Immediate order	Planned order ●
PM04	Unplanned order	Immediate order	Planned order ●
PM05	Unplanned order ●	Immediate order	Planned order
PM06	Unplanned order	Immediate order	Planned order ●
SM01	Unplanned order	Immediate order	Planned order ●
SM02	Unplanned order	Immediate order	Planned order ●
SM03	Unplanned order	Immediate order	Planned order ●

FIGURE 5.65   Assigning planning indicators for order types (© SAP AG)

Order type	Notif.type	Notifctn
MSPM		☐
PM01		☐
PM02		☐
PM03		☐
PM04		☐
PM05	M2	☑
PM06		☐
SM01		☐
SM02		☐
SM03		☐

FIGURE 5.66 Creating a notification and an order at the same time (© SAP AG)

By choosing FUNCTIONS AND SETTINGS FOR ORDER TYPES | CONTROL KEY | MAINTAIN DEFAULT VALUES FOR CONTROL KEYS FOR MAINTENANCE ORDER TYPES, you can assign a combination of maintenance planning plant and order type to control keys that you have defined under MAINTAIN CONTROL KEY. The control key is used to specify how an operation or sub-operation should be handled in the business operations (for example, the orders, costing, or capacity requirements planning). You use the control key of the operation to specify the business functions you want to carry out. The most important parameters for the control key are:

- *Determine capacity requirements*

  You use this indicator to specify that the operation is scheduled and that capacity requirements records are generated for it.

- *Cost*

  You use this indicator to specify that the operation is taken into consideration during costing.

- *External processing*

  You use this indicator to specify that the operation is processed by external companies.

- *Confirmation*

  You use this indicator to specify whether the operation can be confirmed, as well as the type of confirmation for this operation.

- *Print time tickets*

  You use this indicator to specify that time tickets are printed for this operation.

You will find further information on capacity requirements planning, shop paper printing, and confirmations in the following sections of this chapter. A total of three control keys for Plant Maintenance are defined in the standard R/3 System. Control keys PM02 and PM03 are used in external processing, and are described in Chapter 7, 'Special cases'.

Figure 5.67 shows the standard settings for control key PM01 (Plant maintenance – internal), the most frequently used control key for maintenance tasks. Figure 5.68 shows that control key PM01 is assigned to the combination of maintenance planning plant 1000 and order type PM01. This means that plant 1000 uses order type PM01 (and all its control parameters) mainly for internally processed maintenance tasks.

Figure 5.69 provides a graphical overview of all the Customizing settings described above.

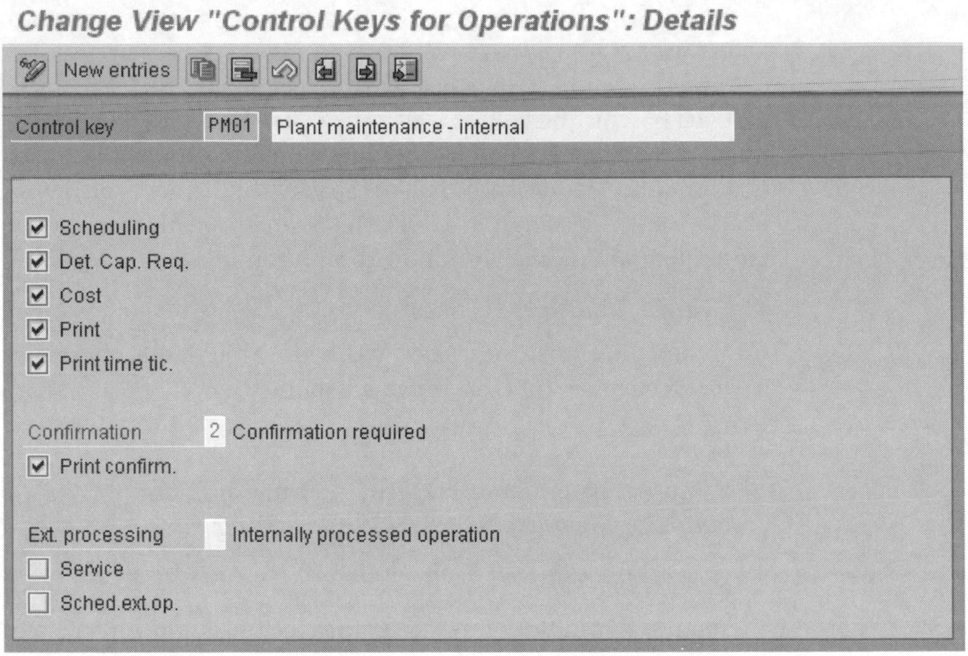

Change View "Control Keys for Operations": Details

New entries

Control key   PM01   Plant maintenance - internal

☑ Scheduling
☑ Det. Cap. Req.
☑ Cost
☑ Print
☑ Print time tic.

Confirmation   2 Confirmation required
☑ Print confirm.

Ext. processing   Internally processed operation
☐ Service
☐ Sched.ext.op.

FIGURE 5.67   Parameters for control key PM01 (© SAP AG)

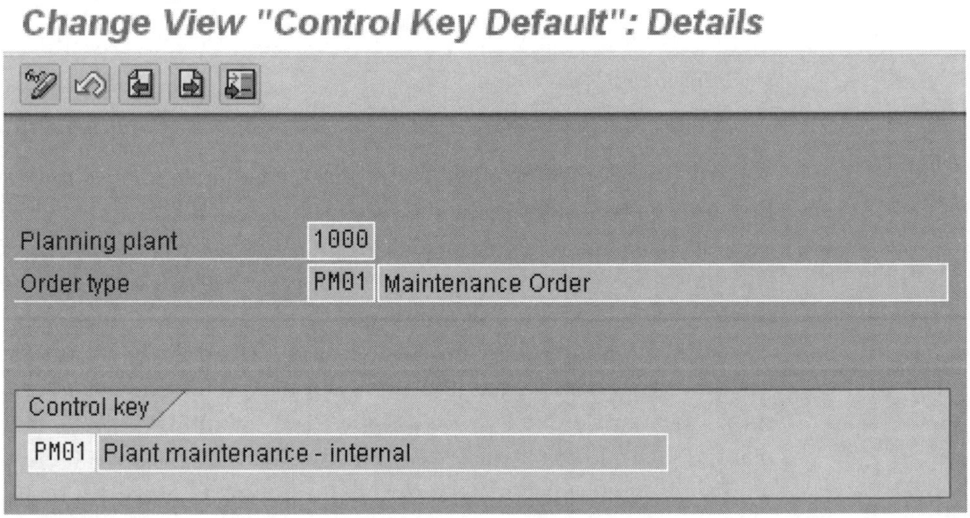

Change View "Control Key Default": Details

Planning plant   1000
Order type   PM01   Maintenance Order

Control key

PM01   Plant maintenance - internal

FIGURE 5.68   Control key for order type PM01 (© SAP AG)

TIP It is advisable to use the default control keys PM01, PM02, and PM03. Before you change or delete existing control keys, you should check whether they are used in the Production Planning (PP) component of the R/3 System, or have already been maintained in the system settings for the maintenance task lists or PM work centres.

5.2.5 Work scheduling

You have created a new order based on a malfunction report from the technician. All the important data from the notification has been copied automatically to the order. You now want to check the tasks entered in the notification and create the appropriate operations or sub-operations for the order. After you have done this, you will assign the PM technician(s) you want to carry out the tasks to the entire order or to the operations.

How to create operations and sub-operations

If the person who reported the notification has already suggested corrective tasks in the malfunction report, you should check these. In our example, the malfunction report contains two items. The technician who noticed the malfunction and created the report has already suggested a task for each item (Fig. 5.70).

You check the tasks and create operations for your order. To do so, you choose the OPERATIONS tab page. If necessary, correct the short text copied from the notification.

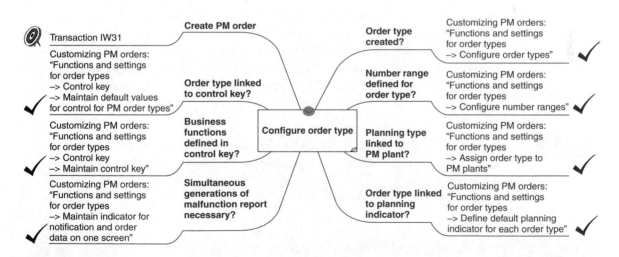

FIGURE 5.69   Customizing settings for order type

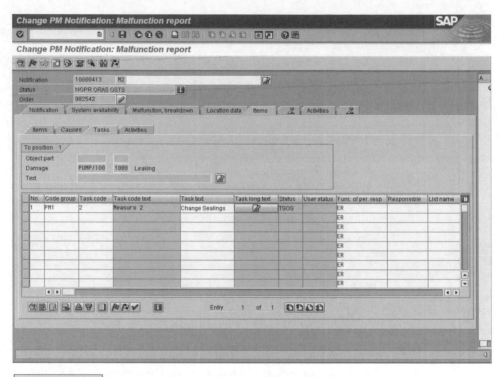

FIGURE 5.70   Outstanding tasks for a notification item (© SAP AG)

Now enter an operation number and a short text for each operation. In the STANDARD TEXT KEY field, you can use F4 to choose standard operations. For each operation, the standard value for the control key is PM01. This is the default value that you set in Customizing for the order type. Enter the amount of work in the WORK field and the activity duration in the DURATION field. The system does not add up the times entered for the sub-operations. You should, therefore, enter the times either at the operation level for all the sub-operations (Fig. 5.71) or separately for each sub-operation.

TIP   Since you cannot assign materials to sub-operations, you should only use sub-operations if the material planning can be combined for the overall operation. If this is not the case, you should create a new operation.

TIP   If you only require one operation, you do not have to use the operation list (OPERATIONS tab page). Enter the necessary data in the header data screen in the FIRST OPERATION group.

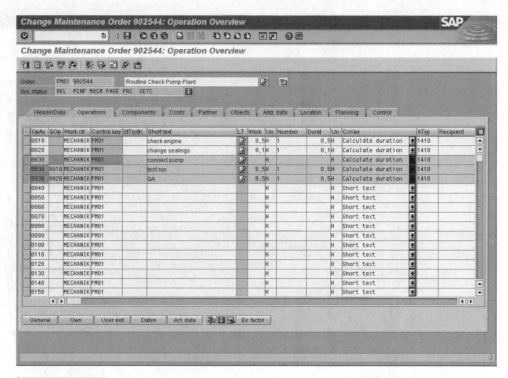

FIGURE 5.71   Operations and sub-operations in an order (© SAP AG)

How to assign technicians to the order

After you have entered all the operations, choose CONTINUE. In the background, the system now uses the data specified in the master record of the PM work centre to calculate the planned costs for the tasks to be performed. The message 'Calculation executed' is displayed.

Where does this information come from? A PM work centre groups together several people (PM technicians) to form a 'maintenance group' (for example, 'Mechanical maintenance' or 'Electrical maintenance'). The work centre has been assigned to the technical object, which is the reference object of the malfunction report, and thus of the order. In the example, the technician work centre 'Mechanik' is assigned to equipment P-1000-n001. This assignment was copied to the malfunction record and the order. In the master record of the PM work centre, specific default values are maintained, which are copied to the operation data of the order. Figure 5.72 shows an example of cost centre assignment of the technician, as well as the default activity type.

You can either keep the default work centre or add a new one. If you change the work centre, the system deletes the work centre-specific data, and determines the defaults from the new work centre (Figs. 5.73 and 5.74). The following fields are defaulted:

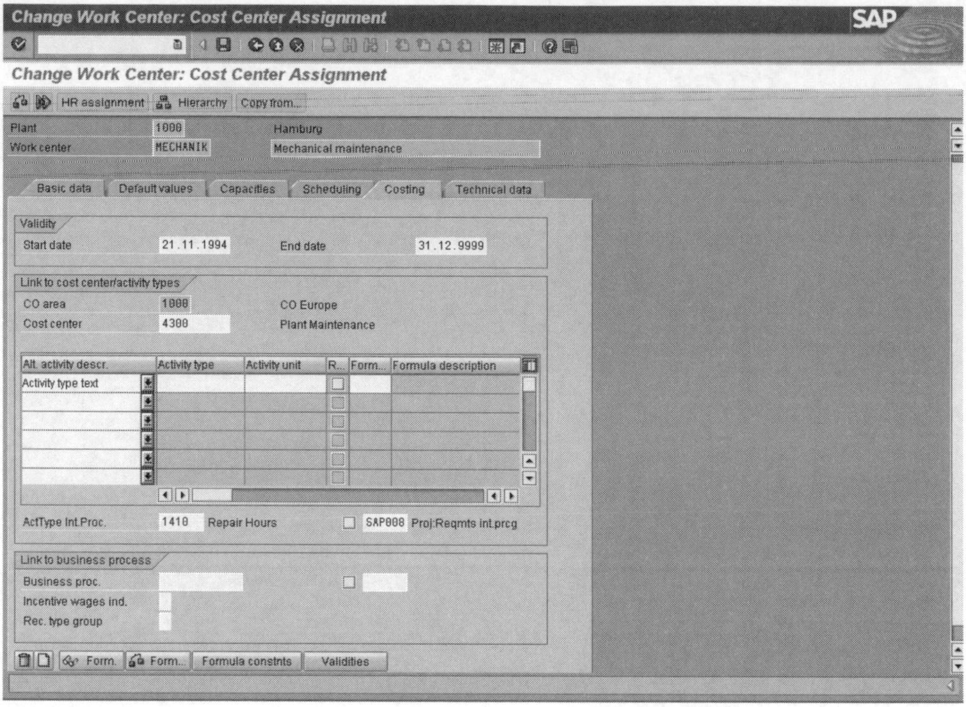

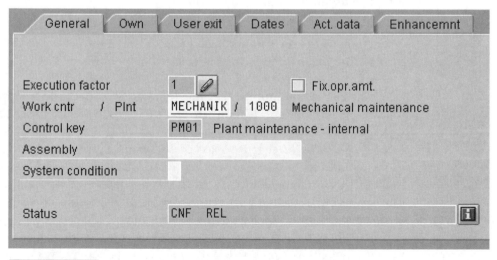

FIGURE 5.72   Cost centre assignment in the PM work centre master record (© SAP AG)

FIGURE 5.73   Determining the default values with changes to the PM work centre (1)
(© SAP AG)

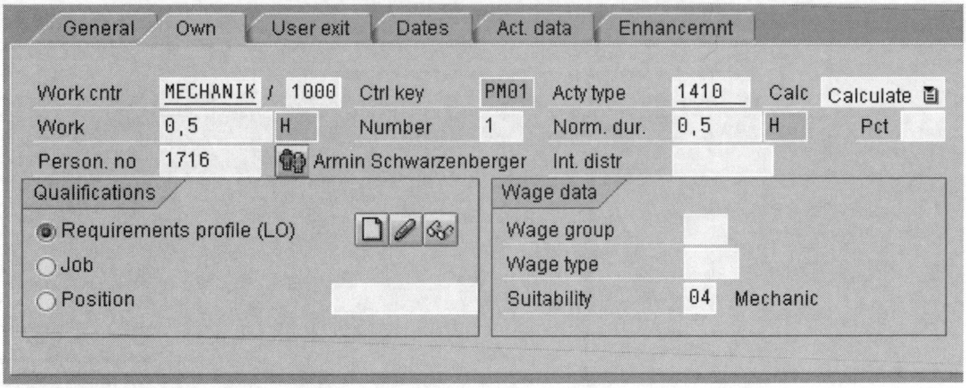

FIGURE 5.74   Determining the default values with changes to the PM work centre (2)
(© SAP AG)

- Wage group
- Wage type
- Suitability
- Number of time tickets
- Activity type

You use the method described above to assign a work centre (in other words, a group of technicians) to the operations. You also have the option of assigning the entire order or one operation to an individual technician (to one personnel number). There are a number of conditions that have to be fulfilled if you want the system to default a personnel number.

You must define a partner determination procedure for Plant Maintenance (for example, 'PM') with associated partner functions. You do this in Customizing for orders, via PARTNER DETERMINATION PROCEDURE | DEFINE PARTNER DETERMINATION PROCEDURE. Examples of partner determination procedures are shown in Figure 5.75.

You then assign the partner function 'person responsible' (VW) to the order types by choosing PARTNER DETERMINATION PROCEDURE | ASSIGN PARTNER DETERMINATION PROCEDURE TO ORDER TYPES. In the PARTNER DETERMINATION PROCEDURES field, you enter the partner determination procedure you have just defined and in the FUNCTION OF ORDER field you enter the partner function 'VW' (Fig. 5.76).

As soon as you enter a partner function, a partner (in other words, a personnel number) can be entered in the RESPONSIBLE PERSON field of the order header. This technician is then personally responsible for executing the order (Fig. 5.77).

Via the F4 help in this field, you can call up the following search functions:

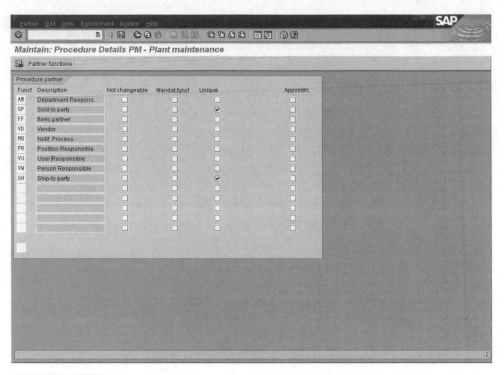

FIGURE 5.75   Partner functions in a partner determination procedure (© SAP AG)

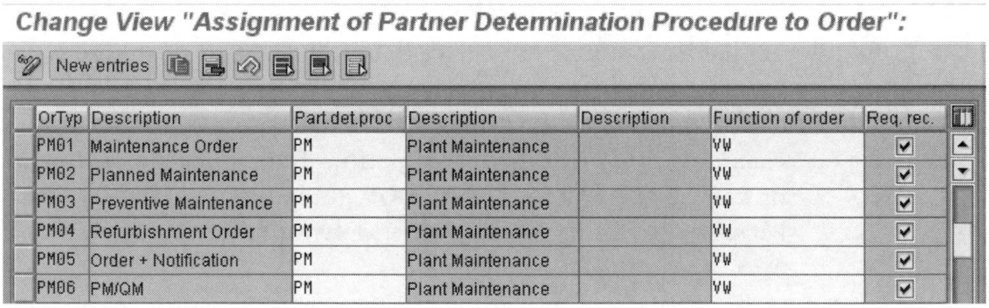

Change View "Assignment of Partner Determination Procedure to Order":

New entries 🗈 🖪 🖾 🖺 🖺 🖺

OrTyp	Description	Part.det.proc	Description	Description	Function of order	Req. rec.
PM01	Maintenance Order	PM	Plant Maintenance		VW	☑
PM02	Planned Maintenance	PM	Plant Maintenance		VW	☑
PM03	Preventive Maintenance	PM	Plant Maintenance		VW	☑
PM04	Refurbishment Order	PM	Plant Maintenance		VW	☑
PM05	Order + Notification	PM	Plant Maintenance		VW	☑
PM06	PM/QM	PM	Plant Maintenance		VW	☑

FIGURE 5.76   Linking partner function and order types (© SAP AG)

1   Display persons (PM technicians) assigned to the selected work centre

2   Display persons for work centre with qualifications

3   Display persons assigned to work centre with qualifications and dates

If you execute the third search function, for example, the system displays a list of employees qualified to carry out the task. You can call up various information on these employees via the pushbuttons (Fig. 5.78). In this context, the most important questions include:

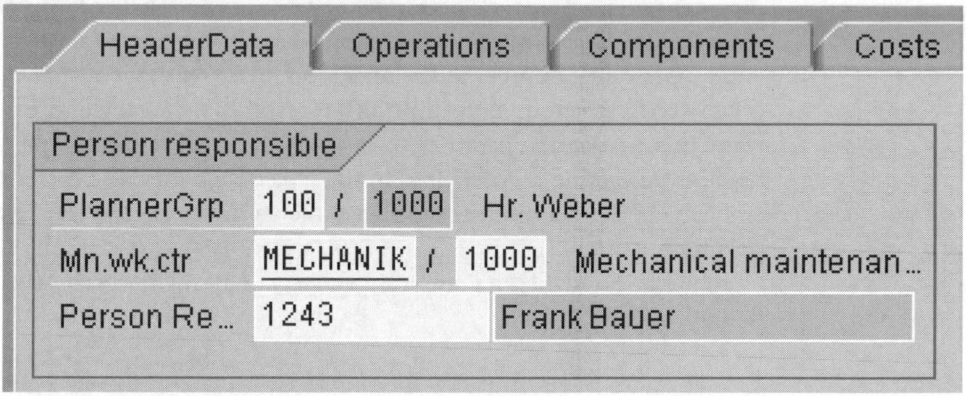

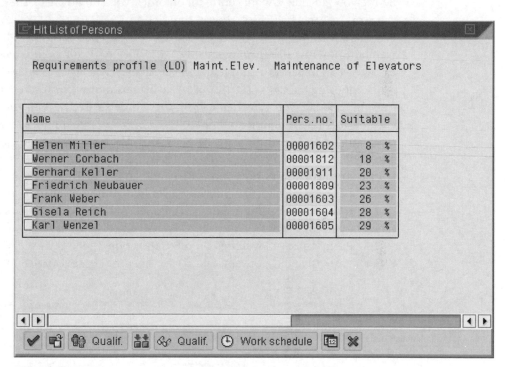

FIGURE 5.77 Person responsible for an order (© SAP AG)

FIGURE 5.78 Persons for a work centre with qualifications and dates (© SAP AG)

- Which orders has the employee already been assigned to?
- On which dates is the employee still available?
- Which qualifications are entered in the employee's HR master record?
- What information does the employee's HR master data contain?

If you enter an employee's personnel number in the PERSON RESPONSIBLE field in the order header, the technician in question is responsible for the entire order. You can also enter a personnel number at the operation level. This means that the work centre (in other words, the group of technicians) is responsible for the entire order, but that you want this particular operation to be carried out by a specific person (for example, because this person is specialized in the type of operations involved). In this case, you enter the personnel number of the technician in the PERSONNEL NUMBER field at the operation level.

Figure 5.79 provides a graphical overview of all the necessary Customizing settings described above.

How to carry out capacity requirements planning

Before you schedule a work centre for an order, you should check the capacity load of the work centre. To do so, choose transaction CM01 (CAPACITY PLANNING, WORK CENTRE LOAD). Enter the desired work centre, and choose the STANDARD OVERVIEW pushbutton. This calls up an overview of the capacity requirements, available capacity, capacity load in per cent, and remaining available capacity in hours (Fig. 5.80).

By choosing the CAPACITY DETAILS/PERIOD pushbutton, you can display the orders causing the load. You can then call up these orders directly from the list by double-clicking them. As a planner, you have to organize a large number or orders, and it is often impossible to distribute the capacity load evenly for all the available work centres and people when you create an order. Planning is generally carried out so that some work centres and people have more capacity than is actually available, while others still have capacity available. To achieve an evenly distributed capacity load, you have to carry out capacity levelling regularly. To do so, you use the graphic planning table or tabular planning table.

To call up capacity levelling, choose transaction CM33 (CAPACITY LEVELLING: PM WORK centre GRAPHIC), or transaction CM34 (CAPACITY LEVELLING: PM WORK CENTRE

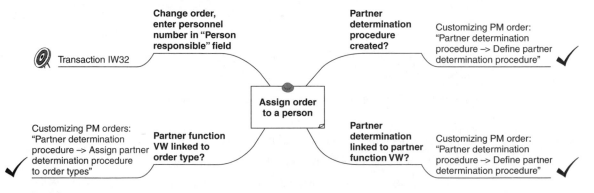

FIGURE 5.79 Customizing settings for assigning personnel to orders

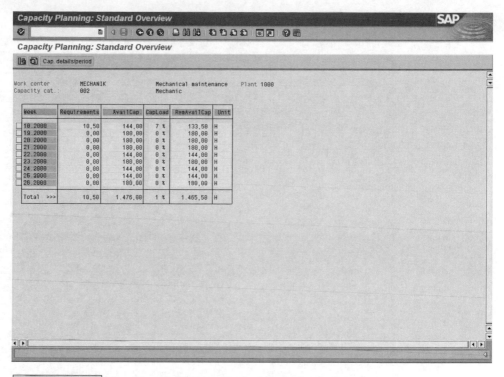

FIGURE 5.80   Capacity load of a work centre (© SAP AG)

TABULAR). Enter the work centre or work centres and the plant. This calls up an overview of the working days on which capacity is still available at the work centre. The planning table also shows you the orders causing the requirement. You can change these orders from the planning table. Figure 5.81 shows an example of the tabular planning table for a work centre. If you display several work centres, you can use the planning table to schedule orders so that all the work centres are evenly loaded.

If you require a clearer overview, you can also use the graphical planning table, or choose EXTRAS | CAPACITY GRAPHIC in the tabular planning table. Using the capacity graphic, you can display specific information on the registered requirements, available capacity, and overload. Figure 5.82 shows an example of the overload for a work centre.

5.2.6 Material planning in orders

For each operation in an order, you can schedule materials required by the technician to perform the task. These materials can be BOM components of the reference object or freely assigned materials. The procedure involved varies depending on whether the scheduled materials are available at the warehouse (stock material) or have to be ordered (non-stock material). The following provides an initial overview of these two procedures, followed by a detailed description of the settings required.

Period Requirements per Resource

🖧 Dispatch	🖧 Deallocate	🖵 Dispatch	🛈	🖧 Strategy	🖫	🖉 Order	🖉 Capacity	🖧 Order	🖨

Plan Work cen Short text	Short text	Cat No P		
☐ 1000 MECHANIK Mechanical main	Mechanic	002 5	🖧🖧🖧🖧	1 / 1

I◀ ◀◀ ◀ ▶ ▶▶ ▶I	☐	☐	☐	☐	☐
Period	29.04.2000	30.04.2000	01.05.2000	02.05.2000	03.05.2000
Avail.capacity	0,0	0,0	0,0	36,0	36,0
Dispatched	0,0	0%	0,0	0%	5,0	*99%	0,0	0%	0,0	0%
Pool/Rqmts.	0,0	0%	0,0	0%	251,0	*99%	1,3	4%	0,0	0%

Requirements

	Tot.req	Order	Op.	Description	P Equip.	System statu	Ctrl	Actual	FunctLocation	Name
☐	1,0	810426	0010		BF-01	CRTD	PM01	0,000	K1-SLB-11	...
☐	0,5	810426	0020		BF-01	CRTD	PM01	0,000	K1-SLB-11	...
☐	1,0	810426	0030		BF-01	CRTD	PM01	0,000	K1-SLB-11	...
☐	5,0	810426	0040		BF-01	CRTD	PM01	0,000	K1-SLB-11	...
☐	1,0	810445	0010		BF-01	CRTD	PM01	0,000	K1-SLB-11	...
☐	0,5	810445	0020		BF-01	CRTD	PM01	0,000	K1-SLB-11	...
☐	1,0	810445	0030		BF-01	CRTD	PM01	0,000	K1-SLB-11	...
☐	5,0	810445	0040		BF-01	CRTD	PM01	0,000	K1-SLB-11	...
☐	1,0	810480	0010	operation 1	EP-EQUI	CRTD	PM01	0,000		...
☐	2,0	810480	0020	operation 2	EP-EQUI	CRTD	PM01	0,000		...
☐	3,0	810480	0030	operation 3	EP-EQUI	CRTD	PM01	0,000		...
☐	1,0	810481	0020	Check .	BF-01	REL	PM01	0,000	K1-SLB-11	...
☐	1,0	810482	0010	operation 1	EP-EQUI	CRTD	PM01	0,000		...
☐	2,0	810482	0020	operation 2	EP-EQUI	CRTD	PM01	0,000		...
☐	3,0	810482	0030	operation 3	EP-EQUI	CRTD	PM01	0,000		...
☐	1,0	810484	0010		BF-01	CRTD	PM01	0,000	K1-SLB-11	...

FIGURE 5.81   Tabular planning table (© SAP AG)

If the materials you schedule for the order are kept in stock, they are reserved for the order in the warehouse (Fig. 5.83). You can set the time for this reservation in Customizing. In Customizing, you specify for each order type whether the system should make the material reservation effective immediately or only when the order is released. You can also change the corresponding indicator in the order when you process the order. You should note, however, that this change cannot be undone. If components are assigned in the order, an availability check can be called up.

When the order is released, an availability check is carried out automatically. Orders can also be released if no availability exists. The papers that can be printed out together with the shop papers include a pull list and material withdrawals slip for the technician. Planned goods issues are entered with reference to the reservations (reservation number), unplanned goods issues are entered with reference to the order number. The goods issues entered can be displayed via the 'Goods movements for order' function.

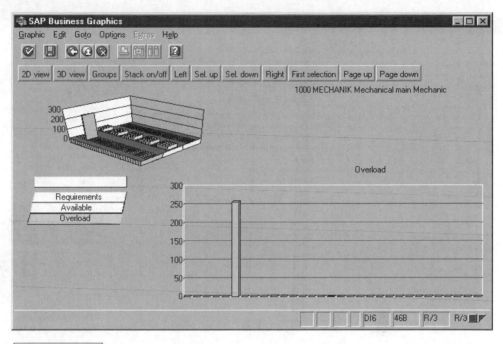

FIGURE 5.82   Capacity graphic (overload) (© SAP AG)

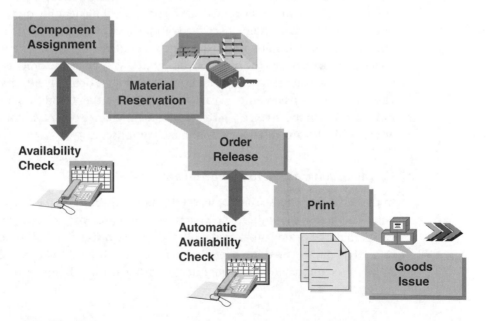

FIGURE 5.83   Process flow with assignment of stock material (© SAP AG)

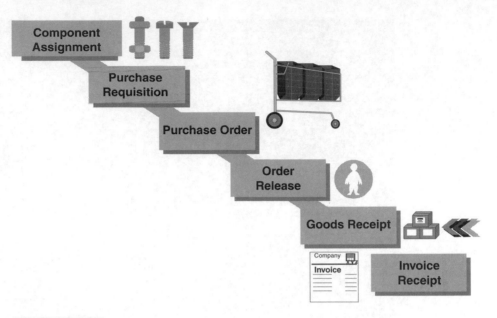

FIGURE 5.84 Assigning non-stock material (© SAP AG)

When you assign components of non-stock materials in the order, you can enter additional purchasing information (see Figure 5.84). The system then generates the purchase requisitions when the order is saved or released (depending on the order type). In purchasing, purchase orders are created on the basis of these purchase requisitions. The purchase order items are assigned to the account for the maintenance order. Goods issues with reference to the order can be entered as soon as the order is released. When the goods issues are entered, the maintenance order is debited with the purchase order value. The goods issues entered can be displayed via the 'Goods movements for order' function. When the invoice is received, the maintenance order is automatically debited or credited with any differences that may have arisen.

How to assign material to the operations

In the order, you choose the COMPONENTS tab page. In the COMPONENT field, you can enter the material number. The system now requires you to enter an item category (stock material or non-stock material) and to assign the material to one of the operations (Fig. 5.85). Enter the operation number, or choose it via the LIST pushbutton. Next, enter the requirement quantity (in other words, the quantity of the required material).

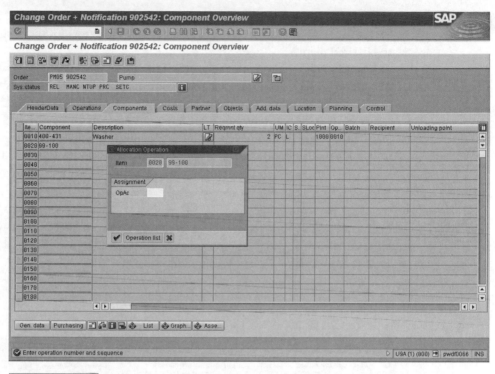

FIGURE 5.85   Assigning a material to an operation (© SAP AG)

TIP

Instead of entering the material number, you can call up the BOM for the reference object. This requires that a BOM exists for the reference object, and that the material required for the order is a replacement part (in other words, an element of the BOM). To call up the BOM from the order, choose EXTRAS | REFERENCE OBJECT | STRUCTURE LIST, or choose the LIST pushbutton in the COMPONENTS tab page. The system then displays the BOM. You can choose the desired material by double-clicking it, and then assign it to an operation. When you do so, the material is copied automatically to the component list, together with its material number, short text, requirement quantity, and item category.

How to generate material reservations and purchase requisitions

When you schedule a stock material in an order, the system automatically generates a material reservation for the planned quantity in the scheduled warehouse. When you schedule a non-stock material, the system automatically generates a purchase requisition (PReq) for purchasing. This requires the following settings to be made in Customizing.

In Customizing for orders, choose FUNCTIONS AND SETTINGS FOR ORDER

TYPES | DEFINE CHANGE DOCS, COLLECTIVE PURC. REQ. INDICATOR, OPERATION NO. INTERVAL. Select the COLLREQSTN and RES/PREQ indicators for the desired order type in the desired plant.

The RES/PREQ indicator specifies the time at which material reservations for stock material become relevant for materials planning, or at which purchase requisitions for non-stock material and external operations are generated. If you flag this indicator, the reservation is relevant immediately for materials planning for each stock material planned and saved; alternatively, a purchase requisition is immediately generated for each non-stock material and each external operation that has been planned and saved. This setting is then copied to the order as a default value, and can be changed in the order.

TIP If you do not set the indicator, reservations become relevant for materials planning (or purchase requisitions are generated) only after the order has been released. You should always deflag this indicator if you are creating orders with a long lead time, during which rescheduling can be expected.

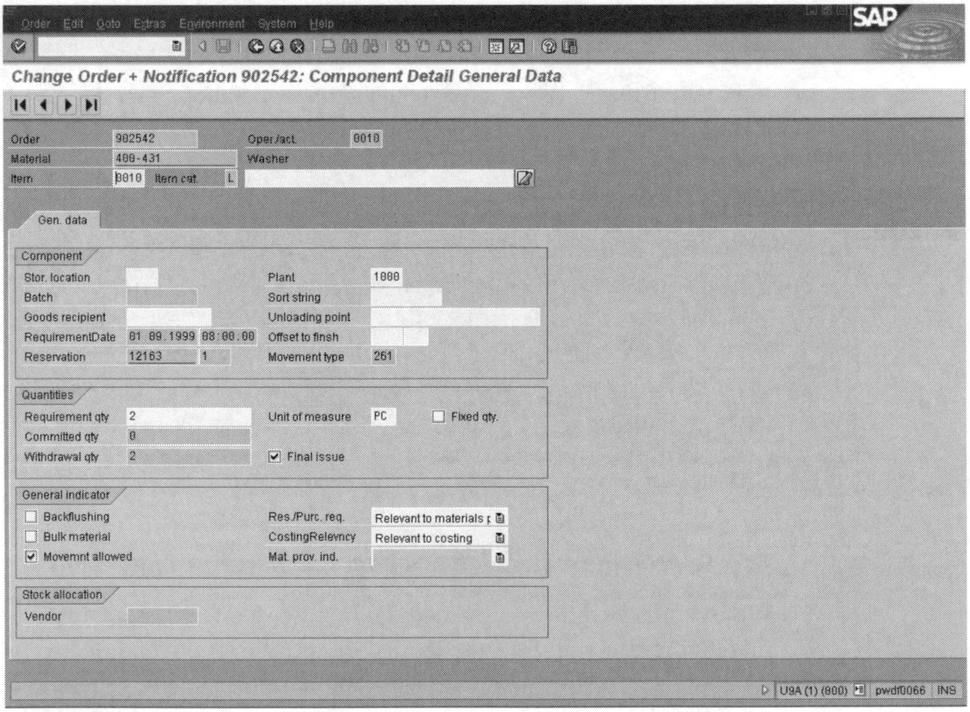

FIGURE 5.86   General data of a material component (© SAP AG)

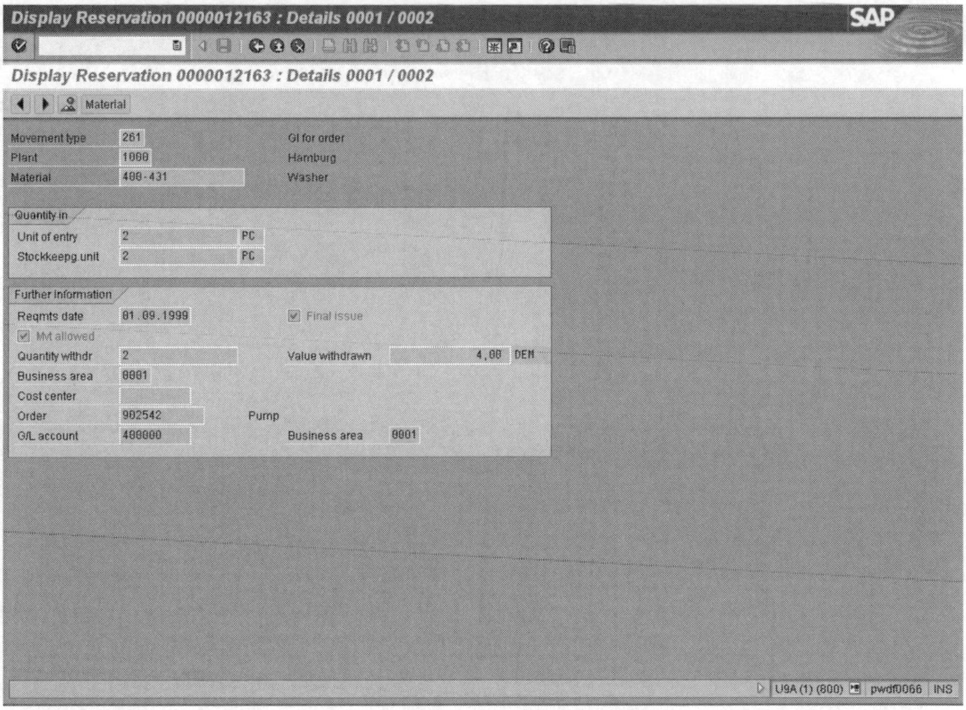

FIGURE 5.87 Master record (material reservation) (© SAP AG)

The COLLREQSTN indicator specifies that a collective purchase requisition should be generated for all externally processed operations or non-stock components in the order. If you do not set this indicator, a separate purchase requisition is generated for each externally processed operation or non-stock component.

The settings made in Customizing are displayed in the order on the CONTROL tab page in the RES./PURC. REQ. field. The number of the reservation generated or of the purchase requisition is also displayed in the order. To display the number of the material reservation, choose the COMPONENTS tab page, select the desired stock material, and choose the GENERAL DATA pushbutton. This screen contains all the material data, including the number (Fig. 5.86). In this case, the number of the material reservation generated is shown in the RESERVATION field. Double-clicking the RESERVATION field calls up the master record of the material reservation (Fig. 5.87).

To display the number of the purchase requisition, choose the COMPONENTS tab page, select the desired non-stock material, and choose the PURCHASING pushbutton. The general data screen contains all the material data, as with the stock material. The purchasing data comprises all the data used as default values for purchasing, including the number (Fig. 5.88). The number of the purchase order requisition generated in this case is in the PREQ field. Double-clicking the PREQ field calls up the master record of the purchase requisition (Fig. 5.89).

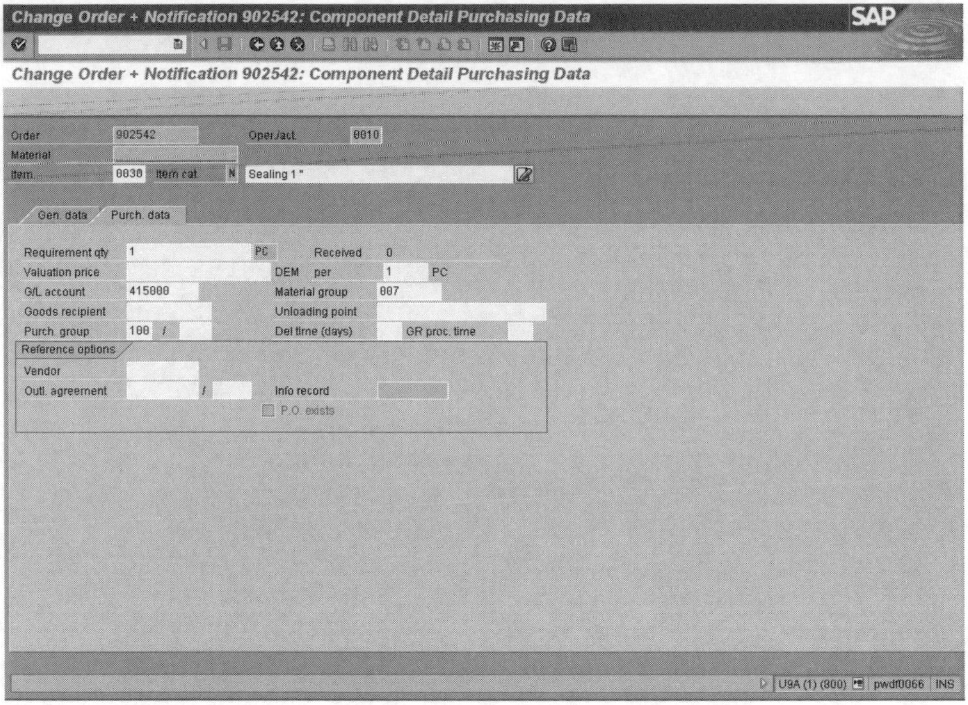

FIGURE 5.88 Purchasing data of a non-stock component (© SAP AG)

How to define default values for material planning

Default values for purchase requisitions: In Customizing for orders, choose FUNCTIONS AND SETTINGS FOR ORDER TYPES | CREATE DEFAULT VALUES FOR EXTERNAL PROCUREMENT. In the external operation profile, you can define the default values for generating purchase requisitions from maintenance orders. In each profile, you can define a default value for:

- A cost element account
- A purchasing organization
- A purchasing group
- A material group

Default values for item categories: In Customizing for orders, choose GENERAL DATA | DEFINE DEFAULT VALUES FOR COMPONENT ITEM CATEGORIES. You can here specify the default values for the item categories of the order components. The default values can be specified according to the material type and maintenance plant. If, for example, your system specifies that raw materials are always stock materials, you can assign the item category for components kept in stock to the material type for raw materials. In the standard R/3 System, the entry for this would be 'ROH' with the item category 'L'.

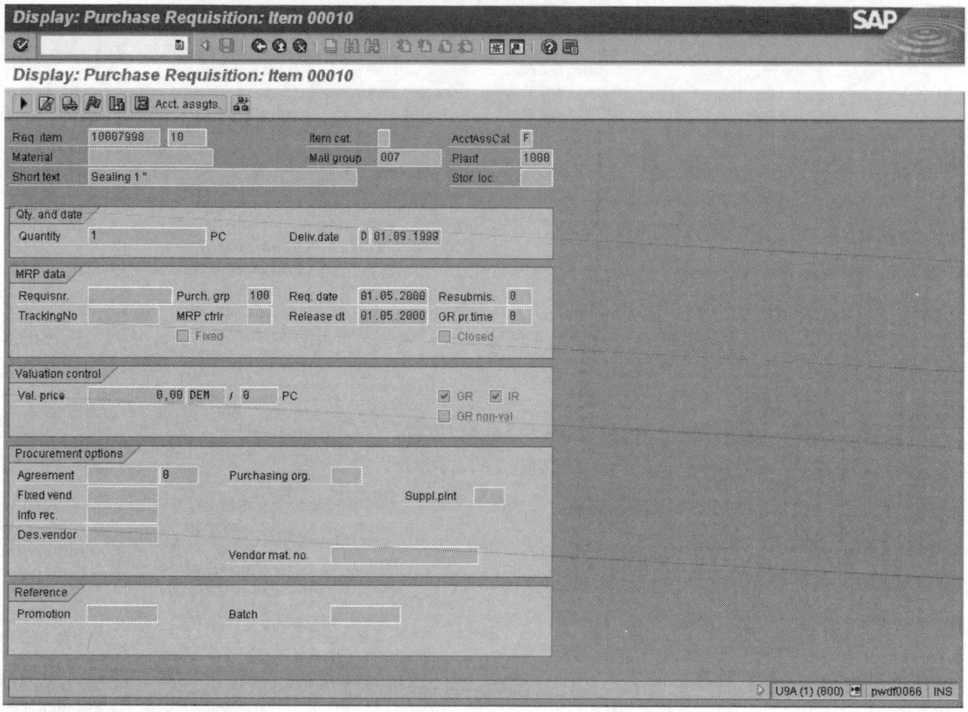

FIGURE 5.89 Master record (purchase requisition) (© SAP AG)

List of goods movements for the order: In Customizing for orders, choose FUNCTIONS AND SETTINGS FOR ORDER TYPES | GOODS MOVEMENTS FOR ORDER | DEFINE DOCUMENTATION FOR GOODS MOVEMENTS FOR THE ORDER. Here, you can specify the types of goods movements that should be documented for each individual maintenance order. You can call up this function as a list from order processing (to do so, choose EXTRAS | ORDER DOCUMENTS | GOODS MOVEMENTS). You can use the settings to specify whether the list should contain the following data:

- Goods receipts for purchase orders created for the order
- Planned goods issues for the order
- Unplanned goods issues for the order

In the standard R/3 System, all types of goods movements for orders are documented.

TIP To receive complete information on all the goods movements for the order, you should deflag an indicator only if you never post purchase orders, unplanned or planned material withdrawals for a particular order type.

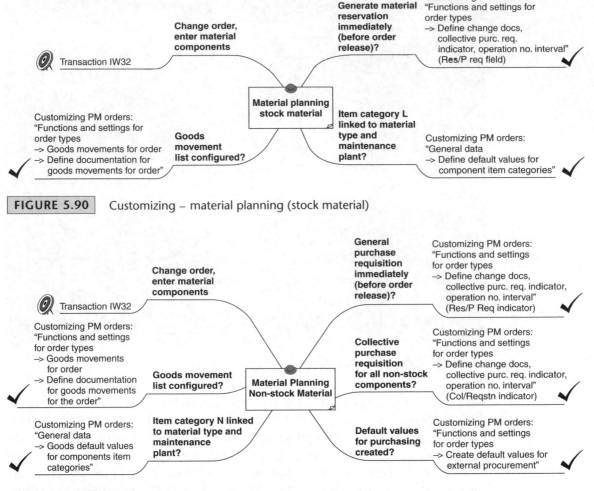

FIGURE 5.90   Customizing – material planning (stock material)

FIGURE 5.91   Customizing – material planning (non-stock material)

Figures 5.90 and 5.91 provide a graphical overview of all the necessary Customizing settings for stock materials and non-stock materials described above.

How to check material availability

You can manually check the material availability for all the scheduled stock materials by choosing the appropriate icon in the standard toolbar. The system carries out the check and then displays a message (for example, 'All checked materials for order 902520 are available'). If some materials are unavailable, call up the log for the availability check by choosing GOTO | LOGS | MATERIAL AVAILABILITY in the order. This contains detailed information on the missing materials.

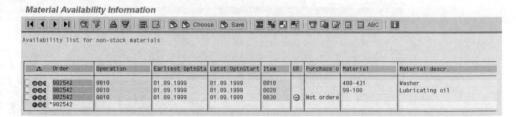

Material Availability Information

Availability list for non-stock materials

△	Order	Operation	Earliest OptnSta	Latst OptnStart	Item	GR	Purchase o	Material	Material descr.
○○○	902542	0010	01.09.1999	01.09.1999	0010			400-431	Washer
○○○	902542	0010	01.09.1999	01.09.1999	0020			99-100	Lubricating oil
○○○	902542	0010	01.09.1999	01.09.1999	0030	⊖	Not ordere		
○○○	*902542								

FIGURE 5.92   Availability list for an order (© SAP AG)

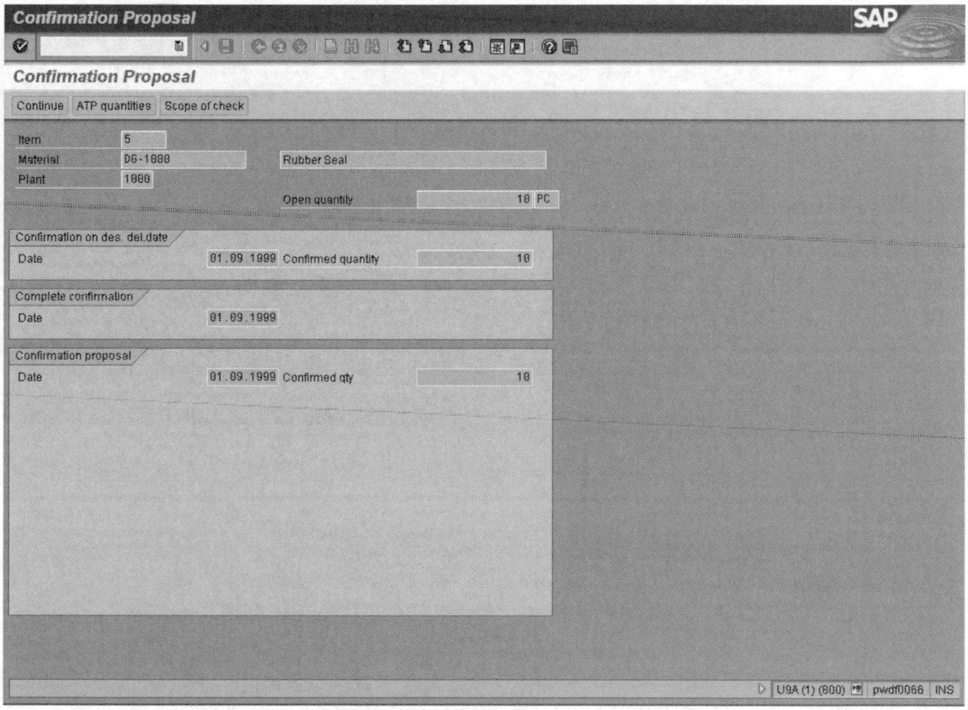

FIGURE 5.93   Availability check (individual material) (© SAP AG)

You display the overview of available materials by choosing ORDER | FUNCTIONS | AVAILABILITY | AVAILABILITY LIST. When you call up this list, the system compares the following data for each planned material:

■ Realistic scheduled delivery date from the current procurement step (purchase requisition or purchase order)

■ Planned earliest start date of the operation

■ Planned latest start date of the operation

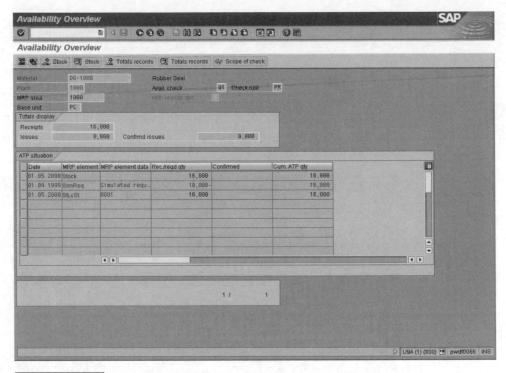

FIGURE 5.94   Availability overview (individual material) (© SAP AG)

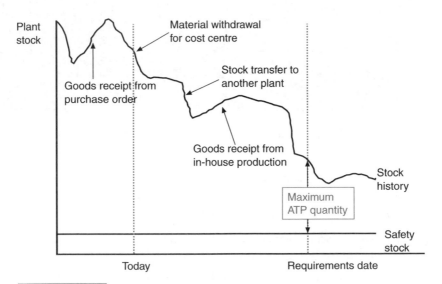

FIGURE 5.95   Calculating the ATP quantity

The data in the list includes answers to the following questions:

- Will the material be available on the earliest operation start date?
- Can the material be delivered before the latest operation start date?
- Why can the material not be delivered on time?
- Does the requirement quantity correspond to the confirmed quantity?

The traffic lights give a clear indication of the current procurement situation (Fig. 5.92).

When you release an order, the system automatically carries out an availability check for the scheduled materials. This check depends on your Customizing settings. If the check reveals that particular scheduled materials are not available in sufficient quantities, your system settings will determine whether you can still release the order.

TIP You can also carry out the availability check for each material individually. To do so, you choose the appropriate icon, but this time at the bottom of the COMPONENTS tab page and not in the standard toolbar. This calls up a screen containing information on the stock data of the material (Fig. 5.93).

The ATP quantities pushbutton enables you to display detailed stock data (Figs 5.94 and 5.95). The ATP quantity is the available quantity from each receipt, which is still available for further requirements (Available to Promise). The ATP quantity is calculated as follows. The ATP quantity of a new receipt is initially the complete quantity received. With an availability check according to ATP logic, only receipt elements that precede a requirement are taken into consideration. A requirement reduces the most recent receipt (and its ATP quantity) first. If a remaining quantity from this receipt is still open, this remaining quantity is retained as the ATP quantity, and can be used to meet another requirement. If one receipt is insufficient to cover the requirement, other receipts (and their ATP quantity) are reduced until the requirement has been met in full. If there is no longer an open ATP quantity for the requirement, or if the requirement can only be met partially, this shortage quantity is displayed in the requirements line as a negative ATP quantity.

How to define conditions for material availability checks

In Customizing for orders, choose FUNCTIONS AND SETTINGS FOR ORDER TYPES | AVAILABILITY CHECK FOR MATERIAL, PRTS AND CAPACITIES. If you choose DEFINE CHECKING RULES, you can define a separate checking rule for plant maintenance (for example, 'PM').

In the next step, choose DEFINE SCOPE OF CHECK (Fig. 5.96). This allows you to specify:

■ Which elements relevant to materials planning (receipts/issues) are taken into account (for example, purchase requisition, purchase order, planned order)

■ Which stock categories are taken into consideration

■ Whether the replenishment lead time is checked

■ Whether the availability check should always be carried at plant level, irrespective of whether a storage location is specified in the reservation

In the final step, choose DEFINE CHECKING CONTROL to specify the following:

■ Whether an availability check should be carried out when an order is created or released

■ Whether an availability check is carried out when a released or created order is saved

■ Which checking rule should be used

■ What effect a lack of availability has on the creation or release of an order

TIP The automatic check at time 1 (create order) is not carried out for maintenance orders. You can only perform the check manually before releasing your maintenance orders. The automatic check at time 2 (release) is always carried out, unless you deactivate it (NO AVAIL. CHECK field). Figure 5.97 shows a setting with checking deactivated.

Figure 5.98 provides a graphical overview of all the necessary Customizing settings described above.

5.2.7 Order release

After you have completed material and personnel planning, release the order. The PM technician responsible then receives the printed shop papers, on the basis of which he begins his work.

When you release an order, the system checks the material availability and the necessary permits. The material reservations become relevant for material planning and withdrawals at the latest when the order is released. This is also the latest point at which purchase requisitions are generated. You can carry out the following actions only after you have released the order:

■ Print shop papers

■ Withdraw material

■ Post goods receipts

■ Enter time confirmations

■ Complete tasks in the notification

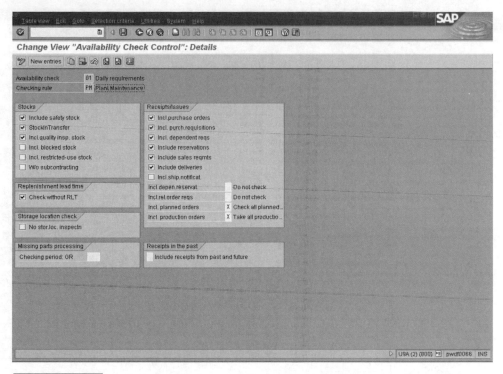

FIGURE 5.96   Scope of check for checking rule (© SAP AG)

How to release orders

From the order, choose ORDER | FUNCTIONS | RELEASE. The order is released as soon as you save it. The order is assigned the system status REL.

> **TIP**
>
> You can also release orders immediately when you create them. This is useful if you generate orders automatically (via maintenance planning) or if you create orders from a notification. To call up this function from Customizing for orders, choose FUNCTIONS AND SETTINGS FOR ORDER TYPES | CONFIGURE ORDER TYPES. Call up the detail screen for the desired order type, and flag the RELEASE IMMEDIATELY checkbox.

If the system is unable to release an order automatically (for example, due to missing permits), the order is automatically assigned the system status 'Release rejected'. The following checks are carried out when orders are released automatically:

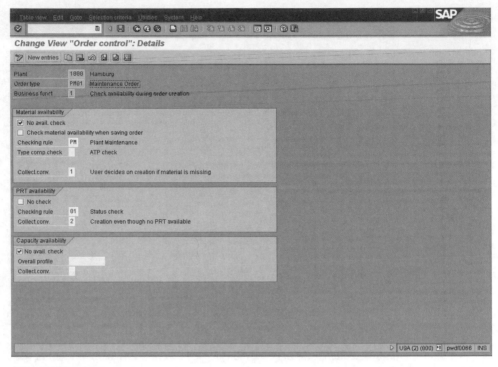

FIGURE 5.97 Checking control for order type PM01 (© SAP AG)

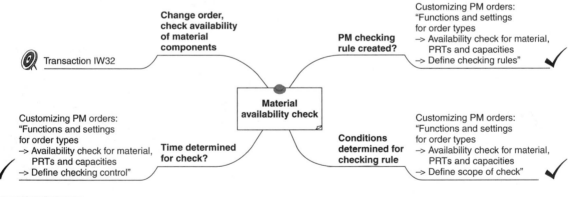

FIGURE 5.98 Customizing – material availability check

- Availability check for material components
- Do permits exist?
- Does a settlement rule exist?
- Consistency check of user status

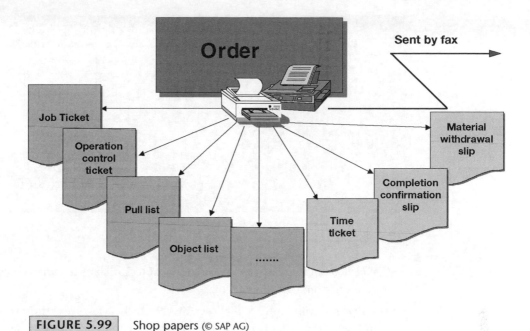

FIGURE 5.99   Shop papers (© SAP AG)

How to print the shop papers

Immediately after the order has been released, you should print out the shop papers for the PM technician. Figure 5.99 shows the shop papers available in the system. Some of the shop papers are intended specifically for the PM technician, while others are used by the planner to improve administration.

- The *job ticket* is an additional shop paper, which provides the PM technician performing the tasks with a complete overview of the order. If the Document Management System is activated in your system, you can also print graphics (for example, engineering/design drawings of the technical object affected).

- The *operation control ticket* provides you (the planner responsible) with a complete overview of the maintenance order. It also contains information on permits.

- The *pull list* shows the warehouse clerk the materials that have been scheduled for each operation in the order.

- The *object list* provides the planner with an overview of all the technical objects and notifications involved in the order.

- *Time tickets* are only printed for operations with a control key that allows this. The number of time tickets specified in the control key is printed out per operation for each of the PM technicians involved in an order. On the time ticket, the PM technician enters the time required to carry out the operation.

Sh...	Description	OutputDevice	Number ...	D...	P...	D...	N...	Output language	Recipient number	
2010	OperationControlTicket vers. 1	A000	1	☐	☐	☐	☑			
2020	Material issue slip vers. 1	A000	1	☐	☐	☐	☑			
2030	Job ticket vers. 1	A000	1	☐	☐	☐	☑			
2040	Pick list	A000	1	☐	☐	☐	☑			
2060	Time ticket vers. 1	A000	1	☐	☐	☐	☑			
1010	Activity report vers. 1	LP01	1		☑	☑	☑			
1020	Downtime report vers. 1	LP01	1		☑	☑	☑			
1030	Notification overview vers. 1	LP01	1		☑	☑	☑			

Print/fax | Multiple fax | Print preview

FIGURE 5.100 Selecting shop papers (© SAP AG)

- *Completion confirmation slips* are used by PM technicians to carry out confirmations if this is not done in the system.
- The *material withdrawal slip* allows the PM technician to withdraw the materials required for the order from the warehouse. One material withdrawal slip is printed for each material component.

To print out or fax shop papers from the order, choose ORDER | PRINT | ORDER. This calls up a dialog box, in which you can select the shop papers required (Fig. 5.100). After you have done this, choose the PRINT/FAX pushbutton.

If you want to call up a preview before printing the shop papers, choose the PRINT PREVIEW pushbutton. You can also print out simultaneously all the shop papers that have not yet been printed for an order (delta printing). To do so, select the DELTA PRINT field. Delta printing can be useful if you want to print out the shop papers for the PM technician first, and then print all the remaining papers for your own administrative purposes. Delta printing has the following results:

- The job ticket and the operation control ticket contain only new operations (in other words, operations that have not yet been printed)
- Time tickets are only printed if they do not yet have the status 'printed'
- Components are only printed if they have not previously been printed on a component slip (such as the material withdrawal slip)
- The printed papers are marked as delta prints

You can only carry out delta printing if it is activated in your system. All the important Customizing settings for printing orders are carried out in Customizing for orders under PRINT CONTROL. To activate delta printing, first choose PRINT CONTROL | DEFINE SHOP PAPERS AND LAYOUT FOR PRINTOUT, and then call up the detail screen for the individual order papers (Fig. 5.101).

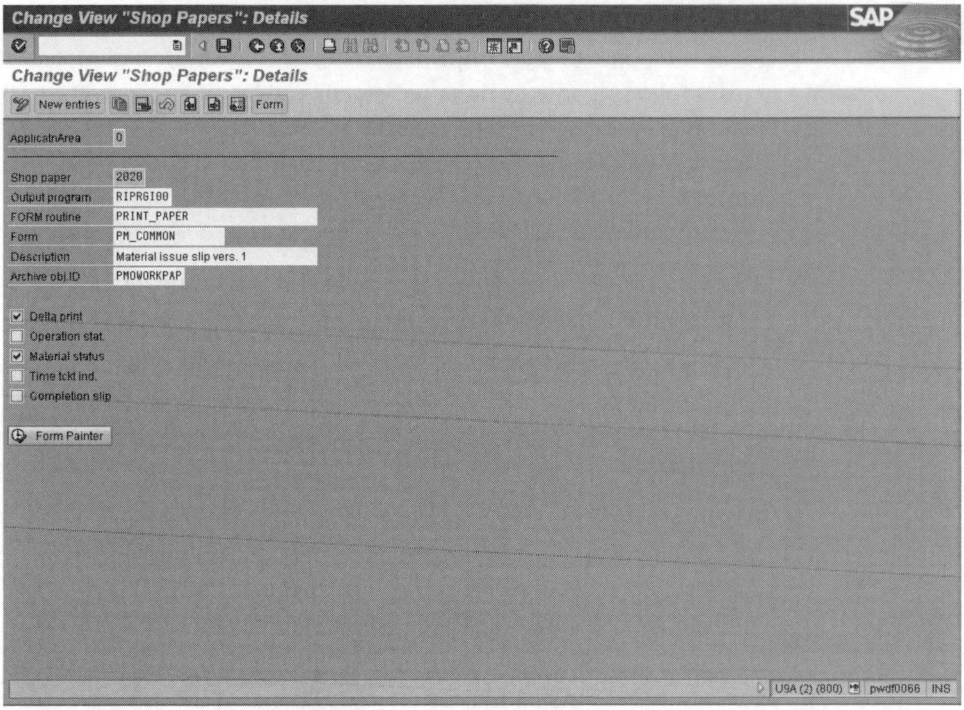

FIGURE 5.101   Activating delta printing (© SAP AG)

As soon as you have printed shop papers for an order, the system assigns the system status PRT to the order and creates a print log. Using this print log, you can determine

- which papers have already been printed for the order
- who printed the papers
- when the papers were printed

You call up the print log by choosing GOTO | LOGS | PRINT.

How to release and print orders at the same time

The R/3 System provides a function that enables you to print shop papers automatically when an order is released. To do so, choose ORDER | FUNCTIONS | PUT IN PROCESS. The order is then assigned the system status REL, and a dialog box is displayed, in which you can enter details for printing.

5.2.8 Technical completion

From the point of view of plant maintenance, technical completion closes the order. This is followed only by order settlement and business completion. Details of the latter process are provided below in section 5.3, 'Tasks of the Controller'. Before you can complete an order technically, the PM technician has to have executed the order. Details of this process can be found above in section 5.1, 'Tasks of the PM technician'.

As the planner, you release the order and only deal with it again

- when the PM technician has provided a time confirmation; in other words, when the order has been finally confirmed
- when all goods movements have been carried out; in other words, when the ordered non-stock materials have arrived (goods receipt), or when the stock materials have been collected from the warehouse (goods issue from warehouse for order).

You now have the task of checking the time confirmations and the document flow of the goods documents. When the order has been completed from your point of view, you set the status to 'technically completed'.

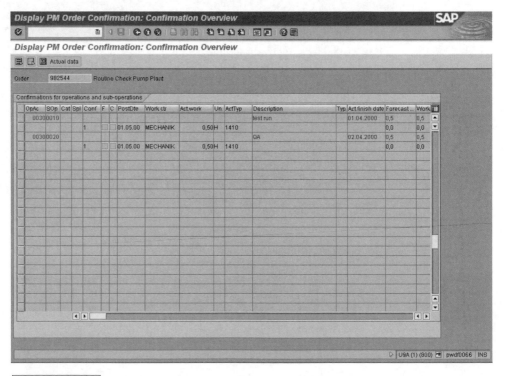

FIGURE 5.102 Displaying time confirmations (© SAP AG)

How to check time confirmations

Choose, for example, transaction IW43, DISPLAY PM ORDER CONFIRMATION. This calls up an overview of all the time confirmations for the individual operations in the order (Fig. 5.102). The overview also displays all the confirmation texts that the PM technician has entered. If necessary, you can use these texts to deduce other defects and create a new order.

TIP You can also check the completion confirmations from the order, by choosing EXTRAS | ORDER DOCUMENTS | COMPLETION CONFIRMATIONS.

How to check document flows

From the order, choose EXTRAS | ORDER DOCUMENTS | GOODS MOVEMENTS. This calls up an overview of all the goods movements for the order.

TIP Choose EXTRAS | ORDER DOCUMENTS | DOCUMENT FLOW. This calls up an overview of all the documents that the system has generated to date for this order; in other words, notifications, goods movements, and completion confirmations. Choosing the DISPLAY DOCUMENT pushbutton takes you directly to the detail data of each document.

How to technically complete orders

In the order, choose ORDER | FUNCTIONS | COMPLETE | COMPLETE (TECHNICALLY).

The order is then assigned the status TECO. As the planner, you can now no longer change the order. The only actions you can carry out are the following:

- Reset technical completion
- Lock and unlock the order
- Set the deletion flag

The location data and account assignment data specified are fixed and can no longer be changed. If the controller has not yet maintained a settlement rule, this is now forced. A deletion flag is set for any purchase requisitions that are still open for the order. Open material reservations are removed. Capacities that were planned for the order and are still open are also removed.

If the order is linked to a notification, you can also complete this notification when you carry out technical completion. This is only possible, however, if the notification no longer contains outstanding tasks. If outstanding tasks still exist, you have two options:

■ You can complete the order without the notification, and then complete the notification task by task in a further operation.

■ You can terminate order processing so that you can first complete the outstanding tasks in the notification. When you have done so, you can carry out technical completion for the order with the notification.

5.2.9 Order status

As part of status management generally, the system sets system statuses internally when specific business transactions are carried out. These statuses inform you that a particular business transaction has been performed on an object, and show you the business transactions that this status permits you to carry out.

Since the system statuses are set automatically by the system when you carry out certain business transactions, and cannot be changed directly by the user, you can only display them.

System statuses and what they mean

■ 'Created' status

The order has been created. Reservations may exist, but are not relevant for withdrawals or materials planning. Purchase requisitions exist, but it is not possible to carry out goods receipt postings. Technical completion can be carried out.

If the appropriate indicator is flagged, reservations and purchase requisitions can be created at a defined time (at latest, however, when the order is released). In Customizing, you can specify that the reference object should be used to create a default settlement rule when the order is created.

■ 'Released' status

The system checks the material availability. It checks whether permits are still outstanding. It also checks what data has been specified in customer exits. This is the latest point at which reservations become relevant for materials planning and withdrawals. Purchase requisitions are written now, at the latest. Goods receipt postings can be carried out. Printing can be carried out. Time confirmations can be made. Settlement can be carried out from this status onwards (for example, to provide an immediate cost display for the receiver).

These checks can be set in Customizing. In Customizing, you can specify that order release is permissible only if the settlement rule is maintained.

■ 'Partially confirmed' status

Individual time confirmations have already been entered for operations or the order header. The planner can see that the maintenance tasks have begun to be carried out. He should only make changes to the order if these are absolutely necessary;

in this case, he must ensure that the PM technician is informed of these subsequent changes.

You can enter partial confirmations for the order header, as well as for the individual operations.

- 'Confirmed' status

The PM technicians have completed their work on the maintenance tasks specified in the order. The final confirmation removes the capacity requirements and sets the status to 'Confirmed' (= finally confirmed).

If the technician selects the COMPLETED field in the order, any capacity requirements that still exist are also removed. The status 'Finally confirmed' can only be set explicitly by the planner.

- 'Technically completed' status

The order is considered completed from the point of view of plant maintenance. Only the following changes can be made to it online:

- You can lock and unlock the order.

- You can post goods receipts for the order.

- You can change the object list entries.

- You can set the deletion flag.

The location data and account assignment data specified for the order are fixed and can no longer be changed. The order can continue to receive costs (for example, via invoice receipts for materials delivered and used). A deletion flag is assigned to all the purchase requisitions that still exist for the order. All the remaining reservations for the order are removed. Capacities that were scheduled for the order and are still open are removed. It is still possible to carry out goods receipts postings. A settlement rule must exist, however, before the technical completion can be carried out.

- 'Locked' status

The order is locked for all changes. It can only be unlocked again. Capacity load records are removed. If purchase requisitions were created when the order was released, these continue to exist, but purchase orders cannot be created for them. To enable changes in planning to be carried out relatively easily, an order is usually locked after it has been released.

- 'Marked for deletion' status

The system checks whether the order can be deleted (for example, the order balance must be zero). The next time the archiving program is run, the deletion flag is set; the order is then deleted from the database and written to the archive.

- 'Not carried out' status

  When evaluations and checks are performed, it is becomes clear that the planned work was not carried out.

How to use the order status for a workflow

You can use a workflow to inform the other planners responsible when the order enters one of the following processing phases:

- Order created
- Order released
- Order finally confirmed
- Order technically completed

If the order has a system status corresponding to one of the above phases, you can inform a person or group of people via workflow (if your system settings permit this). The people that can be involved here are

- The person who created the order
- Another planner
- The controller

These people receive a work item in their SAP Office inbox, where it can be processed directly. When the work item is processed, the change transaction for the order is called up automatically.

How to define user statuses

You set user statuses to allow or prevent specific business transactions for the entire order as well as for individual operations. User statuses for the entire order and for operations do not influence each other. User statuses are defined within a status profile in Customizing for orders. Using this profile, you can further restrict the business operations allowed by particular system statuses. Once a system profile has been assigned, it can no longer be changed. If you have the appropriate authorization, you can assign and delete user statuses defined in Customizing yourself. There are generally two types of user status in a status profile:

- User statuses with status number
- User statuses without status number

The status number is used to specify the possible subsequent status for a specific user status. Only one user status with status number may be active at any one time. If a user status with status number is currently active, and you want to activate one or more user statuses in parallel to this, you must define these as user statuses without status number. Any number of user statuses without status number can be active at the same time.

To define user statuses for orders from Customizing for orders, choose GENERAL DATA | MAINTAIN USER STATUS FOR ORDERS. Choose DEFINE USER STATUS PROFILES, and carry out the following actions for your status profile:

▨ Define separate user statuses and document their functions in a related long text

▨ Specify the status numbers for the user statuses that define the possible sequence of user statuses

▨ Define an initial status that is activated automatically when an object is created

▨ Specify the user status that is activated automatically when a business transaction is carried out

▨ Define the operations that are permitted or forbidden when a specific status is active

Figure 5.103 shows a user status profile to facilitate communication within a team. The user status 'Accepted' should initially be set. As soon as the planner forwards an order to a colleague from planning, he should set the status 'Forwarded to colleague'. As soon as his colleague accepts the order, he sets the 'Accepted' status. Since these two statuses

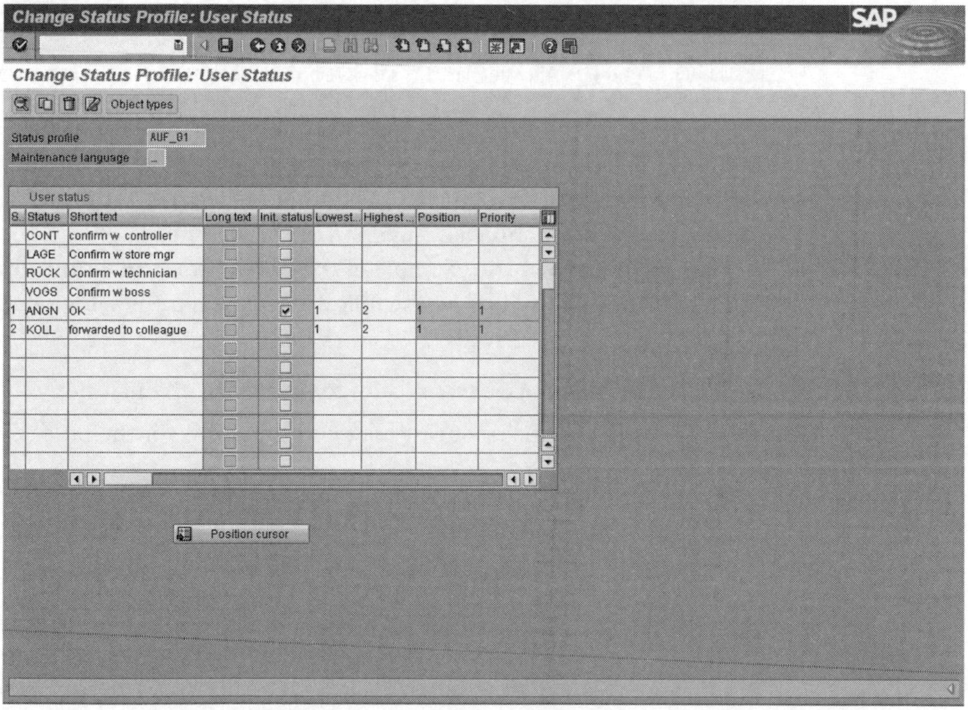

FIGURE 5.103 Defining user status profiles (© SAP AG)

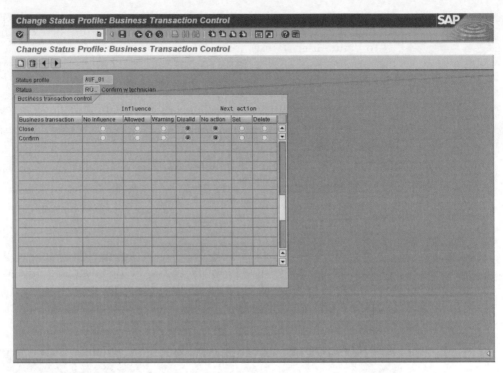

FIGURE 5.104 Allowed and disallowed transactions for defining user status profiles
(© SAP AG)

can never be activated at the same time, they both have status numbers. The statuses without status number can be set in addition, whenever confirmation is required from the controller, PM technician, superior, or the warehouse.

Figure 5.104 shows the example of the status 'Confirm with technician'. Here, you can make settings disallowing the following actions from being performed before confirmation has been received:

- The order may not be technically completed by the planner.
- PM technicians may not carry out confirmations for the order.

After you have defined a status profile, you must assign it to an order type or order operations (Fig. 5.105). To do so, choose USER STATUS PROFILE | ASSIGN USER STATUS PROFILE TO ORDER TYPES.

How to set user statuses

When you create a new order, it automatically has the user status profile set in Customizing. You call up status management from the order by choosing the STATUS icon in the SYSTEM STATUS field. The system then displays an overview of the current

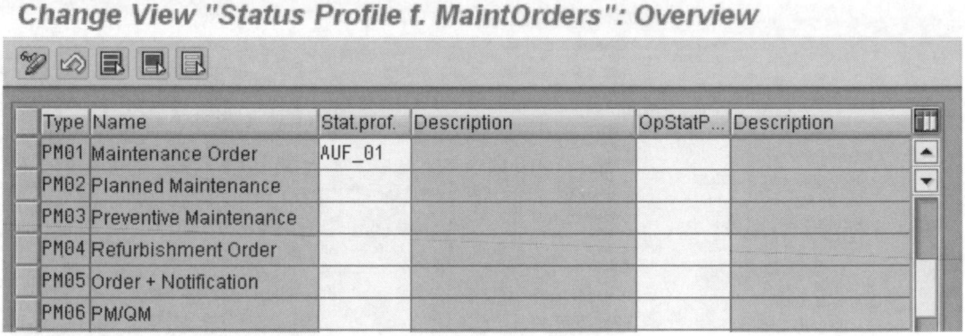

Change View "Status Profile f. MaintOrders": Overview

Type	Name	Stat.prof.	Description	OpStatP...	Description	
PM01	Maintenance Order	AUF_01				
PM02	Planned Maintenance					
PM03	Preventive Maintenance					
PM04	Refurbishment Order					
PM05	Order + Notification					
PM06	PM/QM					

FIGURE 5.105   Assigning a user status profile to an order type (© SAP AG)

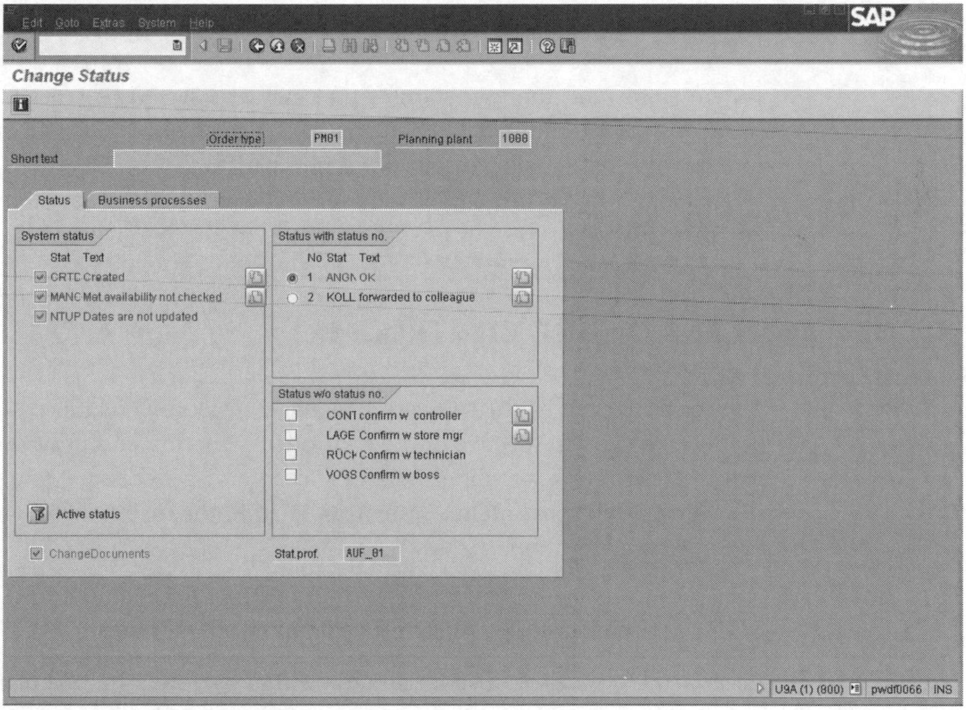

FIGURE 5.106   Status management in an order (© SAP AG)

TIP   A workflow for notification purposes can also be controlled via the user status. If the status 'Confirm with controller' arose in the scenario outlined above, for example, it would be expedient to have the order sent to the controller responsible via an object link/object service.

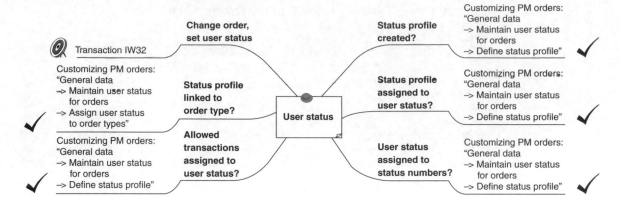

FIGURE 5.107 Customizing – user status

system status and the user statuses that can be selected (Fig. 5.106). You select user status with status number by changing the setting from 1 to 2. You can also select any number of user statuses without status number.

Figure 5.107 provides a graphical overview of all the necessary Customizing settings described above.

5.3 TASKS OF THE CONTROLLER

The controller can be the cost centre manager, personnel manager, a general manager, or PM manager. Irrespective of the controller's function and position within the company, his main task is to monitor the PM costs and, if necessary, to decide whether it is still worthwhile to maintain a system, or whether the maintenance rate of a system justifies a new acquisition.

5.3.1 Estimated costs, planned costs and actual costs

Estimated costs are specified for an order either by you or the PM planner before material planning or personnel planning has been carried out. After the order has been completed, you compare the estimated costs with the costs actually incurred (actual costs). Estimated costs are useful if you want to execute the order as quickly as possible without carrying out detailed planning. Alternatively, you can work without estimated costs and compare the planned costs with the actual costs. Planned costs are incurred as soon as the PM planner has scheduled material or personnel for the order and saved the order. Actual costs are only incurred when material has been withdrawn from the warehouse, or if the PM technician confirms the work performed. Planned and actual costs are determined by the system automatically; you cannot enter them yourself.

TIP If you want to update your costs in the Plant Maintenance Information System (PMIS), you should use planned and actual costs, since estimated costs are not updated in the PMIS.

How to specify estimated costs for orders

In the COSTS field of the HEADER DATA tab page, you can enter estimated costs, which apply to the entire order. The system does not, however, check whether the entry values are valid or consistent. It is not possible to document the estimated costs in a report, nor can an availability control be carried out. The estimated costs entered are subsequently displayed in the ESTIMATED COSTS field of the COSTS tab page (Fig. 5.108).

You can enter estimated costs up to the point when the order is released by the PM planner. If you have entered estimated costs, the order is assigned the status ESTC (ESTIMATED COSTS) when you save it.

FIGURE 5.108 Specifying estimated costs (© SAP AG)

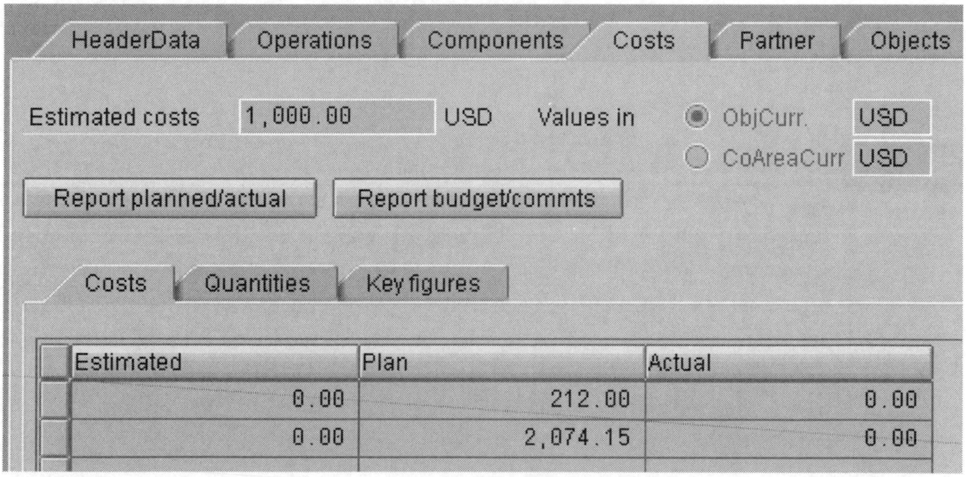

FIGURE 5.109 Cost overview in an order (© SAP AG)

How to read the cost overview

Planned costs are incurred as soon as the PM planner has entered and saved the planned working times in the OPERATIONS tab page, or the planned materials in the COMPONENTS tab page. You can display these planned costs by calling up the cost overview in the COSTS tab page of the order. The cost overview enables you to track all the activities of the PM planner (Fig. 5.109). The cost report in the order represents the technical view of the costs in value categories. You will be shown how to define these value categories in Customizing later in this section.

TIP The cost overview also contains a column for the estimated costs. You can only enter data here if you have configured a cost estimate version in Customizing. Even if you have made the required Customizing settings, the estimated costs are still not updated in the PMIS. The cost estimate version does, however, give you access to more detailed estimates, as well as to displays of the estimated, planned, and actual costs. You define a cost estimate version in Customizing for PM orders under GENERAL DATA | DEFINE VERSION FOR COST ESTIMATES FOR ORDERS. The key defined here is automatically copied to the appropriate table in CO. You can only maintain one entry here, since only one cost version is permissible at any one time.

How to read planned costs and actual costs in the cost report

If you want to break down the costs according to cost elements from CO, you have to use the cost report in the CO component. You call up the cost report via the REPORT PLANNED/ACTUAL pushbutton in the COSTS tab page. The cost report represents the controlling view of the costs and does not, therefore, contain estimated costs (Fig. 5.110).

TIP You also have the option of saving the cost report locally as a file and exporting or sending it to another application. To do so, choose the EXPORT REPORT icon. This calls up the dialog box shown in Figure 5.111, in which you can enter more details. If you want to export the cost report to a Microsoft Excel file, for example, select the appropriate option. You can configure how the data is displayed in Microsoft Excel by choosing CONFIGURE EXPORT TO MS EXCEL, and making the desired entries in the dialog box (Fig. 5.112). Choose CONTINUE in the EXPORT TO PRESENTATION SERVER dialog box. Your data is now copied to an Excel file, where it can be processed as required (Fig. 5.113).

Cost elements		Plan	Actual	Planned qty	Actual quant
* 400000 Consumption, raw material		33,72	33,75		
* 620100 Overhead: Material		6,74			
** Debits		40,46	33,75		
*** Balance		40,46	33,75		

FIGURE 5.110   Cost report in an order (© SAP AG)

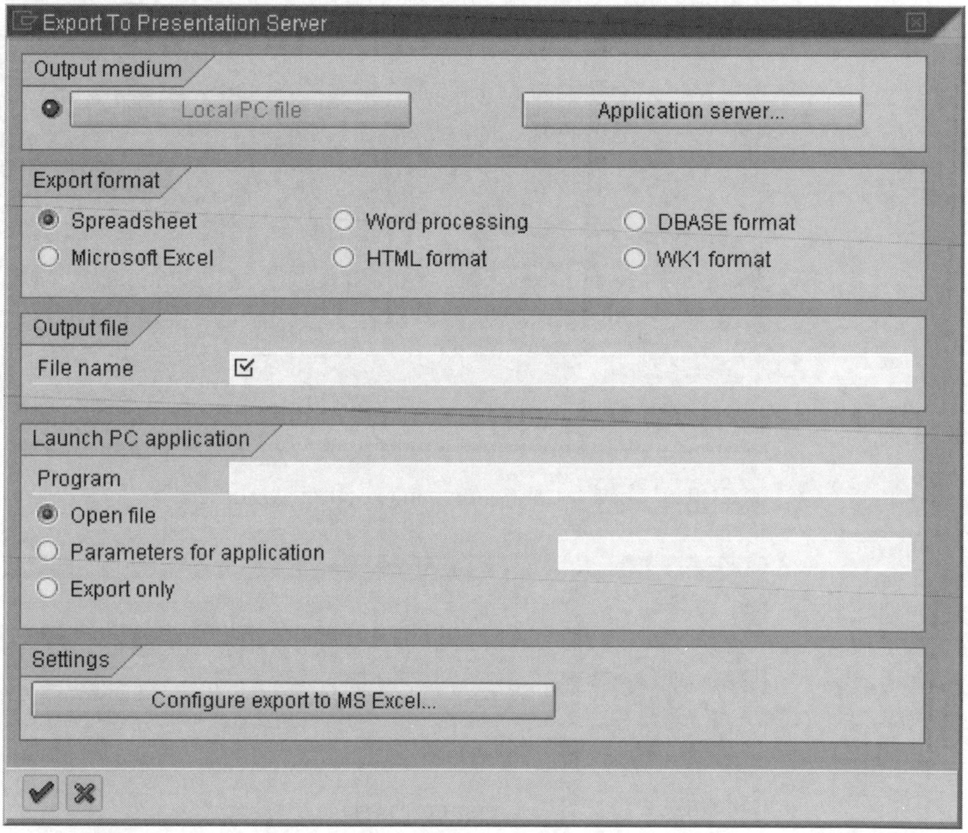

FIGURE 5.111   Exporting a cost report (© SAP AG)

How to group together cost elements in value categories

You use value categories to group together cost elements from a technical point of view. Cost elements are also required for updating in the PMIS. You define value categories in Customizing for maintenance and service processing under BASIC SETTINGS | SETTINGS FOR DISPLAY OF COSTS | MAINTAIN VALUE CATEGORIES.

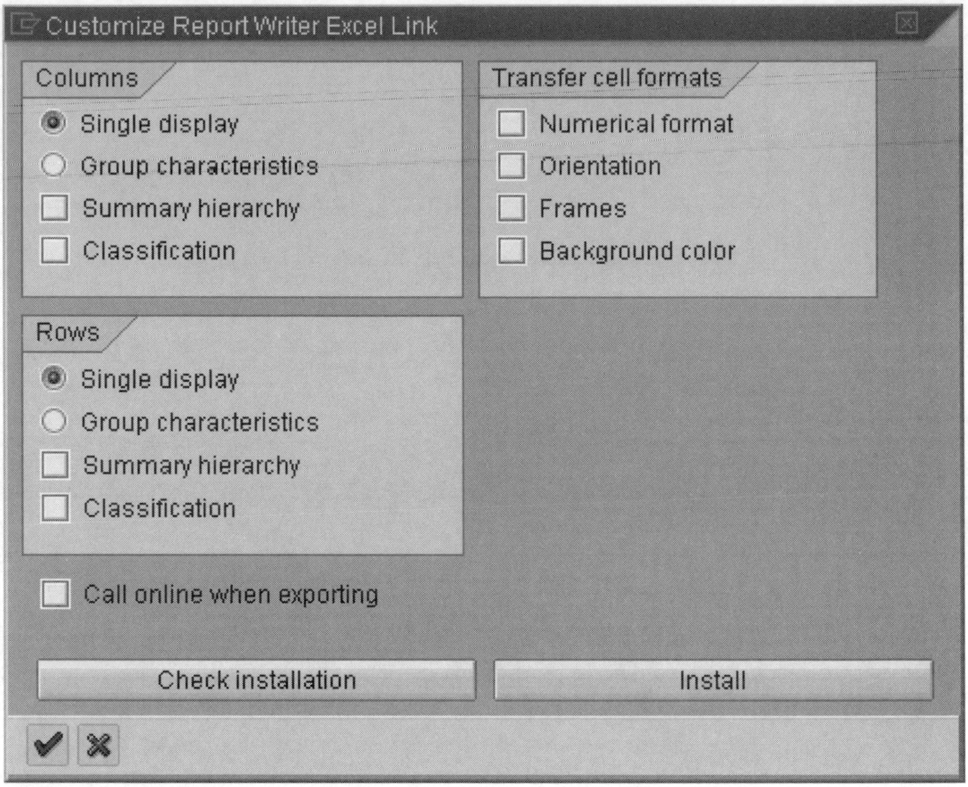

FIGURE 5.112 Configuring an export (© SAP AG)

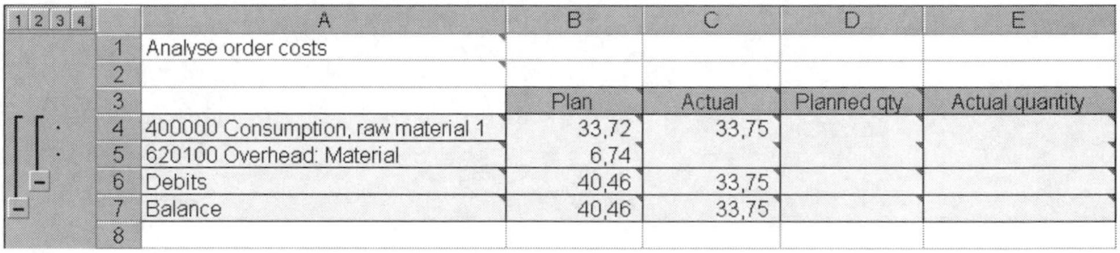

1 2 3 4		A	B	C	D	E
	1	Analyse order costs				
	2					
	3		Plan	Actual	Planned qty	Actual quantity
	4	400000 Consumption, raw material 1	33,72	33,75		
	5	620100 Overhead: Material	6,74			
	6	Debits	40,46	33,75		
	7	Balance	40,46	33,75		
	8					

FIGURE 5.113 Cost report as Excel file (© SAP AG)

1 Define the key and text of the value category (for example, 600 and INTERNAL SERVICES).

2 Specify the debit type of the value category (either COSTS AND OUTGOING PAYMENTS or REVENUES AND INCOMING PAYMENTS).

After you have done this, link the created value categories to cost elements under ASSIGN COST ELEMENTS TO VALUE CATEGORIES.

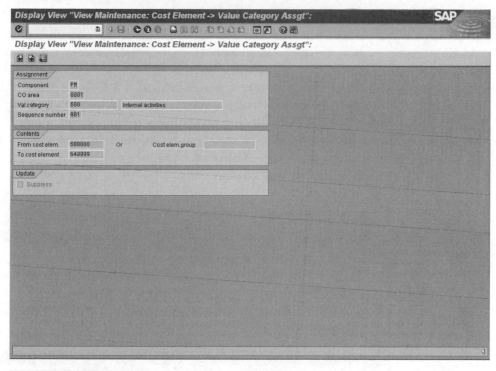

FIGURE 5.114   Linking cost elements and value categories (© SAP AG)

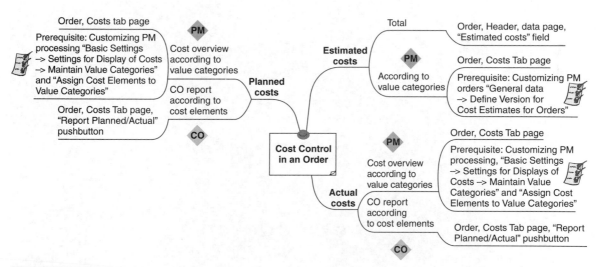

FIGURE 5.115   Cost control in an order

1 Select a value category and call up its detail screen.

2 Enter a cost element, a cost element interval, or a cost element group. Intervals or groups enable you to group together several cost elements (Fig. 5.114).

After you have done this, you should start the CHECK CONSISTENCY OF VALUE CATEGORY ASSIGNMENT report. When you call up the report, specify the controlling area for which you want to carry out the consistency check. When the consistency check is complete, the system outputs a list containing information on the assigned value categories for each controlling area.

Figure 5.115 shows a graphical overview of this process.

5.3.2 Order budget

You can assign a budget for each order. You can do this using the Project System component, but it is easier to assign a budget to the order directly.

You carry out all the settings relevant for budgeting in Customizing for financial accounting: FINANCIAL ACCOUNTING | FUNDS MANAGEMENT | BUDGETING AND AVAILABILITY CONTROL. In the R/3 System, the standard budget profile is profile

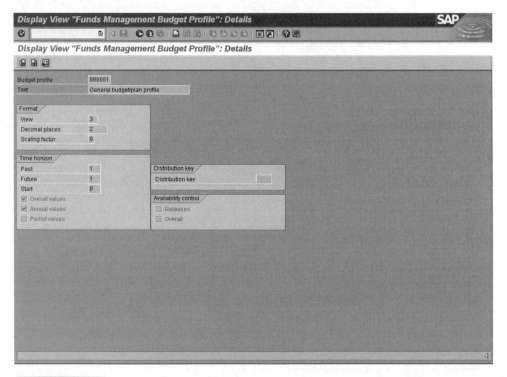

FIGURE 5.116 Defining a budget profile (© SAP AG)

000001. If you want to change profile 000001 or define your own budget profile, you can do so under SET UP BUDGET PROFILES (Fig. 5.116).

The budget with budget profile 000001 is assigned as an overall budget and as an annual budget, where the total of the annual budget may not exceed the overall budget. In the OVERALL checkbox under AVAILABILITY CONTROL, you can specify whether the availability control is carried out with overall or annual values.

Availability control is used to monitor your budget. You can make the relevant settings for this function under AVAILABILITY CONTROL | DEFINE TOLERANCES FOR AVAILABILITY CONTROL. You can change settings for your budget profile here, specifying whether and to what extent variances are permitted, as well as the form in which you want to be notified of these variances (warning with or without mail, error message). Figure 5.117 shows the various options.

You can enter the tolerance as a percentage or an absolute value. For example, if you enter the value '130' in the USAGE IN % field, this means that the funds assigned may exceed the budget by up to 30% before the action is carried out. Alternatively, you can make entries in the ABSOLUTE VARIANCE field. The value '200' in this field, for example, means that with a budget of 1000, the appropriate action is triggered as soon as the sum of all assigned funds exceeds 1200.

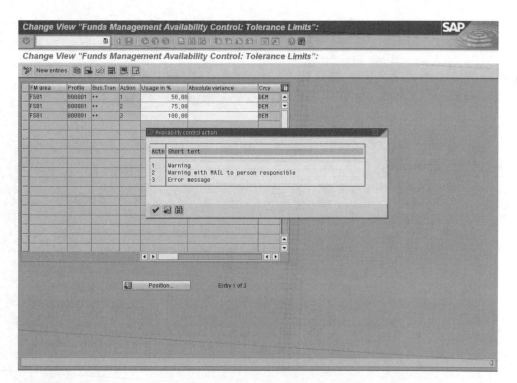

FIGURE 5.117   Notification in the event of budget overrun (© SAP AG)

After you have carried out all the settings in FI Customizing, you must link the budget profile with the corresponding order type in PM Customizing. You do this in Customizing for maintenance orders, under FUNCTIONS AND SETTINGS FOR ORDER TYPES | CONFIGURE ORDER TYPES.

1 Select the desired order type and call up its detail screen.

2 Enter the budget profile (Fig. 5.118).

How to assign a budget for an order

As soon as these settings have been made, you can assign a budget to each order with the appropriate order type. To do so, you use transaction KO22, CHANGE ORDER BUDGET. The original budget is always the first budget assigned that has not been changed. You can update the original budget by means of supplements and returns; in other words, the current budget is the original budget plus all the supplements and minus all the returns.

Depending on your settings for availability control, a budget control is carried out with every actual posting to the order.

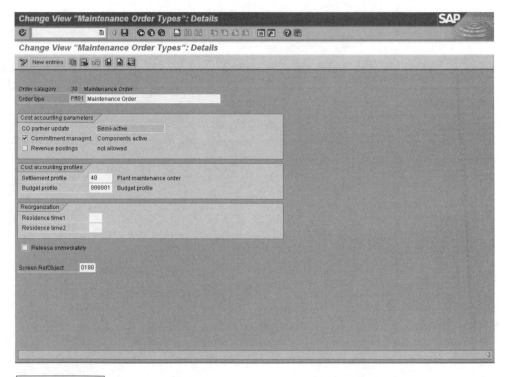

FIGURE 5.118 Linking a budget profile to an order type (© SAP AG)

1   Start transaction KO22.

2   Enter the number of the order and choose ORIGINAL BUDGET.

3   Assign either an overall budget for the current year, or choose the YEARS pushbutton to assign annual budgets. Figure 5.119 shows you how to enter annual budgets.

4   If necessary, have the system check your entries, and then save your data.

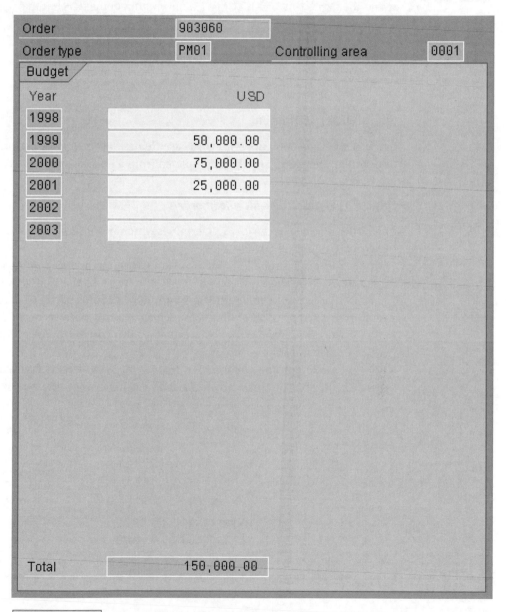

Order	903060		
Order type	PM01	Controlling area	0001

Budget

Year	USD
1998	
1999	50,000.00
2000	75,000.00
2001	25,000.00
2002	
2003	

Total	150,000.00

FIGURE 5.119   Entering annual budgets (© SAP AG)

As soon as the PM planner exceeds the budget, the system outputs a message in accordance with your Customizing settings. In the event of a budget overrun, the costs cannot be posted to the order as actual costs.

TIP You can call up a CO report containing information on the amount of your budget at any time by choosing the REPORT BUDGET/COMMTS. pushbutton in the COSTS tab page of the order.

Figure 5.120 provides a graphical overview of all the necessary Customizing settings described above.

5.3.3 Order settlement

Every business process ends with correct settlement of the service performed. Orders are first settled, therefore, and then completed from a business perspective.

How to map the settlement rule in orders

The settlement rule in the order determines which proportions of a sender's costs are to be settled to which receiver.

You start by defining a settlement rule in Customizing for maintenance processing, under BASIC SETTINGS | GENERAL ORDER SETTLEMENT | MAINTAIN SETTLEMENT PROFILES. For example, in a settlement profile you could specify that 100% of all costs should be settled to precisely one cost centre as settlement receiver. This would normally be the cost centre of the technical object on which the maintenance tasks were performed (Fig. 5.121).

The settlement profile is required to enable you to work with a settlement rule in the order. To do so, you have to assign the settlement profile to an order type in

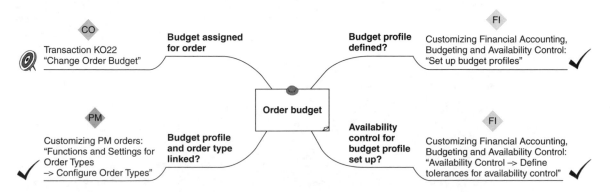

FIGURE 5.120 Customizing settings for an order budget

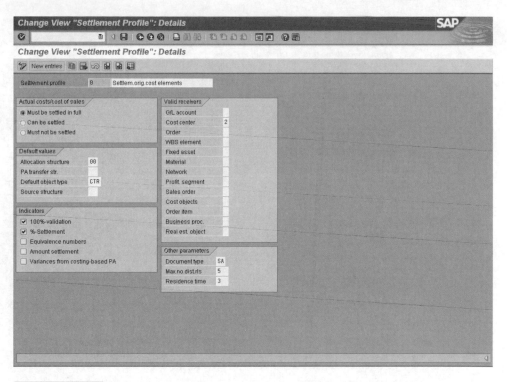

FIGURE 5.121   Defining a settlement profile (© SAP AG)

Customizing for maintenance orders, under FUNCTIONS AND SETTINGS FOR ORDER TYPES | CONFIGURE ORDER TYPES.

For the order type, you can also specify the time at which the settlement rule should be generated during maintenance processing. This can either be when the order is released or when it is completed. You specify this in Customizing for maintenance orders, under FUNCTIONS AND SETTINGS FOR ORDER TYPES | SETTLEMENT RULE: DETERMINE TIME AND DISTRIBUTION RULE.

After you have made these Customizing settings, the settlement rule is mapped automatically in the order. For example, you could specify that the system generates the settlement rule shown in Figure 5.122 in the order as soon as the PM planner releases the order.

This settlement rule specifies that (with full settlement) 100% of the costs are settled to cost centre 4110. This cost centre has been copied from the master record of the technical object. The order receives the status SETC SETTLEMENT RULE CREATED. This settlement rule is generated automatically in an order. If you want to make manual changes to it, choose the appropriate icon. This initially displays the overview screen, from which you can then call up and change the detail view.

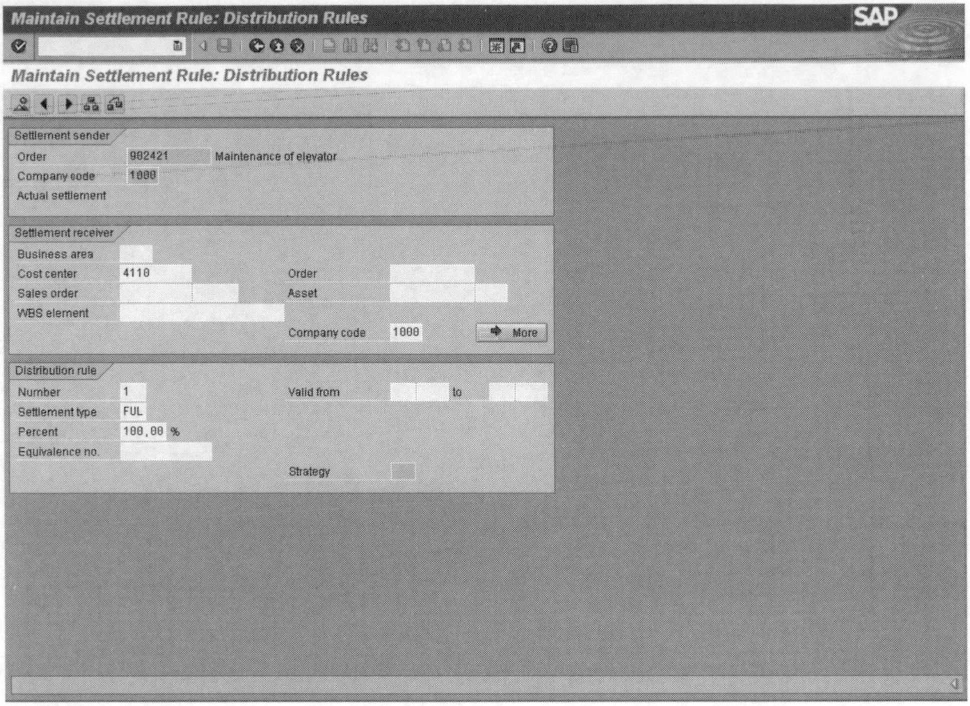

FIGURE 5.122 Settlement rule in an order (© SAP AG)

How to settle orders

The costs for working time and material are initially collected in the order. When settlement is carried out, these costs are forwarded to the settlement receiver named in the settlement rule, with the result that the order balance equals zero. In general, you should carry out periodic settlement of orders automatically, but you also have the option of settling an order individually or performing a settlement test run.

The prerequisites for settlement are:

- The order is released.
- The order has the status SETC SETTLEMENT RULE CREATED.
- The costs collected in the order have not yet been settled.
- The order has not yet been completed from a business point of view.

For example, before an order is settled, its CO report appears as shown in Figure 5.123.

You settle orders using transaction KO88, ACTUAL SETTLEMENT: ORDER. Enter the desired settlement period, and start the test run. A settlement report for the test run is

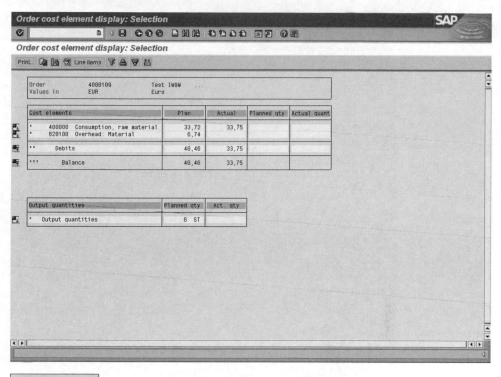

FIGURE 5.123   CO report before order settlement (© SAP AG)

displayed, which shows you whether it was possible to carry out the settlement without errors. If you want to actually settle the order, deflag the TEST RUN checkbox, and start the settlement. The settlement report provides you with information on the settlement you have carried out (Fig. 5.124).

TIP   You can also group together orders to form order groups, and settle them in groups. To group the orders together, you use transaction KOH_1, CREATE ORDER GROUP, and then settle them with transaction KO8G, ACT. SETTLEMENT INT.-/MAINT. ORDERS.

There are no changes in the cost overview of the order after the settlement has been carried out. The result of the settlement (in other words, the credit of the order) is only displayed in the CO report (Fig. 5.125).

Figure 5.126 provides a graphical overview of all the necessary Customizing settings described above.

Actual Settlement: Order Basic list		**SAP**

Actual Settlement: Order Basic list

Selection

Order	902421	Maintenance of elevator
Period	007	
Posting period	007	
Fiscal year	2000	
Processing type	1	Automatic
Posting date	31.07.2000	
Controlling area	1000	CO Europe
Currency	DEM	German Mark
Value date	31.07.2000	

Processing opts

Execution type	Settlement executed
Processing mode	Update run

Result
Processing completed with no errors

Category	Number
Settlement executed	1
No change	
Not relevant	
Inappropriate status	
Error	
* Number of selected objects	1

FIGURE 5.124   Settlement report (© SAP AG)

How to complete orders from a business point of view

If you do not expect any more costs to be posted, settle the order completely, and complete it from a business point of view. The order can then no longer receive postings, and is locked for all changes.

Prerequisites for business completion are:

▓ The order is technically completed.

▓ The order is completely settled (balance equals zero).

▓ No open purchase orders exist for the order (in other words, no more cost postings can be expected).

To carry out business completion of the order, call up the change mode, and then choose ORDER | FUNCTIONS | COMPLETE | COMPLETE (BUSINESS). The order then receives the status CLSD CLOSED.

5.3.4 Order analysis in CO

Numerous reports are available in CO for analysing order costs. You call up these reports via FINANCIAL ACCOUNTING | CONTROLLING INTERNAL ORDERS |

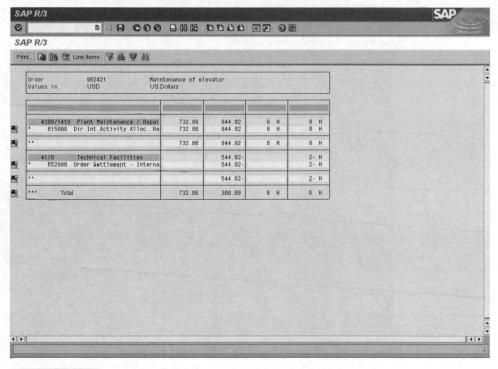

FIGURE 5.125   CO report after order settlement (© SAP AG)

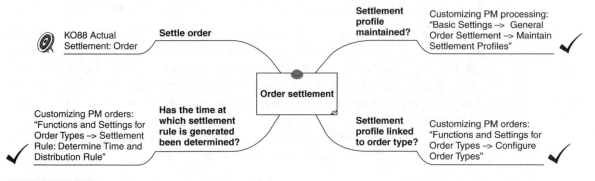

FIGURE 5.126   Customizing settings for order settlement

INFORMATION SYSTEM | REPORTS FOR INTERNAL ORDERS. Since the reports involved here are standard CO reports, they will not be described in greater detail in this book. One example of these reports is report KOB1, which you can use to break down the actual costs for an order or an order interval according to cost elements (Fig. 5.127).

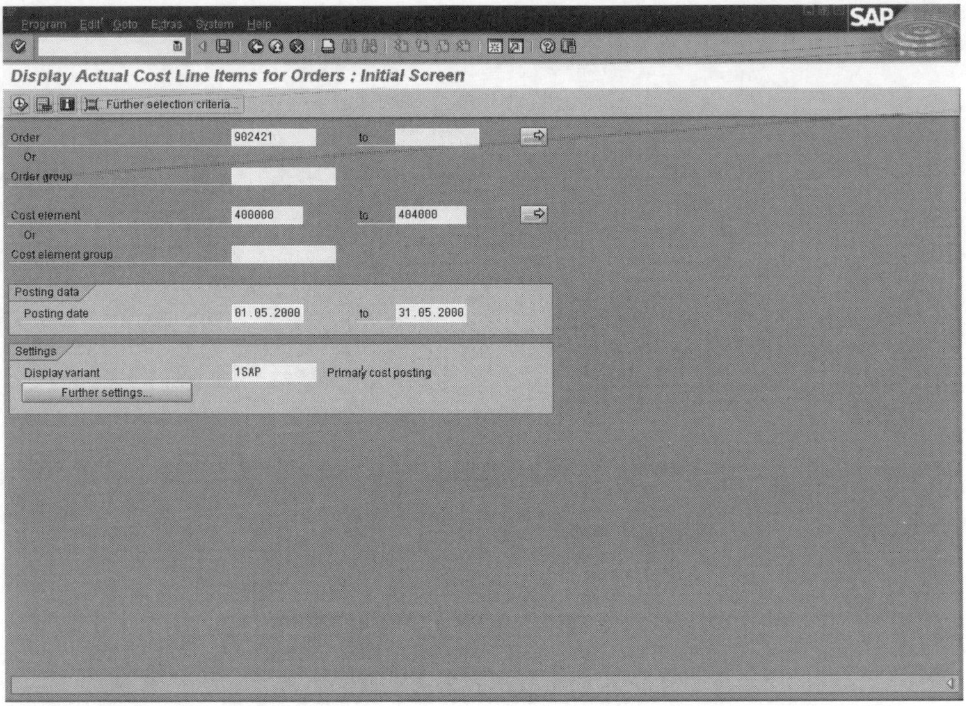

FIGURE 5.127 CO actual costs report (© SAP AG)

5.3.5 Cost evaluation in the Plant Maintenance Information System

As the controller in the area of PM, you require not only detailed cost reports for each order, but also summarized reports on object-based and period-based costs. The Plant Maintenance Information System (PMIS) uses key figures to detect and analyse existing problem areas. In the PMIS, you can collect, summarize, and evaluate data from the productive PM application. In this way, you can constantly check your target criteria and respond in good time.

In the PMIS, data can be analysed by means of a standard analysis or a flexible analysis. In the following, standard analyses will be described, since you can use these directly.

The PM standard analyses

Standard analyses are based on statistics files of the PMIS (information structures), in which important key figures are updated directly from the productive application. In the standard R/3 System, the following information structures are included in the PMIS:

- S061 Location and planning
- S062 Object class and manufacturer
- S063 Damage analysis
- S065 Object statistics
- S070 Breakdown statistics
- S115 Cost analysis
- S116 Customer notification analysis

Table 5.1 shows which transactions in the productive application update which information structures:

TABLE 5.1   Transactions and information structures

Notification	Create, change	S061, S062, S063, S065, S070, S116
Equipment	Create, change	S065
Functional Location	Create, change	S065
Maintenance Orders	Create, change, confirm	S061, S062, S065, S115

Using the example of the data in a maintenance order, the data flow can be represented as shown in Figure 5.128.

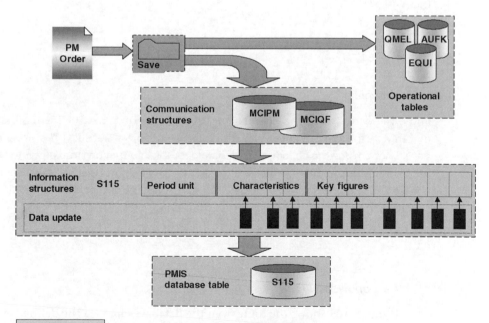

FIGURE 5.128   Data flow in the PMIS (© SAP AG)

When data is saved in a transaction (for example, CHANGE MAINTENANCE ORDER), the system can copy specific field contents to the PMIS. The communication structures MCIPM and MCIQF contain all the fields that can be updated to the PMIS. If a field is not included in one of the communication structures, this means that it cannot be used for the PMIS.

TIP You can display the communication structures in the ABAP Dictionary using transaction SE11. You can use the append function to add new fields.

The information structures define the data tables that transfer the data to the PMIS. The ABAP Dictionary contains a table for each information structure; information structure S115 uses table S115 in the ABAP Dictionary, for example. The data is updated in the PMIS in accordance with the update rules from the information structure (for example, in PMIS database table S115). From there, the data can be accessed to carry out various evaluations, such as standard analysis S115 (cost analysis).

TIP You use the update group to specify the rules for updating the statistics data. Update group 000026 is used for the PMIS. In addition to the type of updating, you can also specify the periodicity of updating (in other words, the time level for which you want the statistics data to be cumulated). You can specify the following periods for each of the information structures in the standard R/3 System:

- Day
- Week
- Month
- Posting period

In the standard R/3 System, information structures S061, S062, S063 and S070 are updated monthly in the PMIS. Information structure S065 (object statistics) has no periodicity. You should not change the periodicity of updating for the information structures into which the cost key figures flow. The prerequisite for changing the periodicity is that no actual data has yet been updated to the information structure. You can configure the periodicity for the information structures in the standard R/3 System in Customizing, under LOGISTICS GENERAL | LOGISTICS INFORMATION SYSTEM (LIS).

Cost analysis S115

Figure 5.129 shows the route from the database table via the defined evaluation structure for the report or standard analysis through to the presentation of the data in a list.

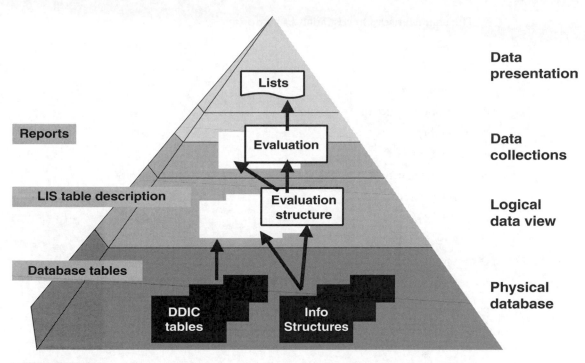

FIGURE 5.129 From the database table through to data presentation (© SAP AG)

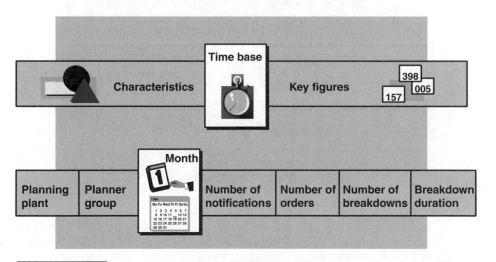

FIGURE 5.130 Characteristics and key figures in the standard analysis (© SAP AG)

What does a standard analysis of this type look like? The basis for cost analysis S115 is provided by data that is updated to information structure S115. In addition to the periodicity mentioned above, this data includes the characteristics and key figures (Fig. 5.130).

The characteristics in cost analysis comprise:

- Object class
- Material
- Manufacturer
- Year of construction
- Assembly
- Key figures
- Completed orders
- Service costs
- Services rate
- Degree of urgency
- Internal wage costs
- Internal material costs
- Internal material rate
- Internal personnel rate
- Number of orders created
- External wage costs
- External material costs
- External material rate
- External personnel rate
- Planned orders
- Total actual revenues
- Total actual costs
- Degree of planning for immediate orders
- Other costs

The following key figures for order costs are updated:

- *Total planned costs for PM tasks*

    When a maintenance order is created or changed, this key figure is updated with reference to the start date of the posting period in which the costs were incurred.

- *Total actual costs for PM tasks*

    This key figure is updated with every cost-relevant operation for a maintenance order (for example, time confirmation, material withdrawal). Updating is carried out on the start date of the posting period in which the costs were incurred. When a historical order is created or changed, the key figure is updated with reference to the start date of the posting period determined for the reference date of the order. From a business point of view, updating this key figure is expedient only with time confirmations.

- *Total actual revenues of the PM tasks*

    This key figure is updated with every revenue posting (for example, billing) for a maintenance order on the start date of the posting period in which the costs were incurred. When historical orders are created or changed, this key figure is updated with reference to the start date of the posting period determined for the reference date of the order.

- *Total actual costs for internal activities of the PM tasks*

    This key figure is updated with every cost-relevant operation for a maintenance order (for example, time confirmation, material withdrawal) with reference to the start date of the posting period determined for the reference date. When historical orders are created or changed, this key figure is updated with reference to the start date of the posting period determined for the reference date of the order. From a business point of view, updating this key figure is expedient only with time confirmations.

- *Total actual costs for external activities of the PM tasks*

    This key figure is updated with every cost-relevant operation for a maintenance order (for example, time confirmation, material withdrawal) with reference to the start date of the posting period determined for the reference date. When historical orders are created or changed, this key figure is updated with reference to the start date of the posting period determined for the reference date of the order. From a business point of view, it is only advisable to update this key figure with confirmation of an external activity (goods/invoice receipt) assigned on the basis of labour hours.

- *Total actual costs for internal material of the PM tasks*

    This key figure is updated with every cost-relevant operation for a maintenance order (for example, time confirmation, material withdrawal). When historical orders are created or changed, this key figure is updated with reference to the start date of the posting period determined for the reference date of the order. From a business point of view, updating this key figure is expedient only with material withdrawals.

- *Total actual costs for external material of the PM tasks*

    This key figure is updated with every cost-relevant operation for a maintenance order (for example, time confirmation, material withdrawal) on the start date of the posting period in which the costs were incurred. When historical orders are created or changed, this key figure is updated with reference to the start date of the posting period determined for the reference date of the order. From a business point of view, updating this key figure is expedient only with goods/invoice receipt for purchased parts (non-stock components).

- *Total actual costs for activities of the PM tasks*

  This key figure 1s updated with every cost-relevant operation for a maintenance order (for example, time confirmation, material withdrawal) on the start date of the posting period in which the costs were incurred. When historical orders are created or changed, this key figure is updated with reference to the start date of the posting period determined for the reference date of the order. From a business point of view, it is only advisable to update this key figure with confirmation of an external activity (goods/invoice receipt) assigned on the basis of the total activity.

- *Total other costs of PM tasks*

  This key figure documents the sum of all the other actual costs for maintenance orders that do not fall into the category of internal personnel, internal material, external personnel, external material, or service. It is updated with every cost-relevant operation for a maintenance order (for example, time confirmation, material withdrawal) on the start date of the posting period in which the costs were incurred. From a business point of view, it is only advisable to update this key figure in the event of surcharges.

The following key figures are subject to a special rule:

- Total actual costs for internal services
- Total actual costs for external services
- Total actual costs for internal material
- Total actual costs for external material
- Total actual costs for services
- Total other actual costs of PM tasks

Actual costs from a cost-relevant operation for a maintenance order (for example, time confirmation, material withdrawal) are assigned in two steps. In CO, all costs are documented under a cost element (for example, 400000 material usage, 615000 internal activities). You carry out the first step in Customizing for the Project System, where you assign cost elements to value categories (Table 5.2).

TABLE 5.2   **Assignment of cost elements to value categories**

Value category	Cost element (from–to)
400 Warehouse issue	400000–499999
600 Internal activity	600000–615000

You carry out the second step in Customizing for Plant Maintenance, where you assign the value categories to the cost key figures of the maintenance order (Table 5.3).

TABLE 5.3	Assignment of value categories to cost key figures
Key figure	**Value category**
Total actual costs for internal material	400
Total actual costs for internal activities	600

With the setting in the second example, the actual costs from the time confirmation for a maintenance order would be included in value category 600, and the key figure 'Total actual costs for internal activities' would also be updated. The actual costs from the warehouse issue would be included in value category 400, and the key figure 'Total actual costs for internal material' would be updated.

When the analysis is performed, the following key figures are calculated:

■ Internal personnel cost rate for maintenance orders

This key figure documents the relationship of the costs for internal activities to the total cost for maintenance orders as a percentage:

$$\frac{\text{Total actual costs for internal activities}}{\text{Total actual costs for maintenance orders}} \times 100$$

■ External personnel cost rate for maintenance orders

This key figure documents the relationship of the costs for external activities to the total cost for maintenance orders as a percentage:

$$\frac{\text{Total actual costs for external activities}}{\text{Total actual costs for maintenance orders}} \times 100$$

■ Internal material cost rate for maintenance orders

This key figure documents the relationship of the costs for internal material to the total cost for maintenance orders as a percentage:

$$\frac{\text{Total actual costs for internal activities}}{\text{Total actual costs for maintenance orders}} \times 100$$

■ External material cost rate for maintenance orders

This key figure documents the relationship of the costs for external material to the total cost for maintenance orders as a percentage:

$$\frac{\text{Total actual costs for external activities}}{\text{Total actual costs for maintenance orders}} \times 100$$

■ Service cost rate for maintenance orders

This key figure documents the relationship of the costs for services to the total cost for maintenance orders as a percentage:

$$\frac{\text{Total actual costs for external activities personnel} + \text{Total actual costs for services}}{\text{Total actual costs for maintenance orders}} \times 100$$

Working with cost analysis S115

You can call up the cost analysis via transaction MCI8 (Fig. 5.131).

Enter the desired order type or PM activity type, and run the report. Figure 5.132 shows the result for order type PM01 in the period from 05/1999 to 05/2000.

From this screen, you can also select another info structure via the appropriate icon (Fig. 5.133).

Choosing the CHOOSE KEY FIGURES icon in info structure S115 enables you to choose other key figures (Fig. 5.134). If you do so, the report then changes in accordance with the key figures you have chosen (Fig. 5.135).

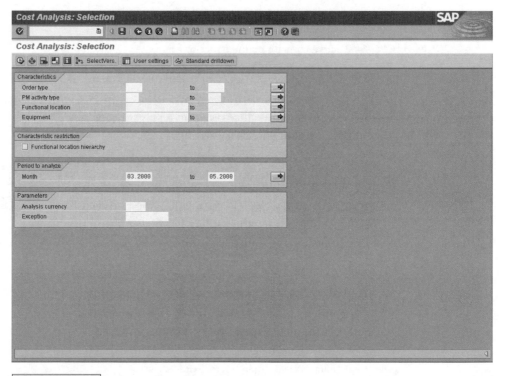

FIGURE 5.131   Cost analysis in the PMIS (© SAP AG)

Month	OrdsCrtd	Immediate	PlanOrders	Unpl.order	Compl.ords	EstTotalCosts
Total	147	89	53	5	4	3.046,00 DEM
05.1999	5	1	4	0	0	0,00 DEM
06.1999	5	2	3	0	0	0,00 DEM
07.1999	12	7	5	0	0	2.800,00 DEM
08.1999	11	5	6	0	0	0,00 DEM
09.1999	25	19	4	2	1	0,00 DEM
10.1999	18	13	5	0	2	0,00 DEM
11.1999	12	8	4	0	0	0,00 DEM
12.1999	21	15	6	0	0	0,00 DEM
01.2000	6	4	2	0	1	246,00 DEM
02.2000	10	6	2	2	0	0,00 DEM
03.2000	4	4	0	0	0	0,00 DEM
04.2000	5	3	2	0	0	0,00 DEM
05.2000	13	2	10	1	0	0,00 DEM

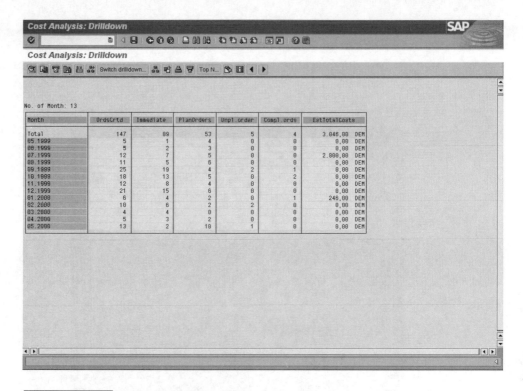

FIGURE 5.132 Cost analysis according to order type and period (© SAP AG)

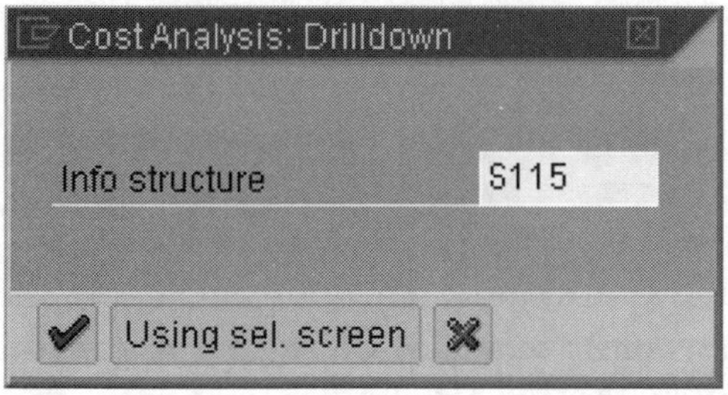

FIGURE 5.133 Changing the info structure (© SAP AG)

You can also carry out a comparison with the previous year with reference to a key figure in the list displayed. This function enables you to compare the data for a key figure currently displayed with the appropriate data for the corresponding selection period in the previous year. For all the characteristic values in the current list, you receive:

- The data for the previous year
- The current data
- The difference between the current and previous year (absolute and as a percentage)

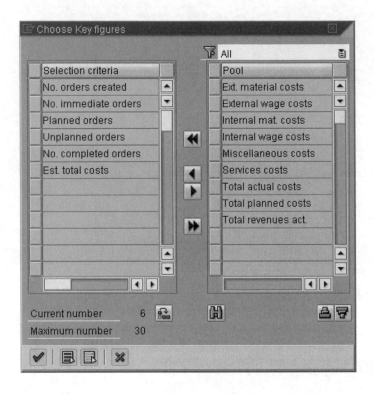

FIGURE 5.134 Choosing other key figures (© SAP AG)

In the basic or drilldown list, position your cursor on the key figure for which you want to carry out a comparison with the previous year. Choose EDIT | COMPARISONS | PREVIOUS/CURRENT. A dialog box containing the comparison data is then displayed.

You can also compare a key figure in the list currently displayed with another key figure. For all the characteristic values in the list, you receive the values for the two key figures compared, as well as the difference between the figures (absolute and as a percentage). Only key figures with a currency, unit of measure, or without a unit can be compared. If you choose a key figure with a currency, for example, the system automatically proposes only other key figures with a currency for comparison.

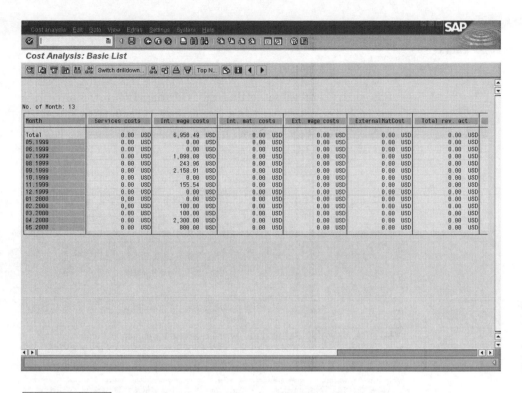

FIGURE 5.135 Cost analysis according to cost elements and period (© SAP AG)

Position your cursor on the key figure in the list, for which you want to carry out a key figures comparison. Choose EDIT | COMPARISONS | TWO KEY FIGURES. This calls up a dialog box, in which you can select the key figures for comparison. Select the desired key figure, and choose ENTER. A dialog box containing the comparison data is then displayed.

How to define PM activity types for cost analysis

In addition to the order type, the PM activity type is an important characteristic in cost analysis. PM activity types are used as grouping elements for maintenance orders, and specify the type of maintenance activity performed. The standard R/3 System distinguishes between activities for repairs, shutdowns, planned activities, and inspections. In Customizing, however, you can specify all other types of activity performed.

In accordance with the settings in Customizing, the PM activity type appears automatically in the HEADER DATA tab page when a maintenance order is created (Fig. 5.136).

TIP PM activity types must not be confused with the activity types in cost accounting and activity allocation in CO.

You carry out these settings in Customizing for maintenance orders, under FUNCTIONS AND SETTINGS FOR ORDER TYPES | MAINTENANCE ACTIVITY TYPE. Choose DEFINE MAINTENANCE ACTIVITY TYPES, and add to the standard PM activity types, if necessary (Fig. 5.137).

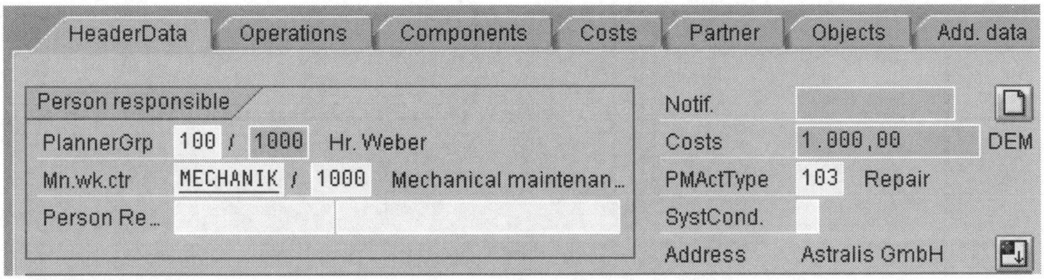

FIGURE 5.136 PM activity type in an order (© SAP AG)

MAT	MAT Description	Warranty case	Insurance case
001	Inspection	☐	☐
002	Regular maintenance	☐	☐
003	Repair	☐	☐
010	Warranty case	☑	☐
011	Insurance case	☐	☑
101	Inspection	☐	☐
102	Regular maintenance	☐	☐
103	Repair	☐	☐
111	Refurbishment	☐	☐
201	Warranty case	☐	☐
202	Insurance case	☐	☐
300	Shut down	☐	☐

FIGURE 5.137 Standard PM activity types (© SAP AG)

Type	Order type text	MAT	MAT Description
PM01	Maintenance Order	001	Inspection
PM01	Maintenance Order	002	Regular maintenance
PM01	Maintenance Order	003	Repair
PM01	Maintenance Order	103	Repair
PM01	Maintenance Order	201	Warranty case
PM01	Maintenance Order	202	Insurance case
PM02	Planned Maintenance	002	Regular maintenance
PM02	Planned Maintenance	101	Inspection
PM02	Planned Maintenance	102	Regular maintenance
PM03	Preventive Maintenance	102	Regular maintenance
PM03	Preventive Maintenance	103	Repair
PM03	Preventive Maintenance	300	Shut down
PM04	Refurbishment Order	111	Refurbishment
PM05	Order + Notification	003	Repair
PM06	PM/QM	102	Regular maintenance
SM01		001	Inspection

FIGURE 5.138   Assigning PM activity types to order types (© SAP AG)

Type	Order type description	MAT	MAT Description
MSPM			
PM01	Maintenance Order	103	Repair
PM02	Planned Maintenance	102	Regular maintenance
PM03	Preventive Maintenance	103	Repair
PM04	Refurbishment Order	111	Refurbishment
PM05	Order + Notification	003	Repair
PM06	PM/QM	102	Regular maintenance
SM01		001	Inspection
SM02		001	Inspection
SM03		003	Repair

FIGURE 5.139   Default value – PM activity type for an order type (© SAP AG)

After you have defined your PM activity types, assign the appropriate PM activity types to each order type. For example, in the ORDER TYPE field of an order with order type PM01, you can use F4 to select the activity types REPAIR, WARRANTY CASE, and INSURANCE CASE. To do so, choose ASSIGN VALID MAINTENANCE ACTIVITY TYPES TO MAINTENANCE ORDER TYPES (Fig. 5.138).

You can define one of these PM activity types as a default value for each order type. To do so, choose DEFAULT VALUES FOR MAINTENANCE ACTIVITY TYPE FOR EACH ORDER. Figure 5.139 clearly shows why, after you create an order with order type PM01, it is automatically assigned the activity type Repair.

Figure 5.140 provides a graphical overview of all the necessary Customizing settings described above.

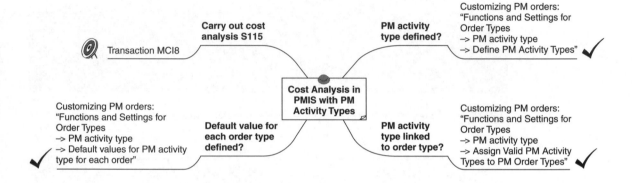

FIGURE 5.140 | Customizing settings for cost analysis in the PMIS with PM activity types

CHAPTER 6

Business process: planned maintenance

TASKS OF THE PM TECHNICIAN

The role of the PM technician has already been described in section 5.1. The tasks of the technician in planned maintenance are identical to those in breakdown and corrective maintenance. For further details, refer to section 5.1.

TASKS OF THE PM PLANNER

The role and tasks of the maintenance planner, as well as the structure of maintenance orders, were discussed in section 5.2.

6.2.1 Preventive versus continuous maintenance

Preventive maintenance comprises all maintenance work that can be planned with respect to the scope of work and the dates involved; in other words, regular inspections, recurring maintenance activities, and planned repairs.

Continuous maintenance denotes maintenance work that is not based on regular planning of tasks. In this case, however, maintenance task lists are also used as the basis for maintenance orders. In addition to this, assigning a maintenance order to a

209

maintenance task list allows the maintenance task list to be used as a reference and entry aid when the order is processed – which considerably reduces the amount of work involved in planning maintenance activities.

In the PM component, the maintenance task lists for preventive maintenance allow you to define the intervals at which you want the individual operations to be carried out. In a second step, you assign these maintenance task lists to a maintenance plan in maintenance planning. This assignment ensures that the correct operations are copied to a maintenance order when the work is scheduled.

The maintenance plan describes the dates and scope of the maintenance and inspection tasks to be carried out on a maintenance object. Maintenance planning will be described in greater detail in section 6.2.3.

You can use maintenance task lists to cut down the time involved in creating maintenance orders and maintenance plans, since the system creates a reference to operations and procedures already entered in the order. You can also integrate inspection characteristics from the Quality Management QM component in maintenance task lists, and include the maintenance task lists in Test Equipment Management. This can be useful if separate data is managed for each individual item of test equipment, or if you want to maintain a results history.

6.2.2 Work scheduling

Maintenance task lists: basics

The purpose of maintenance task lists is to describe a sequence of individual maintenance activities that have to be performed repeatedly in a company. Activities of this type include preventive maintenance, inspections and repairs. Maintenance task lists are used to standardize and plan these processes effectively. A number of manufacturers supply maintenance task lists with their technical objects. It is more common, however, for companies to use their own system to create and process maintenance task lists.

Using maintenance task lists reduces the amount of work required to maintain and process data; for example, if standardized processes are changed due to new legal regulations. In cases of this type, the changes only have to be made at one point in the appropriate maintenance task list. The updated version of the processes is copied automatically to the maintenance orders and maintenance items relating to the changed maintenance task list.

The system contains three types of maintenance task list, which are distinguished from each other by means of an indicator. These task list types can be used for continuous and preventive maintenance:

- *General maintenance task lists*

    These are task lists for general maintenance work that does not refer to a specific technical object. A general maintenance task list allows specific sequences of maintenance tasks to be defined and managed centrally before they are used in work scheduling.

- *Equipment task lists and task lists for functional locations*

    An equipment task list is linked to a specific item of equipment or functional location. Task lists of this type enable maintenance work to be defined and managed centrally, and allow maintenance plans and orders to be prepared for equipment or functional locations.

If you want to use maintenance task lists for preventive maintenance, you can assign a maintenance plan or maintenance item(s) to the task list. The operations described in the maintenance task list are carried out on all the technical objects assigned to the maintenance item. These operations are due at the times calculated by the system when the maintenance plan is scheduled.

Structure of maintenance task lists: Similar maintenance task lists can be grouped together to form a task list group. A group of this type comprises a number of maintenance task lists that describe similar maintenance tasks. The individual elements of the task list are described in greater detail in the following section.

Elements of maintenance task lists

Operations describe the individual maintenance tasks to be carried out. These descriptions comprise information such as time, performing work centre, description of the work to be performed, as well as other control data for individual maintenance tasks. Operations are used, for example, to determine capacity requirements, specify dates at the operation level, specify the spare parts and production resources/tools required, as well as to determine the processing sequence by specifying the relationships between the individual operations.

The control key is used to define the type of operation. The control key specifies the type of operation (internal or external processing), the business function carried out via the operation, and how the operation is processed during the execution time (for example, whether the operation should be printed out and confirmed). Internal as well as external processing data can be entered for any operation. Assigning the control key determines whether the operation is processed internally. As shown in Figures 6.1

General operation overview																
OpAc	SbOp	Work ctr	PInt	Ctrl	Description	L. Work	Un.	No	Duratn	Un.	Calc	Pct	Int. distr	Fct	ATyp	Std txt	Assembly
0010		MECHMNT	3000	PM01	Perform key measurements	0,2	H	1	0,2	H	1	100		1	1410		
0010	0001	MECHMNT	3000	PM01	Check flow pressure against standard	0,3	H	1						1	1410		
0010	0002	MECHMNT	3000	PM01	Measure actual stem valve position		H	1						1	1410		
0010	0003	MECHMNT	3000	PM01	Check actuator pressure	0,5	H	1						1	1410		
0010	0004	MECHMNT	3000	PM01	Check stroking speed	0,5	H	1						1	1410		
0010	0005	MECHMNT	3000	PM01	Determine packing & bearing friction	1	H	1						1	1410		
0010	0006	MECHMNT	3000	PM01	Measure trim wear	2,3	H	1						1	1410		
0010	0007	MECHMNT	3000	PM01	Determine if seat erosion exists	2	H	1						1	1410		
0020		MECHMNT	3000	PM01	Perform key adjustments	1	H	1	1	H	1	100			1410		
0020	0001	MECHMNT	3000	PM01	Adjust bench set	1	H	1						0	1410		
0020	0002	MECHMNT	3000	PM01	Calibrate positioner	1,5	H	1						0	1410		
0020	0003	MECHMNT	3000	PM01	Replace bellows seal	0,3	H	1						0	1410		

FIGURE 6.1 Operation overview (© SAP AG)

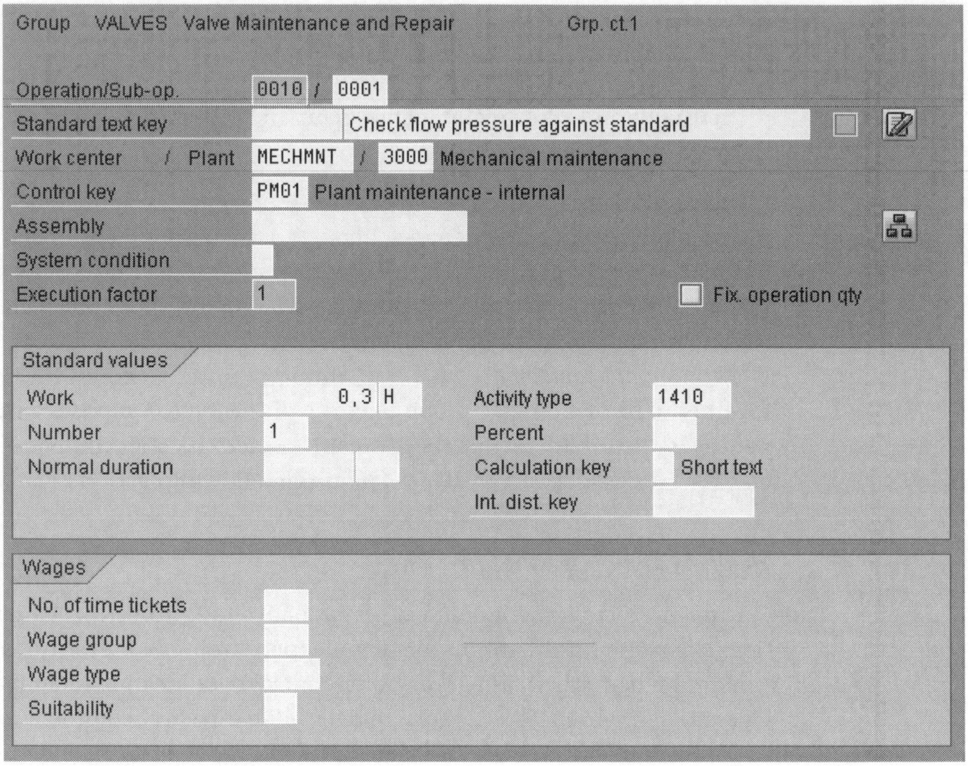

Group	VALVES	Valve Maintenance and Repair	Grp. ct.1

Operation/Sub-op. 0010 / 0001
Standard text key   Check flow pressure against standard   ☐ 🖉
Work center   / Plant   MECHMNT / 3000 Mechanical maintenance
Control key   PM01 Plant maintenance - internal
Assembly   🔗
System condition
Execution factor   1   ☐ Fix. operation qty

Standard values

Work	0,3 H	Activity type	1410
Number	1	Percent	
Normal duration		Calculation key	Short text
		Int. dist. key	

Wages

No. of time tickets
Wage group
Wage type
Suitability

FIGURE 6.2 Operation detail screen (© SAP AG)

and 6.2, the control key can be maintained in the operation overview screen, as well as in the detail screens of the individual operations.

In the PM component, sub-operations can be created to provide an additional level of detail in the maintenance task list. These sub-operations (which can, to a certain extent, contain the same information as the operations) are hierarchically subordinate to the operation. Several sub-operations can be assigned to one operation. This has advantages if several work centres are involved in one operation, or if employees with different qualifications work on one operation.

Material components are materials required for maintenance work. Components from the BOM of the maintenance object (equipment, functional location, or assembly) that are assigned to the maintenance task list, and stock materials not listed in the BOM of the maintenance object, can be assigned to the operations in maintenance task lists. When the task list in the maintenance order is exploded, the system copies the material components assigned to the maintenance task list to the order. Figure 6.3 shows the material components assigned to an operation in a maintenance task list.

Production resources/tools are capacities required to carry out an operation at a work centre. In contrast to machines and technical devices, production resources/tools are

Material component allocations																	
Material	Quantity	Un	B	Component desc.	C	SortStrng	Item	PM	PMAssm	Bulk	PGr	Price	Curr.	per	Del time	Fix	BOMcat	BOM	AltBOM
MR-1000	1,000	PC	☐	Rotor, E-Motor 250 kW	L	STANDARD	0000	☐	☐	☐		0,00		0	0	☐	S	00000021	1
DG-1000	1,000	PC	☐	Rubber Seal	L	Standard		☐	☐	☐		0,00		0	0	☐	S	00000021	1
400-431	2,000	PC	☑	Washer	L	STANDARD	0000	☐	☐	☐		0,00		0	0	☐	S	00000021	1

FIGURE 6.3   Material components for an operation (© SAP AG)

mobile and not restricted to a particular location. Examples of these include tools, load-bearing equipment, or test equipment for carrying out quality inspections. If operations are planned in maintenance task lists, and if you already know the production resources/tools required to perform these operations when you carry out planning, it is expedient to specify these production resources/tools in the maintenance task lists.

In plant maintenance with R/3, four types of master records for production resources/tools are distinguished:

1 *Material*

Creating a production resource/tool as a material enables you to use all the system functions for material master records. The system supports procurement of this PRT category; in other words, the production resource/tool in question can either be procured externally or produced internally. In this case, inventory management can be used on a quantity basis as well as a value basis.

2 *Equipment*

This type of master record enables you to use all the system functions for equipment master records. This is particularly useful for production resources/tools that are maintained independently, have to be maintained at regular intervals, or are required to verify maintenance tasks performed or usage times.

3 *Document*

Creating a document master record for a production resource/tool enables you to manage the PRT as a document in the R/3 System. A document is a data storage medium, which either contains information for the user or is used to transfer data from one system to another. A document can, for example, contain an overview of all equipment that has to be maintained.

4 *PRt master (others)*

In this case, the system cannot support procurement of the production resources/tools in question, nor can inventory management be carried out. The advantage of this PRT type is that this master record requires little data maintenance. Figure 6.4 shows the production resources/tools assigned to an operation.

Item	Cat	Production resources/tools	Plnt	Ctrl	TextKey	Txt	Quantity	Un.	Usage value	Offset	OS	OF	Offset	OF
0010	M	007-240	1000	1		☐	1	PC	0,000	0	☑	☐	0	☑
0020	M	PRÜF.941	1000	1		☐	1	PC	0,000	0	☑	☐	0	☑

FIGURE 6.4   Production resource/tools for an operation (© SAP AG)

Relationships enable you to network operations. Relationships describe the dependency between two operations in a maintenance task list with regard to time. They specify, for example, that a specific operation may only start once another operation has been completed, or that an operation can end only after another operation has been completed.

A relationship defines an operation as the predecessor or successor of another operation. If you use relationships, a maintenance task list is comparable to a standard network in the Project System (PS) component. The maintenance task list thus becomes the basis for planning, describing, and controlling resources.

The type of relationship specifies how individual operations are linked to each other. The various types of relationship are as follows:

- *FS relationship*

  The end of an operation is linked to the start of its successor. For example, the earliest point at which the operation 'Install equipment in a functional location or a higher-level item of equipment' can start is when the operation 'Repair equipment' has been completed. Figure 6.5 provides a schematic illustration of the FS relationship.

- *SS relationship*

  The start of an operation is linked to the start of the subsequent operation. For example, the earliest point at which the operation 'Painting' can start is when the operation 'Erect scaffolding' has been started. Figure 6.6 illustrates the SS relationship.

- *FF relationship*

  The end of an operation is linked to the end of the subsequent operation. The earliest point at which the operation 'Dismantle scaffolding' can end is when the operation 'Painting' has ended. Figure 6.7 illustrates this relationship.

- *SF relationship*

  The start of an operation is linked to the end of the subsequent operation. As the example in Figure 6.8 shows, the earliest point at which the operation 'Start-up' can end is when the operation 'Acceptance' has been started.

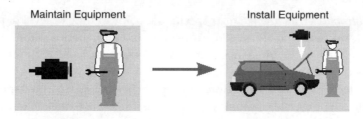

Maintain Equipment   Install Equipment

FIGURE 6.5   FS relationship (© SAP AG)

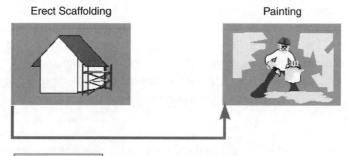

Erect Scaffolding   Painting

FIGURE 6.6   SS relationship (© SAP AG)

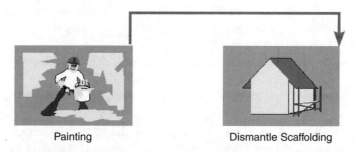

Painting   Dismantle Scaffolding

FIGURE 6.7   FF relationship (© SAP AG)

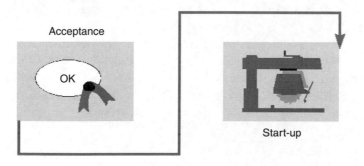

Acceptance

OK

Start-up

FIGURE 6.8   SF relationship (© SAP AG)

Maintenance cycles and packages specify the point in time or level of performance at which maintenance work is to be carried out. In maintenance planning, a distinction is drawn between maintenance plan types created with and without a maintenance strategy.

Maintenance cycles for maintenance plans without a maintenance strategy (for example, single cycle or multiple counter plans) are created directly in the maintenance plan. Templates for maintenance cycles (cycle sets) are provided for creating multiple counter plans. The maintenance plans created with a maintenance strategy (for example, time-based or performance-based strategy plans) contain maintenance packages, which are defined in the maintenance strategy.

Data transfer: If you want to create maintenance task lists for equipment or functional locations with a BOM, you can use a maintenance task list for an item of equipment or functional location with an identical structure as a reference, but with its own BOM number. When you create a maintenance task list of this type, the system transfers only specific materials from the reference.

EXAMPLE The following example illustrates how the system transfers data. Equipment 1, which contains materials and assemblies, has the structure shown in Figure 6.9.

Equipment 2 is purchased subsequently. Since the structure of Equipment 2 is identical to that of Equipment 1, you copy the BOM of Equipment 1. As a result, the BOM of Equipment 2 has a different number than that of Equipment 1. Figure 6.10 shows this structure.

Equipment 1 already has the maintenance task list A, in which materials 1 to 4 from the BOM of Equipment 1 are assigned. You create the maintenance task list B for Equipment 2, using List A as a reference. The result is that List B contains only materials 3 and 4. The reason for this is that when a maintenance task list is created using a reference, the system only copies parts with an identical BOM reference. As Figures 6.9 and 6.10 show, only materials 3 and 4 have the same reference in both equipment BOMs (Assembly 1). Materials 1 and 2 have different references (in the first case, Equipment 1; and in the second structure, Equipment 2).

To enable the system to copy all the materials assigned in the reference when a maintenance task list is created using a reference, you must create a BOM that applies to all identically structured items of equipment. To do so, you specify the construction type for each item of equipment involved, and create a BOM for this construction type. This BOM is identical to the BOM for Equipment 1 in the example. The identical BOM reference is ensured, however, since the new BOM has its own number and is included with this number in the master record of each of the identical BOMs. When a maintenance task list is created using a reference, the system can, therefore, transfer all the assigned materials in the reference.

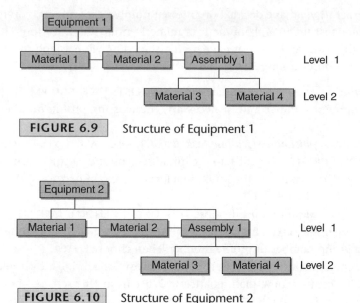

FIGURE 6.9   Structure of Equipment 1

FIGURE 6.10   Structure of Equipment 2

How to create and process maintenance task lists

To create a maintenance task list, choose LOGISTICS | PLANT MAINTENANCE | PLANNED MAINTENANCE | MAINTENANCE TASK LISTS. This calls up the MAINTENANCE TASK LISTS screen.

Number assignment: When you create the first maintenance task list, it is posted with a task list group number and a group counter. Every other task list you create for the same item of equipment or in the same task list group, for example, is saved by the system with a counter.

▩ *For equipment task lists and task lists for functional locations*

The numbers for these maintenance task lists are assigned internally. If you have created an equipment task list or a task list for a functional location, the system tells you the number under which it has saved the task list. The first task list you create for a specific item of equipment or functional location is identified by a task list group number and a counter. Further maintenance task lists for the same item of equipment or functional location are identified by the counter in the group.

▩ *For general maintenance task lists*

Number assignment is carried out here in the same way as for equipment task lists. In the case of general maintenance task lists, however, both internal and external number assignment can be carried out. With general maintenance task lists, the task list group number is of greater importance, since it is required to call up a general task list. If you have decided on internal number assignment, you must assign the general task list an alphanumeric or numeric group identification. The numbers you assign, however, must not have been assigned previously, and must fall within the defined number range.

Creating an equipment task list: Choose TASK LISTS | FOR EQUIPMENT | CREATE. Enter the equipment number and, if necessary, the existing profile number. Then choose ENTER.

Creating a functional location task list: Choose TASK LISTS | FOR FUNCTIONAL LOCATION | CREATE. This calls up the initial screen for creating maintenance task lists. Enter the identification of the functional location and, if necessary, the existing profile number. Then choose ENTER.

Creating a general task list: Choose TASK LISTS | GENERAL TASK LISTS | CREATE. This calls up the initial screen for creating maintenance task lists. Enter either no data or the existing group number or profile number. Then choose ENTER.

If a general maintenance task list already exists, the task list overview screen is displayed. To create a new maintenance task list from this screen, choose EDIT | NEW LINES. This calls up the HEADER GENERAL VIEW screen, where you can process all the relevant data.

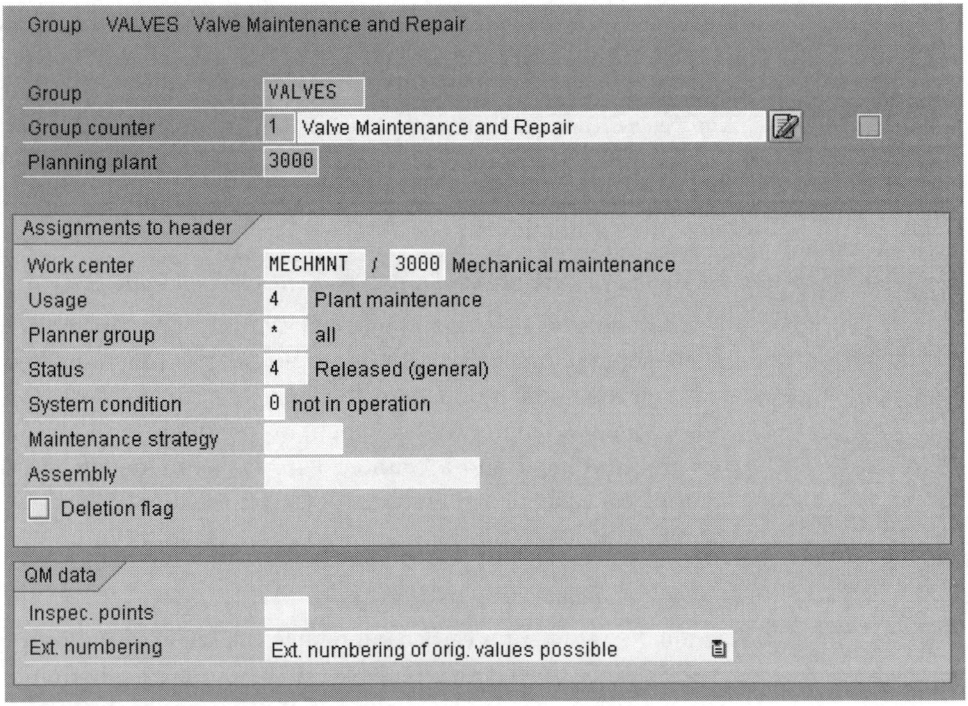

FIGURE 6.11 Header data of a maintenance task list (© SAP AG)

If no general task lists exist, the HEADER GENERAL VIEW screen is displayed as shown in Figure 6.11. To create a new maintenance task list from this screen, enter the header data of the general task list, and then save your data.

Assigning a maintenance strategy: If you want to use a maintenance task list for preventive maintenance, you can assign maintenance packages to the individual operations in the maintenance task list. You should note, however, that you cannot assign maintenance packages to sub-operations. This type of assignment can only be carried out if a maintenance strategy is assigned to the maintenance task list. The ASSIGNMENTS TO HEADER group contains the MAINTENANCE STRATEGY field, which you can use to select the appropriate time-based or counter-based strategy. Examples of time-based strategies include scheduling by calendar or key date; performance-based strategies include scheduling according to operating hours or revolutions.

To assign maintenance packages to the individual operations from the task list header, choose GOTO | OPERATION OVERVIEW and the MAINTPACKAGES pushbutton, or choose OPERATION | OVERVIEWS | MAINTENANCE PACKAGES from the operation overview. This calls up the maintenance package overview screen shown in Figure 6.12.

Assign the maintenance packages for the individual operations, or select one or more operations, and then choose the MAINTENANCE PACKAGES pushbutton to call up the detail view shown in Figure 6.13.

Operat. overview maint. packages

	OpAc	SbOp	Operation description	01	05	10
	0010		Perform key measurements	✔	☐	☐
	0010	0001	Check flow pressure against standard			
	0010	0002	Measure actual stem valve position			
	0010	0003	Check actuator pressure			
	0010	0004	Check stroking speed			
	0010	0005	Determine packing & bearing friction			
	0010	0006	Measure trim wear			
	0010	0007	Determine if seat erosion exists			
	0020		Perform key adjustments	☐	✔	☐
	0020	0001	Adjust bench set			
	0020	0002	Calibrate positioner			
	0020	0003	Replace bellows seal			

FIGURE 6.12 Assigning operations to maintenance packages (© SAP AG)

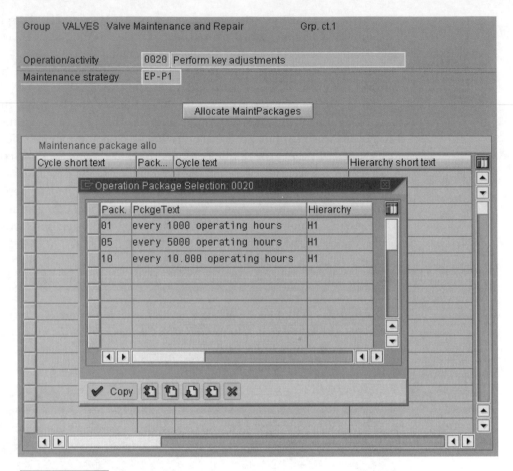

FIGURE 6.13 Detail view of maintenance package allocation (© SAP AG)

By choosing the ALLOCATE MAINTPACKAGES pushbutton, you can call up all the packages of the maintenance strategy assigned earlier, and select a suitable package.

IMPORTANT Once maintenance packages have been assigned to the operation, you can no longer change the maintenance strategy in the maintenance task list.

Creating a maintenance task list or a general task list using a reference: If you want to create a new maintenance task list (irrespective of whether this is a general task list, equipment or functional location task list), you can cut down the time required to do so by using an existing task list as a reference. The system then transfers the data from the reference (such as header data and operations) to the new task list. You can, of course, change this data.

Starting from the menus described above for creating an equipment task list, a functional location task list, or a general maintenance task list, choose one of the following paths:

- ▧ To create an equipment task list: EQUIPMENT TASK LIST | COPY REFERENCE
- ▧ To create a functional location task list: FUNCTLOC TASK LIST | COPY REFERENCE
- ▧ To create a general maintenance task list: GENERAL TASK LIST | COPY REFERENCE

This calls up a dialog box in which you can select the task list type. Select the task list type that you want to use as a reference and choose ENTER.

TIP You can use any task list type when you use a reference to create a maintenance task list or a general maintenance task list.

The system now displays another dialog box containing fields for selecting the maintenance task list or a general task list that you want to use as the reference for the new maintenance task list or general task list. Enter the required data, and choose ENTER.

The system displays another dialog box. This contains a list of the task list groups that correspond to the specified criteria. Select the maintenance task list whose data you want to copy to the new task list you are creating. If only one task list corresponds to the selection criteria, the reference data is displayed automatically in the HEADER GENERAL VIEW screen of the new task list.

Choose ENTER to transfer the data to the new task list. Change or supplement the required data, and save the task list or general task list.

IMPORTANT The system does not transfer the following data from the reference to the new task list:

- ■ Maintenance packages with task lists for preventive maintenance
- ■ Materials assigned as required

Creating operations: The PM component provides two types of operation for maintenance task lists – internal processing operations and external processing operations. The data that the operations contain is mainly relevant for scheduling work if the task list in the maintenance order is exploded and the order is subsequently planned.

Call up the task list in create or change mode, and choose GOTO | OPERATION OVERVIEW. Select the operations for which you want to enter detailed data, and choose one of the following options:

- To enter internal processing data, choose OPERATION | INTERNAL PROCESSING
- To enter external processing data, choose OPERATION | EXTERNAL PROCESSING

Enter the required data, go back to the operation overview, and then save your entries. To call up the next selected operation, choose OPERATION | FURTHER OPERATIONS | NEXT OPERATION. This calls up the entry screen for the next selected operation.

Relevant settings in customizing: You call up the settings for the control key from Customizing by choosing PLANT MAINTENANCE AND CUSTOMER SERVICE | MAINTENANCE PLANS, WORK CENTRES, TASK LISTS AND PRTS | TASK LISTS | OPERATION DATA | MAINTAIN CONTROL KEYS.

The control key of an operation is used to specify the business functions that should be carried out, and how the operation should be treated. The most important parameters are:

- *Capacity requirements planning*

  You use this indicator to specify that the operation is scheduled and that capacity requirements records are generated for it.

- *Costing*

  This indicator is used to specify whether the operation is taken into consideration during costing.

- *External processing*

  You use this indicator to specify that the operation is processed externally.

- *Completion confirmation*

  This indicator specifies whether the operation can be confirmed, as well as the type of confirmation for this operation.

- *Print time tickets*

  You use this indicator to specify whether time tickets are printed for this operation.

- *General costs activity*

  This indicator is used for operations of the Project System (PS) component, and must not be activated for plant maintenance and service orders. If you activate the indicator in the control key, no costs will be displayed for confirmed times or external services relating to the operation in question.

IMPORTANT Please note that the 'milestone confirmation' function is not supported in Plant Maintenance. This means that with control keys that generate a milestone confirmation in the Production Planning (PP) module, each operation subject to confirmation must be explicitly confirmed for maintenance orders.

How to assign material components

As already described in section 6.2.2, under 'Structure of maintenance task lists', components are materials which are required for maintenance work. They are assigned to the appropriate operations: several materials can be assigned to one operation, and one material can be assigned to several operations.

The following material components can be assigned to the operations in maintenance task lists:

▨ Material components from the BOM of the maintenance object (assembly, equipment, or functional location) that is assigned to the maintenance task list.

▨ Stock materials not included in the BOM of the maintenance object.

Prerequisites for assigning components: Material components can be assigned to all three types of maintenance task list (general maintenance task lists, functional location task lists, and equipment task lists). The following two prerequisites apply to all three task list types:

▨ To enable free material assignment for maintenance task lists, a BOM usage for BOMs relevant to maintenance must be specified in Customizing for task lists (usage '4' in the standard R/3 System).

▨ Once free material assignments exist, the assigned usage may no longer be changed. Changing the usage can result in existing material assignments of free materials being lost.

You specify the usage of maintenance task lists via the Customizing path PLANT MAINTENANCE AND CUSTOMER SERVICE | MAINTENANCE PLANS, WORK CENTRES, TASK LISTS AND PRTS | TASK LISTS | GENERAL DATA | DEFINE TASK LIST USAGE. You define the various categories of task list for plant maintenance here.

In the standard R/3 System, the task list usage for plant maintenance is '4'. This task list usage covers all the requirements of plant maintenance.

Assignments to header			
Work center	MECHMNT	/ 3000	Mechanical maintenance
Usage	4	Plant maintenance	
Planner group	*	all	
Status	4	Released (general)	
System condition	0	not in operation	
Maintenance strategy	EP-P1	Electric pumps perf. based OPH	
Assembly	M-1000		Motor, electrical pump 250kW
☐ Deletion flag			

FIGURE 6.14 Assigning components to a task list via the assembly (© SAP AG)

Prerequisites for assigning material components to a general maintenance task list: The assignment of material components in the general maintenance task list is controlled by the assembly in the header data of the list. To enable material components to be assigned to a general task list, you must first specify an assembly.

Starting from the task list overview, choose TASK LIST HEADER | GENERAL VIEW. As shown in Figure 6.14, the ASSIGNMENTS TO HEADER group contains the ASSEMBLY field. You can enter an assembly here. This enables you to use the hierarchy explosion to assign material components from the BOM of the header assembly to the general maintenance task list. You can also assign stock materials not included in the BOM.

IMPORTANT   If material components have already been assigned to the task list, you cannot change the assembly in the header of the task list.

Prerequisites for assigning material components to an equipment task list and a functional location task list: In the header data of an equipment task list or functional location task list, the assembly entry is less important than in the header of a general maintenance task list. Like the assemblies that can be specified in the individual operations of a general task list, this entry is used primarily for detailing.

The material components that you want to assign to an equipment task list or functional location task list do not necessarily have to be in the BOM of the equipment or functional location when the assignment is carried out. You can also assign a free stock material. If a BOM exists for the maintenance object in the equipment task list or functional location task list, and if you assign a stock material not included in this BOM, the system generates a pool of freely assigned materials for the object BOM. If you subsequently assign another free material, the system adds this material to the pool.

TIP   The system does not add the freely assigned material to the BOM. The BOM created previously is retained in its original form, which means that you can call it up again whenever you wish. This is important because assigning a free material can constitute an exception for a specific application case in plant maintenance, and this assignment should not falsify the BOM of the equipment or functional location for subsequent applications.

Call up the maintenance task list in create or change mode, and choose GOTO | OPERATION OVERVIEW. Select all the operations to which you want to assign material components, and then choose OPERATION | OVERVIEWS | COMPONENTS. This calls up the COMPONENT OVERVIEW screen for the first selected operation. Assign the desired material components to each individual operation.

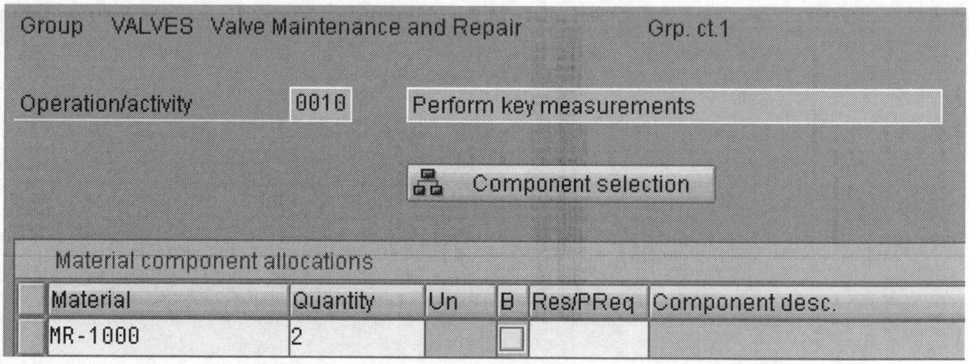

Group	VALVES	Valve Maintenance and Repair		Grp. ct.1

Operation/activity	0010	Perform key measurements

⊞ Component selection

Material component allocations

	Material	Quantity	Un	B	Res/PReq	Component desc.
	MR-1000	2		☐		

FIGURE 6.15 Assigning a component by entering the material number (© SAP AG)

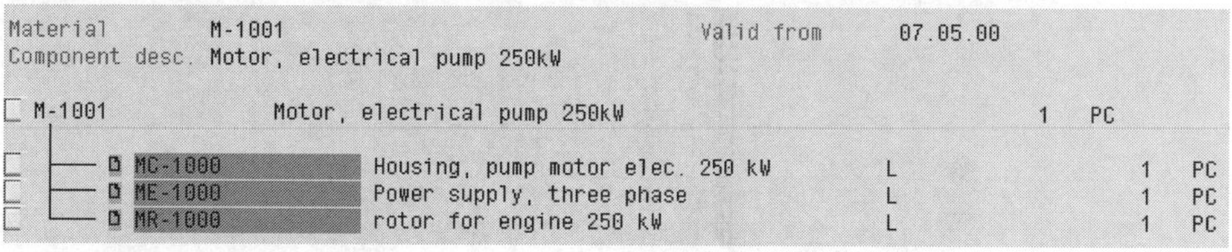

Material	M-1001			Valid from	07.05.00
Component desc.	Motor, electrical pump 250kW				

☐ M-1001		Motor, electrical pump 250kW			1	PC
☐	⊡ MC-1000	Housing, pump motor elec. 250 kW	L		1	PC
☐	⊡ ME-1000	Power supply, three phase	L		1	PC
☐	⊡ MR-1000	rotor for engine 250 kW	L		1	PC

FIGURE 6.16 Structure list of material components (© SAP AG)

Assigning components by entering the material number: If you know the number of the material you want to assign, enter it in the MATERIAL field (as shown in Figure 6.15), and choose ENTER.

The system automatically copies other material data, such as its BOM number and item number, item category, and unit of measurement. Save the maintenance task list.

TIP   If you assign a free material, the item is automatically assigned the sort string STANDARD. This shows you that the item does not come from the object BOM. If you want to include freely assigned materials in the BOM of the object at a later point in time, you can use this sort string to search for the items assigned previously.

Assigning components using the structure list: To call up the structure list, choose EXTRAS | COMPONENT SELECTION | STRUCTURE LIST. The system displays a list of the material components in the BOM assigned to the task list. You can expand or collapse individual BOM levels using the options provided. Figure 6.16 shows this structure list.

Select the material components you require, and assign them to the task list. The COMPONENT OVERVIEW now contains the components you have selected from the list. When you have carried out the assignment, save the maintenance task list.

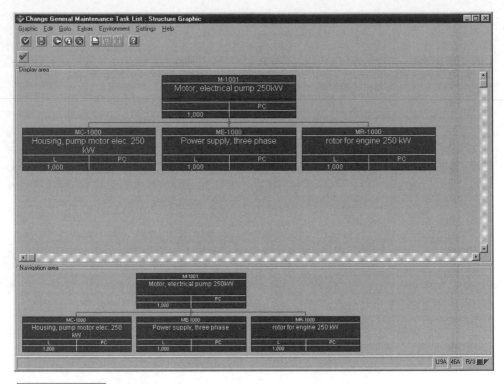

FIGURE 6.17   Structure graphic of material components (© SAP AG)

Assigning components via the structure graphic: If you do not know the material numbers of the components to be assigned, you can select them via the structure graphic of the BOM.

To call up the structure graphic, choose EXTRAS | COMPONENT SELECTION | STRUCTURE GRAPHIC. As shown in Figure 6.17, the system displays a graphic of the material components in the BOM assigned to the task list. Select the material components you require, and assign them to the task list. To do so, select EDIT | CHOOSE.

The component overview now contains the components you selected in the graphic.

How to create and assign production resources/tools

At the beginning of section 6.2.2, under 'Maintenance task lists: basics', we describe how to define and use production resources/tools, as well as the four master record types for PRTs.

Creating a PRT as a material: If you want to create a production resource/tool as a material, you must create a material master record and maintain the production resources/tools view in it. The PRT data is defined for each plant.

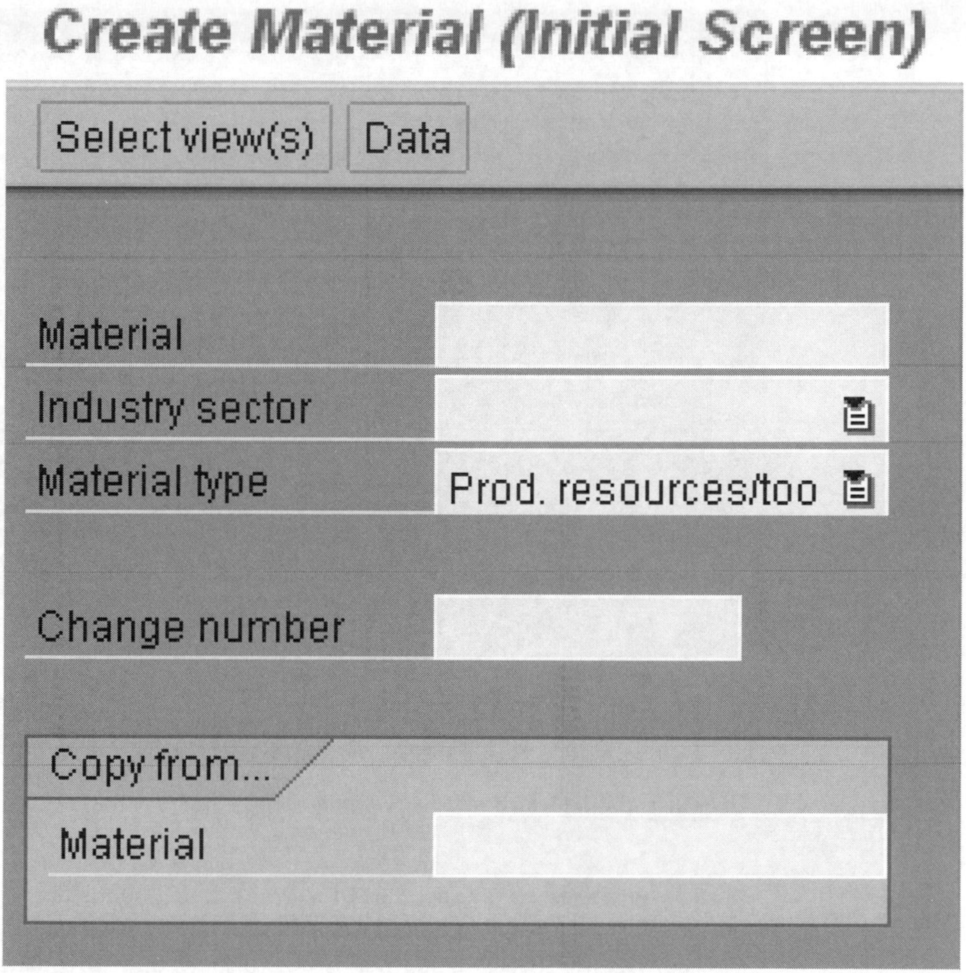

Create Material (Initial Screen)

Select view(s)	Data

Material	
Industry sector	
Material type	Prod. resources/too

Change number	

Copy from...

Material	

FIGURE 6.18   Initial screen for creating a material master record (© SAP AG)

From the MAINTENANCE TASK LISTS node, choose ENVIRONMENT | PRODUCTION RESOURCES AND TOOLS, followed by PRODUCTION RESOURCES/TOOLS | MATERIAL | CREATE. This calls up the initial screen for creating a material master record. Figure 6.18 shows this screen.

TIP   The material type determines the entry fields displayed on the screens, as well as the views that have to be maintained. Enter a material type here that allows the production resources/tools view to be maintained.

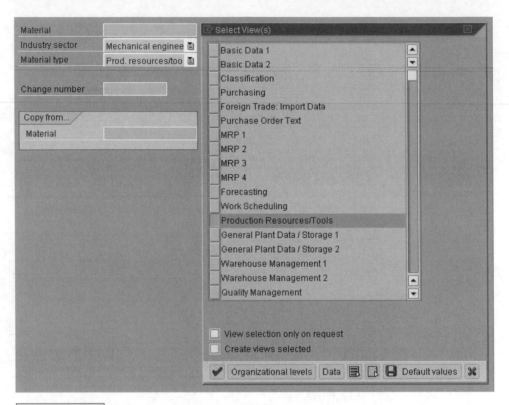

Material	
Industry sector	Mechanical enginee 🖹
Material type	Prod. resources/too 🖹
Change number	

Copy from...
Material

Select View(s)

☐ Basic Data 1
☐ Basic Data 2
☐ Classification
☐ Purchasing
☐ Foreign Trade: Import Data
☐ Purchase Order Text
☐ MRP 1
☐ MRP 2
☐ MRP 3
☐ MRP 4
☐ Forecasting
☐ Work Scheduling
☐ Production Resources/Tools
☐ General Plant Data / Storage 1
☐ General Plant Data / Storage 2
☐ Warehouse Management 1
☐ Warehouse Management 2
☐ Quality Management

☐ View selection only on request
☐ Create views selected

✔ Organizational levels | Data 🖹 🖹 🖫 Default values ✖

FIGURE 6.19 Selecting views when creating a material master record (© SAP AG)

After you choose ENTER, the SELECT VIEW(S) dialog box is displayed. As shown in Figure 6.19, select the PRODUCTION RESOURCES/TOOLS view, and choose ENTER. The ORGANIZATIONAL LEVELS dialog box is now displayed. In this dialog box, enter the plant to which the production resource/tool is assigned, and choose ENTER.

This calls up the PRODUCTION RESOURCES/TOOLS screen. Make all the required and optional entries here, as shown in Figure 6.20, and save the material master record via MATERIAL | SAVE.

Creating a PRT as an item of equipment: If you want to create a PRT as an item of equipment, you must create an equipment master record and maintain the production resources/tools view in it. To do so, choose LOGISTICS | PLANT MAINTENANCE | TECHNICAL OBJECTS, followed by EQUIPMENT | CREATE (SPECIAL) | PRODUCTION RESOURCES/TOOLS.

Alternatively, starting from the MAINTENANCE PROCESSING node, choose ENVIRONMENT | PRODUCTION RESOURCES/TOOLS, followed by PRODUCTION RESOURCES/TOOLS | EQUIPMENT | CREATE. Figure 6.21 shows the initial screen for creating a production resource/tool as an item of equipment.

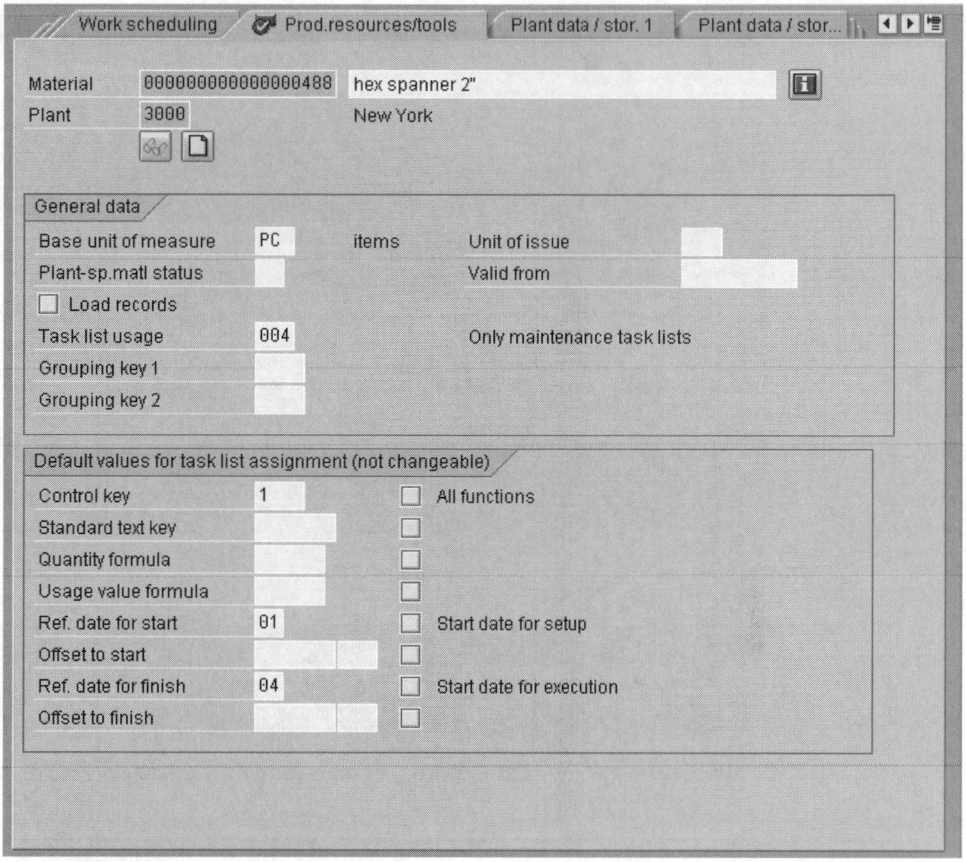

Work scheduling	Prod.resources/tools	Plant data / stor. 1	Plant data / stor...	◄ ►

Material 0000000000000000488 hex spanner 2"

Plant 3000 New York

General data

Base unit of measure	PC	items	Unit of issue	
Plant-sp.matl status			Valid from	
☐ Load records				
Task list usage	004		Only maintenance task lists	
Grouping key 1				
Grouping key 2				

Default values for task list assignment (not changeable)

Control key	1	☐	All functions
Standard text key		☐	
Quantity formula		☐	
Usage value formula		☐	
Ref. date for start	01	☐	Start date for setup
Offset to start		☐	
Ref. date for finish	04	☐	Start date for execution
Offset to finish		☐	

FIGURE 6.20   Production resources/tools view of the material master record (© SAP AG)

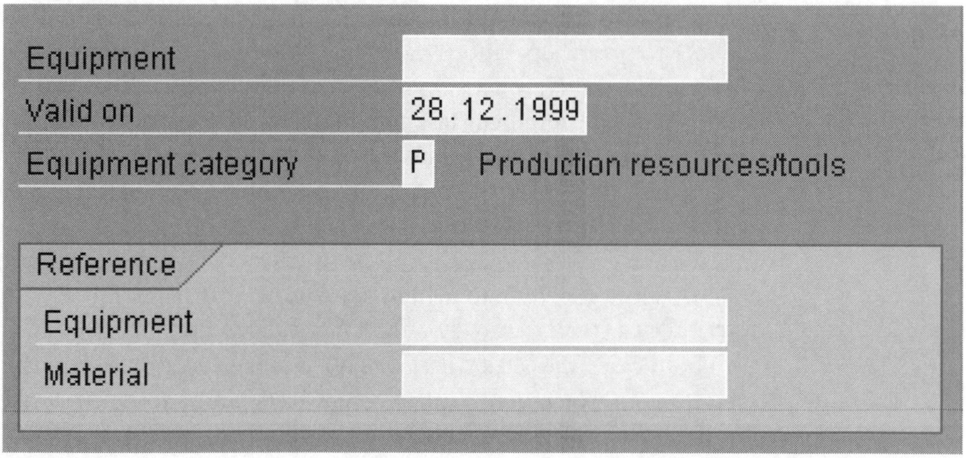

Equipment	
Valid on	28.12.1999
Equipment category	P Production resources/tools

Reference

Equipment	
Material	

FIGURE 6.21   Initial screen for creating a production resource/tool as an item of equipment (© SAP AG)

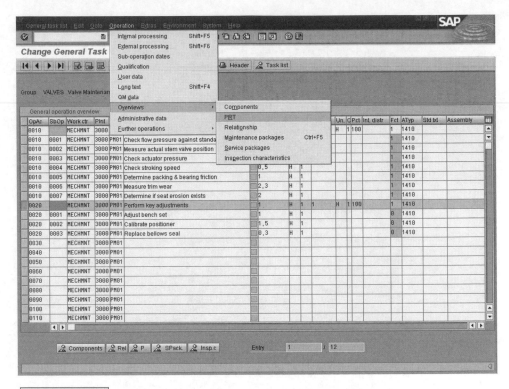

FIGURE 6.22   Assigning production resources/tools to operations (© SAP AG)

Enter all the necessary data in this and the other relevant screens, and then save the equipment master record via EQUIPMENT | SAVE.

Assigning production resources/tools to maintenance task lists: Production resources/tools are assigned to the operations in maintenance task lists. You can assign one PRT to several operations or several PRTs to one operation.

From the MAINTENANCE TASK LISTS node, choose either the CREATE or CHANGE function for an equipment task list, functional location task list, or a general maintenance task list. This calls up the initial screen for creating or changing a task list or a general task list. Enter the necessary data, and choose ENTER. If only one task list matches your entries, the OPERATION OVERVIEW screen is displayed. If several task lists match your entries, however, the TASK LIST OVERVIEW screen is displayed. In this screen, select the task to which you want to assign the PRT, and then choose GOTO | OPERATION OVERVIEW.

In both cases, the OPERATION OVERVIEW screen is displayed. In this screen, select the operations to which you want to assign PRTs, and choose OPERATION | OVERVIEWS | PRT, as shown in Figure 6.22.

If production resources/tools have not yet been assigned, the PRT NEW LINES dialog box is displayed. If PRTs have already been assigned, the PRT OVERVIEW screen is displayed. To assign further PRTs, choose EDIT | NEW LINES | MATERIAL or EQUIPMENT. This calls up the PRT NEW LINES dialog box. Enter the necessary data here. You specify the production resource/tool category you want to include via the MATERIAL, OTHERS, DOCUMENT and EQUIPMENT pushbuttons.

If you only want to assign one PRT, choose CONTINUE. This calls up the PRT OVERVIEW screen. If you want to assign several PRTs, choose INSERT. The PRT NEW LINES dialog box is displayed again. Enter the necessary data for the next PRT you want to assign.

IMPORTANT   You cannot assign PRTs that have been flagged for deletion.

When you have entered all the PRTs you want to assign, choose BACK. This takes you back to the PRT OVERVIEW screen, where all the PRTs you have assigned are displayed. Save the task list or the general maintenance task list.

TIP   If you want to delete an assigned production resource/tool from an operation, first select the operations from which you want to delete the assigned PRT in the OPERATION OVERVIEW screen for the maintenance task list. Selecting OPERATION | OVERVIEWS | PRT calls up the PRT OVERVIEW screen. This contains the PRTs assigned to the first operation you selected.

Select the production resources/tools that you no longer want assigned to the operation, and choose EDIT | DELETE.

The system deletes the selected PRTs, and the next operation you selected is displayed. Delete the PRTs for all the selected operations, and save your changes.

You specify PRT control keys via the Customizing path PLANT MAINTENANCE AND CUSTOMER SERVICE | MAINTENANCE PLANS, WORK CENTRES, TASK LISTS AND PRTS | PRODUCTION RESOURCES/TOOLS | PRODUCTION RESOURCE/TOOL ASSIGNMENTS | DEFINE PRT CONTROL KEYS. When scheduling, costing, production order printing and confirmation are carried out, this key is responsible for including an assignment of production resources/tools in a plan or order.

How to carry out a cost analysis

The Plant Maintenance (PM) component allows you to carry out a cost analysis for maintenance task lists, which shows you the costs incurred by specific operations, and thus enables you to control costs without generating a maintenance order.

The cost analysis can apply either to entire maintenance task lists or to individual operations. All the material costs, as well as all the costs for external and internal processing, are included in the calculation.

How the costs are calculated depends on the costing variants (for example, with or without overheads) that are assigned to the order type, and which form the basis for the cost analysis.

IMPORTANT The program for cost analysis can only be run for one maintenance task list type; if you want to determine the costs for equipment task lists and task lists for functional locations, for example, you must run the program once for the equipment task lists and a second time for the functional location task lists.

As part of cost analysis, you can request a log, which checks the completeness and consistency of all master data relevant to costing. The system checks, for example, whether all the activity types and the valuation segments of the assigned materials are maintained. If data is missing or inconsistent, the system outputs corresponding messages in the cost analysis log. This inconsistency check is useful, since it ensures that the task list is correct before it is included in the order. When maintenance orders are generated, this check prevents problems arising as a result of missing data.

Choose LOGISTICS | PLANT MAINTENANCE | PLANNED MAINTENANCE | MAINTENANCE TASKS LISTS, followed by EVALUATIONS | TASK LIST COSTING. This calls up the TASK LIST COSTING screen shown in Figure 6.23.

Select the task list type for which you want to carry out the cost analysis, and then

Task list type		
○ Funct. loc. task list	○ Equip.task list	● Gen.task list

Task list selection

Functional location		to	
Equipment		to	
Group		to	
Group counter		to	
Key date	07.03.2000		
Class selection	Functnl loc.		Equipment

Costing parameters

Order type	PM01
Business area	0001
☐ Log creation	

FIGURE 6.23 Initial screen for task list costing (© SAP AG)

choose PROGRAM | EXECUTE to call up the OPERATION SELECTION dialog box. Select all the operations you want to include in the cost analysis. Then choose TRANSFER SELECTION. If you want to cost all the operations displayed, choose TRANSFER ALL without selecting individual operations.

TIP During the cost calculation, the system outputs messages containing information on maintenance orders. These messages are not relevant to task list costing. They are only output because the system has to simulate an order in the background to carry out task list costing.

The system creates a list of all the maintenance task lists and operations that meet your selection criteria, and displays the costing result as shown in Figure 6.24.

The display here depends on the underlying cost report. If you want to change the display, choose one via GOTO | OTHER REPORT. The reports available for selection depend on the settings carried out in the CO component.

6.2.3 Maintenance planning

The maintenance planning process

One of the most important tasks of plant maintenance is to maximize the availability of objects. Preventive maintenance is the most suitable strategy for preventing systems or other technical objects from breaking down. This approach helps to save not only

Material	0
Plant	3000 New York
Costing variant	PM01 Maintenance order
Costing version	
Costing date from	07.05.2000
Costing date to	07.05.2000
Lot size	0,000
Cost base	0,000

	Resource	Cost eleme	Quantity	Un		Total		Fixed	Cur...	Resource (text)
E	4300 MECHMNT 1410		0,200	H		0,00		0,00	USD	Perform key measurements
M	3000 M-1001		1	PC		0,00		0,00	USD	Motor, electrical pump 250kW
E	4300 MECHMNT 1410		0,300	H		0,00		0,00	USD	Check flow pressure against standard
E	4300 MECHMNT 1410		1	H		0,00		0,00	USD	Measure actual stem valve position
E	4300 MECHMNT 1410		0,500	H		0,00		0,00	USD	Check actuator pressure
E	4300 MECHMNT 1410		0,500	H		0,00		0,00	USD	Check stroking speed
E	4300 MECHMNT 1410		1	H		0,00		0,00	USD	Determine packing & bearing friction
E	4300 MECHMNT 1410		2,300	H		0,00		0,00	USD	Measure trim wear
E	4300 MECHMNT 1410		2	H		0,00		0,00	USD	Determine if seat erosion exists
E	4300 MECHMNT 1410		1	H		0,00		0,00	USD	Perform key adjustments
M	3000 DG-1000		1	PC		0,00		0,00	USD	Rubber Seal
M	3000 MR-1000		1	PC		0,00		0,00	USD	rotor for engine 250 kW
M	3000 400-431	400000	2	PC		2,92		0,00	USD	Washer
E	4300 MECHMNT 1410		1	H		0,00		0,00	USD	Adjust bench set
E	4300 MECHMNT 1410		1,500	H		0,00		0,00	USD	Calibrate positioner
E	4300 MECHMNT 1410		0,300	H		0,00		0,00	USD	Replace bellows seal
					▪	2,92	▪	0,00	USD	

FIGURE 6.24   Costing result (© SAP AG)

the repair costs associated with breakdowns of this type, but also the follow-up costs incurred due to the resulting production breakdowns, which are often considerably higher.

As explained in Chapter 2, 'Classifying plant maintenance from a business perspective', 'preventive maintenance' is the generic term for inspections, maintenance and repairs, which can be planned in advance as regards dates and scope. Attention must be paid here not only to company-internal aspects of preventive maintenance, but also to external factors. The growing number of legal stipulations requires a greater degree of planned monitoring and maintenance for objects. Examples of external requirements include:

■ *Manufacturers' recommendations*

Procedures or instructions from the manufacturers of technical objects, which are intended to ensure that the operating facilities function optimally.

■ *Legal regulations*

Laws to ensure the safety of objects or relating to industrial safety, which stipulate that systems must be regularly maintained.

■ *Environmental protection requirements*

Preventive maintenance is an effective means of preventing breakdowns that could result in increased environmental pollution.

The demand for quality assurance is another reason for carrying out preventive maintenance, since the condition of a production line can, in certain cases, have a considerable influence on the quality of the products manufactured on it. In addition to this, regularly maintaining objects often saves costs, since it avoids the far greater expense of a breakdown. The data required for this purpose is provided by the system in the form of historical data.

Maintenance planning can be used to specify the scope and dates of plannable maintenance and inspection activities for technical objects. This ensures that technical objects are maintained on time, and function optimally.

When scheduling is carried out, the system generates maintenance call objects. The following provides an overview of the maintenance call objects available in the system:

■ For rough-cut planning of tasks: maintenance notification

■ For detailed planning of tasks: maintenance order

■ For detailed planning of tasks and history for the damage processed in the notification: notification and order

■ For quality management via integration of inspection characteristics: inspection lots

■ For service procurement in purchasing: service entry sheets

One of the most important benefits offered by the Plant Maintenance component is that it enables you to carry out maintenance at various levels. Maintenance plans – and, thus, the maintenance call objects described above – can be created at the following levels:

- Equipment level
- Level of the functional locations
- Material level
- Level of the material/serial numbers
- Assembly level

This enables you to plan and perform maintenance tasks for the following objects:

- Individual items of equipment that are independent of each other (for example, vehicles)
- Functional locations comprising several items of equipment (for example, production lines)
- Assemblies of an item of equipment (for example, pump motors)
- Materials
- Material numbers and serial numbers

Process flow in maintenance planning

1 You create a maintenance plan. A maintenance plan always automatically contains at least one maintenance item.

2 You create the maintenance cycles. With strategy plans, these are the maintenance cycles from the assigned maintenance strategy.

3 You assign other technical objects to the maintenance item, if necessary.

4 You assign a maintenance task list to the maintenance item, if necessary.

5 You assign additional maintenance items to the maintenance plan, if necessary.

6 You maintain the scheduling parameters.

7 You save the maintenance plan.

8 You schedule the maintenance plan, thereby generating maintenance calls. When maintenance is due, these calls are used by the system to generate maintenance call objects (for example, maintenance orders, notifications, or service entry sheets).

Integrative aspects of maintenance planning

Maintenance planning is integrated with the following components and subcomponents of the R/3 System:

- *Plant Maintenance (PM)*
  - Maintenance task lists
  - Maintenance orders
  - Maintenance notifications

- *Customer Service (CS)*
  - Service orders
  - Service notifications

- *Materials Management (MM)*
  - Service procurement
  - Service entry sheets

- *Quality Management (QM)*
  - Inspection characteristics
  - Inspection lots

- *Sales and Distribution (SD)*
  - Outline agreements

For a more detailed discussion of the integrative aspects of the PM component, see Chapter 8.

Maintenance plans: basics

A maintenance plan is a description of the maintenance and inspection tasks to be performed on maintenance objects, which includes the dates and scope. Various types of maintenance plan are distinguished in maintenance planning. The maintenance plan that you use depends on the type of maintenance planning you want to implement:

- *Single cycle plan or strategy plan* (time/performance-based)

  If you want to carry out time-based or performance-based (counter-based) maintenance planning, you can work with either single cycle plans or strategy plans.

- *Multiple counter plan*

  Use multiple counter plans if you want to combine maintenance cycles with different dimensions.

- *Maintenance plan for service procurement in purchasing*

  If you want to use maintenance plans to process services performed regularly, a maintenance plan for service procurement in purchasing is available in the system.

TIP   When you create a maintenance plan, you must specify a maintenance plan category. This category determines, among other things, the maintenance call object (for example, a maintenance order, service entry sheet, or notification) generated by the system when a maintenance call is due.

All maintenance plans comprise the following elements:

■ *Maintenance item(s)*

A maintenance item describes the preventive maintenance tasks to be performed at regular intervals on a technical object or group of technical objects.

A maintenance plan is always automatically assigned at least one maintenance item. Other maintenance items can be created directly in the maintenance plan, and unassigned maintenance objects can also be assigned. Maintenance plans for service procurement and maintenance plans with reference to an outline agreement contain only one maintenance item. The tasks required for the 'maintenance order' call object can be described by a maintenance task list, which is subsequently assigned to the maintenance item.

■ *Maintenance plan*

The maintenance plan contains scheduling information from the following sources:

– The maintenance cycle (with single cycle plans)
– The maintenance cycles (with multiple counter plans)
– The maintenance strategy assigned to the maintenance plan (with strategy plans)
– The scheduling parameters that apply specifically to this maintenance plan

If a maintenance plan is scheduled, this information is used to calculate the due dates for the maintenance operations to be carried out on the assigned technical objects.

Maintenance plan types

■ *Time-based maintenance plans*

With time-based maintenance planning, maintenance is carried out in specific cycles (for example, every two weeks or every six months). Single cycle plans are suitable for mapping simple maintenance cycles. To map complex maintenance cycles, it is more expedient to create a strategy plan on the basis of a time-based maintenance strategy.

To enable a time-based maintenance plan to be scheduled, the plan must contain the following elements:

– Scheduling data
– Scheduling parameters

        – Maintenance cycle (single cycle and multiple counter plans)
        – Maintenance strategy with maintenance packages (strategy plans)
        – Maintenance item(s)

■ *Performance-based maintenance plans*

Performance-based maintenance plans enable you to plan regular maintenance on the basis of counter readings, which are maintained for specific measuring points on equipment or at functional locations. Single cycle plans are suitable for mapping simple maintenance cycles. To map complex maintenance cycles, it is more expedient to create a strategy plan on the basis of a performance-based maintenance strategy.

EXAMPLE A counter is assigned to the maintenance plan. Maintenance work is carried out when the counter of the technical object reaches a certain value (for example, 1000 operating hours, or 500,000 revolutions). The planned date calculated for maintenance depends on the counter reading when planning was carried out, as well as the estimated annual performance specified for the counter.

Section 4.5, 'Measuring points and counters', describes the characteristics of measuring points, how to create them, as well as how to link them to technical objects.

How to create and process single cycle plans

The basic characteristics of single cycle plans have already been discussed at the beginning of section 6.2.2, under 'Maintenance plans: basics'.

To create a single cycle plan, choose LOGISTICS | PLANT MAINTENANCE | MAINTENANCE PLANNING | MAINTENANCE PLANS | CREATE | SINGLE CYCLE PLAN. This calls up the screen for creating a maintenance plan. Enter a maintenance plan type and choose ENTER. The system then displays the single cycle plan shown in Figure 6.25.

Enter the required data. If you specify an activity unit for the cycle, the system automatically defaults the first counter that matches the reference object.

In the SCHEDULING PARAMETERS tab page, maintain the scheduling parameters (such as the shift and cycle modification factors for the maintenance plan), if necessary. Figure 6.26 shows this tab page.

The shift factors in the DATE DETERMINATION group specify the percentage of the shift to be applied to the calculation of the next date if a maintenance task is confirmed too late or too early. The shift factors are only used if the variance between the target and actual date is outside the tolerance range. The tolerance for earlier and later confirmations defines the timeframe in which positive variances between the actual and planned date do not influence subsequent scheduling. The tolerance is defined as the

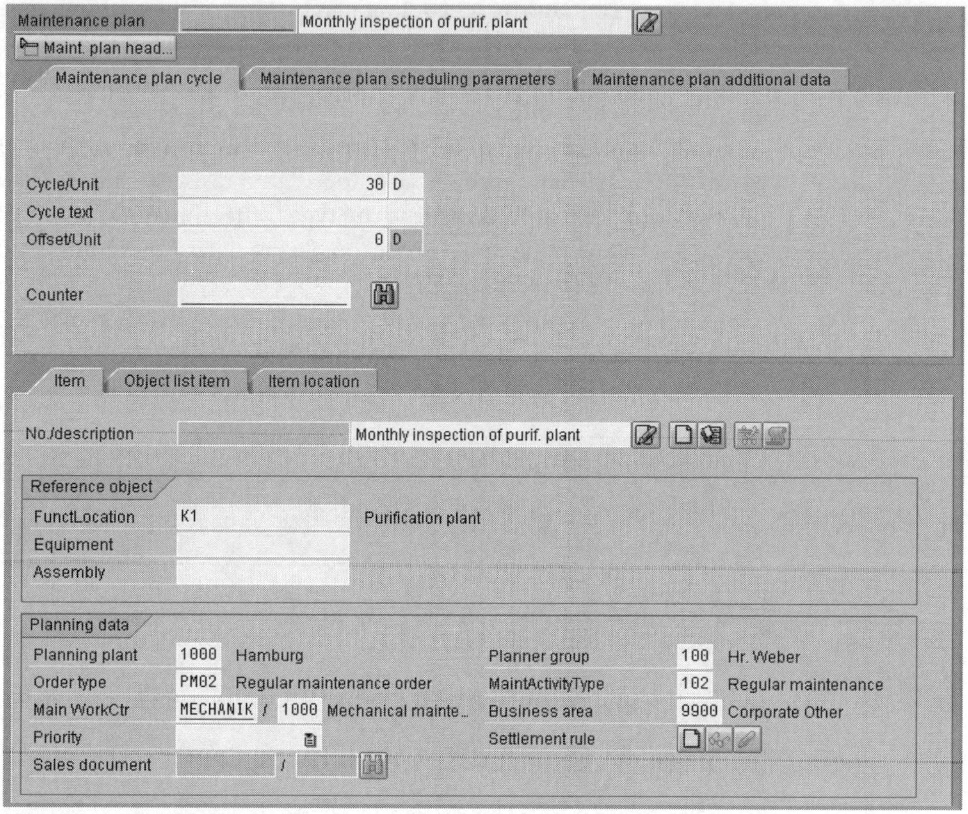

FIGURE 6.25 Creating a single cycle plan (© SAP AG)

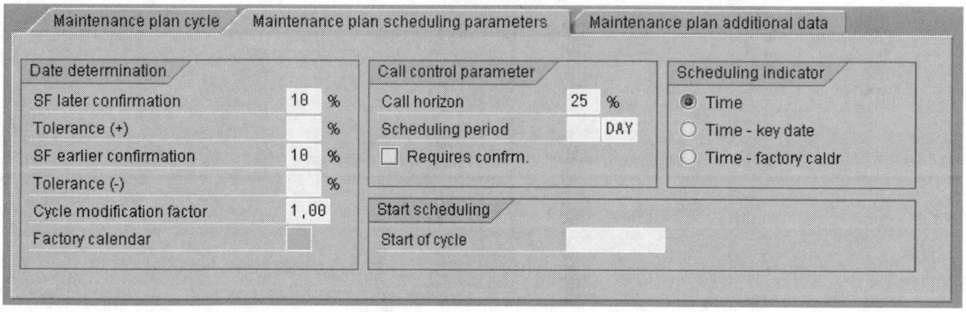

FIGURE 6.26 Scheduling parameters (© SAP AG)

smallest interval between the maintenance cycles of the maintenance strategy. For a detailed discussion of scheduling parameters, refer to 'How to schedule maintenance plans' earlier in this section.

You can maintain the scheduling parameters for the maintenance plan only if you have entered a unit for the cycle. This unit enables the system to detect whether the single cycle plan in question is performance-based or time-based, and to provide the appropriate scheduling parameters.

Enter the data required for the maintenance item, and assign an existing task list to the maintenance item, if necessary. To assign a task list, choose the SELECT TASK LIST pushbutton. To create a task list of the type 'general maintenance task list', choose the CREATE GENERAL TASK LIST pushbutton. Figure 6.27 shows the TASK LIST group, which is located in the ITEM tab page.

If necessary, assign other technical objects to the maintenance item via the OBJECT LIST ITEM tab page, as shown in Figure 6.28.

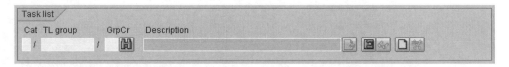

FIGURE 6.27   Selecting and creating a task list (© SAP AG)

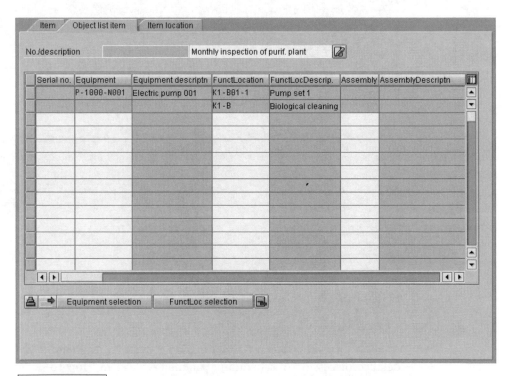

FIGURE 6.28   Assigning objects to a maintenance item (© SAP AG)

If you want to create other maintenance items, choose CREATE OTHER MAINTITEMS, as shown in Figure 6.29. Enter the required data, or use ASSIGN OTHER MAINTITEMS to select an unassigned maintenance item. If necessary, assign the maintenance items to a task list as well as to other technical objects, and then save the maintenance plan.

How to create time-based strategy plans

To create a time-based strategy plan, choose LOGISTICS | PLANT MAINTENANCE | MAINTENANCE PLANS | CREATE | STRATEGY PLAN. This calls up the screen for creating a maintenance plan. Enter the maintenance plan category and a

FIGURE 6.29   Creating and assigning other maintenance items (© SAP AG)

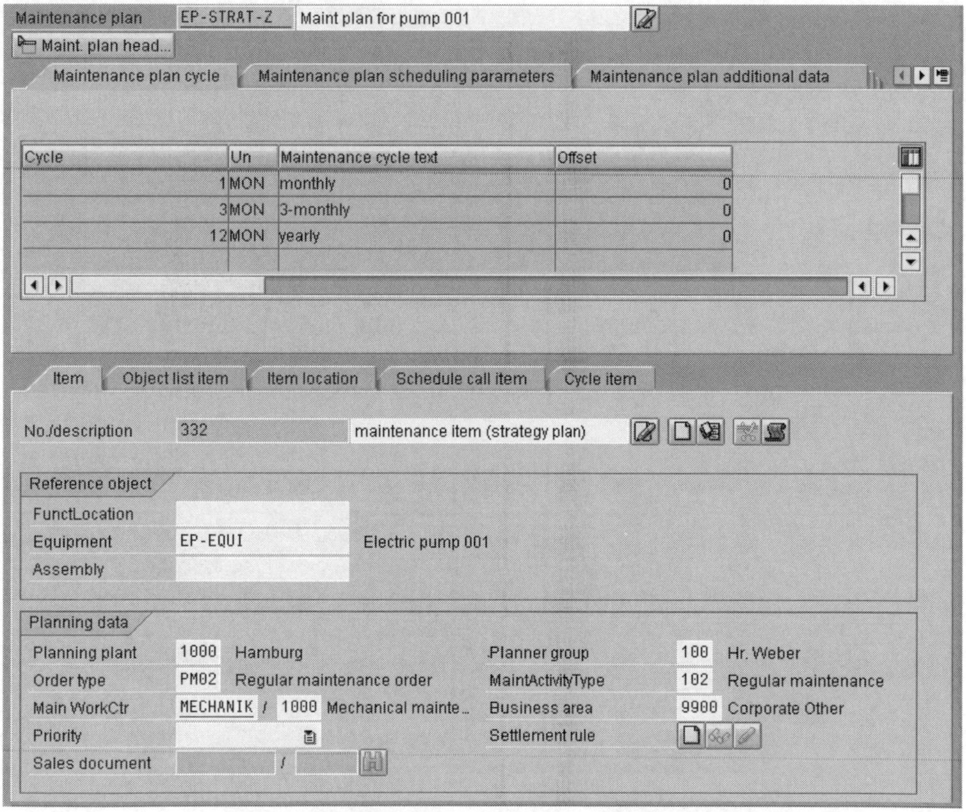

FIGURE 6.30   Creating a time-based strategy plan (© SAP AG)

time-based maintenance strategy, and then choose ENTER. The system then displays the strategy plan shown in Figure 6.30.

Enter the required data for the maintenance plan header and item, and assign the maintenance item to a task list, as described earlier in this section under 'How to create and process single cycle plans'.

After a task list has been assigned, the system displays the following data:

- On the ITEM tab page, the assigned task list, as shown in Figure 6.31
- On the CYCLE ITEM tab page, the maintenance packages from the strategy assigned to the operations in the task list, as shown in Figure 6.32

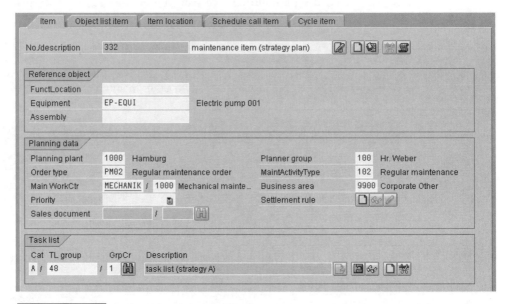

FIGURE 6.31   Assigned task list in the TASK LIST group of the ITEM tab page (© SAP AG)

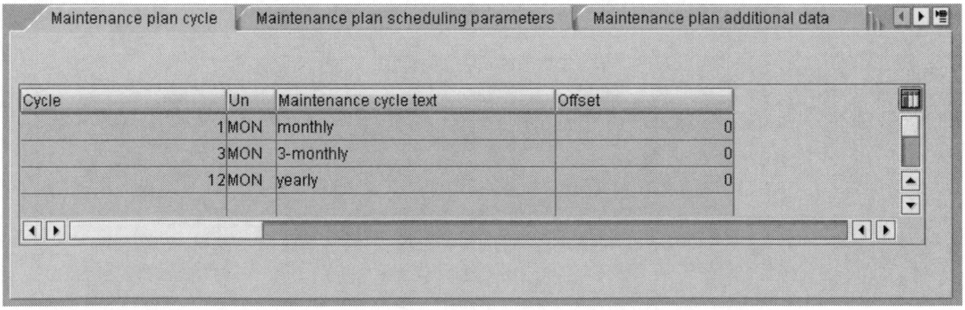

FIGURE 6.32   Overview of the maintenance packages in the MAINTENANCE PLAN CYCLE tab page (© SAP AG)

If necessary, assign the maintenance item other technical objects via the OBJECT LIST ITEM tab page, as described in section 'How to create and process single cycle plans', and shown in Figure 6.28. If you want to create other maintenance items, choose the CREATE OTHER MAINTITEMS pushbutton. Enter the necessary data, or use the ASSIGN OTHER MAINTITEMS pushbutton to select an unassigned maintenance item. If necessary, assign a task list as well as other technical objects to the maintenance items, and then save the maintenance plan.

How to create performance-based strategy plans

To create a performance-based strategy plan, choose LOGISTICS | PLANT MAINTENANCE | MAINTENANCE PLANNING | MAINTENANCE PLANS | CREATE | STRATEGY PLAN. This calls up the screen for creating a maintenance plan. Enter the maintenance plan category and a performance-based maintenance strategy, and then choose ENTER. Note that the strategy you have chosen must have the PERFORMANCE SCHEDULING indicator and contain a dimension other than TIME.

If counters have already been created for the reference object (for example, an item of equipment or functional location) you have specified in the maintenance item, the COUNTER SELECTION dialog box is displayed. Select the counter with the reading you want to use as the basis for scheduling, and choose CONTINUE. Figure 6.33 shows the

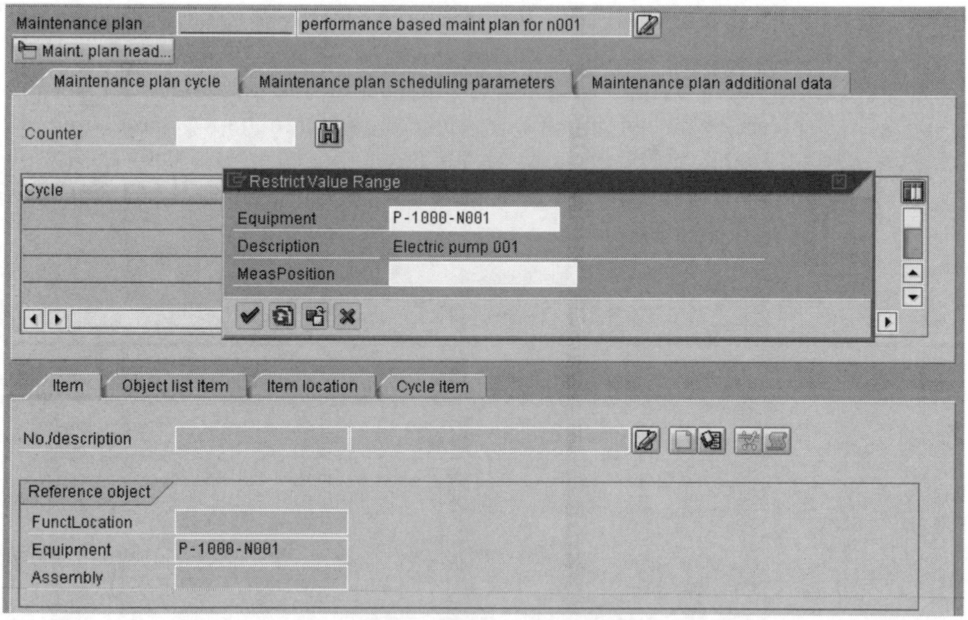

FIGURE 6.33   Detailed information on the counter copied from the reference object
(© SAP AG)

counter copied from the reference object in the maintenance plan, as well as the related information, which you call up by choosing the COUNTER INFO pushbutton.

IMPORTANT The counter unit must have the same dimension as the selected maintenance strategy.

How to create multiple counter plans

To create a multiple counter plan, choose LOGISTICS | PLANT MAINTENANCE | PLANNED MAINTENANCE | MAINTENANCE PLANS | CREATE | MULTIPLE COUNTER PLAN. This calls up the screen for creating a maintenance plan. Enter the maintenance plan category and a cycle set (if you want to create the maintenance plan using a reference for maintenance cycles).

Enter the required data for the maintenance plan header, and create new maintenance cycles in the MAINTENANCE PLAN CYCLE tab page shown in Figure 6.34. If you have used a reference to create the multiple counter plan, you can change or delete existing cycles here.

The subsequent steps in this procedure are the same as for generating time-based and performance-based strategy plans.

How to create and assign maintenance items

A maintenance item describes the preventive maintenance tasks to be performed at regular intervals on a technical object or group of technical objects. The reference objects (such as equipment, functional locations, or assemblies) on which maintenance tasks are to be carried out are assigned to a maintenance item. One or more maintenance items can be assigned to a maintenance plan. All maintenance plans automatically include at least one maintenance item.

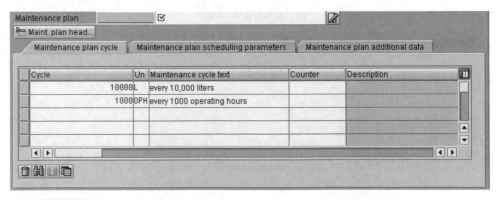

FIGURE 6.34 Assignment of several counters to a maintenance plan in the Maintenance Plan Cycle tab page (© SAP AG)

The system allows you to assign maintenance items to a maintenance plan in the following ways:

- Create a maintenance plan and create a maintenance item directly in the maintenance plan by entering the required data in the ITEM tab page
- Create additional maintenance items in a maintenance plan
- Create a maintenance item without an initial assignment and assign it subsequently to a maintenance plan

IMPORTANT The following constraints apply if you assign a maintenance item to a maintenance plan:

- A maintenance item can be assigned to only one maintenance plan.
- With assignment to a single cycle or multiple counter plan, the maintenance item must have been created without reference to a maintenance strategy.
- With assignment to a strategy plan, the maintenance item must have the same maintenance strategy as the maintenance plan.
- With assignment to a maintenance plan, the maintenance item must have the same maintenance plan category as the maintenance plan.

Maintenance items with a reference object (object-specific maintenance items) can be created for the following reference objects:

- Function locations
- Equipment
- Assemblies of an item of equipment
- Materials
- Material numbers and serial numbers

Maintenance items without a reference object: You can also create maintenance items that do not refer to a technical object (object-independent maintenance items). The location and account-assignment data for maintenance objects of this type can be maintained separately. This enables you to define preventive maintenance tasks that have to be carried out regularly, without specifying the reference object. This is particularly useful for smaller maintenance tasks, such as cleaning work.

Creating maintenance items without assignment: To call up the initial screen for creating a maintenance item, choose LOGISTICS | PLANT MAINTENANCE | PLANNED MAINTENANCE | MAINTENANCE PLANNING | MAINTENANCE PLANS | MAINTENANCE ITEMS | CREATE. Figure 6.35 shows the corresponding initial screen.

Enter a maintenance plan category and, if necessary, a maintenance strategy. If you want to assign the maintenance item to a time-based or performance-based maintenance

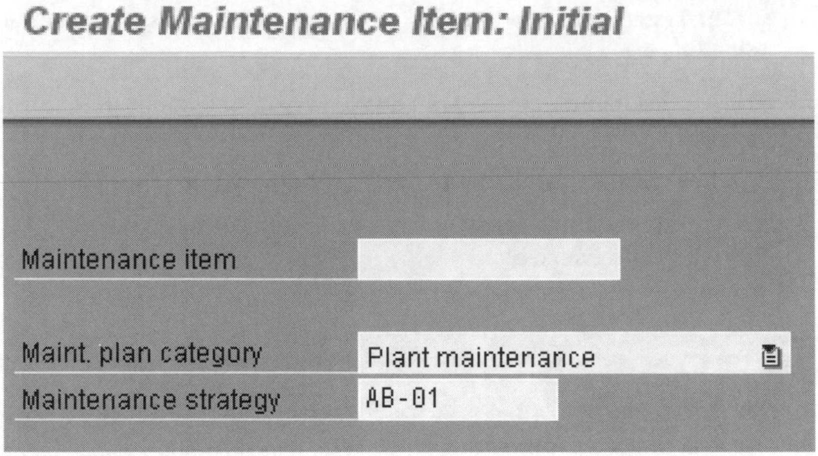

Create Maintenance Item: Initial

Maintenance item

Maint. plan category   Plant maintenance

Maintenance strategy   AB-01

FIGURE 6.35   Creating a maintenance item: initial screen (© SAP AG)

plan, you must specify a corresponding maintenance strategy. If you do not enter a strategy, the maintenance item can only be assigned to a single cycle or multiple counter plan. Choose ENTER, and enter the required data in the screen shown in Figure 6.36.

If necessary, assign other technical objects to the maintenance item via the OBJECT LIST ITEM tab page:

TIP   As shown in Figure 6.36, enter an appropriate text for the maintenance item so that you will recognize it more easily when you assign it to the maintenance plan.

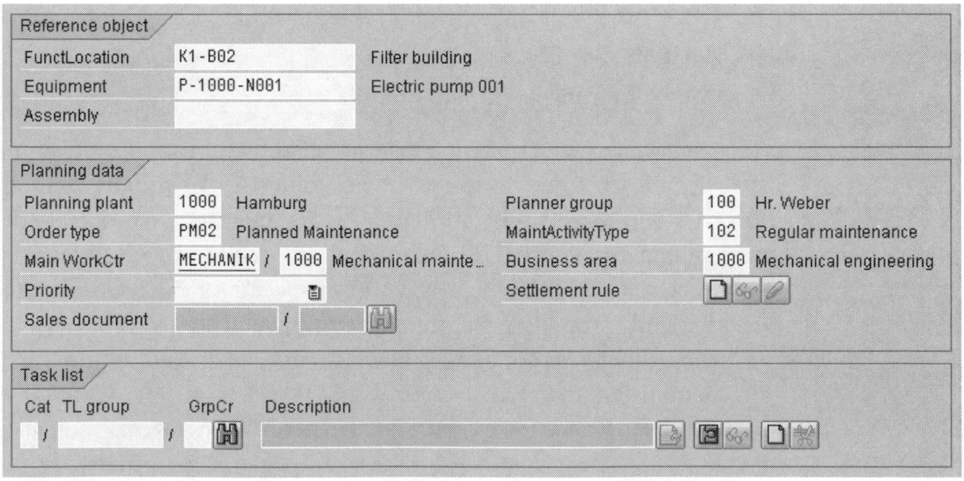

Reference object
FunctLocation	K1-B02	Filter building
Equipment	P-1000-N001	Electric pump 001
Assembly		

Planning data
Planning plant	1000 Hamburg	Planner group	100	Hr. Weber
Order type	PM02 Planned Maintenance	MaintActivityType	102	Regular maintenance
Main WorkCtr	MECHANIK / 1000 Mechanical mainte...	Business area	1000	Mechanical engineering
Priority		Settlement rule		
Sales document	/			

Task list
Cat	TL group	GrpCr	Description
/		/	

FIGURE 6.36   Creating a maintenance item (ITEM tab page) (© SAP AG)

■ To assign an existing task list, choose the SELECT TASK LIST pushbutton.

■ To create a general maintenance task list, choose the CREATE GENERAL TASK LIST pushbutton. If you have created a maintenance item with a strategy, assign maintenance packages to the operations in the task list.

After you have assigned a task list, it is displayed by the system in the ITEM tab page. Save the maintenance item.

Assigning a maintenance item to a maintenance plan: As a rule, you create maintenance items directly in the maintenance plan. It is also possible, however, to assign an unassigned maintenance item to the maintenance plan.

From the create or change mode for the maintenance plan, choose the ASSIGN OTHER MAINTITEMS pushbutton. The system then displays the selection screen shown in Figure 6.37.

Maintenance item selection			
Maint. plan cat.	PM	to	
Maintenance plan		to	
Maintenance item		to	
Maintenance strategy		to	
Description		to	
Functional location		to	
Equipment		to	
Assembly		to	
Material		to	
Serial number		to	
☐ Maintenance plan active			
Settlement rule	◉ with or without	○ with	○ without
MaintPlan assignment	○ with or without	○ with	◉ without
☐ With object list			

FIGURE 6.37 Selecting an unassigned maintenance item: initial screen (© SAP AG)

After you enter the selection criteria, the screen for choosing unassigned maintenance items is displayed (see Figure 6.38). In this screen, select the desired maintenance item.

The procedure for assigning a task list or other technical objects to a maintenance item is described above, under 'Creating maintenance items without assignment'.

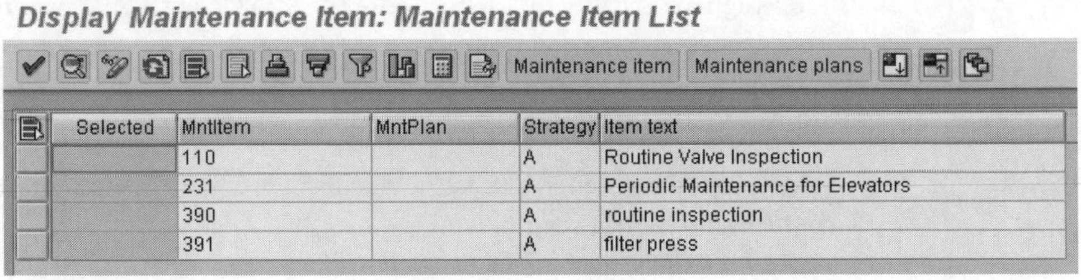

Display Maintenance Item: Maintenance Item List

	Selected	MntItem	MntPlan	Strategy	Item text
		110		A	Routine Valve Inspection
		231		A	Periodic Maintenance for Elevators
		390		A	routine inspection
		391		A	filter press

FIGURE 6.38 Selecting an unassigned maintenance item: selection screen (© SAP AG)

How to create and process maintenance strategies

A maintenance strategy generally specifies the rules for the sequence of planned maintenance tasks. Since maintenance strategies contain general scheduling information, they can be assigned to as many maintenance task lists and maintenance plans as required. A maintenance strategy contains maintenance packages, which specify, among other things, the cycle in which the individual tasks should be carried out.

TIP As of Release 4.0A, maintenance strategies are optional. If you only want to carry out simple preventive maintenance, for which it is sufficient to specify a maintenance cycle, it is expedient to work with single cycle plans. By contrast, strategy plans are used to map more complex maintenance cycles.

The overview in Table 6.1 shows the maintenance plan types that require a maintenance strategy.

TABLE 6.1 Maintenance plan types and maintenance strategies

Maintenance plan type	Maintenance strategy required?
Time-based single cycle plan	No
Performance-based single cycle plan	No
Time-based strategy plan	Yes
Performance-based strategy plan	Yes
Multiple counter plan	No

If you want to use time-based or performance-based strategy plans in your company, you first have to specify

- where regular maintenance is required (mapped as maintenance items in the system)
- in which performance or time intervals the maintenance tasks should be carried out (mapped as maintenance packages)

TIP   You should compare the legal requirements, manufacturer's recommendations, and the costs of preventive maintenance with the costs that would be incurred as a result of a breakdown. One of your first steps should be to consider how the tasks can be grouped together in a maintenance plan so that scheduling and maintenance work are integrated efficiently.

As soon as you have specified the optimal cycles for preventive maintenance, you can define a suitable maintenance strategy. The PM component provides you with the option of creating strategies that map the scheduling rules for all the required preventive maintenance tasks. Since these strategies contain general scheduling information, you can assign them to any number of maintenance plans.

Using maintenance strategies with general scheduling information provides you with the following options and advantages:

▪ The time required to create maintenance plans is reduced: it is not necessary to enter the same information for each maintenance plan.

▪ Scheduling information is updated: maintenance packages are referenced; changes made to maintenance strategies also apply to the assigned maintenance plans; the scheduling parameters, however, are copied to the relevant maintenance plan.

Structure of a maintenance strategy: A maintenance strategy comprises the following elements:

▪ Strategy header

Name of the strategy and short text.

▪ Scheduling parameters

Data that is used to influence the scheduling of maintenance plans for the maintenance strategy. When a strategy plan is created, this data is copied to the strategy plan, where it can be changed.

▪ Scheduling indicators

These indicators are used in a maintenance strategy to specify the required type of scheduling or define a cycle set: time-based scheduling (for example, every 30 days), time-based scheduling with key date (for example, on the fifth of every month), time-based scheduling according to factory calendar (for example, every 10 working days), and performance-based scheduling (for example, every 50,000 operating hours).

▪ Maintenance packages

These are groups of maintenance tasks that have to be carried out on a particular date or at a specific point in time. Maintenance packages contain the cycle duration and measurement unit, for example.

You can assign a strategy several packages, which you want carried out at different intervals. All the packages must have the same dimensions (for example 'time', 'weight', or 'length'). For the purposes of conversion, the packages or maintenance cycles in a strategy share the same unit. This unit corresponds to a particular dimension (for example, the dimension of 'time', 'weight', or 'length').

EXAMPLE Although the packages in a strategy may have different cycle units, they all have the same dimension. For example, a strategy comprises three packages: every two weeks, every four months, and annually. In this case, the 'time' dimension has the cycle units 'week', 'month' and 'year'.

Integrative aspects: In connection with strategy plans, you can, if necessary, assign a maintenance task list to a maintenance item, the operations of which describe the maintenance tasks to be carried out. The same strategy must be specified in the task list and the strategy plan.

This enables you to assign the maintenance packages of the assigned maintenance strategy to the individual operations in the task list. Assigning maintenance packages to operations enables you to define the frequency with which you want the operations to be carried out.

IMPORTANT If you work with hierarchies for packages, and want several packages to be due on the same date, please note that the system does not treat one year as being equal to 12 months: one year equals 365 days, while 12 months are equal to $12 \times 30 = 360$ days.

Creating a maintenance strategy: To call up the overview screen for changing maintenance strategies, choose LOGISTICS | PLANT MAINTENANCE | PLANNED MAINTENANCE | MAINTENANCE PLANNING | MAINTENANCE STRATEGIES | CHANGE.

Choose NEW ENTRIES. This calls up the detail screen for maintenance strategies, as shown in Figure 6.40.

Enter the required data. The necessary scheduling parameters will be discussed in the following section, 'How to schedule maintenance plans'.

Call up the entry screen for maintenance packages by choosing PACKAGES in the tree structure, as shown in Figure 6.41. Next, choose NEW ENTRIES, enter the required data (such as scheduling indicator, cycle duration and cycle hierarchy), and then save the maintenance strategy.

To return to the overview screen, choose MAINTENANCE STRATEGIES in the tree structure.

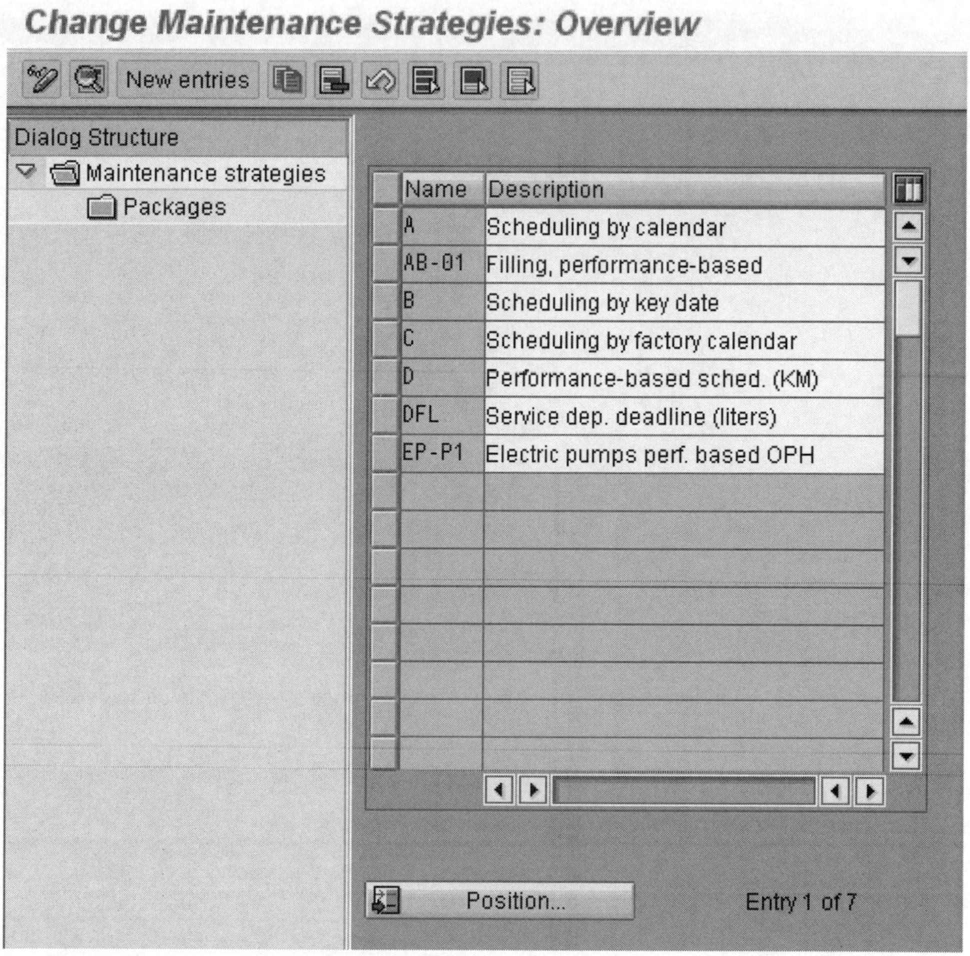

Change Maintenance Strategies: Overview

Name	Description
A	Scheduling by calendar
AB-01	Filling, performance-based
B	Scheduling by key date
C	Scheduling by factory calendar
D	Performance-based sched. (KM)
DFL	Service dep. deadline (liters)
EP-P1	Electric pumps perf. based OPH

Dialog Structure
▽ Maintenance strategies
　　 Packages

Position...　　　Entry 1 of 7

FIGURE 6.39　Selection for creating and changing a maintenance strategy (© SAP AG)

How to schedule maintenance plans

Maintenance plans are scheduled to enable the system to generate maintenance call objects at defined cycles (for example, maintenance contracts). If you are scheduling a maintenance plan for the first time, the start date or start counter reading you specify triggers the maintenance cycle on the time axis.

IMPORTANT If you have entered the start date or the start counter reading in the scheduling parameters, automatic deadline monitoring can be started directly for the maintenance plan. If you do not specify this data, you must start scheduling for the maintenance plan explicitly before you can start automatic deadline monitoring.

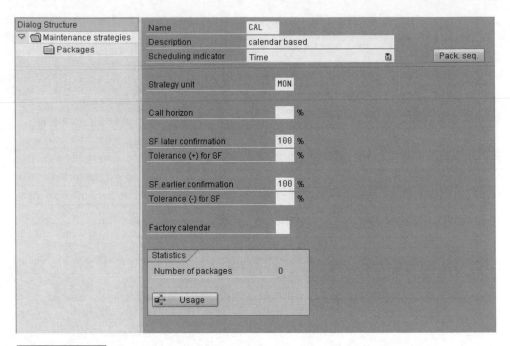

FIGURE 6.40   Creating a maintenance strategy: detail screen (© SAP AG)

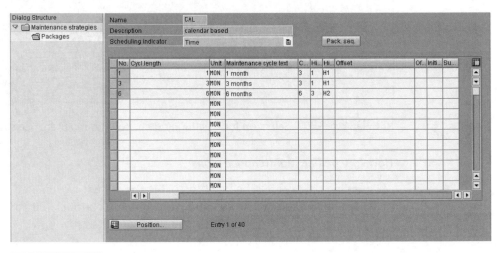

FIGURE 6.41   Creating a maintenance package (© SAP AG)

Every time you carry out scheduling, the system uses the scheduling parameters and maintenance cycles/packages to calculate the due date for the maintenance call object, and generates maintenance calls. It also ensures that at least one maintenance call with WAITING status exists.

When the maintenance call is due, the system generates a maintenance call object for every maintenance item that is due. The call object generated by the system when a maintenance call is due is determined by the maintenance plan category.

Automatic deadline monitoring: This function can be used to simplify generating maintenance call objects for maintenance plans. Start the deadline monitoring function at regular intervals via a report that you program yourself (for example, weekly with a weekly maintenance cycle). The system then generates the maintenance call objects in accordance with the defined cycles. To enable this function to be used, a start date or a start counter reading must have been entered in the scheduling parameters of the maintenance plan, or the maintenance plan must have already been scheduled.

When you run deadline monitoring, all maintenance calls with dates that have been reached with respect to the call horizon are converted to maintenance call objects by the system. The system also completely reschedules the maintenance plan, ensuring that maintenance calls always exist for the period of time you have defined as the scheduling period.

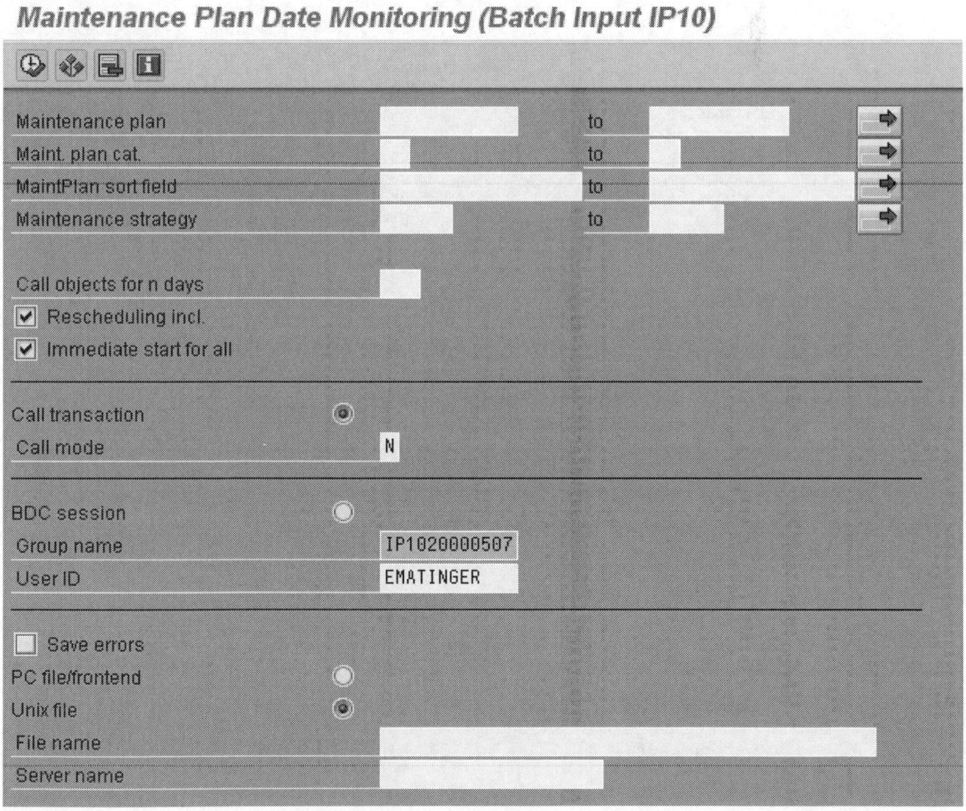

Maintenance Plan Date Monitoring (Batch Input IP10)

Maintenance plan		to	
Maint. plan cat.		to	
MaintPlan sort field		to	
Maintenance strategy		to	

Call objects for n days

☑ Rescheduling incl.
☑ Immediate start for all

Call transaction ◉
Call mode `N`

BDC session ◉
Group name `IP1020000507`
User ID `EMATINGER`

☐ Save errors
PC file/frontend ◉
Unix file ◉
File name
Server name

FIGURE 6.42 Deadline monitoring: initial screen (© SAP AG)

Even if you do not specify a scheduling period in the maintenance plan, scheduling is carried out at least once, and the system generates at least one maintenance call. The maintenance plan is automatically extended. It is no longer necessary to schedule the maintenance plan manually via the scheduling function.

Scheduling: Automatic deadline monitoring enables you to schedule maintenance plans for the first time or to reschedule them. To enable this function to be used, a start date or a start counter reading must have been entered in the scheduling parameters of the maintenance plan, or the maintenance plan must have already been scheduled.

In the maintenance planning menu, choose SCHEDULING FOR MAINTENANCE PLANS | DEADLINE MONITORING. This calls up the initial screen for deadline monitoring shown in Figure 6.42.

Enter the maintenance plans or maintenance strategies for which you want the system to carry out scheduling, and select either CALL TRANSACTION or BDC SESSION.

| Rpt trans.w.errors | Rpt all with errors | Save errors |

```
Message: S CO    085 Order will be released after update
Message: S IW    454 Costs were determined: See cost overview
Message: S IW    182 Default was formed for the distribution rule
Message: S CO    085 Order will be released after update
Message: S IW    454 Costs were determined: See cost overview
Message: S IW    182 Default was formed for the distribution rule
Message: S CO    085 Order will be released after update
Message: S IW    454 Costs were determined: See cost overview
Message: S IW    182 Default was formed for the distribution rule
Message: S CO    085 Order will be released after update
Message: S IW    454 Costs were determined: See cost overview
Message: S IW    182 Default was formed for the distribution rule
Message: S CO    085 Order will be released after update
Message: S IW    454 Costs were determined: See cost overview
Message: S IW    182 Default was formed for the distribution rule
Message: S CO    085 Order will be released after update
Message: S IW    454 Costs were determined: See cost overview
Message: S IP    202 Maintenance plan C1-B01 scheduled

Message: S IP    203 Scheduling data changed for maintenance plan EP-EINZEL-L

Message: S IP    202 Maintenance plan EP-EINZEL-Z scheduled

Message: S IP    203 Scheduling data changed for maintenance plan EP-MFZ

Message: S IP    203 Scheduling data changed for maintenance plan EP-STRAT-L

Message: S IP    202 Maintenance plan EP-STRAT-Z scheduled

Message: S IP    202 Maintenance plan EP-VCI-01 scheduled

Message: S IP    202 Maintenance plan EP-VCI-02 scheduled

Message: S IP    202 Maintenance plan EP-VCI-03 scheduled

Message: S IP    202 Maintenance plan EP-WCI-02 scheduled
```

FIGURE 6.43 System messages that occurred during scheduling (© SAP AG)

CALL TRANSACTION mode is defaulted by the system. Start the program via PROGRAM | EXECUTE. The system generates maintenance calls or maintenance call objects for the selected maintenance plan(s).

Figure 6.43 shows system messages. These indicate, for example, that scheduling or cost determination has been carried out successfully, or provide information on errors and logs. Figure 6.44 shows a list of scheduled maintenance plans.

Scheduling parameters: Scheduling parameters were discussed briefly in the section 'How to create and process single cycle plans'. These parameters enable you to tailor the scheduling process to the specific needs of your company.

```
Maintenance Plan Date Monitoring

Maintenance plan    Strategy        Text

17                  A
18                  A
19                  A
30                  A
40                  AB-01
50                  A
51                  B
60                  A
70                  A               Periodic Maintenance for Elevators
80                                  calibration of multimeter
90
600000000000
600000000010
C1-B01              A               Monthly inspection of pump station
EP-EINZEL-L                         Single Cycle Plan (performance based)
EP-EINZEL-Z                         Single Cycle Plan (time based)
EP-MFZ                              multi counter plan
EP-STRAT-L          D               strategy plan (performance based)
EP-STRAT-Z          A               strategy plan (time based)
EP-VCI-01                           Single Cycle Plan VCI 01
EP-VCI-02                           Single Cycle Plan VCI 02
EP-VCI-03                           Single Cycle Plan VCI 03
EP-WCI-02                           Single Cycle Plan VCI 02
K1                  A
M                                   calibration of multimeter
P                                   calibration of multimeter
P-1000-N005         EP-P1           PM for pump based on operating hours
P-1000-N006                         PM based on operating hours and flow
P-1000-N007                         Flow and op.hours based maintenance
P-3000-N003         A               Time based PM (1,3,12 month)
P-3000-N006                         2200 oph / 600,000 l flow
PUMP01              EP-P1           Performance-Based Maintenance
```

FIGURE 6.44   Scheduled maintenance plans (© SAP AG)

Maintaining scheduling parameters depends on the type of maintenance plan:

■ *Maintenance with single cycle and multiple counter plans*

With single cycle and multiple counter plans, the scheduling parameters are maintained directly in the maintenance plan.

■ *Maintenance with a strategy plan*

With maintenance plans with a maintenance strategy, the system copies the scheduling parameters defined in the strategy to the maintenance plan. The scheduling parameters are default values, which you can, of course, change in the maintenance plan.

IMPORTANT Any changes you make in the maintenance strategy do not affect the scheduling parameters of existing maintenance plans. If you make changes to the maintenance packages (by deleting packages or changing the preliminary or follow-up buffer, for example), these changes also affect maintenance plans to which you have assigned the strategy.

Maintaining scheduling parameters (general): You can maintain scheduling parameters in the maintenance plan or in the maintenance strategy. Table 6.2 shows which scheduling parameters can only be maintained in either the maintenance strategy (MS) or the maintenance plan (MP), and which can be changed in the strategy as well as in the maintenance plan (MS+MP).

TABLE 6.2   **Possible combination of scheduling parameters and maintenance plan types**

Scheduling parameter	Time-based single cycle and strategy plan	Perf.-based single cycle and strategy plan	Multiple counter plan
Scheduling indicator	MS+MP		
Shift factor	MS+MP	MS+MP	
Tolerance	MS+MP	MS+MP	
Cycle modification factor	MS+MP	MS+MP	MS+MP
Call horizon	MS+MP	MS+MP	
Scheduling interval	MS+MP		
Confirmation requirement	MP	MP	
Preliminary buffer	MS	MS	MS+MP
Follow-up buffer	MS	MS	MS+MP
Link type			MS+MP
Maintenance package hierarchy	MS	MS	

In maintenance planning, there are four scheduling indicators, which are used for the following scheduling options:

- Time-based scheduling
- Key-date scheduling
- Scheduling according to factory calendar
- Performance-based scheduling

There are two shift factors in maintenance planning: one for early confirmations and one for late confirmations.

The system provides you with the option of defining the shift factor specifically for a particular maintenance plan. You do this by specifying the shift percentage rate that is to be taken into consideration when the next due date is calculated. The shift factor applies only if the maintenance plan has already been scheduled, and the difference between the planned date and actual date is outside the tolerance range.

EXAMPLE The planned date for a maintenance order was 1 April 2000; the order, however, was confirmed 15 days late, on 16 April 2000. Depending on the specified shift factors, the next planned date can be on various days:

Planned date	01/04/2000
Confirmation	16/04/2000
Next planned date (0% SF)	01/05/2000
Next planned date (50% SF)	08/05/2000
Next planned date (100% SF)	16/05/2000

In maintenance planning, there are two tolerance ranges associated with scheduling parameters:

1 + tolerance
If a confirmation is late, this tolerance defines the timeframe in which a positive variance between the actual and planned date does not influence subsequent scheduling.

2 – tolerance
If a confirmation is early, this tolerance defines the timeframe in which a negative variance between the actual and planned date does not influence subsequent scheduling.

You can define the tolerance as a percentage of the smallest cycle of the maintenance strategy that you have assigned to the maintenance plan.

The smallest cycle in the maintenance strategy assigned to a maintenance plan is 50 days. A tolerance of 10% was defined in the event of a confirmation being carried out early. This yields a tolerance of 3 days. If the confirmation is carried out no more than 5 days before the planned date, the system does not take this variance into account when it calculates the next planned date.

The cycle modification factor is used to individually define the execution time for a maintenance plan. To carry out a definition of this kind, you modify the cycle of the generally valid maintenance strategy so that it takes into account the requirements of the individual system, process, or functional location.

If you specify a cycle modification factor, you can use it to extend or shorten the cycle specified in the maintenance strategy. A cycle modification factor greater than 1 extends the cycle, while a cycle modification factor less than 1 shortens it.

A maintenance strategy with a total cycle duration of 10 days is assigned to the maintenance plan. You want to change this cycle for this plan. To do so, you enter a cycle modification factor of 1.5. The result is $10 \times 1.5 = 15$ days.

The call horizon specifies (as a percentage) when an order should be created for a calculated maintenance date. This controls the time that should elapse between the completion confirmation date or start date and the next planned date of a maintenance plan before the order is created.

You can, therefore, define a specific call horizon for a time-based or a performance-based maintenance plan by entering a particular percentage of the overall maintenance cycle. As soon as the maintenance plan has been scheduled, the system calculates the next planned date.

The overall maintenance cycle is 100 days. If you define a call horizon of 0%, 70%, or 100%, the system will create the maintenance order after the following number of days:

0%	Immediate call
70%	Call after 70% of 100 = 70 days
100%	Call carried out after 100 days, on the day of the planned date

Call horizons cannot be defined for multiple counter plans. To ensure that a maintenance order is created before the start date, you should specify a preliminary buffer in the scheduling parameters. By contrast, a call horizon should always be specified for performance-related maintenance plans.

A scheduling period can be defined for a time-based maintenance plan and specifies the actual length of the scheduling period in days, months or years. For example, if you want a maintenance plan to be scheduled for the entire year and to have this generate all the calls for this year, you specify 365 days or 12 months as the call interval.

The confirmation requirement indicator is used to control when the system generates the next maintenance call object. If you set this indicator, the system generates the next call object only after the preceding call object has been confirmed. As regards the 'maintenance order' call object, this means that the system creates the next order only if the preceding order has been technically completed, or if the call has been confirmed in scheduling.

IMPORTANT This indicator is not equivalent to completion confirmation at the operation level of maintenance orders. These functions are independent of each other.

Preliminary and follow-up buffer: The preliminary and follow-up buffers specify how long before or after the due date of the maintenance packages the execution of the activities can be started or finished, without changing the following due dates.

EXAMPLE You specify a preliminary and follow-up buffer of two days for each maintenance package in the strategy. The planned date calculated by the system is 20 May. The start date proposed in the maintenance order is, therefore, 18 May, and the finish date is 22 May.

The link type is an indicator used to specify the relationship between the maintenance cycles of a multiple counter plan:

- With an OR link, the activity is due as soon as a maintenance cycle ends.
- With an AND link, the activity is only due when the final maintenance cycle ends.

EXAMPLE You want a vehicle to be serviced annually and/or after 20,000 km. If the maintenance cycles are linked with OR, the vehicle must be serviced as soon as one of the two conditions is fulfilled: either a year has elapsed, or the distance driven equals 20,000 km. If the maintenance cycles are linked with AND, the vehicle only has to be serviced if both conditions are fulfilled: a year must have elapsed and the vehicle must have travelled 20,000 km.

The maintenance package hierarchy is a hierarchy that determines which maintenance packages are performed if several maintenance packages are due at the same time.

If the maintenance packages are to be performed together at this time, they must have the same hierarchy number. If only certain maintenance packages are to be performed at this time, these packages must have a higher hierarchy number than the others. The system only selects the packages with the highest hierarchy number.

Completion confirmations: If a maintenance call that is due is called and the system has used it to generate a maintenance call object, the maintenance call has the status CALLED.

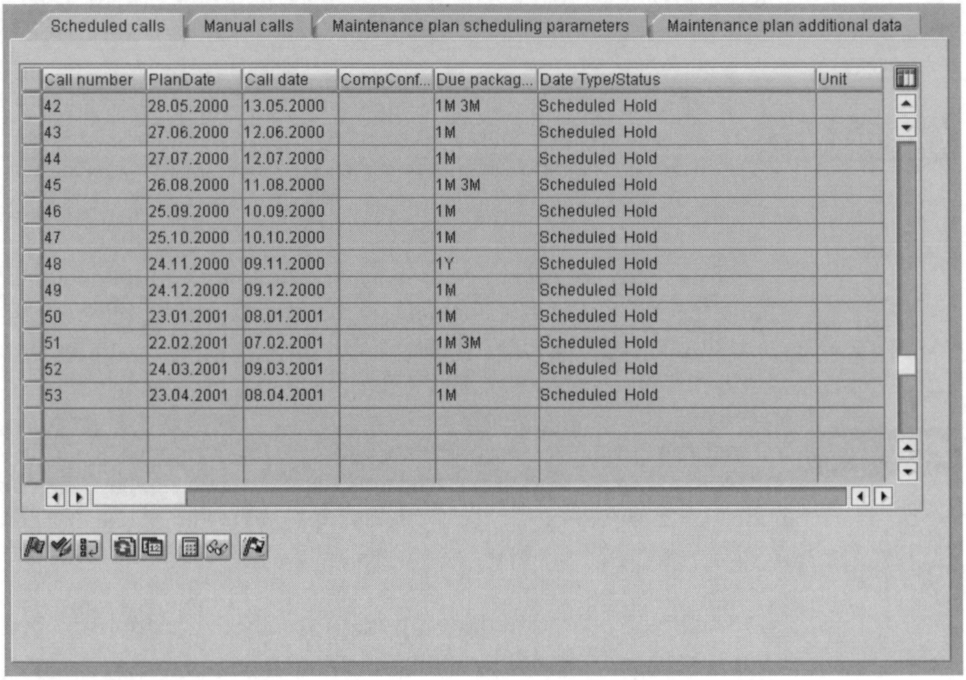

| Scheduled calls | Manual calls | Maintenance plan scheduling parameters | Maintenance plan additional data |

Call number	PlanDate	Call date	CompConf...	Due packag...	Date Type/Status	Unit
42	28.05.2000	13.05.2000		1M 3M	Scheduled Hold	
43	27.06.2000	12.06.2000		1M	Scheduled Hold	
44	27.07.2000	12.07.2000		1M	Scheduled Hold	
45	26.08.2000	11.08.2000		1M 3M	Scheduled Hold	
46	25.09.2000	10.09.2000		1M	Scheduled Hold	
47	25.10.2000	10.10.2000		1M	Scheduled Hold	
48	24.11.2000	09.11.2000		1Y	Scheduled Hold	
49	24.12.2000	09.12.2000		1M	Scheduled Hold	
50	23.01.2001	08.01.2001		1M	Scheduled Hold	
51	22.02.2001	07.02.2001		1M 3M	Scheduled Hold	
52	24.03.2001	09.03.2001		1M	Scheduled Hold	
53	23.04.2001	08.04.2001		1M	Scheduled Hold	

FIGURE 6.45   Scheduled calls of a maintenance plan (© SAP AG)

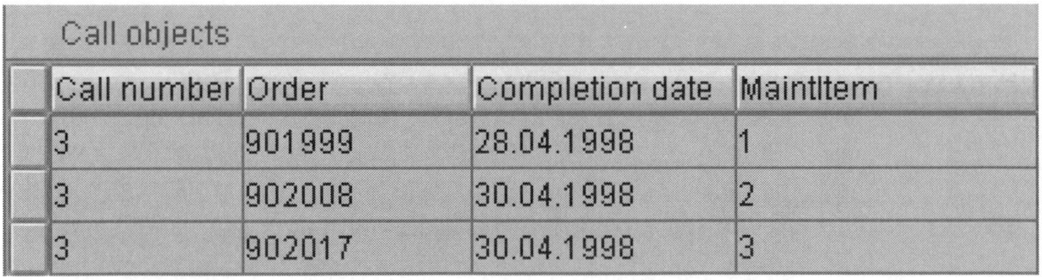

Call objects

Call number	Order	Completion date	MaintItem
3	901999	28.04.1998	1
3	902008	30.04.1998	2
3	902017	30.04.1998	3

FIGURE 6.46   List of call objects of a maintenance plan (© SAP AG)

The maintenance call is only assigned the status COMPLETED, if

- the generated maintenance order has been technically completed
- the generated maintenance notification has been completed
- the generated service entry sheet has been accepted
- the maintenance call has been confirmed in the scheduling functions

Displaying maintenance call objects: As already described, the system generates maintenance call objects when maintenance plans are scheduled. The maintenance call object to be generated for a maintenance plan is specified in the maintenance plan category. Maintenance call objects can be displayed:

- From the maintenance plan
- From the call history
- Via the list function of the maintenance call object

Displaying orders or notifications from the call history: If a maintenance call has the status CALLED or CONFIRMED, a maintenance call object for this call exists in the system. You can display these maintenance call objects either from the call history or from the maintenance plan. Starting from the MAINTENANCE PLANNING menu, choose SCHEDULING FOR MAINTENANCE PLANS | SCHEDULE. This calls up the initial screen for scheduling maintenance plans. In this screen, select the maintenance plan you want to schedule, and choose ENTER. Figure 6.45 shows scheduled calls of a maintenance plan.

In the Schedule maintenance plan screen, choose the SCHEDULED CALLS tab page. This contains the call history with the scheduled maintenance calls up to the current date. Select the call for which you want to display the maintenance call object, and choose DISPLAY CALL OBJECT. Depending on the number of maintenance items assigned to the maintenance plan, this calls up either the order header or the list of all the maintenance call objects. Figure 6.46 shows this list.

Select the maintenance item for which you wish to display a maintenance call object, and choose the DISPLAY ORDER pushbutton. It will then be displayed as a complete maintenance order.

6.3 TASKS OF THE CONTROLLER

The role of the controller was covered in section 5.3. Since the tasks of the controller in planned maintenance are the same as in breakdown and corrective maintenance, refer to section 5.3 for further details.

CHAPTER 7

Special cases

REFURBISHMENT PROCESSING

High-quality material components (such as motors) are often used in production systems. In the event of damage, components of this type are replaced by a functioning repairable spare, and then refurbished in the maintenance department on the basis of a separate order. Refurbishing defective high-quality repairable spares is extremely important from an economic point of view, and is often a core process in maintenance. Refurbishment is frequently considerably more cost-efficient than purchasing a new material component.

The refurbishment process supplements the business processes already described, and is carried out as follows. During a maintenance or repair task, a defective item of equipment is replaced. The maintenance or repair order, however, contains only the material consumption for the new item of equipment. If it is intended to repair (in other words, refurbish) rather than scrap the defective item of equipment, the refurbishment process begins. The defective item of equipment is posted to stock as a material number (assigned previously to the item of equipment via a serial number), and is stored in the spare parts warehouse. When the stock of defective parts reaches a certain level, the PM planner creates a refurbishment order (an order type of the standard maintenance order). After the refurbishment tasks have been planned and controlled, the PM planner releases the order. The PM technician then withdraws the defective item of equipment from the spare parts warehouse and refurbishes it. Finally, he confirms the working time and materials required via completion confirmation, and returns the refurbished item of equipment to the spare parts warehouse. From the point of view of plant maintenance, this completes the business process. The refurbished item of equipment is now available for installation in a system.

7.1.1 Inventory management and condition-based material valuation

In addition to the functions of Plant Maintenance, functions from inventory management and material planning are used for refurbishing repairable spares. Inventory management maps physical stocks by entering all operations that change the stock and the resulting stock updates in real time. This provides you with a constant overview of the current stock situation of a material. This applies, for example, to stocks

- that are currently stored in the warehouse
- that have already been ordered, but have not yet been received
- that are currently stored in the warehouse, but are already reserved for production or a customer
- that are currently undergoing quality inspection

The stocks are managed on a value basis as well as a quantity basis. With every goods movement, the system updates the following data automatically:

- Quantity and value update for inventory management
- Account assignment for cost accounting
- G/L accounts for financial accounting via automatic account determination

The organizational level at which the material stocks are managed on a value basis is the valuation area. The valuation area can be a plant or a company code. Inventory management is always carried out at the plant and storage location level. When you enter a goods movement, therefore, you only need to enter the plant and the storage location of the material. The company code is derived from the plant via the valuation area.

In the material master record, a price is defined for the material for each valuation area. In the case of materials that can be refurbished, you require several prices per material within one valuation area. This split material valuation is intended to value the stocks of a material according to their condition. The prerequisite for split valuation is that a valuation category has been entered in the accounting data of the material master record (for example, 'C' for the status). The valuation category is a key, which specifies the criterion according to which the partial stocks are to be differentiated (for example, status, procurement type, origin). Within the valuation category, each partial stock of a material must also be assigned to a valuation type.

For example, a pump is mapped as a material master record with the number 'P-2001'. This pump is scheduled for refurbishment. 'C' (for status) is entered as the valuation category (Fig. 7.1). The following three material conditions are defined:

1 New part

2 Refurbished part

3 Defective part

Within valuation category C, three valuation types are created for these three conditions: C1 for a new part, C2 for a refurbished part, C3 for a defective part. In the life cycle of the material, pump P-2001 is thus initially installed in a system as a new part (C1). From the point of view of plant maintenance, the material then becomes an item of equipment. If the pump is defective, it is replaced and put into the spare parts warehouse as a defective part (C3). The valuation type changes, therefore, from C1 to C3. If the pump is refurbished, the valuation type changes again, from C3 to C2.

If split valuation is scheduled for a material, the material is managed in various partial stocks, each of which is valued separately. Each valuation-relevant operation (whether this be goods receipt, goods issue, or physical inventory) is carried out at the level of the partial stock. When one of these operations is carried out (for example,

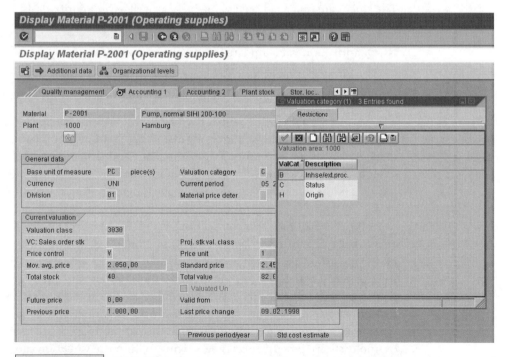

FIGURE 7.1   Valuation category in a material master record (© SAP AG)

when goods are issued for refurbishment from the spare parts warehouse), you must always specify the partial stock affected. This ensures that only the value of the affected partial stock changes. In addition to the partial stocks, the total stock is updated. The value of the total stock is calculated from the sum of the stock values and stock quantities of the individual partial stocks.

Depending on the condition of pump P-2001, three partial stocks are defined. At storage location 0001 in plant 1000, there is a total of 40 parts (total stock). In partial stock C1 for new parts, there are 10 parts; in C2 for refurbished parts, there are 20 parts; and in C3 for defective parts, there are 10 parts (Fig. 7.2).

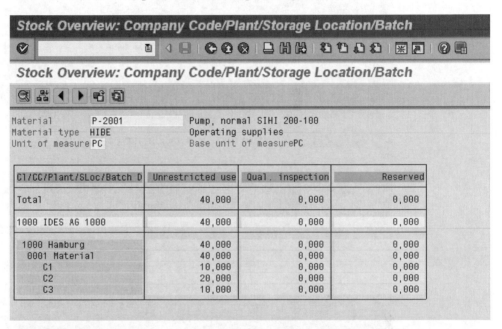

Stock Overview: Company Code/Plant/Storage Location/Batch

Material	P-2001	Pump, normal SIHI 200-100
Material type	HIBE	Operating supplies
Unit of measure	PC	Base unit of measure PC

C1/CC/Plant/SLoc/Batch D	Unrestricted use	Qual. inspection	Reserved
Total	40,000	0,000	0,000
1000 IDES AG 1000	40,000	0,000	0,000
1000 Hamburg	40,000	0,000	0,000
0001 Material	40,000	0,000	0,000
C1	10,000	0,000	0,000
C2	20,000	0,000	0,000
C3	10,000	0,000	0,000

FIGURE 7.2 Stock overview of partial stocks (© SAP AG)

Organizational Levels

Organizational levels	
Plant	1000
Stor. location	0001
Valuation type	C3

☐ Org. levels/profiles only on request

✔ Select view(s)   💾 Default values   ✖

FIGURE 7.3 Display material according to valuation type (© SAP AG)

7.1.2 Standard price and moving average price

Due to the split valuation, each valuation type has its own standard price. You can call up the standard price if you display the material not only according to plant and storage location, but also according to valuation type (Fig. 7.3). For example, pump P-2001 is

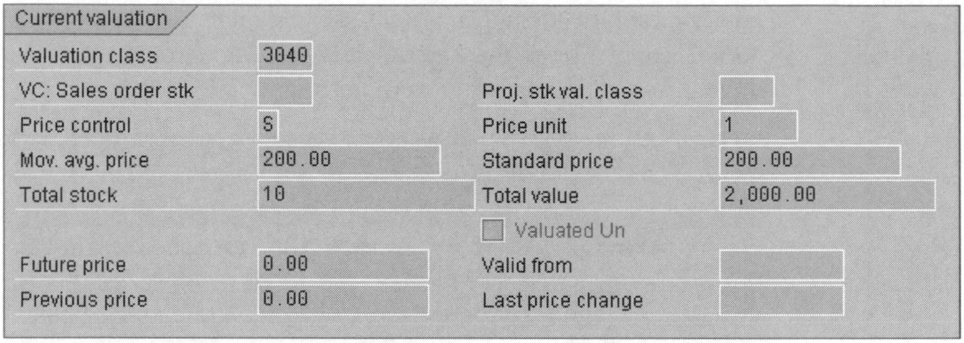

Current valuation			
Valuation class	3040		
VC: Sales order stk		Proj. stk val. class	
Price control	S	Price unit	1
Mov. avg. price	200.00	Standard price	200.00
Total stock	10	Total value	2,000.00
		☐ Valuated Un	
Future price	0.00	Valid from	
Previous price	0.00	Last price change	

FIGURE 7.4   Standard price with valuation type C3 (© SAP AG)

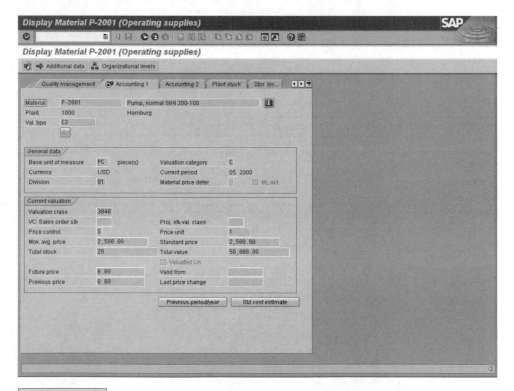

FIGURE 7.5   Standard price with valuation type C2 (© SAP AG)

valued as a defective part in partial stock C3 with a standard price of $200.00. There is an 'S' in the PRICE CONTROL field, which means that this is the standard price, and not the moving average price. For this reason, the standard price of $200.00 is also displayed in the MOVING AVERAGE PRICE field (Fig. 7.4). By way of comparison, Figure 7.5 shows the standard price in partial stock C2 for refurbished parts. The standard price here is $2,500.00. When a defective part is refurbished, therefore, its value increases by $2,300.00. This means that a refurbishment measure will only be expedient if the personnel and material costs for refurbishment are considerably less than $2,300.00 per part.

At the valuation area level, the stock quantity, stock value, and valuation price of all valuation types are managed cumulatively, and then yield the moving average price for the material. You can call up the moving average price by simply choosing ENTER without entering a valuation type.

Pump P-2001 is valued at $3,000.00 in partial stock C1. Ten pieces exist. In partial stock C2, the pump is valued at $2,500.00. Twenty pieces exist here. In partial stock C3, the pump is valued at $200.00. Ten pieces exist here. The value of the partial stocks is now cumulated. This yields a moving average price of $2,050.00, which is displayed in the corresponding field. The PRICE CONTROL field contains the letter 'V', which shows that the price here is not the standard price (Fig. 7.6).

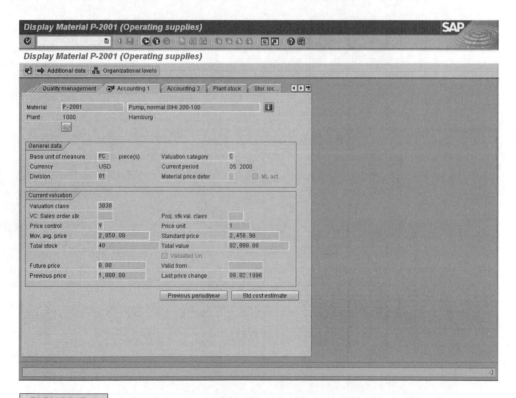

FIGURE 7.6 Moving average price (© SAP AG)

7.1.3 How the PM planner creates refurbishment orders

A refurbishment order is a standard maintenance order type. In Customizing for orders, you first create an order type (such as PM04). To do so, choose FUNCTIONS AND SETTINGS FOR ORDER TYPES | CONFIGURE ORDER TYPES. You now flag this order type as a refurbishment order. To do so, choose FUNCTIONS AND SETTINGS FOR ORDER TYPES | INDICATE ORDER TYPES FOR REFURBISHMENT PROCESSING, and flag the indicator for PM04 (Fig. 7.7).

You can create a refurbishment order directly via transaction IW81. The order type flagged in Customizing (PM04) has already been proposed by the system (Fig. 7.8). Enter the material for refurbishment as well as the maintenance planning plant in which you work as PM planner.

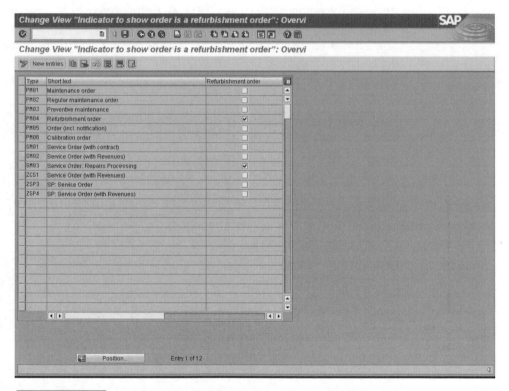

FIGURE 7.7 Order type for refurbishment order (© SAP AG)

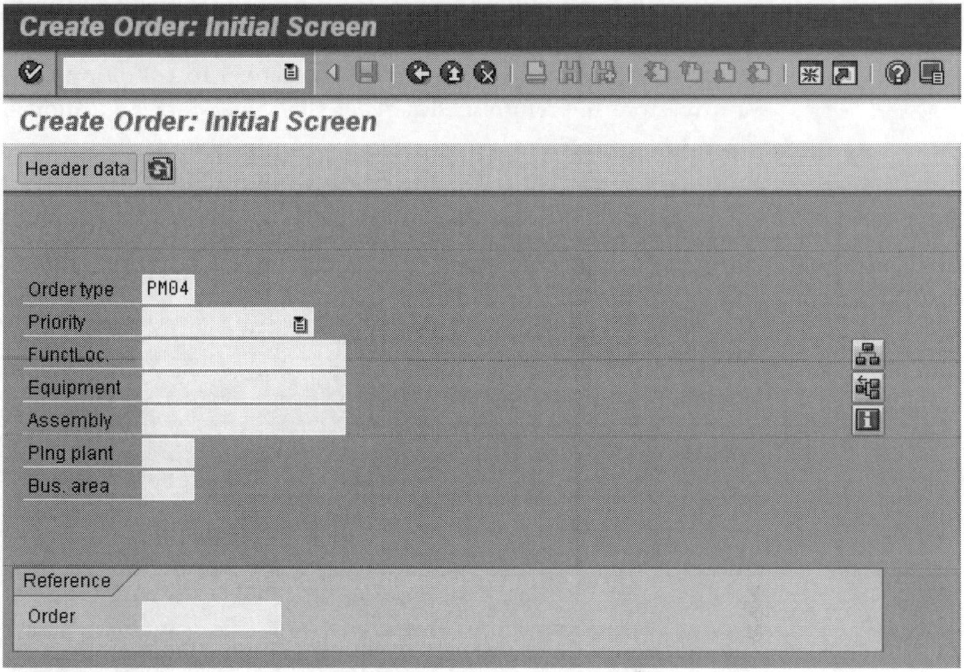

Create Order: Initial Screen

Create Order: Initial Screen

Header data

Order type	PM04
Priority	
FunctLoc.	
Equipment	
Assembly	
Plng plant	
Bus. area	

Reference

Order

FIGURE 7.8   Creating a refurbishment order (© SAP AG)

You treat a refurbishment order like any other order type. Figure 7.9 shows the header data of a refurbishment order. The only difference here is that you have to enter some additional refurbishment-specific data for the material. The relevant required entries are:

▪ The quantity of parts to be refurbished with this material number

▪ The actual condition of the material (for example, C3 for defective parts)

▪ Plant and storage location at which the material is stored in its actual condition

▪ The target condition that should be achieved following refurbishment (for example, C2 for refurbished parts)

▪ Plant and storage location at which the material should be stored in its target condition

You want to refurbish a total of five parts of material P-2001. At present, these are stored at storage location 0001 in plant 1000. This refurbishment order is intended to transfer the parts from condition C3 (defective) to condition C2 (refurbished). You want to store the refurbished parts at the same storage location in the same plant (Fig. 7.10).

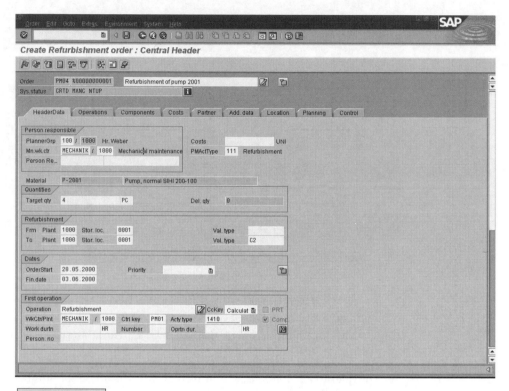

FIGURE 7.9   Header data of a refurbishment order (© SAP AG)

Quantities						
Target qty	5		PC		Del. qty	0

Refurbishment						
Frm	Plant	1000	Stor. loc.	0001	Val. type	C3
To	Plant	1000	Stor. loc.	0001	Val. type	C2

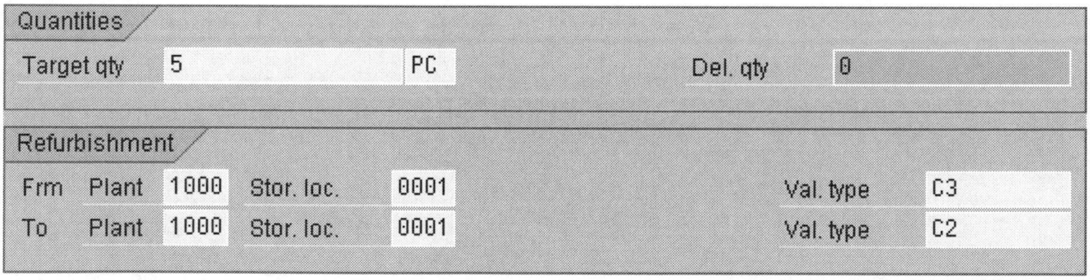

FIGURE 7.10   Material-specific information in a refurbishment order (© SAP AG)

As the PM planner, you now carry out the required personnel and material planning, and then release the order. The material to be provided is entered automatically as a material component in the COMPONENTS tab page. A material reservation is generated automatically for these materials.

The system has generated a material reservation in plant 1000 for the required quantity of five pieces of material number P-2001 in valuation type C3 (actual condition). The specified movement type is 261 (Fig. 7.11).

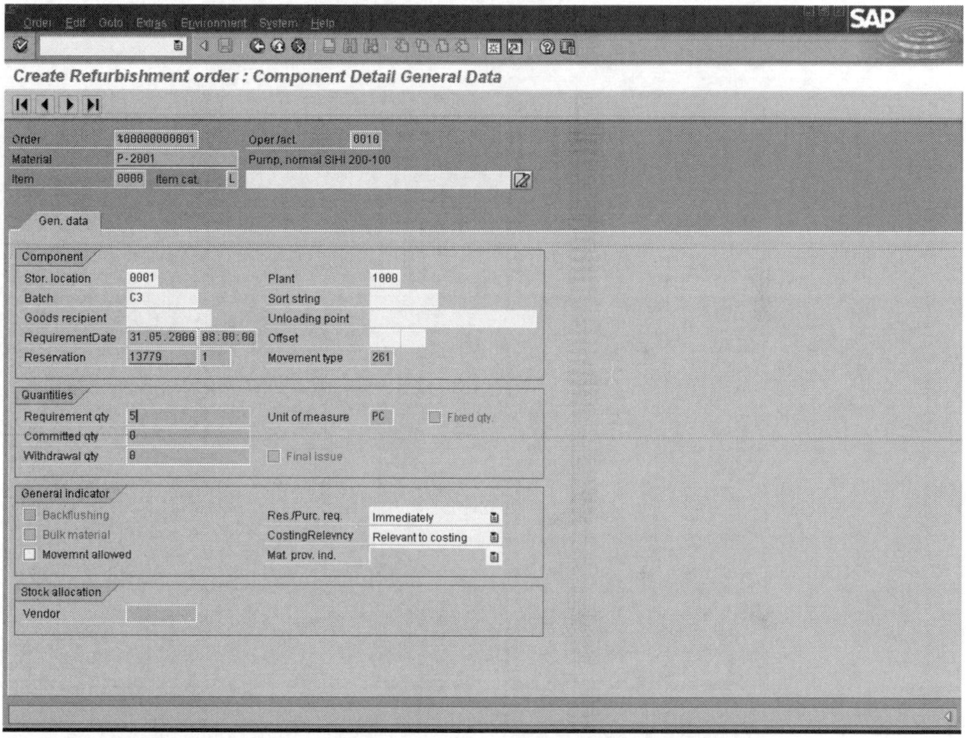

FIGURE 7.11 Material reservation in a refurbishment order (© SAP AG)

7.1.4 How PM technicians carry out refurbishment

As the PM technician, you first withdraw the reserved material from the warehouse. In the present example, the reserved material corresponds to the five reserved pumps with material number P-2001. To carry out the material withdrawal with movement type 261 (goods issue for order), use transaction MB1A. The goods issue applies to materials with valuation type C3 (Fig. 7.12).

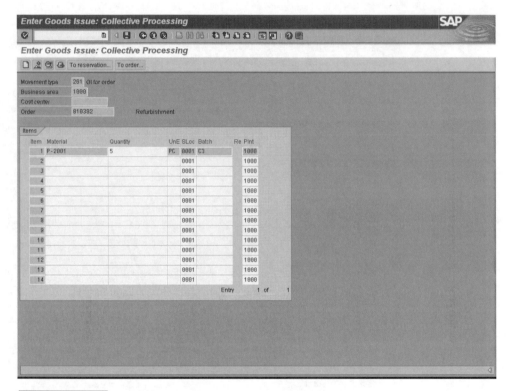

FIGURE 7.12   Goods issue for reserved material (© SAP AG)

After you have withdrawn the materials, carry out the refurbishment tasks. When you have done this, enter a time confirmation. In the example, you have not exceeded the scheduled working time for refurbishment (one hour). Spare parts and production resources/tools were not required. Enter a confirmation text, and then flag the FINAL CONFIRMATION indicator (Fig. 7.13).

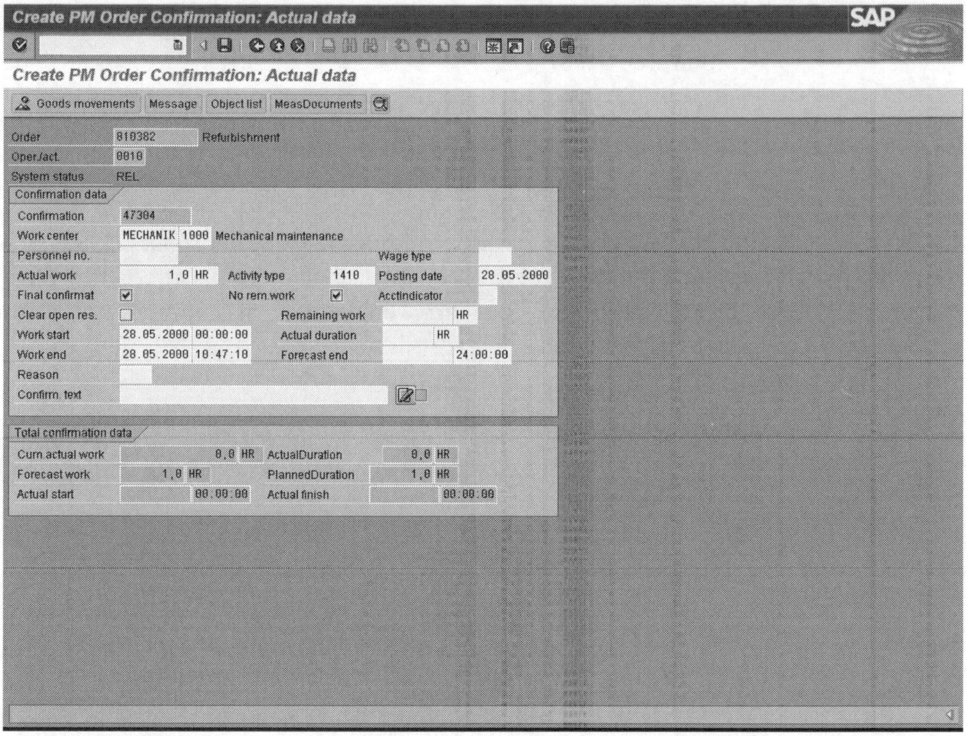

FIGURE 7.13 Time confirmation for a refurbishment task (© SAP AG)

7.1.5 How the PM planner technically completes orders

After the PM technician has carried out final confirmation, you (in your role as the planner) can check and technically complete the refurbishment order. You must assign the order a settlement rule, which has been agreed on with the Controller. The default settlement rule normally comes from the technical object, and contains the cost centre to which the technical object is assigned. Since P-2001 is a material master record, no value is defaulted here.

To maintain the settlement rule from the order, choose GOTO | SETTLEMENT RULE. In the example, you then enter cost centre KST 1410 for systems.

You can then use transaction MMBE to call up the stock overview. Before the five parts were refurbished, there was a total of 31 parts (total stock) at storage location 0001 in plant 1000. In partial stock C1 (new parts) there were 10 parts; in C2 (refurbished parts) there were 11 parts; and in C3 (defective parts) there were 10 parts.

After refurbishment, the stock is as follows (Fig. 7.14):

- Total stock of 31 parts
- Partial stock C1 with 10 new parts
- Partial stock C2 with 16 refurbished parts
- Partial stock C3 with 5 defective parts

Since the material is valued at $2,500.00 in partial stock C2, and at $200.00 in partial stock C3, the stock value of the total stock increases after refurbishment.

From the order, you carry out technical completion by choosing ORDER | FUNCTIONS | COMPLETE (TECHNICALLY).

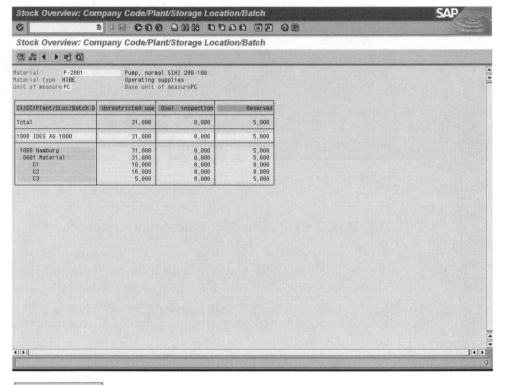

FIGURE 7.14   Stock overview after refurbishment (© SAP AG)

7.1.6 How the controller checks the cost flow in refurbishment

After the order has been released, you (in your role as controller) can check the planned costs. A refurbishment order is debited with the planned costs the for work performed and spare parts used, as well as the planned costs for parts to be refurbished.

One working hour is planned for the refurbishment of the five P-2001 pumps, and the order is consequently debited with $116.15. In addition to this, there is the debit due to the five parts, which were each valued at $200.00 in their defective condition. The order is, therefore, debited with total planned costs of $1,327.77. At the same time, the refurbishment order is also credited with the five parts, which are valued at $2,500.00 in their refurbished condition. The order is, therefore, credited with a total of $12,500.00 (Fig. 7.15).

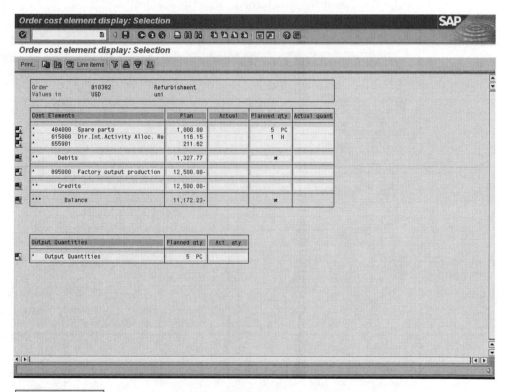

FIGURE 7.15   Planned cost in a refurbishment order (at the time of release) (© SAP AG)

In the next stage, the PM technician withdraws the five defective parts from the warehouse, and posts this withdrawal as a goods issue. After he has carried out the refurbishment tasks, he confirms his working time, and flags the final confirmation indicator. As a result, the order is debited with the following costs (Fig. 7.16):

- Goods issue of five defective parts (in the present example, each valued at $200.00)
- Work performed in hours (in the example, the planned working time of one hour corresponds to the actual working time)

When refurbishment is complete, the refurbished parts are posted back to the warehouse, and the PM planner technically completes the order. For you, as the controller, the cost situation at this point in time is as follows. The debits of the order remain constant. As specified in the planned costs, the order is credited after goods receipt with the total value of the refurbished parts (Fig. 7.17).

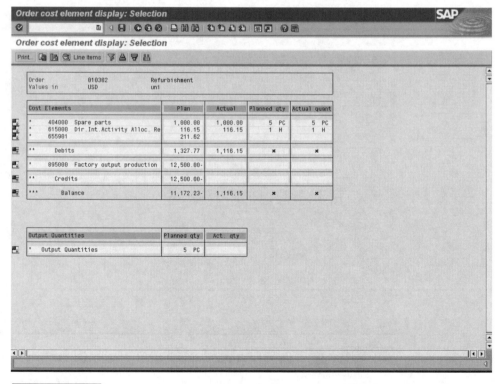

FIGURE 7.16 Actual costs after material withdrawal and final confirmation (© SAP AG)

After technical completion has been carried out by the PM planner, the order is transferred to you (the controller) for settlement. You carry out order settlement via transaction KO88. After the order has been settled, you complete the refurbishment order from a business point of view. In the cost report, the order is displayed as shown in Figure 7.18.

Refurbishment orders are settled directly to the material stock. When settlement is carried out, the order is debited with the actual outlay, which replaces the temporary debit of the order and related increase in the material stock value. This total is then settled directly to the material. As a result, the total stock value (and thus the moving average price) increases.

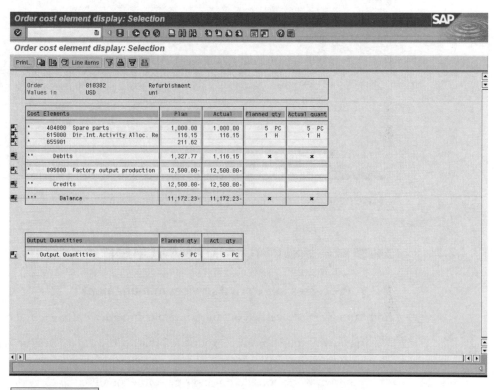

FIGURE 7.17   Actual costs after goods receipt (© SAP AG)

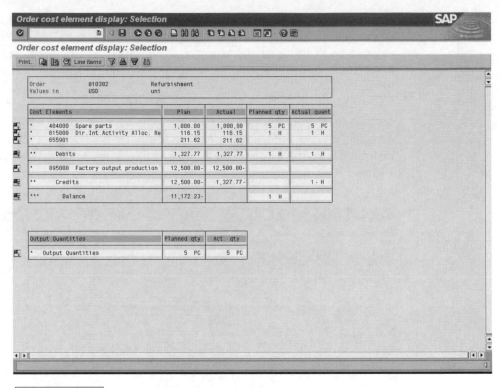

FIGURE 7.18 Actual costs after order settlement (© SAP AG)

7.2 EXTERNAL SERVICES MANAGEMENT

7.2.1 Processes in external services management

You can have tasks carried out by external companies if, for example:

▨ Your own workshops are overloaded due to the capacity situation (for example, during revisions, shutdowns, or year-end closing operations)

▨ Your own workshops do not have personnel qualified to carry out specialized tasks (for example, specialized tasks for air-conditioning systems, elevator systems, or electronic control units)

▨ Consideration of the primary costs (invoiced amount) and secondary costs (for example, order planning, purchase order, acceptance of service performed, or invoice verification) shows that it would be more cost-intensive to have the task carried out by your own workshops

With external service management in the R/3 System, a distinction is always drawn between short-term requirements for different vendors, and long-term relationships with a specific vendor. The system provides you with the following forms for managing external services:

- Management with an external company as a work centre for long-term vendor relationships

- Management with individual purchase order for short-term requirements

- Management with service specifications

The process steps involved in management with external work centres are described below.

To manage external services in this way, you first have to set up a cost centre for each external company individually, or for all the external companies together. After you have done this, you set up a CO activity type and a price for the cost centre of the external company in Controlling (CO), which reflects the conditions of the individual purchase order. You also set up a work centre for the external company, which is linked to the cost centre and the CO activity type.

1. You set up an individual purchase order with a validity period (for example, quarter, year), and in which the purchase order conditions are defined. You assign this individual purchase order to the cost centre of the work centre that you have created for the external company.

2. You create the order containing the operations to be processed externally in exactly the same way as you would create orders with operations to be processed internally.

3. You request the external company to carry out maintenance tasks by sending/faxing the order papers to the external company, or by distributing them to employees of the external company.

4. The tasks are carried out by the external company.

5. You confirm the externally processed operations of the order in exactly the same way as you would confirm internally processed operations.

6. The time confirmation of the operations results in the cost centre of the external company being credited.

The cost centre of the external company can be debited by invoices issued periodically (for example, monthly). The invoice here comprises all the orders executed in this period. After the invoice has been paid, the balance of the cost centre is equal to 0. The costs are initially collected in the order, and are then settled to the receiver named in the settlement rule.

In the following, the process steps for handling external services with individual purchase orders are described.

1 You create the order with the operations to be processed externally, exactly as you would create an order for internal processing.

2 The system creates a purchase requisition automatically for the operations that you have flagged with a control key for external processing (the system does this when the order is released, at latest).

3 If necessary, the person responsible in the purchasing department carries out source determination, and creates a purchase order.

4 The following settlement types are available:

– Settlement according to resources (examples 1 and 2).

– Settlement based on the total expected output (example 3).

EXAMPLE 1 You have agreed on a direct labour hour rate of $80.00, and assume that executing the task will take four hours. In fact, five hours are required: you settle $400.00.

EXAMPLE 2 You have agreed on a fixed price of $10.00 for laying one metre of cable, and assume a total cable length of 40 m. In fact, only 35 m of cable has to be laid: you settle $350.00.

EXAMPLE 3 You have agreed on a flat-rate price of $400.00 for laying 40 m of cable, and assume that the task will take four hours. In fact, five hours and 50 m of cable were required: you settle $400.00.

5 The tasks are carried out by the external company.

6 The completion confirmation is entered by internal personnel in the form of a goods issue for purchase order.

7 The resulting costs are initially collected in the order and then settled to the receiver named in the settlement rule.

8 The offsetting entry is initially charged to a clearing account and is then written off automatically when the invoice is received, since the vendor's invoice is generally received after his delivery. Any variances between the purchase order value and the invoice value are subsequently debited or credited to the order.

9 In the operation processed externally, the status EXTERNAL OPERATION PARTLY DELIVERED is set. If you have flagged the final delivery indicator, the status EXTERNAL OPERATION FINALLY DELIVERED is set.

The process steps for handling external services with *service specifications* are as follows:

1 You create the order with the operations to be processed externally, exactly as you would create an order for internal processing.

2 The PM planner creates service specifications for the operations to be processed externally.

3 The system creates a purchase requisition automatically for each operation with service specifications. Each service specification is linked to the item of the corresponding purchase requisition.

4 On the basis of the purchase order, the system automatically creates service entry sheets, on which the services can be confirmed as with internally processed orders.

5 You have the following ordering options:
  – Individual purchase order
  – Framework order

Purchasing skips all the phases of source determination and the purchase order. The framework order can have an extended validity period, and can, therefore, be used several times (in other words, whenever services are requested from the vendor for whom the framework order was created). The purchase requisitions are linked to the framework order.

6 The tasks are carried out by the external company.

7 The services performed are recorded in the service entry sheets for the purchase order.

8 The services entered previously are accepted by a member of staff, who has checked that they have been performed correctly. This acceptance is the basis for settling the services, and is posted in an acceptance document.

9 In invoice verification, the information from the purchase requisition and service entry sheets is compared. The invoice should contain the amount that was previously accepted. If there are variances, the invoice is blocked until the variances have been clarified.

10 Externally processed operations are assigned the status PARTIALLY DELIVERED or FINALLY DELIVERED.

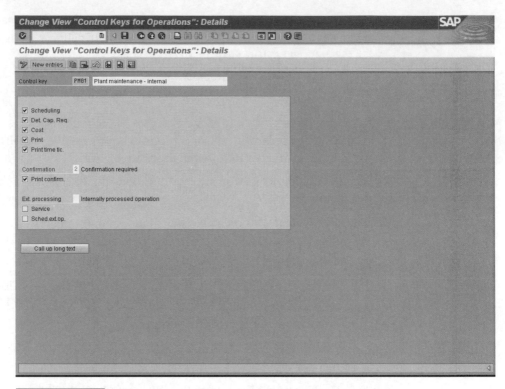

7.2.2 How the PM planner uses control keys

In the R/3 System, external assignment is always triggered via the control key in the order. A separate control key is available for each of the three forms of processing discussed above:

- Control key PM01 for processing with external work centres
- Control key PM02 for processing with individual purchase orders
- Control key PM03 for processing with service specifications

You maintain the control keys in Customizing for orders, under FUNCTIONS AND SETTINGS FOR ORDER TYPES | CONTROL KEY | MAINTAIN CONTROL KEYS. Figures 7.19, 7.20 and 7.21 show the detail screens of the three control keys. Control key PM01 was used to control all of the maintenance orders that have so far been described in connection with breakdown, corrective and planned maintenance. With control key PM02, the EXTERNAL PROCESSING field is flagged, and with control key PM03 the SERVICE indicator and the EXTERNAL PROCESSING field are both flagged.

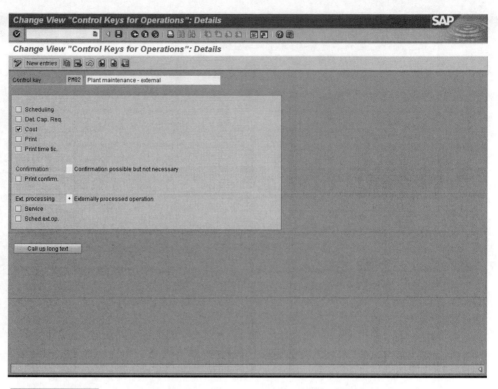

FIGURE 7.20   Detailed data for control key PM02 (© SAP AG)

In maintenance orders, you generally enter the control key for each operation in the CONTROL KEY field of the operation detail screens (Fig. 7.22). You can also select the control key in this field by choosing F4. This calls up information on the control key from the detailed data in Customizing (Fig. 7.23).

7.2.3 How the PM planner uses external work centres

Before you (as the PM planner) can use external work centres to carry out planning, the controller has to have created the following data sets for the external company:

- A separate cost centre
- An activity type for the cost centre
- A price for the current fiscal year for the cost centre and activity type

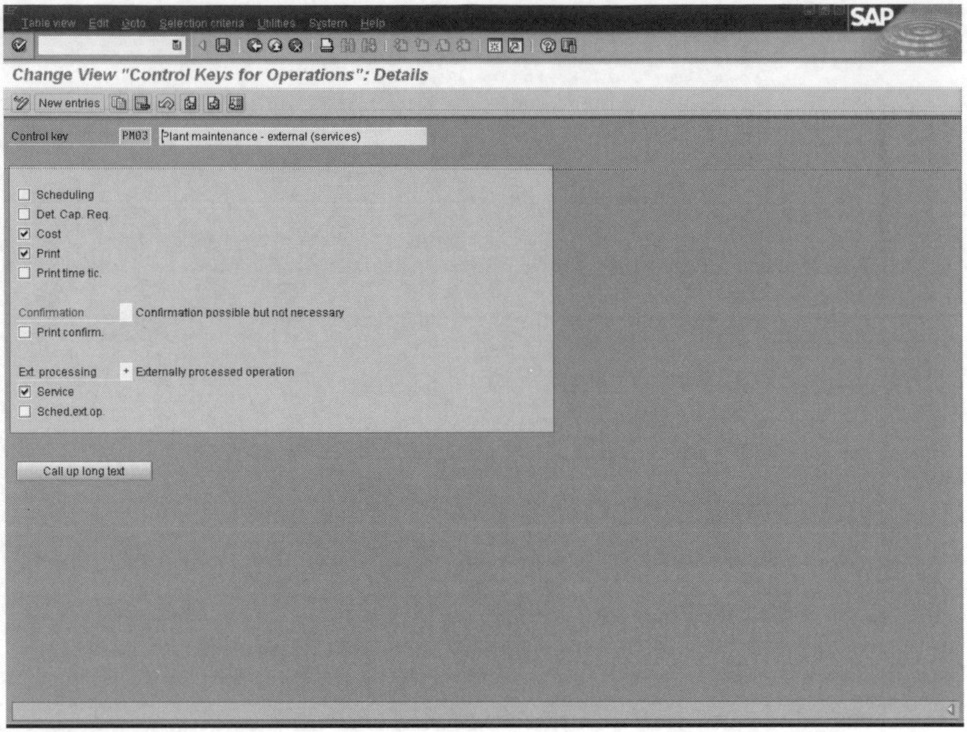

FIGURE 7.21 Detailed data for control key PM03 (© SAP AG)

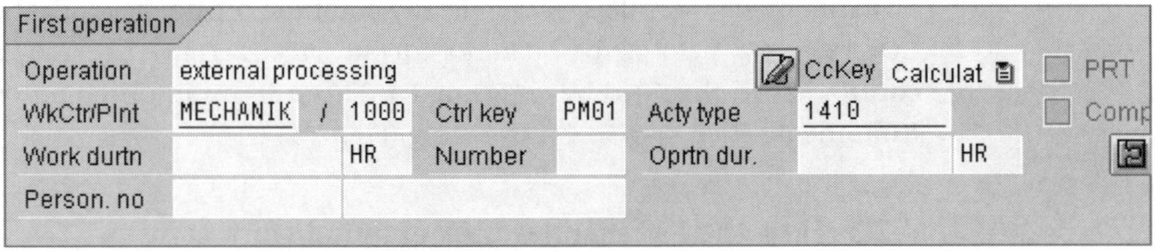

FIGURE 7.22 Control key in an order operation (© SAP AG)

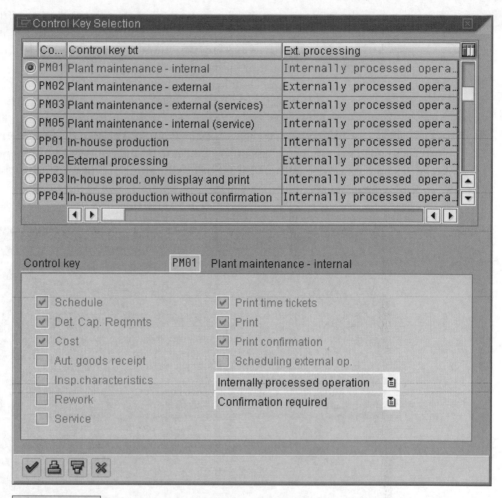

FIGURE 7.23   Selecting a control key in an order operation (© SAP AG)

For example, you want an external company to carry out maintenance on the cooling systems in the ice-cream production plant. The external cost centre T-PM00 and activity type 1610 ('External hours') are set up for this purpose. As the PM planner, you map the external company, for which a vendor master record (number 1000) already exists, as work centre master record T-FR00. To do so, use transaction IR01.

In the DEFAULT VALUES tab page, enter PM01 as the control key. In the COST CEN-TRES tab page of the work centre, enter the external cost centre T-PM00 in the COST CENTRE field, and activity type 1610 in the ACTTYP INT.PROC. field (Fig. 7.24). You can display the assigned price via transaction KP27.

You link work centre T-FR00 with purchase order 4500004891 via the classification function. To do so, choose the CLASSIFICATION pushbutton in the BASIC DATA tab page. Assign the class PM_WORK_ CENTRE_EXT to the work centre (Fig. 7.25). In the classification system, you have already linked this class to the characteristic PUR_ORDER, which permits a purchase order number to be entered (Fig. 7.26). You now integrate the purchase order 4500004891 in the classification data of work centre T-FR00 directly as a characteristic value (Fig. 7.27).

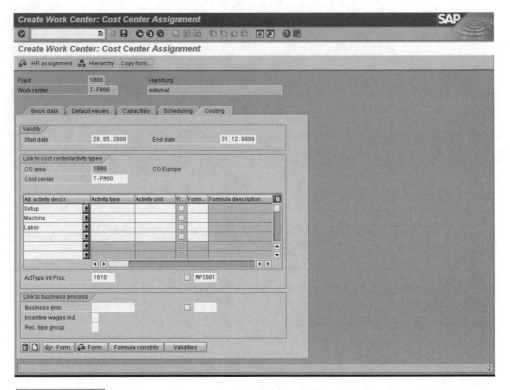

FIGURE 7.24   Linking cost centres and activity types in a work centre (© SAP AG)

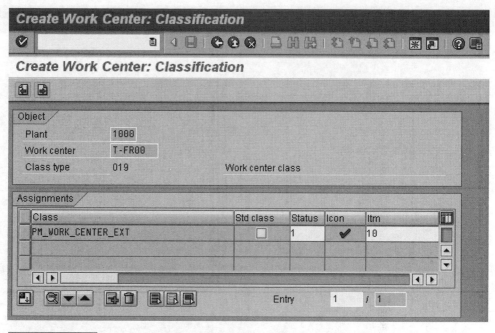

FIGURE 7.25   Classifying a work centre (© SAP AG)

Purchase order 4500004891 was created by your purchasing department. This purchase order must be assigned to the external cost centre T-PM00 and have a specific validity period. The item price of the purchase order must contain the price of the activity type. You can display the purchase order via transaction ME23. Purchase order 4500004891 comprises 200 operating hours for a mechanic from vendor 1000 (Fig. 7.28).

The actual process steps for order entry, release, execution, confirmation (by the PM technician) and technical completion (by you, as the PM planner) are no different from those process steps already described for orders. The only thing you have to note here is that the defined external work centre must be entered at the operation level. You also have the option of assigning the entire order to the external company. To do so, you create an order with only one operation, and assign this operation to the external work centre. You can also assign parts of the order externally by creating one order with several operations. You then enter the external work centre for some of the operations, and an internal work centre for all the others.

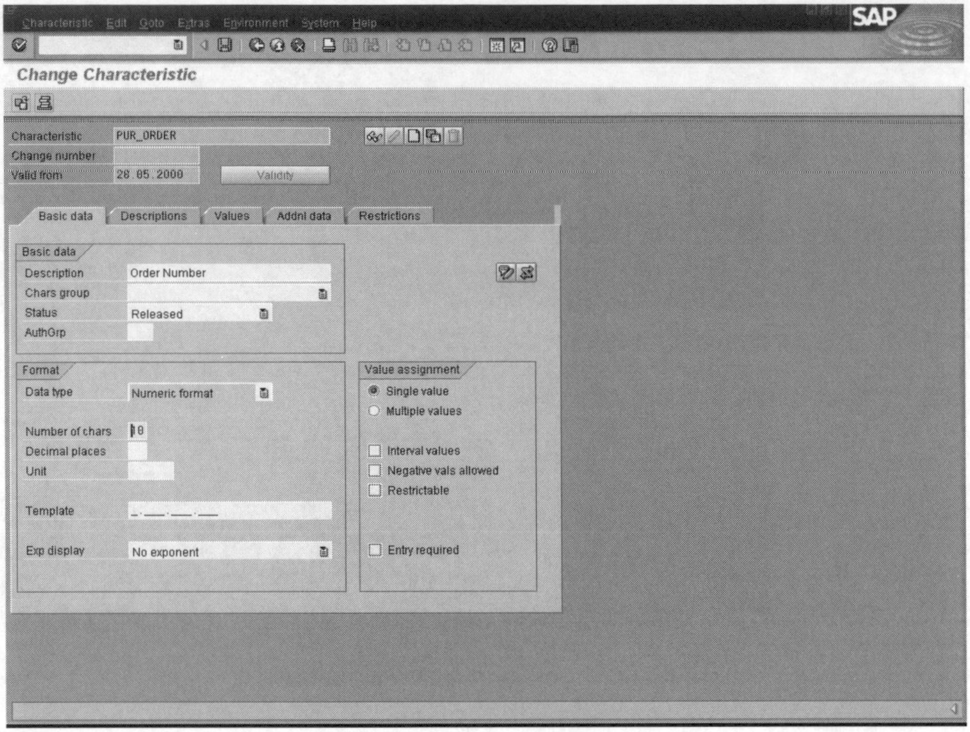

FIGURE 7.26 Characteristic for a work centre class (© SAP AG)

For example, you want to assign an entire order in your ice-cream production plant externally. To do so, you enter the external work centre T-FR00 in the WKCTR/PLANT field for the first and only operation (Fig. 7.29). In the PERSON RESPONSIBLE screen area, you should enter an internal work centre as the main work centre, which supervises the execution of the tasks or accepts the activity (Fig. 7.30).

7.2.4 How the PM planner uses individual purchase orders

If you want to order specific services from various external companies, rather than using one external work centre, you use individual purchase orders. To do so, you create a maintenance order and change the control key to PM02. Other operation data (such as the work centre, amount of work, operation duration, or activity type) do not have to be entered (Fig. 7.31). From the order, choose the OPERATIONS tab page, select the external operation, and choose the EXTERNAL pushbutton. In the screen that is now displayed, you can enter the detailed data for the external service (Fig. 7.32).

In the OPERATION QUANTITY and PRICE fields, you have two options:

1   You can enter, for example, 20 hours as the operation quantity and $100.00 as the price. This would mean that you pay a total of $2000.00 for 20 hours.
2   You can enter, for example, a service unit as the operation quantity and $300.00 as the price. This means that you pay a fixed price of $300.00, irrespective of the hours actually worked.

In the current example, 417000 is automatically defaulted as the cost element for externally processed services, and 007 as the material group for external services.

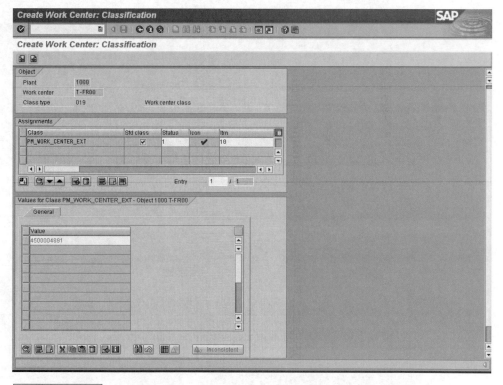

FIGURE 7.27 Assigning a purchase order to a work centre via characteristic value assignment (© SAP AG)

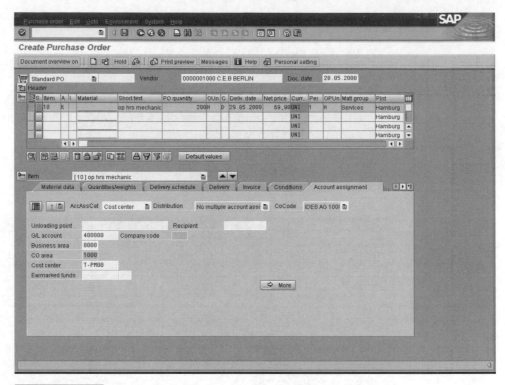

FIGURE 7.28 Purchase order for external work centre (© SAP AG)

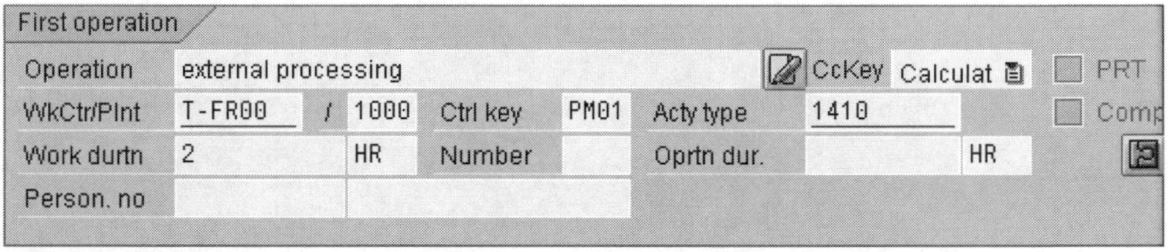

First operation					
Operation	external processing				☑ CcKey Calculat 🗒 ☐ PRT
WkCtr/PInt	T-FR00 / 1000	Ctrl key	PM01	Acty type	1410 ☐ Comp
Work durtn	2	HR	Number	Oprtn dur.	HR 🗒
Person. no					

FIGURE 7.29 External work centre in an order operation (© SAP AG)

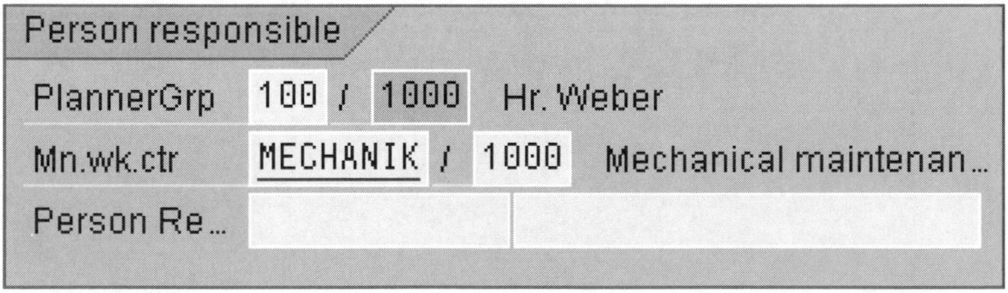

Person responsible			
PlannerGrp	100 / 1000	Hr. Weber	
Mn.wk.ctr	MECHANIK / 1000	Mechanical maintenan...	
Person Re...			

FIGURE 7.30 Main work centre in an order header (© SAP AG)

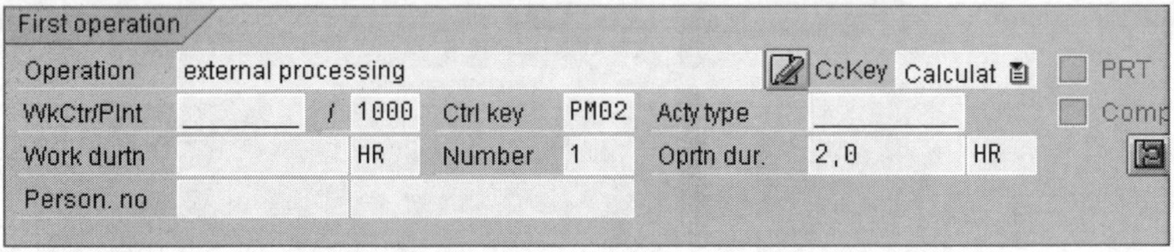

FIGURE 7.31 Control key PM02 in an order (© SAP AG)

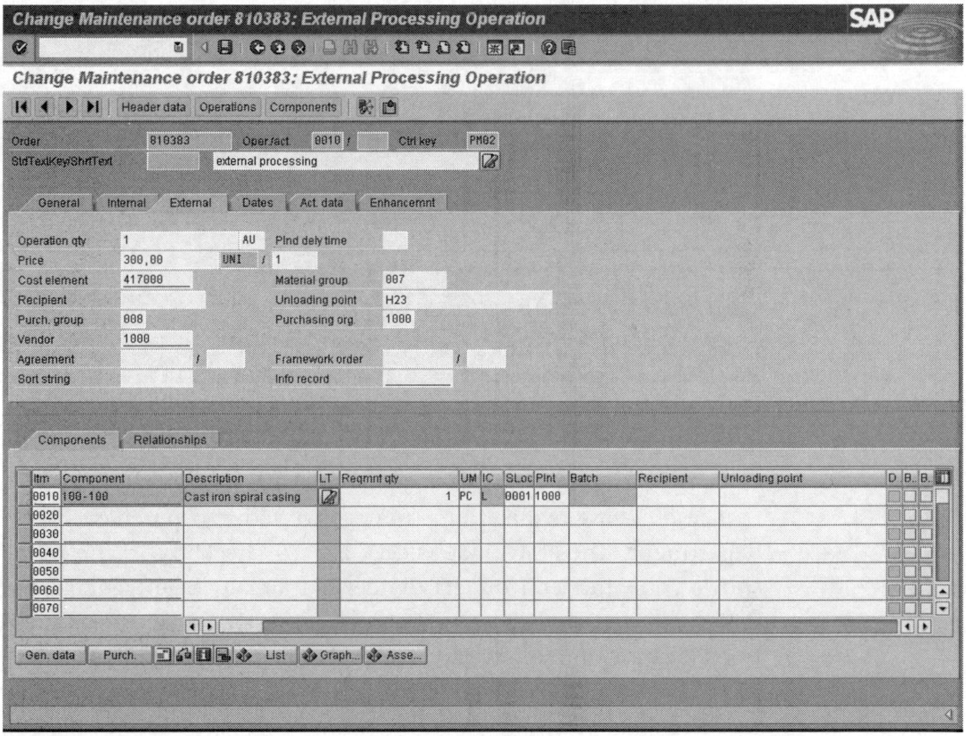

FIGURE 7.32 Detailed data: external processing for order operation (© SAP AG)

As soon as you plan an order with control key PM02, a purchase requisition is automatically triggered in the background. The number of the purchase requisition is displayed in the REQUISITION field in the ACTUAL DATA tab page of the detailed data for external processing in the order operation (Fig. 7.33). From this tab page, you can also call up the master record of the purchase requisition (Fig. 7.34). Alternatively, you can also display the purchase requisition in the document flow for the order. To do so, choose EXTRAS | ORDER DOCUMENTS | DOCUMENT FLOW.

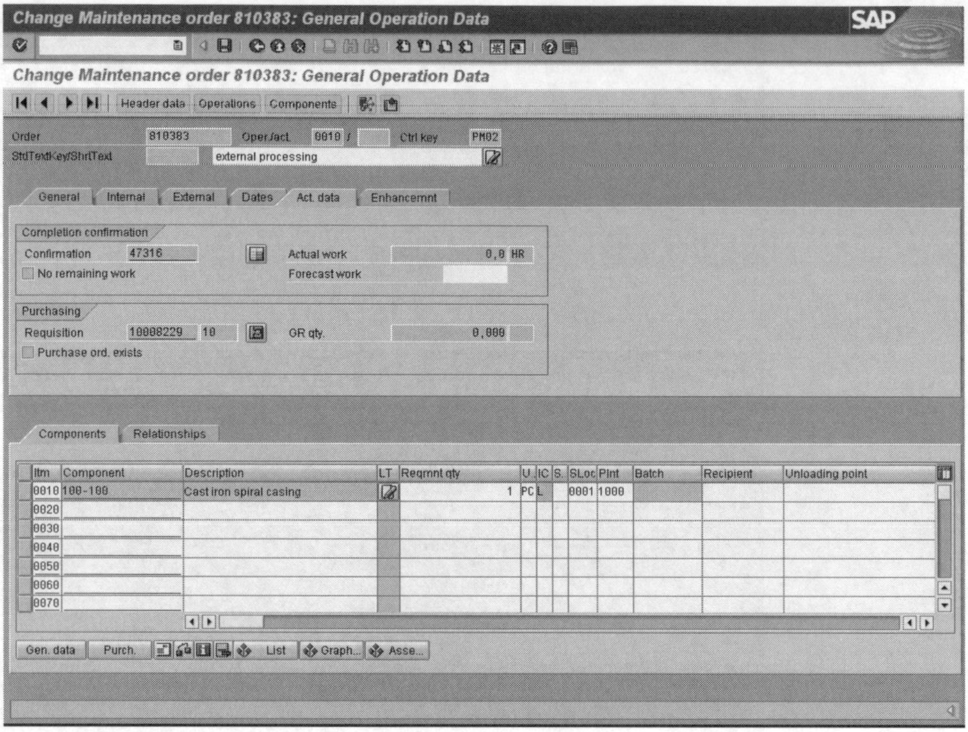

FIGURE 7.33 Detailed data for purchase requisition (external processing) (© SAP AG)

The purchase requisition is now converted to a purchase order in the purchasing department. The PURCHASE ORDER EXISTS checkbox in the ACTUAL DATA tab page shows you whether a purchase order has already been generated for your order (Fig. 7.35). External services are not confirmed in the same way as normal time confirmations, but are entered as goods receipts for purchase orders. The GR QTY field in the ACTUAL DATA tab page shows you whether goods have been received and, if so, how many (Fig. 7.36).

If the final delivery indicator is flagged with goods receipt, the order operation is assigned the status EODL (EXTERNAL OPERATION DELIVERED). If a goods movement has already been carried out, but has not yet been completed, the order operation is assigned the status EOPD (external operation partially delivered). As the PM planner, you thus receive constant confirmation of how work is progressing. The operation status is displayed in the STATUS field of the GENERAL tab page (Fig. 7.37). After the external service has been checked and accepted, you technically complete the order.

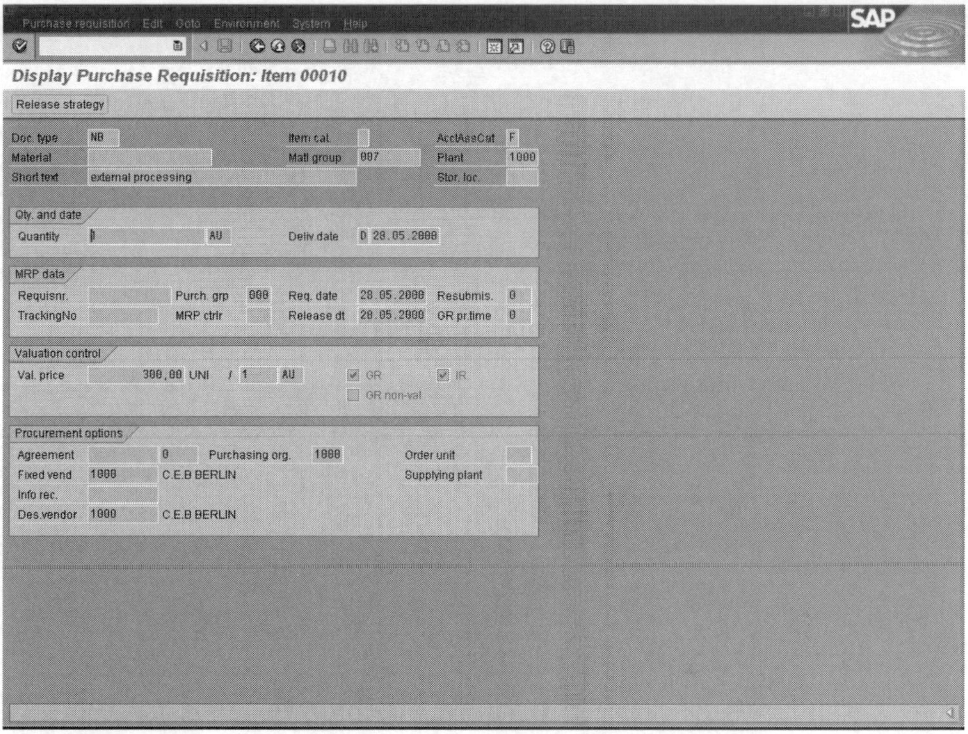

FIGURE 7.34   Master record (purchase requisition) (© SAP AG)

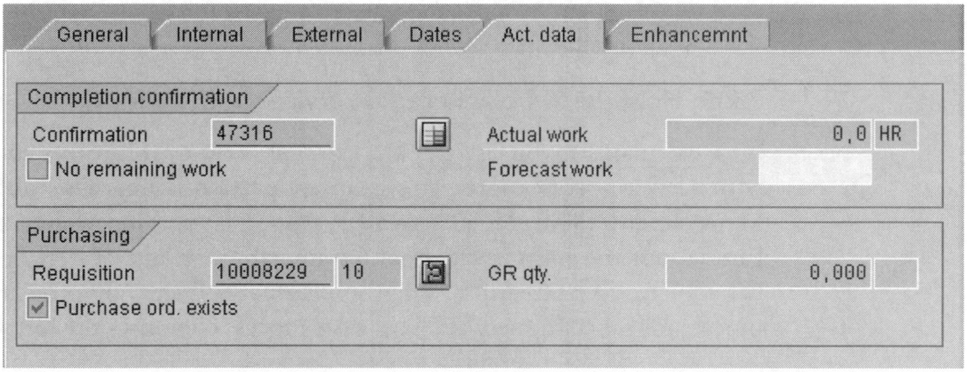

FIGURE 7.35   Purchase order exists for order (© SAP AG)

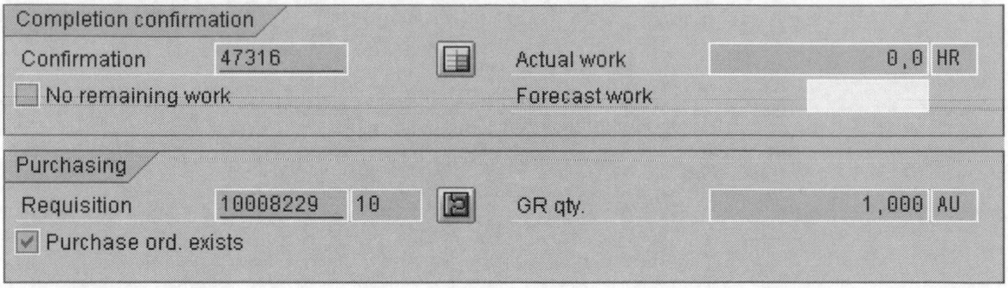

Completion confirmation

Confirmation	47316	▦	Actual work	0,0 HR
▢ No remaining work			Forecast work	

Purchasing

Requisition	10008229	10	▣	GR qty.	1,000 AU
☑ Purchase ord. exists				

FIGURE 7.36   Goods have been received (© SAP AG)

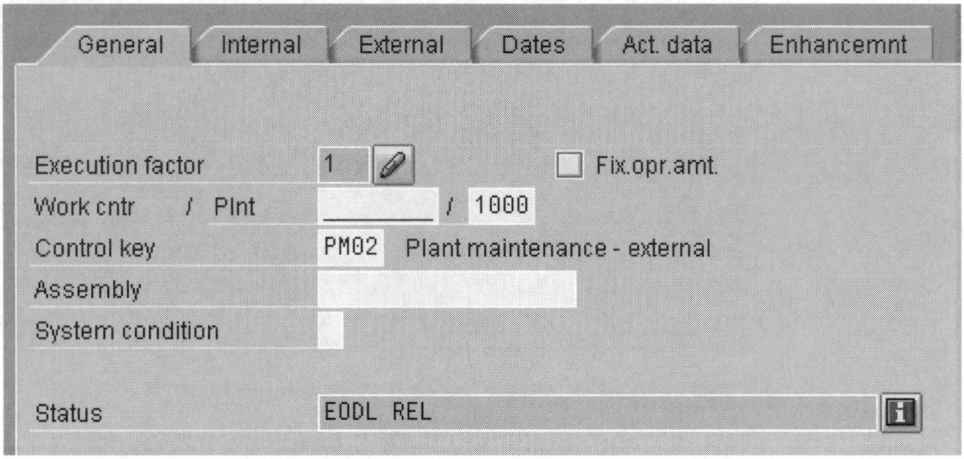

General	Internal	External	Dates	Act. data	Enhancemnt

Execution factor   1 ✎   ▢ Fix.opr.amt.

Work cntr   / Plnt   _____ / 1000

Control key   PM02   Plant maintenance - external

Assembly   _____

System condition   ▢

Status   EODL REL   ℹ

FIGURE 7.37   External operation delivered (© SAP AG)

7.2.5 How the PM planner uses service specifications

As a PM planner, you use the R/3 External Services (MM-SRV) component to work with service specifications. This is an application component within the Materials Management (MM) module, which supports your maintenance planning tasks throughout the entire cycle, from bid invitation, award, and acceptance of services, through to invoice verification. The External Services component provides a basic process for procuring services. This basic process comprises the following functions:

▨ You can use SERVICE MASTER RECORDS, in which you can store the descriptions of all the services to be procured. In addition to this, a standard service catalog and model service specifications are available.

▨ You can create separate SERVICE SPECIFICATIONS for each planned procurement in the desired document; for example, in the maintenance plan, maintenance order, PS network, MM purchase requisition, request for quotation, contract, purchase order, or service entry sheet.

In addition to items with services, you can also enter items with materials in service specifications.

When you create extensive service specifications, you can use the reference method and selection function to copy documents quickly and easily from existing master records and documents. This means that you do not always have to list the services again manually.

- You can evaluate data that already exists in the system to find suitable sources of supply for specific services.

- You can also carry out a bid invitation, use a price comparison list to evaluate the quotations received, and then award the purchase order to the desired vendor.

- While the service is being performed, lists and totals displays provide you with a constant overview of your service specifications, how performance is progressing, as well as the costs incurred.

- You can document services performed in service entry sheets.

- Acceptance can be issued in various ways for the service entry sheets.

- After acceptance, the invoice can be checked and payment made.

As alternatives to this basic process, the system also provides you with various accelerated and simplified processes. You can use these processes as you wish, in accordance with the individual procurement transaction.

The External Services component provides two basic options for entering services performed:

1 *Planned services with details of specification, quantity and price*
Planned services are services that are already known at the start of the planned procurement. When the request is made, the specifications are entered either using a service master record or via short/long text directly in the service specifications. In both cases, the price and quantity are specified.

2 *Unplanned services with details of a value limit only*
Unplanned services are services that cannot (or should not) be specified, since the specific individual services that will constitute the planned procurement (for example, building an office block) are not known when the request is made. These can also be services that you do not want to plan for various reasons. Unplanned services do not, therefore, contain service descriptions, and are entered in the form of value limits in $. Services may be performed up to this value limit, which ensures that costs are monitored.

The External Services component is fully integrated in the Materials Management component. The master data for procuring services can be stored in service master records, which subsequently provide default data for the purchasing documents. The service specifications for a specific planned procurement are not entered and processed separately for each document (for example, as bid invitation specifications or contract service specifications), but are generated directly in the purchasing documents (for example, in a request for quotation, quotation, purchase order, or a contract). In addition to this, the External Services component is linked to the Plant Maintenance (PM) and Project System (PS) components. This enables purchase requisitions to be created for services as part of a maintenance task or a project, and then transferred to purchasing with no additional effort required to maintain the data.

The service master

In a service master, you can maintain all the services that have to be repeatedly procured in your company. In addition to the unique description of the particular service, a service master record contains further information required for procurement (for example, texts, or units of measure). You can store price information at various levels. For example, you can store a 'market price' or 'own estimated price' of $100.00 per hour for service A, or $98.00 with vendor Smith and $105.00 with vendor Jones. The individual service master records can be grouped according to various service types (for example, industry sectors or trades).

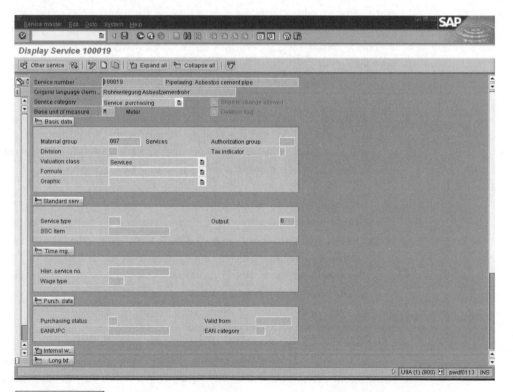

FIGURE 7.38   Service master (© SAP AG)

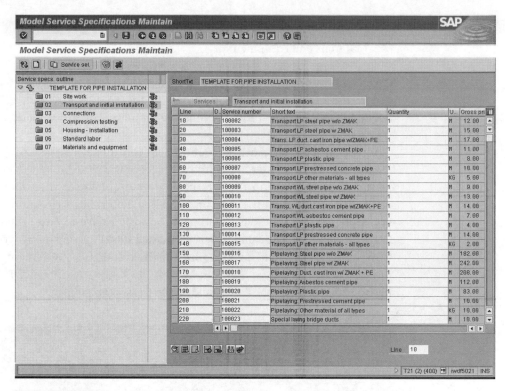

FIGURE 7.39   Model service specifications for pipe laying (© SAP AG)

For example, in your ice-cream production plant, you want to install an asbestos cement pipe. You want to transfer this task to an external company. In the MM component, a service master record already exists for this purpose (100019, Pipe laying: asbestos cement pipe). Call up the master record via transaction AC03 (Fig. 7.38).

This service master record is an element of the model service specifications for pipe laying generally. You can display these model service specifications via transaction ML12 (Fig. 7.39). In the model service specifications, the individual service master records are grouped together under the following service types:

1 Site work

2 Transport and initial installation

3 Connections

4 Compression testing

5 Housing installation

6 Standard labour

7 Materials and equipment

Service master record 100019 is listed as line 180 under the transport and installation area in the model service specifications. In the BASIC DATA tab page of the related detailed data, you can see that laying one metre of asbestos cement pipe should cost $112 (Fig. 7.40).

You create a maintenance order and assign control key PM03 to the order operation. It is not necessary to enter the technical object or the performing work centre here (Fig. 7.41). When you call up the external processing data for the order operation, the service specifications for the order are displayed. Enter the service number of the desired service master in the SERVICES tab page. You then have to enter the quantity of the desired service. Since the unit in service master 100019 is one metre, you have to enter '4' in the QUANTITY field if you require four metres of asbestos cement pipe (Fig. 7.42). The price for one metre is then displayed in the GROSS PRICE field. The price for four metres is displayed in the PRICE field of the EXTERNAL tab page.

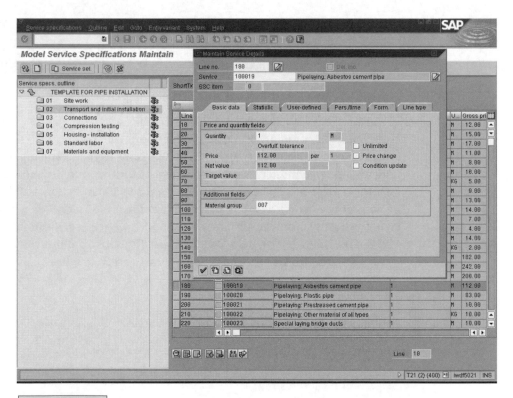

FIGURE 7.40   Service master in model service specifications (© SAP AG)

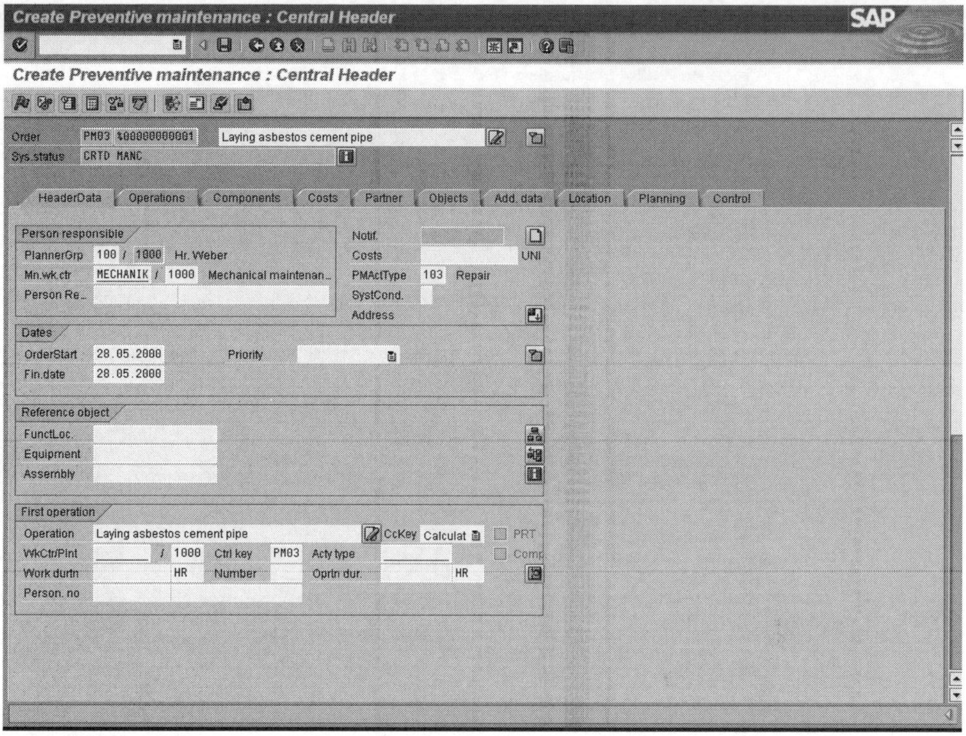

FIGURE 7.41   Order with control key PM03 (© SAP AG)

The system automatically generates a purchase requisition. In purchasing, this purchase requisition is used to generate a purchase order. As the PM planner, you create a service entry sheet for this purchase order. To do so, use transaction ML81. Enter the number of the purchase order in the PURCHASE ORDER field. Select the ADOPTION OF PLANNED SERVICES indicator in the ADOPT PLANNED SERVICES screen area so that the details are copied from the purchase requisition order. In the SEQUENTIAL CONTROL area, select ADD. If you do not do this, you cannot create a new service entry (Fig. 7.43).

The service entry sheet is a list in which you can document all the services that were planned in the purchase order and have actually been performed. The service entry sheet also specifies unplanned services that have been performed, and which were not specified when the purchase order was generated. After consulting with the vendor, you can also copy the service entry information from the vendor rather than entering it yourself. For this purpose, the R/3 System provides you with an interface for importing external data.

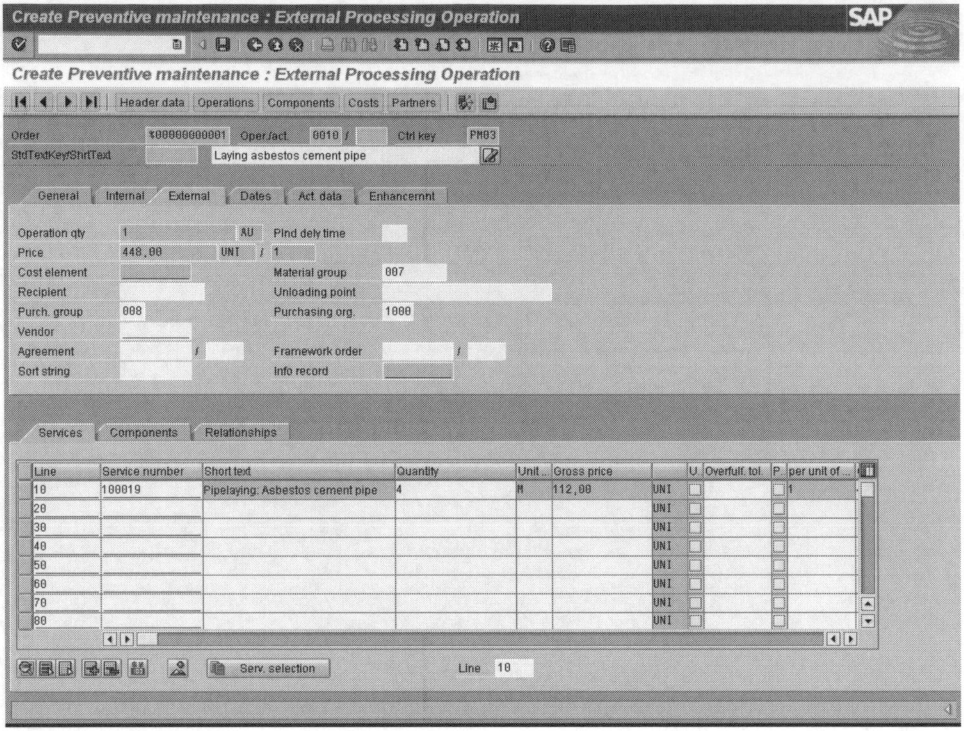

FIGURE 7.42 Service specifications for order (© SAP AG)

In our case, the service entry sheet only contains service master 100019 (Fig. 7.44). Enter all the necessary data, and accept the service by choosing the appropriate icons. The system now posts the acceptance document. In the maintenance order, this is equivalent to the goods receipt for individual purchase orders; in other words, the order header contains the status GMPS (Goods movement posted). You can now technically complete the order.

7.2.6 How the controller checks external processing

In the following, the cost flow for processing with external work centres will be described.

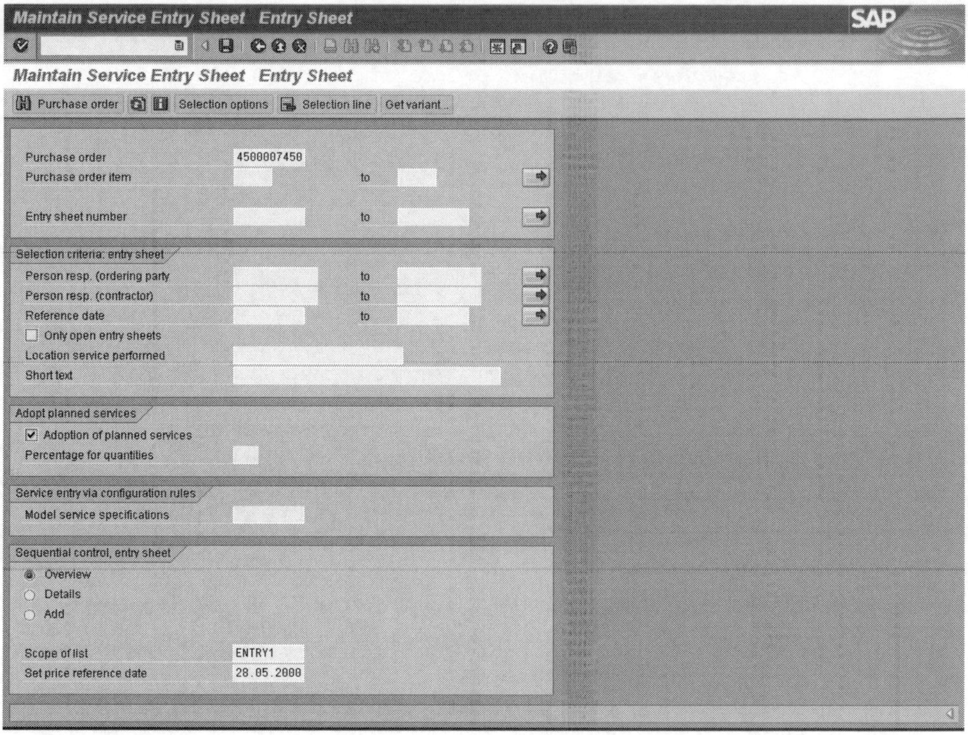

FIGURE 7.43   Creating a service entry sheet (© SAP AG)

As soon as services are performed by an external work centre, the associated external cost centre is credited, and the maintenance order is debited. Invoice receipt is carried out periodically (for example, monthly), not for each individual service. The invoice total comprises the value of all the services that have been performed since the last invoice was issued. Account assignment here is always carried to the external cost centre, and not to the individual orders. In the mid-term, the external cost centre has to balance its books; in other words, the total credits caused by the maintenance orders must be equal to the total debits caused by the invoices.

In the following, the cost flow for processing with individual purchase orders will be described.

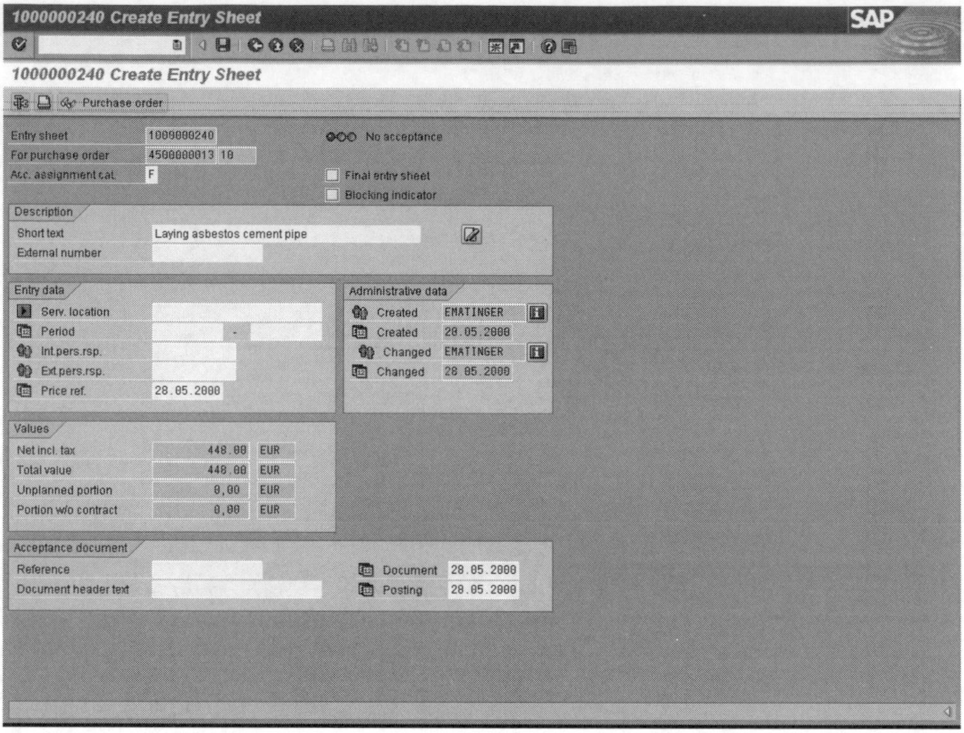

FIGURE 7.44 Accepting a service in the service entry sheet (© SAP AG)

As soon as the external service order is posted as a goods receipt, the service is valued with the purchase order price and entered in the accounts of financial accounting. The maintenance order with control key PM02 is then debited with this value (Fig. 7.45).

The invoice from the external company is generally received after the service has actually been performed. As a result, the offsetting entry is posted to a clearing account and then written off automatically when the invoice is received. Any variances between the purchase order value and the invoice value are subsequently debited or credited to the order. The maintenance order is then settled in the usual way, via the receiver named in the settlement rule. In this example, the DM 300 with cost element 417000 (purchased services) is charged to offsetting account 191100 (goods received/invoice received – offsetting: external processing), where it remains until the invoice is received.

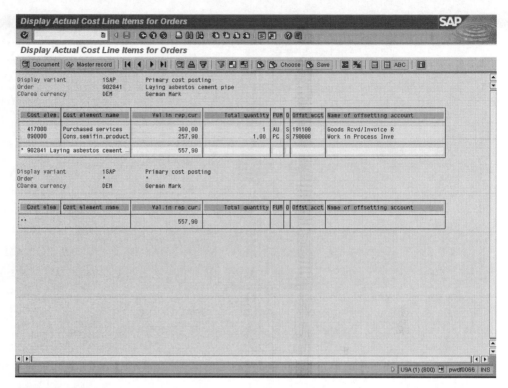

FIGURE 7.45 Cost report in order after debit due to goods receipt (© SAP AG)

The cost flow for processing with service specifications is as follows. As soon as the PM planner has accepted the service entry sheet, the acceptance document is posted. This results in the actual costs being posted to the maintenance order (Fig. 7.46). The maintenance order is then settled in the usual way to the receiver named in the settlement rule.

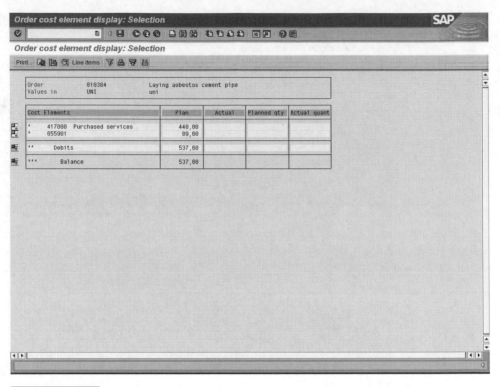

FIGURE 7.46 Cost report in an order after posting of acceptance document (© SAP AG)

CHAPTER 8

Integrative aspects

8.1 INTEGRATION OF THE PM COMPONENT: GENERAL

The exceptional features of the PM component are to a great extent based on the integration of other R/3 components. For example, PM is equipped with links to the Logistics components, such as Materials Management (MM) (in the context of purchase requisitions and ordering), or to the PP component (with regard to capacity requirements planning). The integration of the Project System (PS) component enables you to manage plant maintenance projects. In addition to this, integrating the Controlling (CO), Asset Accounting (FI-AA) and Investment Management (IM) components provides comprehensive coverage for all your business requirements. The most important aspects of integration will be discussed in the following sections.

8.2 INTEGRATION OF THE MATERIALS MANAGEMENT (MM) COMPONENT

The issue of spare parts planning has already been covered in section 5.2, 'Tasks of the PM planner'. The process flows for purchase requisitions and purchase orders were also discussed in this section.

The use of service specifications was described in Chapter 7, 'Special Cases' (section 7.2.5, 'How the PM planner uses service specifications').

INTEGRATION OF THE PRODUCTION PLANNING (PP) COMPONENT

Capacity requirements planning has already been covered in section 5.2, 'Tasks of the PM planner' (under 'How to carry out capacity requirements planning').

INTEGRATION OF THE QUALITY MANAGEMENT (QM) COMPONENT

The integration of the PM and QM modules can be subdivided into the areas of test equipment management and extended measurement reading entry. The master data necessary for integration (such as equipment, measuring points and counters) has already been discussed in Chapter 4, 'Objects in R/3 PM'.

8.4.1 Process flow in test equipment management

Maintenance task lists are used to plan and carry out regular inspections. These lists include the operations in quality inspection, as well as maintenance plans, from which maintenance call objects can be generated in the form of orders. The basics of work scheduling, as well as creating and maintaining maintenance task lists, have already been covered in section 5.2.5, 'Work scheduling'.

In the first step, a maintenance task list containing the inspection operations is generated for the work to be performed. These operations are assigned master inspection characteristics (language-independent inspection characteristics that can be used frequently in inspection plans). In the QM data of the operations, inspection point completions are defined (for example, automatic valuation). The master inspection characteristic, which also establishes the link to the measuring point, is assigned a defect code. If a measurement reading is outside the tolerance range, this code is copied to the notification generated by the system.

For test equipment management to be carried out efficiently, it is essential that the test equipment to be inspected is created as a production resource/tool. If the measurement readings are to be updated, measuring points must also be assigned to this equipment.

The maintenance plans described in section 5.2, 'Tasks of the PM planner', are created to plan and monitor inspection dates. These maintenance plans are assigned a maintenance cycle or a maintenance strategy, as well as the maintenance task lists created previously, and the technical objects to be inspected. As with the process flow in maintenance planning, an order with inspection lot is created as a result of scheduling.

The measurement readings yielded by the inspection are entered in the QM component as an inspection result, and are used as a basis for making usage decisions. If measurement readings for an item of equipment are outside defined tolerance ranges, for example, the usage decision 'Adjust' can be made. To prevent the item of equipment from being used in production, its status can be changed and a maintenance notification with an appropriate error code generated.

8.5 INTEGRATION OF THE PROJECT SYSTEM (PS) COMPONENT

8.5.1 Basics of project planning

Projects are tasks with specific characteristics:

- They are, as a rule, complex, one-off tasks, and are associated with a relatively high risk.
- They have precisely defined objectives, which must be agreed on by the customer and contractor.
- They are of limited duration and are particularly cost- and resource-intensive.
- They are usually of strategic importance for the company that carries them out.

Projects are generally integrated in the internal processes of a company. To control all the tasks that occur in project implementation, a project-specific form of organization is required, which should be located between the departments affected. To enable an entire project to be carried out, the aims of the project must be described in detail, and the project tasks to be performed must be structured. A clear and uniquely structured project is the basis for planning, monitoring and control.

8.5.2 Planning structures and schedules

Structural planning, which is implemented in the Project System (PS) component via the work breakdown structure, specifies the structures for organizing and controlling the project, and subdivides the project into individual, hierarchically organized structure items. This subdivision can be carried out according to various criteria, depending on the type and complexity of the particular project (for example, depending on the responsibility and structure of the departments involved, or the relationships attributable to production and assembly).

In the work breakdown structure, the individual operations and tasks required to carry out the project are described in separate structure items, and related to one another hierarchically. Depending on the particular project implementation phase, the individual structure items can be further structured step by step via individual levels, until the desired level of detail is reached. The elements of the work breakdown structure (called WBS elements in the Project System) describe a task or project within the work breakdown structure. WBS elements can be tasks, part tasks or work packages.

In the Project System, you can plan the processes and sequence of tasks with *networks*. This form of planning specifies, for example, which events in the project are interdependent, and which additional activities are required or have to be detailed. A network maps the schedule of a project or an activity in the project. The various structural elements of the project and their interdependencies can be displayed graphically.

During the life of a project, networks are used as a basis for planning, analysing, describing, controlling and monitoring dates, costs and resources (such as personnel, machines or materials). Networks consist essentially of activities and relationships.

8.5.3 Processing plant maintenance projects

Plant maintenance projects are defined and planned in the Project Information System, where the project structure and WBS elements are specified. Using the integration between the PM and PS components is expedient because it enables:

■ Coordination of complex logistical processes: dates in WBS elements are copied as basic dates of an order.

■ Shared administration and monitoring of funds: the budget for the WBS element is copied as available funds and compared to the costs for the order.

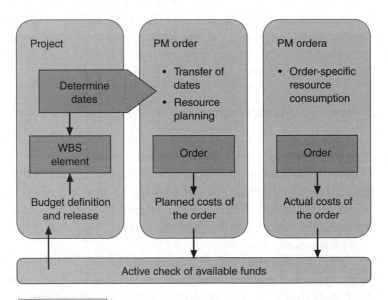

FIGURE 8.1   Schematic illustration of processing for PM projects

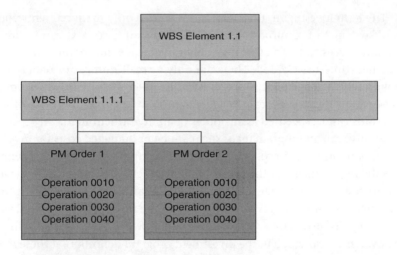

FIGURE 8.2   Schematic illustration of project management (© SAP AG)

The link between the maintenance order and the WBS element enables you to check resource utilization against the current budget. Figure 8.1 provides a schematic illustration of processing for plant maintenance orders.

Budgets and dates are planned and monitored at the level of WBS elements. Scheduling and resource planning for the individual tasks, however, is carried out at the level of the particular maintenance order.

The project-related maintenance tasks that have been performed are settled to the related sub-projects (the WBS elements) (Fig. 8.2). The incurred costs of the order are 'forwarded' to the WBS element, which results in the order being credited and the WBS element debited. When settlement is complete, the balance of the maintenance order is zero.

8.6   INTEGRATION OF THE INVESTMENT MANAGEMENT (IM) COMPONENT

8.6.1 Basics of Investment Management

The functionalities of the Investment Management component support the planning, investment and financing processes in your company when you carry out:

- Investments in tangible fixed assets, such as acquisitions of fixed assets (produced internally or purchased)
- Investments in research and development
- Projects which primarily incur overhead costs
- Maintenance programs

The term investment, therefore, is not limited only to investments you capitalize for bookkeeping or tax purposes. An investment in this context can be any measure that initially causes costs, and that may only generate revenue or provide other benefits after a certain time has elapsed. There are only a small number of data objects specific to Investment Management, since most of its objects are borrowed from other components. Maintenance orders can be assigned to an investment item, and functional locations can be specified as attributes of an investment item.

An investment program maps the planned or budgeted costs for investments within a company in the form of a hierarchical structure, which can be defined to meet the specific requirements of the company. Investment programs can be structured according to the organizational structure of a company, and according to the scale of the allocated measures. An investment program can be used to manage all the tasks, orders or projects located in one controlling area, and which have the same currency and fiscal year variant as specified in the investment program definition. If these requirements are met, cross-company code programs can also be defined.

Within the hierarchy of an investment program, you can also plan and budget the costs for investments. Individual measures can be assigned to the investment program positions at the bottom of the hierarchy. As shown in Figure 8.3, the possible measures are internal orders, WBS elements, and maintenance orders.

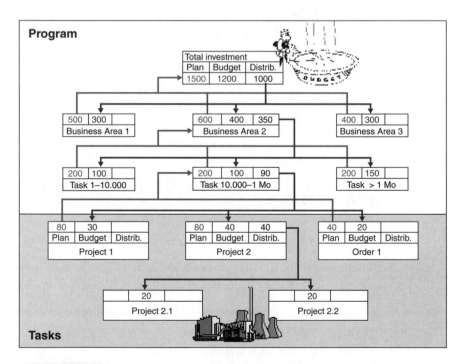

FIGURE 8.3   Structure of an investment program with planning and budgeting of the program positions and measures (© SAP AG)

8.6.2 Processing maintenance orders as investment measures

The scenario outlined in Figure 8.4 assumes that funds budgeted for an investment are to be compared with the planned and actual values of the individual investment measures in Reporting.

Using the IM information system, the planned and actual costs of the order can be rolled up and compared with the budget.

The scenario illustrated in Figure 8.5 assumes that the funds budgeted for an investment measure are to be compared with the planned and actual values of the individual investment measures in Reporting. As in the scenario outlined in Figure 8.4, the

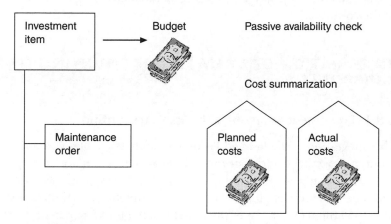

FIGURE 8.4   PM-IM scenario without budget distribution

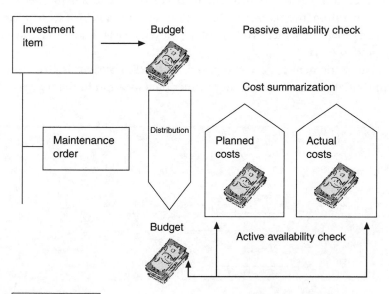

FIGURE 8.5   PM-IM scenario with budget distribution

planned and actual costs of the order are rolled up using the IM information system and can be compared with the budget.

8.7 INTEGRATION OF THE CONTROLLING (CO) COMPONENT

The subject of *cost control* has already been discussed in section 5.3, 'Tasks of the controller' (under 'Estimated costs, planned, and actual costs'). *Budget allocation* was discussed in Section 5.32, 'Order budget'.

For a detailed description of settling maintenance orders, refer to section 5.3, 'Tasks of the controller'.

8.8 INTEGRATION OF THE ASSET ACCOUNTING (FI-AA) COMPONENT

8.8.1 Equipment as an object in Asset Accounting

The integration of the PM and FI-AA components enables you to form asset units by grouping together equipment for maintenance from an accounting point of view. In this case, the higher-level (technical) system is regarded as a tangible asset. Grouping equipment to form tangible assets enables comprehensive evaluations to be carried out on a level higher than that of the individual items of equipment.

As shown in Figure 8.6, the PM and FI-AA components are linked via the asset number in the 'Account assignment' group of the equipment master.

In maintenance processing, assets can also be specified as receivers when maintenance orders are settled. This enables maintenance activities that must be capitalized to be settled to assets.

The settlement receiver proposed by the R/3 System is the asset assigned to the appropriate item of equipment or functional location in the master record.

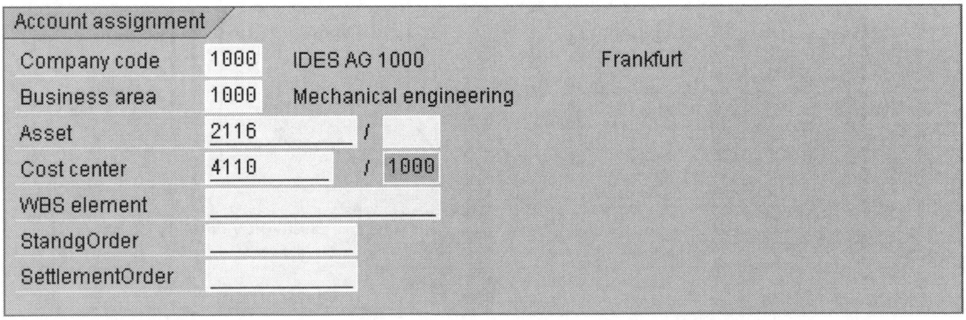

FIGURE 8.6 Integration PM – FI-AA via asset number (© SAP AG)

8.8.2 Workflow for data synchronization

The integration of the PM and FI-AA components is supported by the ability to create and change equipment and assets synchronously via workflow. The workflow can be configured so that the system automatically generates an equipment master record when an asset is created.

The equipment category is determined via the asset class. Consistency of the data in the asset and equipment is also ensured by the fact that fields in the equipment master record are updated when changes are made to the asset master record. The system also allows you to specify that when an item of equipment is created or changed an asset master record is automatically created or changed.

| 8.9 | **INTEGRATION OF THE HUMAN RESOURCES (HR) COMPONENT (EXAMPLE: TIME SHEET)** |

8.9.1 Time sheets: basics

The SAP Time Sheet component (CATS – Cross Application Time Sheet) is a cross-application transaction which enables actual times for individual employees to be entered in a central time sheet. The layout of the Time Sheet can be specified via data entry profiles.

Reports transfer the data to the various applications. The actual times involved can be relevant for different applications simultaneously. The CATS functionality enables time data for the following target applications to be entered in or transferred to the Time Sheet:

- Human Resources (HR): attendances, absences and employee remuneration information
- Controlling (CO): internal activity allocation
- External Services (MM-SRV): entry of services performed
- Plant Maintenance (PM), Customer Service (CS): completion confirmations for orders
- Project System PS: confirmations for networks

IMPORTANT Confirmations in Production Planning (PP) are not supported by CATS, since only time data is recorded, not machine and quantity data.

The prerequisites for using CATS are:

- A 'mini-master' in Human Resources with the personnel numbers and HR data of the employees for whom the times are to be entered.

- A data entry profile for entering person-related time data.
- The appropriate authorizations for working with the CATS Time Sheet.

The CATS process comprises the following steps:

1. Entering data in the Time Sheet
2. Releasing time data
3. Approving time data
4. Transferring CATS time data to target applications

8.9.2 CATS and Plant Maintenance

Completion confirmations for maintenance orders can be carried out via the Time Sheet. The following points present the interrelated assignments and relationships between Plant Maintenance and Human Resources step by step. Figure 8.8 provides a schematic representation of these relationships.

- A maintenance order is used to plan the performance of maintenance orders, track the progress of work and allocate the costs for the task. The individual activities required by an order are described by operations. The duration and work, as well as the type of activity expected to be required to carry it out, is planned for each operation. The actual times involved in the operation are confirmed in an order.
- An operation is assigned to a work centre. Operations in one order can be assigned to various work centres. The work centre is assigned to a cost centre. Activity types are planned for cost centres and map the activity performed within the cost centres. Activity types are assigned to operations (for example, in orders).
- In addition to this, the work centres in an organizational unit can be assigned to an organizational unit from Human Resources. Positions are assigned to an organizational unit and are, in turn, occupied by people who carry out the work.

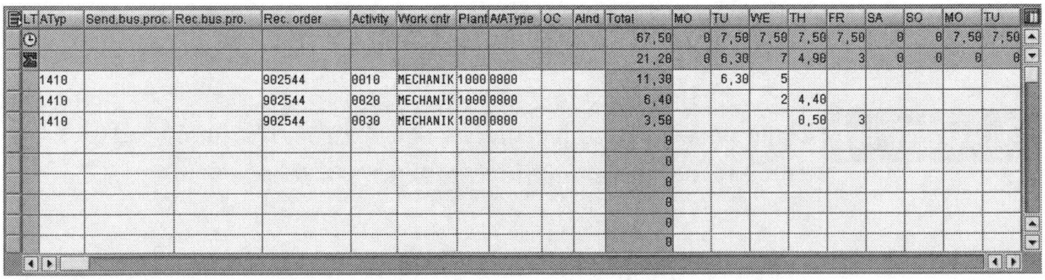

LT	ATyp	Send.bus.proc.	Rec.bus.pro.	Rec. order	Activity	Work cntr	Plant	A/AType	OC	AInd	Total	MO	TU	WE	TH	FR	SA	SO	MO	TU
											67,50	0	7,50	7,50	7,50	7,50	0	0	7,50	7,50
											21,20	0	6,30	7	4,90	3	0	0	0	0
	1410			902544	0010	MECHANIK	1000	0800			11,30		6,30	5						
	1410			902544	0020	MECHANIK	1000	0800			6,40			2	4,40					
	1410			902544	0030	MECHANIK	1000	0800			3,50				0,50	3				
											0									
											0									
											0									
											0									
											0									
											0									

FIGURE 8.7 Time recording in the Time Sheet (© SAP AG)

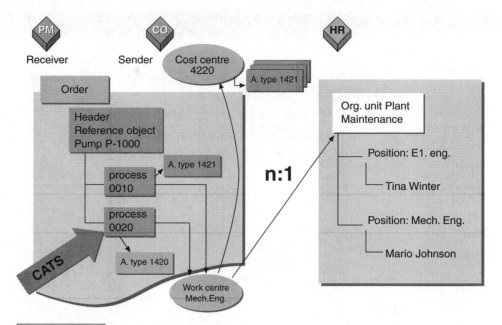

FIGURE 8.8 Integration of PM-HR (example: maintenance order) (© SAP AG)

8.9.3 Prerequisites for using CATS

Person-related time data is entered in the cross-application Time Sheet. A mini-master is required for each employee affected, who is identified by a unique personnel number. This mini-master is defined in entry screens in Human Resources (also known as info-types). Infotypes are entry screens for storing employee data. They are logically classified according to various contents, and contain both optional and required entry fields.

The CATS mini-master must contain at least the following Human Resources info-types:

▓ Actions (0000)

This infotype is required for hiring an employee (in other words, the initial entry of an employee's data).

▓ Organizational Assignment (0001)

This infotype comprises information for incorporating the employee in the organizational structure and personnel structure of a company.

▓ Personal Data (0002)

This infotype comprises personal employee data, such as name, date of birth and so on.

It is recommended that you use the 'Time Sheet Defaults' infotype (0315). This infotype saves data used as default values in the Time Sheet. Various entries can be made here:

- Account assignments (such as sending cost centre or activity type) are used in Logistics and Controlling.

- The plant is used as the default plant for Logistics.

- Vendor, sending purchase order, sending purchase order item, and service number are used as defaults for using the service orders.

CHAPTER 9

Interfaces to non-SAP systems

INTERFACE TO PROCESS CONTROL SYSTEMS AND BUILDING CONTROL SYSTEMS

9.1.1 How process control systems and building control systems can contribute to plant maintenance

Process control systems are used to monitor, regulate, control and optimize specific technical processes (for example, the cooling system in an ice-cream production plant). Building control systems are used to monitor, control, regulate and optimize specific technical processes within a building (for example, air-conditioning). You can transfer data relevant to plant maintenance that has been acquired in these systems to the R/3 System via an interface (PM-PCS interface). The R/3 System uses this data to generate a measurement document, which you can then use as the basis for a maintenance task, or for documentation purposes.

Process control systems and building control systems provide a variety of data acquired in a process, a building or an infrastructure. In this context, SCADA (Supervisory Control And Data Acquisition) systems function as filters, filtering out data relevant to maintenance, and thereby preventing the R/3 System from being flooded with process data. In addition to this, SCADA systems provide the basis for communication between the R/3 System and one or more process control systems.

If a cooling system breaks down in the ice-cream production plant, the process control system recognizes this and responds appropriately by transferring the ice-cream to another cooling system, or interrupting production. Via the PM-PCS interface, the process control system can notify the R/3 System that the cooling system has broken down. If the appropriate settings have been carried out, the R/3 System can then generate a malfunction report including the data of the cooling system.

Figure 9.1 shows R/3 integration via a SCADA system with a direct field bus connection; in other words, the process control system does not require a SCADA interface. Figure 9.2 shows R/3 integration via a process control system equipped with its own SCADA interface. Figure 9.3 shows R/3 integration to a process control system equipped with the required filter and interface functions, which enables the process control system to be connected directly to the R/3 System without an intermediate SCADA system. Figure 9.4 shows how different process control systems can use a shared SCADA system to establish R/3 integration. In each case, R/3 integration is implemented via Remote Function Call (RFC).

9.1.2 The PM-PCS interface

The PM-PCS interface is an integral element of the R/3 System, and is used to record data from non-SAP systems. This data can be entered from process control systems, as

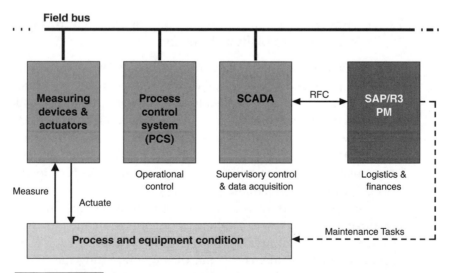

FIGURE 9.1   R/3 integration with a process control system without SCADA interface
(© SAP AG)

well as via laptops or barcode scanners. All of the individual functions are implemented in the R/3 System via RFC-compatible function modules (Remote Function Call):

▨ Function module MEASUREM_DOCUM_RFC_SINGLE_001

▨ Function module MEASUREM_DOCUM_RFC_SINGLE_002

▨ Function module MEASUREM_POINT_RFC_SINGLE_002

▨ Function module FUNC_LOCATION_RFC_002

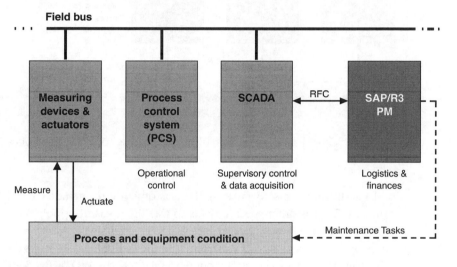

FIGURE 9.2   R/3 integration with a process control system with SCADA interface
(© SAP AG)

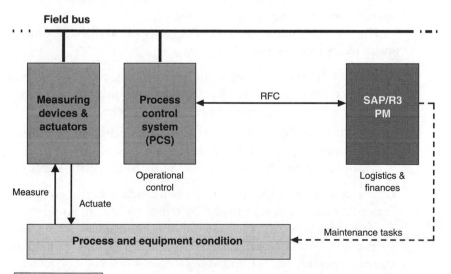

FIGURE 9.3   R/3 integration with a process control system without a SCADA system
(© SAP AG)

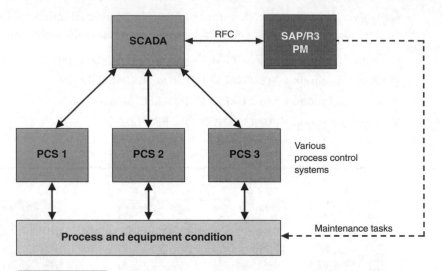

FIGURE 9.4 R/3 integration of various process control systems via a SCADA interface (© SAP AG)

In addition to this, by creating the Customizing to include CI_IMPTT or CI_IMRG, you can add customer-specific fields to IMPTT (measuring point) or IMRG (measurement document) tables. This enables you to control these customer-specific fields in all three of the above customer exits. Since all the individual functions can be called up via RFC, the calls can also be carried out with OLE (via the WDTFUNCS.OCX from SAP). All the function modules are online interfaces. If the R/3 System is not available for some reason, the process control system or SCADA system must be capable of buffering the measurement readings to be transferred.

The following additional customer exits are available for measuring points and measurement documents:

- IMRC0001 runs before updating is carried out, and enables you to define specific field contents in measuring points and measurement documents, generate workflow events, and update customer-specific tables.

- IMRC0002 and IMRC0003 provide you with menu exits during online processing of measuring points and measurement documents, thereby enabling you to trigger customer-specific functions or call up customer-specific screens.

Customer exit IMRC0001 is particularly important in this context, since it can automatically trigger actions in the R/3 System if specific threshold values are exceeded or specific valuation codes occur. You can define measurement range limits for every technical object. Measurement range limits are value ranges within which measurement results are permissible. In Customizing for measuring points, counters and measurement documents, you can configure the system to output a warning or an error message whenever results exceed or fall below the measurement range limits. In addition to this, you can specify that a malfunction report is triggered automatically whenever a specific threshold value is exceeded. Other tasks can be triggered via customer exits in the report (for example, order creation).

The valuation code is a standardized code for evaluating the measurement reading, and is specified in addition the measurement reading. For example, measurement reading 100 degrees centigrade with valuation code 0001 (= 'Measurement reading OK'), measurement reading 105 degrees centigrade with valuation code 0002 ('Measurement reading not OK'). In certain cases, specifying a valuation code alone can be sufficient (for example, 1000 'Fire door OK', 1001 'Fire door damaged', 2001 'Fire door: no local alarm', 2002 'Fire door: no alarm in control room'). When you define valuation codes, the system can automatically trigger a malfunction report containing the text for the valuation code as the malfunction description.

EXAMPLE One of the tasks of your building control system is to monitor continuously the building's air-conditioning. You also use a SCADA system, which recognizes events you have defined (Fig. 9.5). One of the events you have defined specifies that the loss of pressure in an air filter may not exceed 50 mbar. Although all the air filters are replaced once a year, some may have to be replaced earlier than scheduled due to excessive loss of pressure, which contaminates the air filter. You use the R/3 System to carry out condition-based maintenance. The loss of pressure in an air filter is recognized by the building control system and reported to the R/3 System, where it generates a malfunction report and an order.

1 Whenever the pressure exceeds 50 mbar, the SCADA system transfers this as a measurement value (for example, 52 mbar) to the R/3 System via the PM-PCS interface.

2 The R/3 System generates a measurement document for the measurement reading of 52 mbar.

3 The R/3 System identifies 52 mbar as exceeding the threshold value of 50 mbar, or as the valuation code 'Measurement reading not OK'.

4 Via customer exit IMRC0001, the R/3 System generates a malfunction report and an order to replace the air filter.

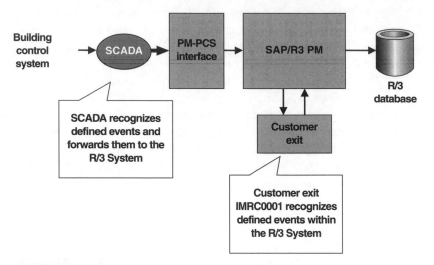

TIP

You can call up the system documentation for each customer exit and each of the function modules that support them. With customer exits, you do so as follows:

1   Choose TOOLS | ABAP WORKBENCH.

2   Next, choose UTILITIES | ENHANCEMENTS | PROJECT MANAGEMENT.

3   Enter 'IMRC0001' or another customer exit, and select DOCUMENTATION as sub-object.

4   Choose DISPLAY. This calls up the online documentation.

With function modules, you use the following procedure (Release 4.5B):

1   Choose TOOLS | ABAP WORKBENCH.

2   Next, choose DEVELOPMENT | FUNCTION BUILDER.

3   Enter 'EXIT_SAPLIMR0_001' or another function module and select INTERFACE as the subobject.

4   Choose DISPLAY.

5   Choose GOTO | FURTHER OPTIONS | DOCUMENTATION | FUNCTION MODULE DOC. This calls up the online documentation.

The implementation of the PM-PCS interface is as follows. To monitor an interface between two systems, logging is generally required at these points:

■ In the source system (PCS/SCADA). For retrospectively entering events that have occurred during a phase in which the target system was not available.

■ In the target system (SAP R/3)
  – For storing all the incoming events if processing is not carried out synchronously.
  – For monitoring event processing if this is carried out in separate steps (transactions), as with workflow, for example.
  – For monitoring database updates (asynchronous update in the R/3 System).

With the PM-PCS interface, however, logging is not required under the following conditions.

■ Event processing in the R/3 System is carried out synchronously.

  Each event results directly in an entry being made in an R/3 application table (in other words, each event generates a measuring document in the R/3 System).

■ Event processing in the R/3 System is carried out in a single transaction.

  Malfunction reports are generated at the same time as the measurement document, in one R/3 transaction.

■ The R/3 application tables are updated synchronously.

During normal operation, logging is carried out only in the source system (process control system or SCADA), where the R/3 measurement document number is logged for each event transferred. This enables the completeness of the transfer to be checked at any time. When the R/3 System returns the document number to the source system, the R/3 database has already been updated. This also applies if a malfunction report has been created in addition to the measurement document.

If the R/3 System is not available, the source system must deal with the following scenarios:

■ The measuring point for which the event is to be transferred is currently locked in the R/3 System.

■ In the source system log, the exception POINT_LOCKED, which is returned by the R/3 System, is logged for the event record.

■ The R/3 System is not currently available.

  The exception ZZ_SAP_NOT_AVAILABLE is written to the log.

■ For some reason, event processing in the R/3 System takes too long.

The exception ZZ_SAP_TIME_OUT is written to the log. The source system no longer waits for confirmation from the R/3 System, and the work process in the source system is released.

The PM-PCS interface enables automatic completion of the event transfer. For this purpose, the log in the source system must be continuously monitored. If necessary, events are transferred to the R/3 System again. The missing R/3 document number in the log enables the source system to identify events that have not yet been transferred. After the exceptions POINT_LOCKED and ZZ_SAP_NOT_AVAILABLE, transferring the event again is not critical, since event processing has not yet been carried out in the R/3 System. After the exception ZZ_SAP_TIME_OUT, it must be ensured that the event is not processed twice in the R/3 System after it has been transferred to the R/3 System again (duplicate records).

Since every incoming event usually results in a new measurement document, duplicates are not immediately identifiable in the R/3 System. For this reason, the source system must transfer each event with a customer-specific document ID. This document ID enables the R/3 System to recognize incoming events that have already been processed, thus avoiding duplicate processing.

■ *Transfer of customer-specific document ID*

You can create a field ZZ_CUST_ID of any format in the prepared customizing include CI_IMRG, for this purpose.

■ *Activation of duplicate recognition*

When you call up the R/3 function module MEASUREM_DOCUM_RFC_SINGLE_001, set the parameter CHECK_CUSTOM_DUPREC = X.

■ *Response of R/3 System after duplicates have been recognized*

The function module sets the indicator CUSTOM_DUPREC_OCCURRED = X. Instead of giving a new measurement document number, the function module returns the number of the measurement document that already exists. As in normal operation, this number is logged for the event in the source system.

9.2 INTERFACES TO CAD SYSTEMS[1]

9.2.1 How CAD systems can contribute to plant maintenance

Examples of CAD drawings include process and instrumentation diagrams (PIDs) in system engineering and plant maintenance. Since planners and technicians constantly

---

1 The authors wish to express their thanks to Mr Jürgen-Peter Brettschneider of PIA GmbH (www.pia.de), who kindly provided the material for this section.

work with PIDs, they usually find it easier to locate a malfunction in a familiar PID than in the R/3 System. For this reason, an existing PID in a CAD system can be used as a user interface for carrying out day-to-day work. From this interface, objects in the R/3 System are to some extent, created or displayed 'in the background'.

Further application areas for CAD systems include building plans, room logbooks, or verifications in facility management, or CAD displays of complex equipment (for example, aircraft and industrial robots) for improved diagnosis of the individual parts affected. In all cases, either the CAD interface is used as a familiar user interface for the R/3 System, or the objects are displayed and processed as CAD drawings from the R/3 System.

Established CAD systems (such as Microstation, PCCAD400 or AutoCAD) communicate with the R/3 System via its integrated CAD interface (unidirectional OCX interface). The following scenarios can be mapped:

1   From his CAD application, the user selects a graphical object, for which he wants to call up the linked data in the R/3 System. To do so, he clicks the mouse to initiate a request from his client to the SAP application server. The result is then displayed in a SAPGUI screen in parallel to his CAD application (Fig. 9.6).

2   From his CAD application, the user selects a graphical object, for which he wants to call up the linked data in the R/3 System. To do so, he clicks the mouse to initiate a request from his client to the SAP application server. In this case, the result is displayed in his CAD application (Fig. 9.7).

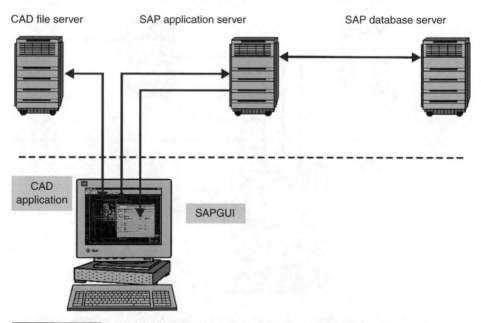

CAD file server   SAP application server   SAP database server

CAD application

SAPGUI

FIGURE 9.6   Calling up SAP data from a CAD system (display in SAPGUI) (© SAP AG)

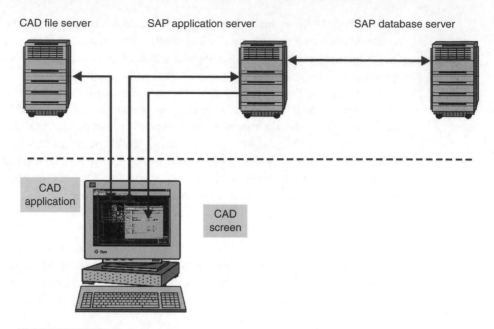

CAD file server   SAP application server   SAP database server

CAD application

CAD screen

FIGURE 9.7   Calling up SAP data from a CAD system (display in CAD) (© SAP AG)

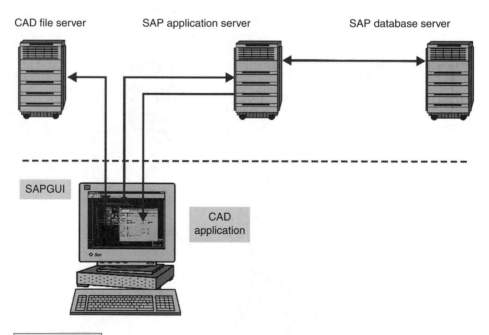

CAD file server   SAP application server   SAP database server

SAPGUI

CAD application

FIGURE 9.8   Calling up a CAD drawing from SAP (display in SAPGUI) (© SAP AG)

3 From the SAPGUI screen of the R/3 System, the user calls up a technical object (functional location or equipment) for which he wants to display the corresponding CAD drawings. The technical object he has called up should be highlighted in the CAD drawing. The user clicks the mouse to initiate a request from his client to the SAP application server. The CAD system then loads and displays the CAD drawing, and also zooms in on and highlights the technical object (Fig. 9.8).

Workshops

A.1   ROLE-BASED WORKSHOP

A.1.1 The basic concept

This appendix is intended to provide the basis for a two-day role-based workshop involving students who already have a basic knowledge of the R/3 System and want to acquire an overview of the R/3 PM component. The chapter is aimed at instructors or team leaders.

TIP   You can also use the information provided in this appendix to carry out training in a project team. For employees in a project team, simply omit phase 1 and expand phase 2 to meet the specific requirements of your company. In this case, the supplementary integration workshop should be held as soon after the role-based workshop as possible.

The PM component is particularly suited for teaching students how to use Logistics functionalities in the R/3 System, since it comprises fewer functions than the PP or MM components. You can easily work through the core processes in PM in two days, using practical examples to teach students how the R/3 System works and the logical processes involved in operating it.

TIP Even if the PP and MM components are included in your syllabus, you should begin by introducing PM.

The workshop is particularly useful for the following departments:

- Computer science (SAP R/3)
- Information management (SAP R/3)
- Business administration, with emphasis on information management (ERP systems)
- Business administration, with emphasis on logistics (logistics systems)

To reduce the amount of preparation required to hold the workshop, the students should already have a certain amount of prior knowledge. If you are working with a group that does not have knowledge of this type, you should schedule an additional half-day of preparation before phase 1 to provide the prerequisites described below. You can also use Chapter 4, 'Objects in R/3 PM', as a source of material for this additional phase.

The participants should have the following prerequisites:

- Basic knowledge of the R/3 System (client/server structure, component structure)
- Basic knowledge of the user interface (possibly based on earlier releases)
- Basic knowledge of the organizational structures in the Logistics components of the R/3 System (the plant concept, controlling area, company code)
- Basic knowledge of logistical processes in manufacturing companies

The aims of the workshop are as follows:

- Students should acquire in-depth knowledge of how to operate the R/3 System and how the system works.
- The small PM component should be used to prepare students for the larger PP and MM components.
- Students should use the example of Plant Maintenance to work through the core processes in Logistics.
- Students should be introduced to the benefits of role-based learning.
- Students should be familiarized with the classification of plant maintenance from a business perspective, and discuss modern concepts in maintenance management.
- Students should develop problem-solving skills in practical project work.

A.1.2 Procedure and schedule

The workshop comprises the following three phases:

- Short presentations and demos on plant maintenance
- Group work on requirements and tasks
- Role-based project work using the R/3 System

Due to the group work involved, the group as a whole should consist of no more than 18 people (in other words, a maximum of six people per team). Each team should ideally be provided with its own computer. No more than three computers are required; if there are fewer than three computers, the teams will have to reckon with extended periods during which they will not be able to work.

The planned timeframe is two days. If it is not possible to work for two whole days, the workshop can also be carried out in two steps, each comprising four classes. Since four classes are required for the practical work with the R/3 System, this is the minimum time unit for phase 3.

EXAMPLE
- Four classes on Friday afternoon for phase 1 (two classes) and phase 2 (two classes)
- Four classes on Saturday morning for phase 3 (3.5 classes) and a brief final feedback session

A.1.3 Tasks in phase 1 – short presentations and demos on plant maintenance

In this phase, you provide the students with a brief overview of how plant maintenance is classified from a business perspective. You can design this phase as a presentation (with or without demos using the R/3 System). You should cover the following topics from Chapters 1, 2 and 4:

- Plant maintenance as a management task (goals and tasks of plant maintenance, traditional and modern forms of organization)
- Modern plant maintenance concepts (such as TPM)
- Business processes
- The PM component and how it is integrated in the R/3 System
- Processing maintenance tasks in PM using the example of planned maintenance with a maintenance plan (demo)

A.1.4 Tasks in phase 2 – group work on requirements and tasks

In phase 2, you divide the students into three groups of equal size. Each group should find answers to the questions listed below. This phase concludes with each group presenting its findings, which are then discussed in a plenary session. The groups should record their findings in writing for the final feedback session in phase 3.

- What are the requirements in the plant maintenance department of your company?
- What are your requirements as regards a plant maintenance system in the ERP environment?
- Who is involved in the plant maintenance process in your company?
- Can these people be grouped together as roles?
- Formulate specific tasks for each of the roles you have defined.

A.1.5 Tasks in phase 3 – role-based project work using the R/3 system

In this phase, you introduce the three roles of PM planner, PM technician and Controller. You should derive these roles from the roles that the students defined in phase 2. Each of the three teams now represents one of the three roles. In phase 3, you should work through the business process of corrective maintenance with the students. Use examples from Chapter 5, and introduce the scenario of a defective pump in the cooling system of an ice-cream production plant. In this scenario, you should play the part of the contractor or sold-to party, and allow the teams to work through the business process in the system with as little input as possible.

An IDES system is a prerequisite for carrying out the project work with groups that have little experience of R/3. If you do not have access to an IDES system, you should ensure that the organizational structures exist (maintenance plant, maintenance planning plant, controlling area, company code, and so on). Map the pump as an item of equipment, and the cooling system as a functional location. Create at least one PM work centre. With experienced groups, you can let the participants create the organizational structures and master data themselves.

The technician team, the planner team and the controller team first have to agree on who should perform what work. The technician team ideally reports a malfunction by creating a notification. The planner team carries out planning and control of the maintenance task in consultation with the technician team (for example, as regards capacities), and with the controller team (for example, as regards the order budget). The technician team then performs and confirms the maintenance task. The completion confirmation is, in turn, checked by the planner team and the controller team. When the planner team technically completes the order, the controller team settles it.

The students should find out for themselves which actions they have to perform in the R/3 System to carry out the tasks they have defined. If a team is unable to continue, you can copy the appropriate procedures from Chapter 5 and distribute them to the students. The teams will soon learn that a new action can only be carried out successfully by one team if another team has already carried out an earlier action successfully.

EXAMPLE
- The technician team cannot confirm the task until the planner team has released the order.
- The technician team cannot withdraw material from the warehouse unless the planner team has reserved the material or ordered it via purchase requisition, or if unplanned material withdrawals are not permitted.
- The planner team cannot release the order unless the controller team has increased the planned costs budget for the order.
- The planner team cannot technically complete the order unless the controller team has entered a settlement rule.

The business process has been successfully completed when the controller team has settled the order and completed it from a business point of view. You can use the order status to check whether the business process has been carried out successfully.

A.1.6 Final feedback session and planning a follow-up workshop

At the end of the workshop, the individual teams present the work they have carried out together on the business process. They can do so, for example, by breaking down the process into individual steps and presenting each step from the point of view of the team affected.

The final feedback session is intended to identify and record any outstanding points on which you should provide additional information. If necessary, you should copy the appropriate sections from Chapter 5, or deal with the outstanding points in a follow-up workshop. You can also use a follow-up workshop to work through the business processes in Chapters 6 and 7.

A.2   INTEGRATION WORKSHOP

A.2.1 The basic concept

This section provides you with a basic framework for a two to three-day case study for internships, which consolidates the knowledge of plant maintenance with the PM component that participants have acquired in standard or in-house training courses. The workshop provides an example of the part of a typical implementation project that is relevant to plant maintenance. The aim of this case study is to map enterprise structures in the system, and to configure the most important business processes in plant maintenance as well as in the relevant 'adjoining' enterprise areas.

The data in section A.2.5, 'Background information on the model company FreezeMe Inc.', has been designed to give participants sufficient scope for their own decisions and views. In 'real-life' implementation projects, the necessary data and information is often unavailable, available too late, or redundant. The workshop concept is intended to take these circumstances into account.

The workshop supervisors should provide support and assistance if questions arise and also carry out moderation tasks. They should play the role of customers but not that of a hotline or the project management.

A.2.2 Procedure and schedule

Participants in this workshop have two to three days to configure a system and implement specific business processes on the basis of the following project description. The participants are also responsible for planning and managing the project.

The workshop comprises the following two phases:

■ *Defining the enterprise structures*

As in a real project, the aim of the first phase is to reach agreement between the project team and a (notional) steering committee as regards the enterprise structure.

■ *Creating the business processes*

The second phase comprises mapping and adjusting the business processes. On the final day of the project, the participants present specific business processes to a 'steering committee', and discuss the practicability of the implementation chosen.

The following schedule is suggested for the case study:

Day 1
- Assemble project team
- Define enterprise structures and discuss in steering committee
- Create project plan

Day 2 (and 3)
- Adjust system
- Map business processes in system

The participants in the workshops and the supervisors regularly take part in steering committee meetings, at which potential problems are discussed. The presentation of a configured prototype has highest priority here. This presentation focuses on integrating the PM module within a streamlined business process flow within the supply chain.

A.2.3 Tasks in phase 1

■ Assemble and structure the project team(s)

■ Define enterprise structure and give reasons for choosing particular structures

- Define standards for naming conventions and master data
- Present enterprise structure to steering committee

You should only begin configuring the enterprise structure after it has been discussed with and approved by the steering committee.

A.2.4 Tasks in phase 2

- Create a project plan and specify milestones
- Manage project plan using ASAP method and Business Engineering Workbench tools
- Take integrative aspects of PM module into account
- Define processes in the business transactions and describe potential problems and difficulties during creation of prototype
- Compile a report for meeting with steering committee clarifying following questions:
  - Which functions and processes are installed?
  - Which problems arose?
  - Can the schedule be met?

A.2.5 Background information on the model company FreezeMe Inc.

FreezeMe Inc. is a medium-sized company specializing exclusively in producing and selling ice-cream machines. In addition to this, the company provides repair and maintenance services. The company is headquartered in Smallsville, USA.

The management has decided that the company (which already uses the FI, CO, MM, SD and PP modules) also requires software for handling internal plant maintenance and external services. Various executive employees have been delegated to form a steering committee and carry out an extensive examination. A comparison of different solutions has shown that the PM module is best suited to the company's requirements and plans for growth – not least because the 'new' module is integrated in the existing system landscape.

The corporate financial manager has sent the consultancy company DoIT a request for quotation. DoIT has decided to put forward its quotation in the form of several presentations. The group(s) have been given the task of creating a prototype for this purpose and presenting it to the steering committee of FreezeMe Inc. On the basis of these presentations, FreezeMe Inc. will decide whether to award the contract to DoIT or to a competitor.

All the products sold by FreezeMe Inc. are produced in plants 1000 and 1200 in Smallsville. Plant 1000 contains various storage locations for purchased material and semifinished goods produced internally, as well as for spare parts for the production systems. Plant 1200 is assigned storage location 0002, which is used as a warehouse for replacement equipment.

The following information on FreezeMe Inc. has been gathered by the steering committee and an independent auditing company, which is not competing for the

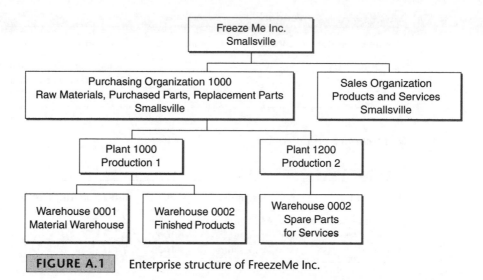

FIGURE A.1   Enterprise structure of FreezeMe Inc.

contract. Using this information from the customer, the team has to define and configure the enterprise structure, and gather the master data.

FreezeMe Inc. has two plants in Smallsville, USA. Shop floor areas 1 and 2 are located in plant 1000, while plant 1200 produces mechanical equipment exclusively. Internal maintenance of the production systems is planned centrally in plant 1000.

Purchasing organization 1000 is responsible for raw materials, purchased parts, and replacement parts, while sales organization 0001 sells products and services. The enterprise currency is UNI; the fiscal year comprises 12 months, and ends in December. The fixed assets have to be administered in accordance with the company guidelines and cost accounting rules. Apart from the management, the employees of FreezeMe Inc. are paid according to pay scale.

A.2.6 Data to be defined by the workshop participants

Materials management

TABLE A.1   Material

Material type	Material ID	Plant	Storage location	Comments
Comp., purchased	Electric motor	1000	0001	Characteristics: connected load, weight
Comp., purchased	Terminal	1000	0001	BOM item for electric motor Standard price 4.5 UNI
Comp., purchased	Loop	1000	0001	BOM item for electric motor Standard price 2 UNI
Comp., purchased	Casing	1000	0001	BOM item for electric motor Standard price 175 UNI
Comp., purchased	*	1000	0001	BOM item for electric motor

TABLE A.2	Vendor		
Name of vendor	Location	Purch. org.	Comments
ELECTRO PLUS	Bigtown, USA	1000	Vendor number assigned internally GR-based invoice verification Term of payment ZT01

Maintenance organization

TABLE A.3	Work centres			
Work centre	Description	Plant	Indiv. capacities assigned	Cost centre
Preventive maintenance	Main work centre	1000	3	*
ME-EL	Work centre	1000	4	*
Foreman	Work centre	1000	1	*

Master data in maintenance

TABLE A.4	Equipment and functional locations			
Structure element	Description	ID	Plant	Comments
Functional location	Unit production line1	*	1000	Measuring points, counters; Measurement reading inheritance to ELECTRIC MOTOR
Functional location	Unit production line 2	*	1000	Measuring points, counters; Measurement reading inheritance to ELECTRIC MOTOR
Equipment	Electric motor	internal	1000	Generated from material ELECTRIC MOTOR
Equipment	Hex wrench	internal	1000	Production resource/ tool

TABLE A.5	Equipment category	
Equipment category	Reference	Comments
E	Machines	Change documents should be generated "Serial data" view should be displayed in the application

TABLE A.6	Maintenance task lists and maintenance plans	
Element	**Object**	**Specifications**
Maintenance task list	ELECTRIC MOTOR	Only FOREMAN work centre may enable system and put it in operation Work centre ME-EL carries out work System is not available during repair tasks
Maintenance plan	ELECTRIC MOTOR	Maintenance call every 700 operating hours Performance of motor = approx. 95 operating hours/week

Maintenance processing

The participants must generate movement data such as postings of goods issues and goods receipts. Data marked * must also be defined by the participants.

A.2.7 Business process prototypes for the presentation

Structuring technical objects

1. Three electric motors for use in plant 1000 are procured at a price of 670 UNI. The goods receipt is to be mapped. When the material with the description *electric motor* is created, equipment must be generated automatically with the goods receipt. Equipment category E should be defined in accordance with the specifications in section A.2.6.

2. One of these items of equipment is installed at the functional locations unit production line *1* and unit production line *2*. A maintenance order should be created for this purpose, a goods issue for the order carried out, and functional locations created with an appropriate predefined structure indicator. The structure of the functional locations begins with the plant description. Work centre ME-EL performs the work.

3. The remaining equipment is placed into stock in warehouse 0002 of plant 1000.

4. The equipment should be classified according to the categories *connected load* and *weight*. Characteristic values are to be assigned. In the event of malfunctions, it is useful to be able to address queries directly to the vendor *Electro Plus*, as well as the main work centre *Preventive maintenance*. Both should be included in the equipment master.

5. A BOM for the item of equipment *electric motor*, which includes the materials *terminal* and *loop*, should be defined. Four items of each material are installed in the equipment. Other relevant materials (including a *casing*) should be entered in the BOM.

6. The equipment and functional locations are subject to performance-based maintenance. The measuring points and counters are located in the production lines. The measurement readings entered for the operating hour counter are inherited by the electric motors.

Work scheduling, work centres

1. The procured and installed equipment should be maintained in accordance with a maintenance task list defined by the participants, which should provide only rough specifications.

2. Only the work centre foreman may enable the system and, therefore, release it for maintenance. While the repairs are being carried out, the system is not available. When the activities performed by work centre ME-EL have been completed, the system is checked by the foreman and put into operation.

Maintenance processing

1. An employee reports a malfunction at the functional location *unit production line 1*. After closer examination, the cause is identified as one of the items of equipment that you procured and installed.

2. As specified in the maintenance task list, the item of equipment is repaired on site and without being dismantled. Two items of each of the replacement parts *terminal* and *loop* are used for this purpose. In accordance with the principle 'If you break it, you pay for it', the internal service (3.5 hours at an hourly rate of 85 UNI) and the materials used are settled to the cost centre of the functional location after the order has been completed.

3. Some hours later another malfunction is reported in the item of equipment that was repaired. To avoid costly downtimes, the defective item of equipment is dismantled and replaced by the remaining (third) item of equipment, which is removed from storage for this purpose.

4. The dismantled item of equipment is refurbished by work centre ME-EL and put back into storage with the condition 'refurbished' (C2) (0001 in plant 1000). The operations here include dismantling and cleaning the rotor and lubricating the connection between the bearing and shaft.

5. The costs incurred for internal service and the spare part used (*casing*) are settled to an internal order.

Maintenance planning

1. To prevent malfunctions of this type from occurring in future, a performance-based maintenance plan is generated. The tasks to be carried out every 700 operating hours are based on the maintenance task list that you generated earlier.

2. The production tools/resources required include a *hex wrench*, which is removed from stock in warehouse 0001 and returned again. Data on this tool/resource can also be found in section A.2.6.

Bibliography

Biedermann, Hubert (1990) *Erfolgspotentiale für Unternehmer und Führungskräfte – Anlagenmanagement, Managementwerkzeuge zur Rationalisierung.* Köln.

Biedermann, Hubert (1998) Benchmarking. Chancen und Risiken für die Instandhaltung. In: *Benchmarking. Auf dem Weg zu Best Practice in Produktion und Instandhaltung. 12. Instandhaltungs-Forum.* Hrsg. Österreichische Technische Wissenschaftliche Vereinigung für Instandhaltung und Anlagenwirtschaft (ÖIVA). Köln.

Feldmann, Klaus, Thomas Collisi and Jürgen Wunderlich (1999) Simulationsgestütztes Instandhaltungsmanagement. Nutzeffekte in der Praxis. In: *Industrie Management* 15.

Gamweger, Jürgen and Gerhard Grill-Kiefer (1998) Kennzahlengestütztes Controlling in der Instandhaltung. In: *Benchmarking. Auf dem Weg zu Best Practice in Produktion und Instandhaltung. 12. Instandhaltungs-Forum.* Hrsg. Österreichische Technische Wissenschaftliche Vereinigung für Instandhaltung und Anlagenwirtschaft (ÖIVA). Köln.

Geipel-Kern, Anke (1999) Profitieren von der Betriebsstörung. In: *Chemie Produktion*, October, 108–109.

Grobholz, Harald R. (1988) *Managementaufgabe Instandhaltung* 2. Auflage.

Günther, Thomas and Catharina Kriegbaum (1997) Life Cycle Costing. In: *Das Wirtschaftsstudium* 10.

Hartmann, Gernot, Friedrich Härter and Heinrich Schmitz (1995) *Spezielle Betriebswirtschaftslehre der Industrie* 8. Auflage, Rinteln.

Matyas, Kurt (1999) Von der präventiven Instandhaltung zu TPM. In: *Industrie Management* 15.

Nolden, Rolf-Günther (1996) *Industriebetriebslehre* 7. Auflage, Köln.

Schierenbeck, Henner (1995) *Grundzüge der Betriebswirtschaftslehre* 12. Auflage, München.

Sokianos, Nicolas, Helmut Drüke and Claudia Toutatoui (1998) *Lexikon Produktionsmanagement.* Landsberg.

Steinbuch, Pitter A. (1997) *Organisation.* 10. Auflage, Ludwigshafen.

Stender, Siegfried (1999) Von TPM bis zur DAPV. In*: Instandhaltungsmanagement in neuen Organisationsformen.* Hrsg. Engelbert Westkämper, Wifried Sihn, Siegfried Stender. Berlin, Heidelberg, New York.

Stender, Siegfried and Rüdiger Proksch (1999) Innovative Instandhaltungskonzepte. In: *Industrie Management* 15.

Stoll, Volker (1999) Technologische Trends für die Überwachung und Diagnose komplexer Systeme. In: *Instandhaltungsmanagement in neuen Organisationsformen.* Hrsg. Engelbert Westkämper, Wifried Sihn, Siegfried Stender. Berlin, Heidelberg, New York.

Warnecke, Hans-Jürgen (1992) *Handbuch Instandhaltung – Instandhaltungsmanagement.* Band 1. Köln.

Index

ABAP Dictionary 196
ABSENCES 110
account assignment data 84
accounting data 53, 62
actions, documenting 95
activity confirmations 103–8
activity data 86, 87
activity reports 79, 82, 88–95
  automatic task determination 92
  documenting actions 95
  documenting tasks 90–2
  entering in the system 89
  follow-up tasks 94
  linking to maintenance orders 132–6
actual costs 178, 180–1, 198–200
analysing order activity types 205–8
analysing order costs 192–208, 231–3
assembly master data 64–5
Asset Accounting (FI-AA) 53, 80, 312–13
asset management 13, 22
assigning maintenance strategy 219–20
assigning materials 154–5, 223–6
assigning planning indicators 139
assigning production resources/tools 226–31
assigning technicians 145–50
ATTENDANCES 110
automatic deadline monitoring 253–4
automatic task determination 92
availability of materials 152, 160–4

backflushed materials 101
benchmarking xiii, 21–3
Biedermann, Hubert xii, 21, 22
bills of materials (BOM) 64–5, 68–70, 155
BPR (Business Process Reengineering) xiii
breakdowns see malfunctions
budgets 184–8
building control systems 7–8, 27, 317–24

business completion 192
Business Process Reengineering (BPR) xiii
business processes 1–2, 18–21
Business Workplace 32–5
  folder contents lists 34
  mail processing 33
  preview function 34
  structure 33

CAD systems 324–7
CALCULATE PERFORMANCE 115
call history 261
call horizons 258
cancelling completion confirmations 102,
    113–14
capacity requirements planning 14, 141,
    150–2, 222
Case-Based Reasoning Systems (CBR) 28
catalog system 86–8
CATS-Cross Application Time Sheet 313–16
cause catalogs 132
causes data 97
centralized planning 50
CIP (continuous improvement programs) xii
CO (Controlling) component 81, 192–4, 312
collective time confirmations 108–11
  with selection 111
  without selection 109–10
completion confirmations 100–12, 141, 168,
    222, 260–1
  activity confirmations 103–8
  CALCULATE PERFORMANCE 115
  cancelling 102, 113–14
  collective time confirmations 108–11
  control parameters 114–16
  cost displays 102
  creating 100–3
  displaying 102, 112–13